KU-661-289

For Maija, Brad, and Aksel
Bethany, Carrie, Charlie, Damon, and Dara
Erin, Kate, Kelly, Renée, and Sarah

Public Opinion and American Foreign Policy

Revised Edition

OLE R. HOLSTI

The University of Michigan Press
Ann Arbor

Copyright © by the University of Michigan 2004
All rights reserved
Published in the United States of America by
The University of Michigan Press
Manufactured in the United States of America
⊗ Printed on acid-free paper

2007   2006   2005   2004   4   3   2   1

No part of this publication may be reproduced, stored in a retrieval system, or
transmitted in any form or by any means, electronic, mechanical, or otherwise,
without the written permission of the publisher.

A CIP catalog record for this book is available from the British Library.

Library of Congress Cataloging-in-Publication Data

Holsti, Ole R.
    Public opinion and American foreign policy /
Ole R. Holsti.— Rev. ed.
        p. cm. — (Analytical perspectives on politics)
    Includes bibliographical references and index.
    ISBN 0-472-03011-6 (pbk. : acid-free paper)
    1. United States—Foreign relations—1989— —Public opinion.
    2. United States—Foreign relations—1945–1989—Public opinion.
    3. Public opinion—United States.   I. Title.   II. Series.

E840.H592   2004
327.73—dc22   2004000622

ISBN13 978-0-472-03011-8 (paperback)
ISBN13 978-0-472-02230-4 (electronic)

UNIVERSITY
OF SHEFFIELD
LIBRARY

Public Opinion and American Foreign Policy

DATE OF RETURN
UNLESS RECALLED BY LIBRARY

2 3 OCT 2015

PLEASE TAKE GOOD CARE OF THIS BOOK

Analytical Perspectives on Politics

ADVISORY EDITORS:

John Aldrich, Duke University
Bruce Bueno de Mesquita, Hoover Institution and New York University
Robert Jackman, University of California, Davis
David Rohde, Michigan State University

Political Science is developing rapidly and changing markedly. Keeping in touch with new ideas across the discipline is a challenge for political scientists and for their students.

To help meet this challenge, the series Analytical Perspectives on Politics presents creative and sophisticated syntheses of major areas of research in the fields of political science. In each book, a high-caliber author provides a clear and discriminating description of the current state of the art and a strong-minded prescription and structure for future work in the field.

These distinctive books provide a compact review for political scientists, a helpful introduction for graduate students, and central reading for advanced undergraduate courses.

Robert W. Jackman, *Power without Force: The Political Capacity of Nation-States*

Linda L. Fowler, *Candidates, Congress, and the American Democracy*

Scott Gates and Brian D. Humes, *Games, Information, and Politics: Applying Game Theoretic Models to Political Science*

Lawrence Baum, *The Puzzle of Judicial Behavior*

Barbara Geddes, *Paradigms and Sand Castles: Theory Building and Research Design in Comparative Politics*

Rose McDermott, *Political Psychology in International Relations*

Ole R. Holsti, *Public Opinion and American Foreign Policy, Revised Edition*

Contents

Preface to the Revised Edition

The first edition of *Public Opinion and American Foreign Policy* was generally well received, but that is not sufficient reason to bring out a revised and updated version of the book. The rationale for a new edition can be found in a number of developments since 1995, when the first edition went to press. In addition to important evidence about public attitudes provided by the Gallup Organization and other major polling firms, the Chicago Council on Foreign Relations, the Program on International Policy Attitudes, the Pew Research Center for the People and the Press, the Foreign Policy Leadership Project, and the Triangle Institute for Security Studies have undertaken major surveys that focus on various important aspects of America's foreign relations. These have been especially helpful because each of them has included samples of opinion leaders, a sector of American society that has not frequently been the subject of special attention from Gallup and other commercial polling firms. Almost all of the tables appearing in the first edition have been redone to reflect new evidence from these surveys.

A second important development has been the recent publication of major studies that have probed the most difficult and complex issue regarding public opinion—its impact on the political process. Steven Kull, I. M. Destler, Lawrence Jacobs, Robert Shapiro, Richard Sobel, Douglas Foyle, and others have been at the forefront of efforts to combine archival research with interviews of public officials and in some cases of pollsters, thereby providing a better understanding of how public opinion enters the policy-making process, the uses to which it is put, and its impact on policy outcomes. These works and other works have provided important new evidence for the discussions in chapter 3 and elsewhere.

The end of the Cold War and increasing democratization are

among the developments that have opened up opportunities for public opinion studies in countries where such research, especially by Westerners, would have been quite unthinkable even a few years ago. This book focuses on the United States, but the growth of comparative cross-national research provides a much richer understanding of the relationship between public opinion and foreign policy—for example, which findings about that relationship are limited to the American political context, and which may have more universal validity?

A major theme of the first edition of this book is that research and theory on public opinion and foreign policy have often been shaped by such key events as the two world wars of the twentieth century and the war in Vietnam. Several studies have shown that many post-Vietnam aspects of public attitudes have persisted beyond the end of the Cold War. However, the enormity of the September 11, 2001, terrorist attacks on New York and Washington raises anew questions about continuity and change. As many analysts have asserted, has everything changed since 9/11, including public attitudes toward foreign affairs, much in the way that the attack on Pearl Harbor six decades earlier drove a stake through the heart of the isolationist argument that national interests, geographical realities, and commonsense prudence dictated a policy of limiting contacts with belligerents or potential belligerents abroad? It is clearly far too early to assess the long-term impact of 9/11 on the American public and its attitudes toward global engagement. Chapter 6, which is wholly new in this edition, nevertheless undertakes at least an interim assessment of the role, if any, that public opinion has played in promoting or sustaining the Bush administration's pronounced preferences, during both the nine months before September 11 and the first two years following the terrorist attacks, for a unilateralist approach to world affairs. The post-9/11 period includes debates and frequent polling on the issue of Iraq, culminating in the March 2003 invasion of that country and the destruction of Saddam Hussein's regime in Baghdad.

In this undertaking I have been extraordinarily fortunate in receiving the counsel, insights, assistance, and encouragement of many persons. I reiterate the many debts acknowledged in the preface to the first edition. Many of those cited there have continued to provide help far beyond the call of collegiality and friendship, and my gratitude for their assistance persists unabated. I have also benefitted immensely from those who pointed to ways in which the first edition might be improved, including Richard Eichenberg, Beth Fischer, Maxine Isaacs, Brigitte Nacos, and Richard Sobel. As noted earlier, chapter 6 is wholly new in this edition. Comments and suggestions from Bruce Jentleson and Bob Lieber, when some parts of it were discussed at a June 2000 conference at the Woodrow Wilson Center in Washington, D.C., were most useful. John Aldrich, Peter Feaver, Kal Holsti, Bruce Jentleson, Bob Keohane, and Richard Sobel read an initial draft of chapter 6 and provided incisive and useful suggestions for improving it. I am also indebted to two anonymous reviewers who read the entire manuscript and offered their suggestions for revisions. Steve Kull was generous in offering advice and sharing data from his Program on International Policy Attitudes; Chris Whitney was most helpful in providing data from the 2002 Chicago Council on Foreign Relations survey; and Steve Casey provided some useful information about Franklin Roosevelt's views on polling.

Dan Harkins, my friend and associate for more than two decades; Christy Hamilton, Carrie Liken, Janet Newcity, and Kuba Stolarski provided invaluable computer programming assistance on the Foreign Policy Leadership Project and Triangle Institute for Security Studies data sets.

Since August 2000 I have benefitted immensely from Anne Marie Boyd's assistance on all aspects of this project. She is a genius at finding sources, even obscure ones, in the library and on the Internet. Her many talents have had an impact on formatting tables, clarifying sentences, proofreading, indexing, and many other aspects of the project. She has done all these things with such unfailing energy, enthusiasm, good nature, and good humor that working with her has always been a great pleasure.

Working with the University of Michigan Press has also been a pleasant experience. The first edition began with the support of political science editor Malcolm Litchfield and was completed under his successor, Chuck Myers. Jeremy Shine, political science acquisitions editor, provided initial support for this revised edition, and it has been a pleasure working with Jim Reische, Kevin Rennells, and Sarah Mann in bringing this book to fruition.

My heartfelt thanks to all of the above. They are absolved from responsibility for errors that remain. My apologies to anyone whose contributions I may inadvertently have overlooked.

This book has a double dedication. The first is to my wonderful daughter, Maija; her devoted husband, Brad; and their delightful son, Aksel Eric Anderson, who was born as this project was nearing completion. It is also dedicated to some outstanding undergraduate students whom I had the privilege of teaching during the past decade. They have also demonstrated an extraordinary commitment to public service, both at Duke and after graduation. The greatest joy of E-mail is that they have kept in touch, sharing with me news of their activities in settings as diverse as the Peace Corps; classrooms in Japan, South Korea, and inner-city Boston; NATO headquarters; all three branches of the U.S. government; and a wide range of volunteer undertakings that have helped others and made the world a better place. At a time when every day seems to bring news of still further outrageous misconduct by top leaders in churches, business, finance, accounting, and government, their idealism and energy are a source of great hope for the future of the country and of humankind. The achievements of these exceptional people are a constant source of inspiration, and I cherish their friendship.

Preface to the First Edition

Ours is appropriately called the "age of polling." Few aspects of contemporary life have eluded the public scrutiny of the survey. Polls are regularly conducted to determine what the general public thinks about issues, parties, candidates, presidents, institutions, and other countries, to say nothing of products, pastimes, and popular personalities. As this is being written, the public is being asked whether the Miss America Pageant should continue to judge contestants in bathing suits and how retired general Colin Powell would fare as a presidential candidate in 1996. Other surveys rely on expert opinion to answer some variant or another of America's favorite question: "Who is number one?" Which college football team is the best this week in the opinion of sportswriters and coaches? How do academic specialists rank graduate programs in their disciplines?

Foreign affairs, once considered the private preserve of small groups of knowledgeable and interested elites, have also been the subject of repeated surveys. Although those surveys have consistently revealed that the average American is poorly informed about international affairs, opportunities for the public to become engaged in foreign policy have increased. For example, new communications technologies permit the public to observe important events as they unfold. The Cable News Network (CNN) brought the Persian Gulf War into the world's living rooms in real time, and it did the same with the mission of Jimmy Carter, Sam Nunn, and Colin Powell to persuade Haiti's ruling junta that stepping down voluntarily was the only way to avert an American military invasion to force it out of power. These technologies can also make the public a quasi participant in such episodes by almost simultaneous polling to determine reactions to and assessments of events as they take place.

The impact and consequences of these developments are not

free of controversy, but many of the issues that have surfaced are in fact variants of venerable debates about the role of the public in international affairs. Is foreign policy "different" from other aspects of public policy? How can a poorly informed public make any coherent sense of the complex issues that constitute international relations? Can it make any constructive contribution to foreign policy? Can great powers in the nuclear age afford to take public sentiments into account when the consequences of policy choices may determine the continued existence of the country, or perhaps even of the human race? Can they afford not to? Has the end of the Cold War increased the likelihood that public passions will drive governments into well-meaning but hopeless undertakings that have little relationship to the national interest? Conversely, will a public suffering from "compassion fatigue" insist that an agenda of domestic problems be given priority over the vision briefly articulated by former President Bush—a "new world order" in which the United States would play a leading role?

More basically, what is the proper role of public opinion in the conduct of foreign affairs in a democratic polity? What do we know about the nature and impact of public opinion on foreign and defense policy? Philosophers have debated the first question for centuries, but twentieth-century conflicts have played a crucial role in framing the key questions and research agendas in the search for answers to the second one. World War I transformed the question of public participation in foreign affairs from a theoretical issue into a practical one that many postwar leaders had to confront. World War II was equally significant. For many leaders and public opinion analysts, a key question arising from that conflict was whether the public would permit the United States to play a constructive leadership role in the postwar international order. Answers to many of the normative and empirical questions that emerged from extensive research during the two decades following World War II came to be reexamined as a consequence of the long and failed U.S. effort in Vietnam. The end of the Cold War has raised new questions, including the extent to which our understanding of American public opinion and foreign policy may need to be modified in the light of a world that has in many ways been transformed since the late 1980s. The chapters that follow will attempt to examine and evaluate some of the theory and evidence concerning these issues.

John Zaller (1992) has appropriately argued that our knowledge about public opinion has suffered from a tendency to organize research around policy issues, including foreign policy. While this book is focused on opinions about international affairs, I have also made some effort to draw upon theory and evidence from other issues and such related aspects of political behavior as voting.

In the course of writing this book, I have received invaluable help from many persons and institutions. John Aldrich, Ronald Hinckley, Layna Mosely, and Jim Rosenau read the entire manuscript in draft form and provided many helpful comments, cogent criticisms, and constructive suggestions for improving it. Peter Feaver did the same for the final chapter. Jim Rosenau has also been a collaborator for more than two decades on a related project concerning the political beliefs of American opinion leaders. This book, which originated in a suggestion by John Aldrich, is far better than it would have been without their help.

I am also indebted to those who read and commented on an earlier and much briefer effort to review the literature on public opinion and foreign policy: Stephen Earl Bennett, Bill Chittick, Thomas Graham, Jon Hurwitz, Ben Page, Mark Peffley, Philip Powlick, Bruce Russett, and Gene Wittkopf. Many stimulating conversations with Gene Wittkopf about most of the topics discussed here have invariably been enlightening.

Four National Science Foundation (NSF) grants made it possible for me to conduct surveys of American opinion leaders in 1980, 1984, 1988, and 1992. Some of the resulting data are reported in chapters 4 and 5. The NSF also provided a Research and Training Grant (RTG) in political psychology to the Mershon Center at the Ohio State University. The frequent meetings of faculty and doctoral students under the auspices of the Mershon RTG have provided an exceptional interuniversity, multidisciplinary, and cross-generational setting in which to further my education.

The Duke Arts and Sciences Research Council provided a grant to undertake the initial survey of opinion leaders in 1976, and since that time it has frequently provided additional support for my research on American public opinion and foreign policy.

Any reader will quickly come to appreciate that this book could not have been written without the efforts of many people who have written about public opinion and foreign policy. It is thus appropriate for me to express my gratitude to all of the authors cited in the bibliography. Three of them—Ronald Hinckley, Alan Kay, and Steven Kull—also have generously shared the results of their own surveys with me.

For many years I have relied on the expert programming skills of Daniel F. Harkins. As the entire computing system at Duke has undergone immense changes on an almost annual basis, Dan's patience and ingenuity have been almost as important as his immense technical abilities. The many drafts of the manuscript and tables were skillfully typed by Rita Dowling. Not even the most daunting table ever caused her to lose her excellent sense of humor. Layna Mosely and Elizabeth Rogers provided outstanding assistance in searching through memoirs and biographies of presidents and secretaries of state for materials related to public opinion. Justine Lapatine diligently checked the quotations and citations.

Finally, I wish to thank several persons at the University of Michigan Press: Colin Day, Malcolm Litchfield, and Charles T. Myers, who supported this project from its inception.

All those who have so kindly contributed to this book are, of course, absolved from blame for any remaining deficiencies.

Tables

Figures

CHAPTER 1

Introduction

In one of several public addresses on the appropriate prerequisites for deployment of American combat forces abroad, Secretary of Defense Casper Weinberger in 1984 specified six requirements for any such U.S. military intervention. According to Weinberger, one of those preconditions was that "there must be some reasonable assurance that we will have the support of the American people" (Weinberger 1984, A5). His cabinet colleague, Secretary of State George Shultz, publicly disagreed with the "Weinberger Doctrine," characterizing it both at that time and later in his memoirs as an unreasonably stringent set of preconditions that would rarely, if ever, be met. Consequently, Shultz argued, these restrictions effectively would serve as an excuse for inaction, even when vital American interests abroad were potentially threatened (Shultz 1993, 84, 103, 649–51). The public disagreement between Weinberger and Shultz may be seen as one of many arguments about the ends and means of foreign policy that have marked the decades since the American intervention in Vietnam ended in defeat. Varying interpretations of the Vietnam War, why it was lost, and the appropriate lessons to be drawn from that conflict, especially with respect to the deployment of troops abroad, have continued to generate heated debates more than three decades after the last Americans were evacuated from Saigon. Post–Cold War interventions in Somalia, Haiti, and parts of the former Yugoslavia have, if anything, sharpened rather than tempered debates about the use of American armed forces abroad. Even though Saddam Hussein was an enemy with few redeeming features, the decision to expel Iraqi troops from Kuwait in 1991 came within only a few votes in Congress from setting the stage for a potential constitutional crisis. It took the enormity of the September 11, 2001, terrorist attacks on New York and Washington to create overwhelming support for sending U.S. troops to

Afghanistan to seek out the perpetrators of the attack and to overthrow the Taliban regime that had provided a haven for members of al Qaeda. The insurgency against American forces in Iraq has reignited debates about interventions abroad.

The differences between Weinberger and Shultz may be seen as part of the "Vietnam syndrome"—the propensity to perceive and assess international undertakings through the prism of the war in Southeast Asia. These differences also may be viewed as part of a more basic and venerable debate about some central issues regarding the theory and practice of democratic government: namely, what is the proper role of public opinion in the conduct of foreign affairs? Is public opinion an obstacle in the definition of vital national interests and in the implementation of appropriate foreign and defense policies to pursue those interests? Have publics in democratic countries hamstrung military operations by failing to exhibit sufficient patience to support important undertakings that fail to produce quick results or by insisting that such undertakings be conducted without casualties? Alternatively, does public opinion play an indispensable role in legitimating and sustaining long-term efforts to pursue and protect vital interests abroad? Can it serve as a valuable constraint against policies that have at best a tenuous relationship to such interests? Understandably, a great deal of research on public opinion and foreign policy has been driven by issues of the moment. Almost any dramatic international development will immediately give rise to surveys directed at discovering public attitudes and preferences for dealing with it. Indeed, major U.S. television networks conduct regular surveys in cooperation with national newspapers, and it is now even possible to report how the public is reacting to events as they unfold.[1] Air attacks against Iraq during the 1991 Gulf War could be viewed in real time, even as polling organizations were conducting surveys to assess, for example, the level of public support for the war effort. The terrorist attacks on New York and Washington stimulated a flood of surveys concerning questions ranging from the appropriate U.S. responses to the emotional impact of the events on respondents.

One of the themes to be developed in this and the following two chapters is that research and theory on public opinion and foreign policy have been heavily influenced by major international developments and by normative preferences for the ways the United States should deal with them. Despite the heavy emphasis in most surveys sponsored by the popular media on public reactions to current issues—or perhaps because of this emphasis— there is value in linking the issue of public opinion and foreign policy to broader questions about the conduct of public affairs. This examination of the linkage between public opinion and foreign policy will begin with a review of historical controversies regarding the issue. A good starting point is the long-standing debate between proponents of two quite different philosophical approaches to international relations.

Public Opinion in the Realist-Liberal Debate

Although other major theoretical contenders have claimed to provide empirical and/or normative guides to international relations—for example, several variants of Marxist-Leninist dependency theories and, more recently, postmodern attacks on virtually every effort at systematic analysis—the rival assertions by proponents of realism and their liberal critics have tended to dominate debates among theorists, reformers, and policymakers.[2] Realists can properly claim the longest intellectual lineage, tracing their roots to Thucydides, if not earlier. Most liberal theories are of more recent vintage, dating to the seventeenth century and more or less coinciding with the creation of the modem state system with the 1648 Treaties of Westphalia. Although realist-liberal differences extend across virtually all central questions of foreign policy, international relations, and statecraft, the appropriate role for public opinion in the making of foreign policy is at the center of persisting debates between these two approaches to international affairs. Is public opinion a force for enlightenment—indeed, a necessary if not sufficient condition for sound foreign policy and thus a significant contributor to peaceful relations among nations—as celebrated by Woodrow Wilson and many other liberals? Alternatively, is the public more appropriately described as a source of emotional and shortsighted thinking that can only impede the effective pursuit and defense of vital national interests?

There is a long liberal tradition, dating back at least to Jeremy Bentham, that places public opinion at the center of legitimate and effective public policy. Bentham described public opinion, or the "Public-Opinion Tribunal," as the "sole remedy" for many problems of government. His "Plan for an Universal and Perpetual Peace" also proposed removing the veil of secrecy from the conduct of foreign affairs: "That secresy in the operation of the foreign department ought not to be endured in England, being

equally repugnant to the interests of liberty and those of peace"
(1962, 8:561, 2:547). James Mill effectively summarized the liberal
case for public opinion as a repository of wisdom:

> Every man, possessed of reason, is accustomed to weigh ev-
> idence, and to be guided and determined by its preponder-
> ance. When various conclusions are, with their evidence, pre-
> sented with equal care and with equal skill, there is a moral
> certainty, though some few may be misguided, that the great-
> est number will judge aright, and that the greatest force of
> evidence, wherever it is, will produce the greatest impres-
> sion. . . . When all opinions, true and false, are equally de-
> clared, the assent of the greater number, when their interests
> are not opposed to them, may always be expected to be
> given to the true. These principles, the foundations of which
> appear to be impregnable, suffice for the speedy determina-
> tion of every practical question. (1913, 16, 18)

Jean-Jacques Rousseau and Immanuel Kant developed similar
themes specifically with respect to foreign policy and war. Mon-
archs may engage in wars for reasons that have nothing to do with
the interests of their subjects. In contrast, the foreign policies of
republics are more peaceful, at least in part because the public can
play a constructive role in constraining policymakers; accountability to the public can restrain any war-making proclivities of
leaders. Kant based his argument on the constraints that republics
and nonrepublics face when they contemplate engaging in war.
The former are likely to be more peaceful because the public,
which bears most of the costs, will be cautious about engaging in
war: "If (as must inevitably be the case, given this form of constitution) the consent of the citizenry is required in order to determine whether or not there will be war, it is natural that they consider all its calamities before committing themselves to so risky a
game" (Kant 1983, 113). The situation is quite different under non-
republican constitutions, according to Kant, because the

> easiest thing in the world to do is to declare war. Here the
> ruler is not a fellow citizen, but the nation's owner, and war
> does not affect his tables, his hunt, his places of pleasure, his
> court festivals, and so on. Thus, he can decide to go to war
> for the most meaningless of reasons, as if it were a kind of
> pleasure party, and he can blithely leave its justification

(which decency requires) to his diplomatic corps, who are always prepared for such exercises. (113)

Among nineteenth-century statesmen, William Gladstone most explicitly adhered to the liberal vision "which favors the pacific, not the bloody settlement of disputes, which aims at permanent and not temporary adjustments; above all, which recognizes as a tribunal of paramount authority, the general judgement of civilized mankind" (quoted in Kissinger 1994, 164). The essence of the liberal thesis is thus a distinction between the peaceful public and leaders who may, for a broad range of reasons, pursue policies that lead to war. British Foreign Minister Ernest Bevin succinctly summarized the Kantian case for public opinion as a barrier to war when he told Parliament in November 1945, "There has never been a war yet which, if the facts had been put calmly before ordinary folk, could not have been prevented. The common man is the greatest protection against war."[3]

Although the liberal position on the desirability of engaging the public in the conduct of foreign affairs boasts a distinguished lineage, an equally formidable array of theorists and statesmen in the realist tradition has taken a much more skeptical stance on the public's contribution to enlightened and effective diplomacy. In contrast to most liberal theories, realism has generally been grounded in a pessimistic theory of human nature, either theological (for example, St. Augustine and Reinhold Niebuhr) or secular (for example, Machiavelli, Thomas Hobbes, and Hans Morgenthau). Humans are by nature self-regarding and are largely motivated by such passions as greed and fear, qualities that are not lost when people are aggregated into political units such as nation-states.

Because realists are skeptical of institutional arrangements for promoting international cooperation in an anarchical system—to say nothing of philosophers' blueprints for regulating international relations or ensuring peace—they typically rely on balance-of-power strategies for defending national interests. Viscount Palmerston's widely quoted aphorism that Great Britain has no permanent friends or enemies, only permanent interests, summarizes a cardinal rule of realist statecraft. But the flexibility required effectively to pursue balance-of-power politics may run contrary to public sentiments. Because the public is likely to be interested in "nationality, justice, or traditional friendships and enmities," selling the proposition that yesterday's friend is today's enemy, or vice versa, may not be easy (Wright 1965, 265). Realists have typically viewed both friends and enemies from an instrumental perspective: they are means to the common end of defending vital national interests. One of the realist rules of thumb is that "my enemy's enemy is my friend," though acting on that dictum may involve at least temporary alliances with unsavory regimes. On the eve of Nazi Germany's invasion of the Soviet Union in 1941, Winston Churchill asserted, "I have only one purpose, the destruction of Hitler, and my life is simplified thereby. If Hitler invaded Hell, I would make at least a favourable reference to the Devil in the House of Commons" (1951, 370). In contrast, according to realist critics, the public is more likely to view relations with other countries as ends in themselves and to be more critical of alliances with brutal dictatorships. This is but one of the reasons why realists usually describe public opinion as a barrier to any thoughtful and coherent foreign policy, hindering efforts to promote national interests that may transcend the moods and passions of the moment.

The skepticism of the realists could also be found among the founding fathers who formulated and debated the U.S. Constitution. Alexander Hamilton and others expressed grave doubts about the wisdom of the general public. The authors of the *Federalist Papers* argued that the Senate (an appointed body until early in the twentieth century) was better suited than the directly elected House of Representatives to play a key role in the conduct of foreign affairs. Because a reliable and stable government is necessary to gain the "respect and confidence of other nations," the Senate is to be preferred to the "numerous and changeable" House. "Without a select and stable member of the government, the esteem of foreign powers will . . . be forfeited by unenlightened and variable policy." Moreover, to enact foreign policies that will be in the interest of the country as a whole, it is best to rely on a body of the legislature that is not as directly responsible to the public as is the House. In foreign policy matters, the Senate can serve as a "defence to the people against their own temporary errors and delusions." Senators are also in a better position to gain the expertise and preserve the secrecy essential to the effective conduct of foreign policy. Finally, according to Hamilton, the fluctuating character of the House makes it the less suitable body for ratifying treaties: "Accurate and comprehensive knowledge of foreign politics; a steady and systematic adherence to the same views; a nice and uniform sensibility to national character; decision, *secrecy,* and dispatch, are incompatible with the genius of a body [the House of Representatives] so variable and so numerous." Taken together, these arguments add up to a concise statement of the realist case for shielding the nation's foreign and security policy from the assumed vagaries of the public and the institution, the House of Representatives, that most directly represented it (Hamilton, Jay, and Madison 1937, nos. 62–64, 75).

Several decades later, Alexis de Tocqueville, a sympathetic French analyst of American society and politics, questioned whether democracies could satisfy the requirements for the effective conduct of diplomatic affairs. After admitting that it is "very difficult to ascertain, at present, what degree of sagacity the American democracy will display in the conduct of . . . foreign policy," he nevertheless expressed his own judgment in terms applicable not only to the United States but to all democracies: "As for myself, I do not hesitate to say that it is especially in the conduct of their foreign relations that democracies appear to be decidedly inferior to other governments." His analysis went on to identify the "propensity that induces democracies to obey impulse rather than prudence, and to abandon a mature design for the gratification of a momentary passion" as the essential barrier to the effective making of foreign policy. In contrast to the aristocracy—"a firm and enlightened body"—the "mass of the people may be led astray by ignorance and passion" (Tocqueville 1958, 1:243–45). These putative qualities of the general public—ignorance and passion—lie at the heart of virtually all realist critiques of public opinion.

At this point it is appropriate to introduce a question that I will later revisit. Do domestic and foreign policy differ so sufficiently that they require separate normative and empirical theories? More specifically, do these differences extend to the role of public opinion in these two realms of policy? Realists and liberals often vary in their approaches to this question as well. Realists generally answer the question in the affirmative, asserting that foreign affairs are indeed sufficiently unlike domestic issues to require differences in the processes by which policy is formulated; even some liberals—for example, John Locke—would accept this distinction.[4] According to realists, the public might be sufficiently informed and motivated to deal with schools, zoning, and other local issues that impinge on their daily lives, but foreign affairs are too far removed from the public's experiences, and in any case, the masses have little time or inclination to become sufficiently informed about such complex and remote issues. Moreover, realists may sometimes concede that the quality of domestic policy might be enhanced by public deliberations, but the benefits of public participation do not extend to foreign affairs. The effective conduct of diplomacy, these realists assert, must often be based on sensitive intelligence or other confidential information that cannot be shared with the public. Diplomacy usually requires secrecy, flexibility, speed of action, and other qualities that would be seriously jeopardized were the public to have a significant impact, and public passions would often make it impossible to conduct sensitive negotiations with either friends or adversaries abroad.

Thus, to permit the public a strong voice in policy would be to place democracies at a distinct disadvantage in their relations with other nations; doing so would perhaps even put the stability of the international system at risk. In this vein, Theodore Lowi (1967) has argued that democracies perform most effectively during crises, precisely the circumstances that reduce the impact of domestic "politics as usual." Democracies perform less effectively in other circumstances; therefore, an important challenge is to "make democracy safe for the world." Morgenthau summarized the case against an active role for public opinion in words that would gain the approval of most realists: "The rational requirements of good foreign policy cannot from the outset count upon the support of a public opinion whose preferences are emotional rather than rational" (1978, 558).

These differences between liberals and realists often have been intensified by wars and major conflicts. Historians of various perspectives still argue about many questions relating to the impact of public opinion. Did angry farmers drive the Madison administration into an unnecessary war with Great Britain in 1812? Did public opinion, aroused by William Randolph Hearst, Joseph Pulitzer, and other masters of "yellow journalism," push the United States into war with Spain in 1898? Did the public, still scarred by the horrors of World War I, prevent Britain and France from realistically facing up to the threats posed by the expansionist dictatorships during the 1930s? Was Franklin Roosevelt forced to back off from his efforts to warn the world about the growing dangers of fascism—for example, by his "quarantine" speech in 1937—because of an outpouring of negative reaction from some prominent opinion leaders and several isolationist segments of the American public? Had the existence of public opinion polls "blocked the war with Hitler that it was critically important to win" while sanctioning "a war that the country could not afford against a great power [Japan] that it had no immediate need to fight?" (O'Neill 1993, 73). Was the Truman administration "compelled by stiffening American opinion — vocally expressed in the Republican-controlled Eightieth Congress — to adopt the containment strategy?" (Crabb 1976, 91). In his efforts to gain public support for aid to Greece and Turkey in 1947 and other aspects of the containment policy, did Truman help to create a hypervigilant public mood that ultimately made him a captive of his own rhetoric? Did public aversion to casualties force the U.S. military to rely excessively on high-altitude bombing in the Kosovo war, even though the inevitable result was higher civilian casualties? Was this aversion to casualties also a factor in the war in Afghanistan against the Taliban regime and members of al Qaeda, resulting in large numbers of civilian deaths?

World War I, which might be described as the first public relations war, was an especially significant event in the liberal-realist debate on the proper role of public opinion in diplomacy. From the war's inception, the Allied and Central Powers tried to win over "world opinion" in various ways, including publication by many foreign offices of highly selective document collections — the "color books" — that were intended to absolve their authors from responsibility for the war while placing the entire blame on their adversaries. The propaganda war during the conflict was almost as intense as that on the battlefield. As the most powerful nonbelligerent, the United States was an especially important target of vigorous propaganda efforts by both sides until it entered the war in April 1917.[5]

President Wilson's hopes for a new postwar world order depended significantly on democratizing foreign affairs and diplomacy. In his April 2, 1917, war message, he declared, "A steadfast concert for peace can never be maintained except by partnership of democratic nations. No autocratic government could be trusted to keep faith within it or observe its covenants. It must be a league of honor, a partnership of opinion. . . . Only free people can hold their purpose and their honor steady to a common end and prefer the interests of mankind to any narrow interest of their own" (1917, 1). "Open covenants openly arrived at," an important feature of Bentham's blueprint for perpetual peace, was the first of Wilson's Fourteen Points and among his most important procedural prescriptions for reforming an international order in which secret diplomacy allegedly had dragged nation after nation into the catastrophic war against the will and interests of its ordinary citizens. The last of the Fourteen Points, the creation of a general international organization, had a similar goal of bringing diplomacy within the purview of world public opinion. During the war Wilson had stated,

> The counsels of plain men have become on all hands more simple and straightforward and more unified than the counsels of sophisticated men of affairs, who still retain the impression that they are playing a game of power and are playing for high stakes. That is why I have said that this is a people's war, not a statesman's. Statesmen must follow the clarified common thought or be broken.[6]

Wilson's faith in the public was not limited to abstract political theory. Throughout his career he had looked to the public as the court of final appeal for his most important projects. When faced with Senate opposition to the Treaty of Versailles, within which the League of Nations Covenant was embedded, he believed that direct appeals to the public would force the Senate to accept the treaty without the modifications proposed by Senator Henry Cabot Lodge and many other Republicans.

In September 1919, the president undertook a nationwide speaking tour, intending to go over the heads of the Senate by taking his case for the League of Nations directly to the people.[7] However, three weeks after leaving Washington, after a well-received speech in Pueblo, Colorado, Wilson suffered a serious stroke. His illness ended the tour and reduced his effectiveness for the remainder of his presidency. The Senate initially defeated the treaty by a vote of thirty-nine to fifty-five, as forty-two Democrats loyally followed Wilson's request to reject it because of the Lodge reservations. In a later Senate vote, the Versailles Treaty was approved by a margin (forty-nine to thirty-five) that fell short of meeting the constitutional requirement of a two-thirds favorable majority, again in large part because of the president's unwillingness to accept the Lodge package of reservations on the league covenant.

Yet Wilson optimistically staked his hopes for a reversal of that verdict by relying once again on the public. The 1920 presidential election would serve, he hoped, as "a great and solemn referendum" on the League of Nations. In fact, the campaign predictably revolved around a wide variety of issues, ranging from prohibition to independence for Ireland. The 1920 Democratic platform and presidential candidate, James M. Cox, supported the league, but the Republican platform was sufficiently ambiguous such that both the league's supporters and its opponents could believe that the party followed their preferences. The resulting landslide victory for the Republican ticket headed by Warren G. Harding effectively ended the debate on American participation in the League of Nations.

Although Wilson's faith in the wisdom and power of public opinion did not save the Treaty of Versailles, his hopes for the beneficial effects of democratizing the making of foreign policy were not merely the lonely, utopian longings of a former college professor. Elihu Root, arguably the most distinguished Republican foreign policy leader of the time—he was a former secretary of war, secretary of state, and U.S. senator as well as the winner of the 1912 Nobel Peace Prize—effectively summarized the reasoning of those who welcomed an increasing public role in the conduct of foreign affairs. In the lead article of the initial issue of *Foreign Affairs*, published by the Council on Foreign Relations, Root (1922, 5) eloquently expressed the case for democratizing foreign policy.

> When foreign affairs were ruled by autocracies or oligarchies the danger of war was in sinister purpose. When foreign affairs are ruled by democracies the danger of war will be in mistaken beliefs. The world will be the gainer by the change, for, while there is no human way to prevent a king from having a bad heart, there is a human way to prevent a people from having an erroneous opinion.

By more effective international education, "the people themselves will have the means to test misinformation and appeals to prejudice and passion based on error."[8] Root was not alone among notable conservatives in emphasizing public opinion as a force for peace. Frank Kellogg and Henry Stimson, Republican secretaries of state, counted on public opinion as a pillar of support for the Kellogg-Briand Pact (also known as the Pact of Paris).

But not all observers of postwar world affairs joined Wilson and Root in applauding the prospect of popular diplomacy. A young journalist, Walter Lippmann, was among the leading skeptics. Lippmann had accepted appointments in the Wilson administration during World War I—first as an assistant to Secretary of

War Newton D. Baker and later on a secret committee to plan for the postwar world—that gave him insight into the uses and effects on public opinion of wartime propaganda. Disillusioned by the compromises that President Wilson made at the Paris Peace Conference, Lippmann and his colleagues at the *New Republic* unanimously opposed the Versailles Treaty on grounds quite similar to those of the most irreconcilable isolationists in the Senate: "Americans would be fools if they permitted themselves now to be embroiled in a system of European alliances" (Steel 1980, 159).

During the next few years, Lippmann undertook a full-scale attack on the liberal case for public opinion. In two book-length treatises (1922, 1925) that adopted a sociopsychological perspective on politics, he challenged the core premises of classical liberal democratic philosophy. Liberal theory assumed that, if given the facts, the public could and would make reasonable decisions. In contrast, Lippmann emphatically questioned whether the average citizen could make any constructive contribution to world affairs: "He lives in a world which he cannot see, does not understand, and is unable to direct" (1925, 14).

Liberal theory was, according to Lippmann, wrong on several counts. In his view, common people are too fully involved in the requirements of earning a living and in otherwise attending to their most immediate needs to have the time or inclination to satisfy the heroic but clearly unrealistic assumptions about the informed and engaged citizen celebrated in classical democratic theory. The chasm between theory and reality is especially wide in the realm of foreign affairs, which are typically far removed from the direct experiences of the general public. Because the "pictures in the head" of the average citizen are unlikely to have much correspondence to the real world of international affairs, according to Lippmann, even if the public were inclined to take an active part in foreign affairs, it could scarcely make an informed and constructive contribution. In fact, these "pictures" are likely to be little more than stereotypes that color the manner in which reality is perceived. Thus, average citizens are not unlike those portrayed in Plato's allegory of the cave; instead of directly observing reality, they can see only indirect and inadequate representations of it. Lippmann's remedy was also not unlike Plato's: the salvation of the democratic polity requires greater reliance on experts.

Finally, journalist Lippmann was not notably sanguine when he contemplated the role that his profession could play in bridging the gap between the real world and the average citizen's stereotypes. In a short book published in 1920, he had outlined the inadequacies of the press and questioned "whether government by consent can survive in a time when the manufacture of consent is an unregulated private enterprise. For in an exact sense the present crisis of western civilization is a crisis of journalism" (1920, 5). He also presented some proposals for improving the performance of the media.

With his *New Republic* colleague Charles Merz, Lippmann also undertook an empirical analysis of the press, focusing on the Russian Revolution as depicted on the pages of America's "newspaper of record," the *New York Times,* during 1917–20. As a standard against which to measure the performance of the *Times,* Lippmann and Merz's assessment included only events that unquestionably had occurred: the failure of the July 1917 Russian offensive in Galicia; the Bolshevik overthrow of the Kerensky provisional government in November 1917; the Russian-German peace treaty of Brest-Litovsk in March 1918; the failure of the White generals' campaign against the Bolsheviks; and the Bolshevik maintenance of power through March 1920. The study did little to assuage Lippmann's pessimism about the media's ability to serve as a source of valid information about the world for the public. Lippmann and Merz concluded that coverage of these events was inadequate and misleading: "In the large, the news about Russia is a case of seeing not what was, but what men wished to see. . . . From the point of view of professional journalism the reporting of the Russian Revolution is nothing short of a disaster. On the essential questions the net effect was almost always misleading, and misleading news is worse than none at all. . . . The Russian policy of the editors of the *Times* profoundly and crassly influenced their news columns" (1920, 2, 3, 42).

Although Lippmann's books were written long before public opinion polling had become a "science" and a pervasive feature of American society—and before he had achieved the status of a widely read, frequently quoted, and immensely influential syndicated columnist—they have had an extraordinary and continuing impact on students of public opinion and the role of the media. As one reviewer put it, "Lippmann's theories are the diving board from which scholars in these two disciplines take their plunge" (Isaacs 1994, 2–3).[9]

As has often been the case, the ebb and flow of the liberal-realist debate depended at least as much on the course of contemporary world events as on the eloquence and logic of supporters and critics of one side or the other. The events leading up to the outbreak of World War II, which seemed to raise serious questions about the optimistic Wilsonian premises while apparently providing compelling empirical confirmation for the realist approach to international politics, further tipped the balance in the debate on public opinion and foreign policy in favor of the skeptics. Hitler's ability to arouse public support for breaking out of the international order established at the Versailles Peace Conference as well as for more aggressive subsequent steps; the tepid response of the British and French publics to Japanese, German, and Italian expansion during the 1930s; and American isolationism in the face of mounting evidence that the post–World War I international order was collapsing were among the developments realists cited to sustain their doubts about the general publics' ability to contribute constructively to foreign policy.

A realist British diplomat and historian, Edward Hallett Carr, wrote perhaps the most savage attack on Wilsonian liberalism and its nineteenth-century intellectual foundations, with a special emphasis on what Carr called the liberal "doctrine of salvation by public opinion" (1946, 33). While his polemics were aimed at a wide array of liberal targets, including those who supported the League of Nations or who asserted that world public opinion would provide an effective sanction against aggression, Carr's most powerful attacks were directed at the Wilsonians and their faith in public opinion.

> Woodrow Wilson's "plain men throughout the world," the spokesmen of "the common purpose of enlightened mankind," had somehow transformed themselves into a disorderly mob emitting incoherent and unhelpful noises. It seemed undeniable that, in international affairs, public opinion was almost as often wrong-headed as it was impotent. . . . Governments of many countries acted in a sense precisely contrary to this [expert] advice [on how to conduct foreign policy], and received the endorsement of public opinion at the polls. . . .The breakdown of the post-War utopia is too overwhelming to be explained merely in terms of individual action or inaction. Its downfall involves the bankruptcy of the postulates [about public opinion] on which it is based. (1946, 50–53)

The Inception of "Scientific" Opinion Polling

The period encompassing World War II and its immediate aftermath coincided with the inception of "scientific" public opinion polling. The 1936 presidential election provided something of an unplanned critical experiment on two approaches to polling. The *Literary Digest* used a method that had enabled it correctly to predict the winner in several previous presidential elections, including Franklin Roosevelt's victory over Herbert Hoover in 1932. In the 1936 Roosevelt-Landon election, the magazine sent out ten million ballots, describing its poll as the "most extensive straw ballot in the field—the most experienced in view of its twenty-five years of perfecting—the most unbiased in view of its prestige—a Poll that has always been correct." From its returns of more than two million ballots, it confidently forecast a Landon victory of landslide proportions: the Kansas governor was predicted to win 57 percent of the popular vote and 370 votes in the electoral college (*Literary Digest* 1936, 5–6). In fact, Landon carried only Maine and Vermont, and the *Literary Digest* folded before it could try to salvage its reputation in the 1940 presidential election.[10]

In contrast, the recently established American Institute of Public Opinion, more popularly known as the Gallup poll, used a sampling design that yielded far fewer respondents but a more representative sample. Gallup correctly predicted the outcome, but even his poll underestimated the magnitude of the Roosevelt electoral avalanche. Nevertheless, we can date the beginning of the era of scientific surveys from the establishment of the Gallup poll in 1935 or of the *Public Opinion Quarterly* three years later.[11]

Polling also became a part of the policy process. In an effort to influence public attitudes on foreign policy, the State Department had established a Division of Information before World War I. The State Department later undertook its own polling to assess public attitudes (see Elder 1957; White 1959; Chittick 1970; Foster 1983). Despite his avid interest in polling and Gallup's correct call in the 1936 election, President Roosevelt nevertheless entertained doubts about the nonpartisanship of the Gallup organization. In a meeting with Democratic congressional leaders a month before the 1940 election, FDR asserted,

You watch these polls, you watch the Republican timing of the campaign. . . . They're going to show Willkie—ah—in pretty good shape the first part of August. Then they're going to put him through a bad slump, *bad slump,* so that I'll be well out ahead on the first of October. And my judgment is that they are going to start Willkie—pickin' up! pickin' up! pickin' up!—from the first of October.... In the Gallup poll, we'll have a great many—too many—votes handed to us.[12]

Consequently, Roosevelt also turned to other sources. He was a pioneer in the use of a professional public opinion consultant—Hadley Cantril, one of the founding fathers of the new science—for guidance on policy on both domestic and foreign policy. Roosevelt had an extraordinary interest in public opinion, and there is ample evidence that his foreign policy actions were significantly shaped and constrained by his sense of what was politically feasible given the climate of domestic opinion (Dallek 1979; Casey 2001). Virtually all presidents since Roosevelt—even those who have expressed disdain for "policy by polls"—have engaged the services of public opinion specialists. Cantril not only advised FDR in this capacity but went on to serve as a consultant to the Eisenhower and Kennedy administrations.

Theory and research on international relations have almost always been shaped by contemporary events in the real world. It is impossible to understand the agenda that dominated research and writing on public opinion and foreign policy during the first quarter century after the inception of scientific polling without reference to the central policy question of the period: namely, what role would the United States play in the postwar international system? Members of the Roosevelt administration and many others who felt that an irresponsible American isolationism after 1919 had contributed to the breakdown of the Versailles world order and the consequent outbreak of war feared that after World War II, the public mood might trace out a pattern resembling the experience of the earlier conflict: that is, wartime idealism and internationalism, followed soon thereafter by cynicism and disenchantment with active American leadership in efforts to create a new and more stable international order, and concluding ultimately with withdrawal.

During the decade before Pearl Harbor, the essential lessons of World War I for many Americans could be summarized by two words: never again! When war broke out in Europe in 1939, an overwhelming proportion of the public favored the Western allies over Germany—even a Soviet victory was seen as preferable to a German one — but sentiments for staying out of the war were even stronger.[13] Isolationists, Anglophobes, revisionist historians, and the congressional hearings conducted by Senator Gerald Nye had persuaded many Americans that the nation's entry into World War I — a "war to end all wars" — had more to do with the machinations of American munitions makers, bankers, and other wealthy holders of British bonds than with the prudent pursuit of national interests. Consequently, many Americans came to hold highly skeptical views of the nation's participation in that conflict and a resulting determination never again to become embroiled in war for reasons short of a direct attack on the United States. Indeed, in a 1937 Gallup poll, 70 percent of the respondents answered in the affirmative when asked, "Do you think it was a mistake for the United States to enter the World War?" That opinion remained virtually unchanged as late as a month after the German invasion of Poland in 1939, when 68 percent of respondents stated that entering World War I had been a mistake.

Perhaps of even greater importance, much of the public looked to the experience of World War I as a rich source of "lessons" to guide U.S. foreign policy. During the 1930s, Congress had regularly passed neutrality legislation aimed at preventing a recurrence of the policies and actions that, according to many isolationists, had led the United States into war in 1917. The Ludlow Amendment to the Constitution, which required a national referendum before any declaration of war unless it was in response to an invasion of the United States, failed in the House of Representatives by only a handful of votes despite diligent lobbying against it by the president and Secretary of State Cordell Hull. A series of Gallup surveys conducted between 1935 and 1939 revealed consistently strong support for several key propositions that, according to isolationists, would prevent the nation from being unwisely dragged into war, as had been the case in 1917.[14] These were, specifically:

Restraints on the executive

To declare war, the Congress should be required to obtain approval of the people in a national referendum. Seventy-five percent of respondents to a September 1935 Gallup survey agreed with this proposition, and it gained the approval of 71 and 73 percent of those taking part in surveys during the next two years. By February 1939, after the Ludlow Amendment had been defeated in the House of Representatives and seven months before World War II began in Europe, this proposal still had the support of almost 60 percent of the public.

In March 1939, 61 percent of respondents supported a constitutional amendment to require a national vote before Congress could draft men to fight overseas. Support for such an amendment declined to 51 percent six months later.

According to more than two-thirds of those taking part in a 1937 survey, Congress was more to be trusted than the president to keep the United States out of war.

Restraints on Americans abroad

Americans should not be permitted to engage in certain types of risky behavior because doing so might drag the United States into war. For example, only 18 percent agreed in September 1939 that American citizens should be allowed to travel on ships of warring countries. The same survey revealed that even fewer respondents (16 percent) agreed that American ships should be allowed to carry goods anywhere rather than be kept out of war zones.

American citizens in China should be warned to leave, and the troops protecting them should be withdrawn, according to 54 percent of respondents in August 1937. A similar proposal garnered even higher support (70 percent) four months later.

Restraints on arms and arms makers

The manufacture and sale of war munitions for private profit should be prohibited, according to 82 percent of those to whom the question was posed in January 1936.

In surveys conducted in 1937 and 1938, two-thirds of the public favored a world disarmament conference.

Almost two-thirds of the public opposed arms shipments to China in February 1938. Five months earlier, an overwhelming 95 percent had opposed any bank loans to China or Japan.

By early 1939, a very small majority (52 percent) agreed that the United States should sell arms to Britain and France. However, after war had broken out in Europe in September 1939, 90 percent of respondents wanted Great Britain and France to pay cash for American goods rather than allowing those countries to buy on credit. An even greater proportion (94 percent) agreed that Britain and France should be required to carry the goods away on their own ships.

Internationalists regarded the outbreak of World War II as the direct result of a shortsighted and futile isolationist agenda. Even some devout isolationists experienced a conversion. For example, Senator Arthur Vandenberg, a leading isolationist and Republican presidential hopeful, began his diary on December 7, 1941, with the observation, "In my own mind, my convictions regarding international cooperation and collective security for peace took form on the afternoon of the Pearl Harbor attack. That day ended isolationism for any realist" (1952, 1). But there could be no assurance that others would read the lessons of the interwar period in the same manner. Because the Senate's rejection of the Treaty of Versailles symbolized for many internationalists the abdication of a responsible U.S. role in the postwar international order, a central question was whether the United States would join or again turn its back on membership in a general international organization after World War II.

Interest in the postwar state of American public opinion was reflected in the frequency with which the Gallup and other polling organizations asked respondents general questions about the United States taking an active role in or staying out of world affairs and more specific queries about support for or opposition to American membership in a general international organization. These surveys seemed to indicate that substantial majorities among the general public in fact rejected a return to isolationism after the war. A January 1942 Office of Public Opinion Research survey revealed that, by a margin of 71 to 24 percent, Americans preferred taking "an active role" rather than "staying out" of postwar international affairs. The same question was posed nine additional times between February 1942 and November 1946, a period that included the Normandy invasion, the defeat of Nazi Germany, the atomic bomb attacks on Japan, the end of World War II, and the first signs that wartime cooperation among the victorious Allies would not extend into the postwar period. Responses to each of those surveys indicated, by margins ranging between three and four to one, that the public rejected an American retreat from an active international role. Further evidence that the public might reject isolationism emerged from a question posed just as the guns were being stilled in Europe. A strong majority of

Americans supported the reciprocal trade agreement program as well as its use for further reductions of tariffs in the United States and abroad (Gallup 1972, 505).

Public sentiments on another key issue should also have provided some comfort for internationalists, as Gallup surveys revealed comparably strong support for U.S. membership in some kind of general international organization. As early as July 1941, several months before the attack on Pearl Harbor brought the United States into the war, almost three-fourths of the general public favored American entry into such an organization. Although the name and nature of the organization and the specific obligations of membership could not have been known at that time, these results appear to have reflected a rather sharp shift in public sentiment since the mid-1930s. Interestingly, only a month later, a survey of leaders drawn from *Who's Who in America* revealed that elite support for U.S. participation in an international organization fell somewhat short of that among the general public.

A June 1944 Gallup poll also suggested that President Roosevelt's efforts to avoid some of Woodrow Wilson's mistakes in dealing with the League of Nations issue were bearing fruit: 72 percent of the respondents favored American membership in a successor to the League of Nations, and differences between Democrats and Republicans were negligible (Gallup 1972, 451–52). Wilson had broken a tacit wartime agreement to mute partisanship by asking the electorate to support him with Democratic House and Senate majorities in midterm elections held just as peace was settling over Europe in 1918; he failed to include any prominent Republicans in the American delegation to the Versailles Peace Conference; he allowed his deep personal animosity toward Republican Senator Henry Cabot Lodge, chairman of the Foreign Relations Committee after the 1918 elections gave the Republicans majorities in both the House and Senate, to color the administration's strategy for guiding the Versailles Treaty through the Senate; and, finally, Wilson rejected even moderate compromises on the treaty in the hopes of ultimately winning on all its features. As he put it, "I would rather be defeated in a cause that will ultimately triumph, than to win in a cause that will ultimately be defeated" (quoted in Kegley 1993, 131).

Unlike Wilson, Roosevelt had engaged such leading Republicans as John Foster Dulles in planning for a postwar international organization and had avoided casting the issue in partisan terms. Indeed, the agreement between Secretary of State Hull and

Dulles, the foreign policy adviser to Republican candidate Thomas Dewey, to keep the United Nations issue out of the 1944 presidential campaign is often cited as the genesis of bipartisanship in foreign policy. The June 1944 Gallup survey revealed Republicans were scarcely less inclined than Democrats to support American membership in the United Nations. Even respondents from the Midwest, often considered the most congenial region for isolationism, did not in fact differ on this issue from those living in other sections of the country.

This reassuring survey evidence notwithstanding, fears of a postwar return to isolationism persisted. Roosevelt's concerns in this respect were amplified by a memorandum that Cantril gave the president just before he left for the Yalta Conference with Churchill and Stalin early in 1945. According to Cantril,

> Although the overwhelming majority of the American people now favor a strong international organization necessarily dominated by the big powers, it is unrealistic to assume that Americans are international-minded. Their policy is rather one of expediency, which, at the moment, takes the form of internationalism. The present internationalism rests on a rather unstable foundation: it is recent, it is not rooted in any broad or long-range conception of self-interest, it has little intellectual basis. (1967, 76)

This advice reinforced Roosevelt's judgment. He said privately, "Anybody who thinks that isolationism is dead in this country is crazy. As soon as this war is over, it may well be stronger than ever" (quoted in A. Schlesinger 1995, 4). Roosevelt also told his allies that public opinion would not permit American occupation troops to remain in Europe for more than two years after the end of the war.

Although attended only by the soon-to-be victorious Allies, the 1945 San Francisco conference from which the United Nations Charter emerged was marked by disagreement on a number of issues. American participation in the United Nations nevertheless won overwhelming support in the Senate, with only two dissenting votes cast. Thus, the United States joined the United Nations when that organization came into existence in October 1945. Despite success in the campaign to bring the United States into the United Nations, proponents of an active American role in postwar international affairs continued to worry that there might soon be a reversion to withdrawal, and they usually focused their attention on public opinion as the most likely driving force behind any return to isolationism. Consequently, research on the relationship of public opinion to foreign policy emerged as a growth industry during the period immediately following World War II. Much of the analysis and writing on the question was marked by two features: an empirical approach that relied heavily on the growing body of polling data, and a normative concern that mood swings among the public might lead the United States to repeat the failed isolationist policies of the interwar years. Both these features may be found in three of the pioneering works on public opinion and foreign policy: Thomas A. Bailey's *The Man in the Street* (1948), Lester Markel's *Public Opinion and Foreign Policy* (1949), and Gabriel Almond's *The American People and Foreign Policy* (1950). Each of these works examined the growing body of evidence produced by the Gallup Poll, the Office of Public Opinion Research at Princeton, the National Opinion Research Center, and other major survey organizations. These authors found very little in the data to assuage their concerns and came to share a distinctly skeptical view of average people and their potential contributions to the conduct of postwar American foreign policy. Fears that an ill-informed and emotion-driven American public would force the country back into an irresponsible isolationism generated a substantial postwar research effort.

An Overview

The consensus that emerged from much of this research during the two decades following the end of World War II, which I will review in chapter 2, painted an unflattering portrait of the general public. Public opinion was described not only as ignorant about international realities but also as volatile, reflecting unstable moods of the moment rather than an understanding of international realities as well as lacking in any structure or coherence. Although some observers feared that a feckless public would severely damage the prospects for a coherent foreign policy, other commentators assured these critics that public opinion seldom if ever has a significant impact on actual policy decisions.

Just as the two world wars stimulated interest in the public's impact on foreign policy, the Vietnam War served as a catalyst for serious reexamination of the post–World War II consensus on the nature and effects of public opinion. Although these more recent studies continued to show that the public is often poorly informed about international affairs, the evidence nevertheless challenged the theses that public opinion on foreign policy issues is volatile, structureless, and without significant impact on policymaking. Following a summary of these research efforts, chapter 3 then turns to some further evidence about the nature of public opinion by examining survey data on attitudes toward several of the most important clusters of issues of the Cold War and post–Cold War eras: namely, the nature of the Soviet Union (Russia after 1991) and China and their foreign policy goals; prospects for conflict or cooperation between Washington and Moscow and the United States and China; and appropriate U.S. foreign policy goals.

Chapter 4 compares the general public and opinion leaders—the relatively small stratum of the public that is most likely to be interested in, informed about, and influential in the way in which the United States copes with international challenges and opportunities. The chapter first examines data on the content of opinions about several international issues, including the appropriate U.S. role in the world, trade and protectionism, economic and technical assistance, military assistance, deployment of U.S. troops abroad, and foreign policy goals. The analysis then turns to the structure of foreign policy beliefs, presenting evidence about appraisals of the international system, future threats to U.S. national security, the Persian Gulf War, and the sources of change in Eastern Europe and the former Soviet Union. The chapter concludes with an examination of the relationship between opinion leaders' domestic and foreign policy beliefs.

Chapter 5 focuses on the sources of foreign policy beliefs among both the general public and opinion leaders. The chapter examines in some detail the hypothesis that partisan and ideological differences have, since the Vietnam War, increasingly become the driving forces behind debates on the conduct of American foreign policy. The chapter also presents evidence about other background factors that are often identified as important sources of foreign policy attitudes, including generation, gender, education, occupation, region, and race.

According to some observers, the end of the Cold War marked the end of public support for the internationalist and multilateralist impulses that had dominated U.S. foreign policy for more than a half century after the attack on Pearl Harbor in 1941. For some analysts, that change is a source of great concern, whereas for others it is a long overdue retrenchment made possible by the disintegration of the Soviet Union at the end of 1989. Chapter 6 addresses the validity of the thesis that such a transformation of public preferences has occurred, either before or after the 2001 terrorist attacks. It is no doubt too early to assess the long-term impact of the September 11 attacks and the 2003 invasion of Iraq, but it is possible to undertake at least an interim analysis that focuses on continuities and changes in public opinion.

Chapter 7 addresses the question "Where do we go from here?" It develops the thesis that public opinion is likely to play a more rather than less potent role during the post–Cold War era, at least in part because the "new" issues that are likely to gain prominence on foreign policy agendas—including but not limited to trade, immigration, the environment, and civil wars arising from nationalism, religion, and ethnicity—are more likely to be resistant to executive arguments that the requirements of secrecy, speed, and flexibility justify excluding the public and its representatives from the policy process. The chapter then turns to some of the ways in which our understanding of public opinion and its impact might be strengthened. The conclusion adduces some anecdotal evidence to suggest that although there is compelling evidence that the public is often ill informed about specific aspects of world affairs, there is nevertheless more to fear from processes and policies that blatantly disregard public sentiments than from those that make a serious effort to engage the public in discussions of such central questions as the scope and nature of American interests in developing situations.

CHAPTER 2

The Post–World War II Consensus

Among the social scientists enlisted into the effort to win World War II were survey researchers. Their most notable contributions included classic studies of morale among American soldiers (Stouffer et al. 1949) and the impact of strategic bombing on Germany (U.S. Strategic Bombing Survey 1947).[1] Julian Woodward, who had worked in the Office of War Information, believed that such surveys ultimately would become a routine function of government:

> Sooner or later the government itself will have to go into the polling field and provide both its administrators and its legislators with adequate and sound information on what the public thinks. Eventually this sort of information will become as necessary as census data and will be provided by an agency with a reputation for unbiased research equal to that now enjoyed by the Census Bureau. (1945, 245)

The inception of scientific public opinion polling was not universally applauded, however. Congress, suspicious of the political and social uses to which surveys could be put, dismantled much of the wartime apparatus for such studies. Even George Gallup, whose surveys had underestimated the Democratic vote in 1944 – as they had also done in 1936 and 1940 – was called before Congress to explain the errors of his ways (J. Converse 1987, 207–10). Survey skeptics also existed outside Congress. One of them, Lester Markel, welcomed the startling failure of the Gallup and other polls to predict Harry Truman's victory over Thomas Dewey in the 1948 presidential election, and Markel ventured the judgment that as a result, the practice of polling would be permanently discredited: "The poll, then, fortunately, has been dethroned from its high place. Government, Congress and the people will be better off" (1949, 31). But even Markel conceded that surveys might be useful for gaining some insight into the average citizen's knowledge—or lack of knowledge—about international affairs.

All of the many surveys undertaken during the years immediately following World War II to assess the level of public knowledge about international affairs came to essentially the same two conclusions. First, among the general population there is a wide variation in the level of factual information about world affairs, and the average citizen is remarkably uninformed, even about institutions, events, and personalities that have been the focus of current news and controversies. Soon after the United States joined the United Nations as a charter member, a National Opinion Research Center survey in Cincinnati revealed that few citizens had much interest in or knowledge about that international organization. Even a rather simple six-question test found that 30 percent of the respondents were "uninformed" about the United Nations and another 27 percent were "poorly informed" (National Opinion Research Center 1947).[2] Other evidence indicated that the citizens of Cincinnati were not unusual in this respect (Cottrell and Eberhart 1948).

In the same manner, Thomas Bailey's (1948) pioneering study of public opinion and foreign policy, based on the growing archives of survey evidence at the Gallup Organization and elsewhere, sketched a distinctly unflattering portrait of *The Man in the Street.* Bailey's chapter titles—for example, "The Perils of Apathy," "The Incubus of Ignorance," "The Curse of Caprice," and "The Fruits of Isolation"—provide ample clues to the substance of his main fears and findings. Martin Kriesberg (1949) undertook a similar study of the survey evidence and, in a chapter entitled "Dark Areas of Ignorance," emerged with conclusions that sustained those of the Cincinnati and Bailey studies. Gabriel Almond's *The American People and Foreign Policy* (1950), the most important and systematic analysis of survey data on the topic to that point, reinforced the conclusion that despite the dramatic events of the previous decade—including World War II, the start of the nuclear era, the nation's emergence as a world leader, and the onset of the Cold War—many Americans remained remarkably uninformed about even the most elementary aspects of international affairs.

Research undertaken by educators would be unlikely to applaud widespread ignorance about the world, and indeed, all these studies pointed to the need for better international education. The mere fact of public ignorance, however, was not the sole reason for worry. Concerns about the lack of basic information about international affairs were reinforced—perhaps even magnified—by a second finding that emerged consistently from the survey data. One's level of knowledge about the world was typically correlated with attitudes toward many important aspects of international affairs, including global institutions, other nations, and appropriate U.S. foreign policies for coping with postwar issues. For example, the Cincinnati study found that among the better-informed respondents, 76 percent thought that America should take an active part in world affairs, 55 percent mentioned an international problem as among the most important confronting the United States, and 61 percent agreed that they would benefit personally from increased foreign trade. Among the "uninformed," the comparable figures were 41 percent, 29 percent, and 41 percent (National Opinion Research Center 1947).

More generally, respondents within the least informed strata of the public were also most likely to be isolationist, chauvinist, suspicious of other nations, and generally opposed to policies that involved international cooperation, whether in the United Nations, through the Marshall Plan, or in the North Atlantic Treaty Organization. Conversely, the most informed strata of the public also tended to provide the strongest support for the wide array of international undertakings that constituted what was often described as the post–World War II "revolution in U.S. foreign policy."

In short, much of the research during the years immediately following the end of the World War II was driven by the same normative concerns that had engaged internationalists during the war—the fear that the public would in fact validate Hadley Cantril's warning to President Roosevelt, cited in chapter 1, by retreating from its temporary and shallow enthusiasm for an active international role once the fighting had ended. Thomas Bailey expressed views that more or less represented a shared outlook among many pioneers in the study of public opinion and foreign policy:

> The statesmen in charge of American foreign policy, as well as the better-informed citizens, know that isolation is not only dead but dangerous; that we must learn to see the other nation's problems as they appear to its eyes; that we must cultivate tolerance and understanding; that we must sublimate suspicion and ill-will; that we must yield pride and

prestige; that we must meet the other fellow half way, sometimes more than half way; and that we must invest some of our precious sovereignty in effective world organization—perhaps some kind of world government. But the average citizen—indifferent, ignorant, or misled by ill informed and sometimes unscrupulous editors, columnists, radio commentators, and politicians—does not see all these things. Yet, as we have repeatedly observed throughout this book, American public opinion in the long run determines basic foreign policies. If the American people, through their Congress, insist upon isolation, non-cooperation, ruinous tariff barriers, and other impediments to world recovery, they will have their way—with consequent disaster. (1950, 907)

The availability after World War II of growing archives of polling data and the institution of systematic studies of voting behavior, combined with the U.S. assumption of a leadership role in world affairs, served to stimulate many additional analyses of public opinion. A general consensus about the nature, structure, and impact of public opinion seemed to have emerged from those who focused on international affairs between the end of World War II and the escalation of the American military effort in Vietnam. This consensus centered on three major propositions.

> Public opinion is highly volatile and thus provides very dubious foundations on which to develop and sustain sound foreign policies.
> Public attitudes on international affairs are so lacking in structure or coherence that they might best be described as nonopinions.
> At the end of the day, however, perhaps the deficiencies of the general public will not be so damaging because public opinion has a very limited impact on the conduct of foreign policy.

Let us examine in more detail each of these propositions and the evidence on which they rest.

Public Opinion Is Volatile

In an early analysis of the sources and nature of public opinion, Gabriel Almond argued that most Americans invest their intellectual and emotional energies in private pursuits, to the neglect of public policy concerns. Policy issues that impinge directly on daily life may generate some interest and attention among the public, but remote international events rarely do so. Consequently, foreign policy issues give rise to mass indifference, punctuated by occasional apprehension or anger in response to international crises. Almond described these "superficial and fluctuating responses" as "plastic moods which undergo frequent alteration in response to changes in events" (1950, 53). Lacking any firm foundations in knowledge of or interest in international affairs, these moods are highly unstable but are not necessarily random or unpredictable. Owing to some central tendencies in the American national character, Almond suggested that public mood swings would take place along several dimensions of direct relevance to foreign policy:

Withdrawal/ intervention
Unstructured moods/policy simplification
Optimism/pessimism
Tolerance/intolerance
Idealism/cynicism
Superiority/inferiority

Almond proposed the hypothesis that these mood fluctuations are related to the business cycle. Specifically, he suggested that an economic depression would impair national self-confidence, weaken foreign policy resolution, result in feelings of international overextension, and lead ultimately to withdrawal (1950, 54–65).

To substantiate the thesis that public moods are highly volatile, Almond turned to one of the questions that had been posed repeatedly by Gallup surveys between 1935 and 1949: "What is the most important problem facing the United States today?" The evidence revealed striking shifts in the percentage of respondents who identified any foreign policy issue as most important. Between November 1935 and January 1939, that figure ranged between 11 and 26 percent. During the first year after Hitler's invasion of Poland, the figure rose to just under half of the respondents, and by November 1941 (just prior to the Japanese attack on Pearl Harbor), 81 percent of the public placed a foreign policy issue first on the agenda of the nation's most important problems. A month after the Japanese surrender in 1945, domestic issues again took top priority for an overwhelming proportion of the public, as only 7 percent identified a foreign policy issue as the most important problem. During the next four years, the comparable figures ranged from a low of 11 percent in June 1946 (ten months after the Japanese surrender but before the Cold War) to a high of 73 percent less than two years later, when the Soviets had just instituted the Berlin blockade.[3]

Interpreting these data, however, is not unlike deciding whether a glass is half full or half empty. From Almond's perspective, the surveys revealed a fickle public whose limited attention span precluded a steady focus on important international problems. But the same figures do not automatically exclude an alternative and somewhat more flattering interpretation of shifts in public identification of the most serious problems: the public reasonably focuses its attention on external problems when wars, crises, and confrontations pose a major threat to the United States. When these international threats appear to have faded or disappeared (for example, with the Japanese surrender that ended World War II) public attention turns to more proximate problems and threats that originate in the domestic arena (for example, unemployment, inflation, race relations, or crime). Some economists feared that postwar cuts in military spending and demobilization of millions from the armed forces would throw the United States into a recession or even a depression. Thus, concerns about the state of economy following the end of hostilities do not necessarily serve as powerful evidence of public ignorance or fickleness.

The explanation for these mood swings resembled those proposed by Tocqueville in the nineteenth century and Lippmann during the 1920s. It could be found, according to Almond, in general American value orientations:

> The average American is so deeply and tensely involved with immediate, private concerns that any diversion of attention meets with powerful resistance. When political issues impinge, or threaten to impinge, upon these concerns, public attention broadens to include them. But the moment the pressure is reduced there is a swift withdrawal, like the snapping back of a strained elastic. (1950, 76)

Although the half decade prior to Almond's study had witnessed a number of major international commitments by the United States, including membership in the United Nations, the

World Bank, the International Monetary Fund, the North Atlantic Treaty Organization, the Truman Doctrine, and the Marshall Plan, Almond drew some sober policy conclusions from his analysis. The possibility of a relapse into mindless isolationism could not be ruled out because only a thin veneer of postwar internationalism covered a thick bedrock of indifference to the world. Most leaders might understand that isolationism was no longer a viable option for the United States, but public opinion could serve as a volatile and mood-driven constraint on foreign policy: "The undertow of withdrawal is still very powerful. Deeply ingrained habits do not die easy deaths. The world outside is still very remote for most Americans; and the tragic lessons of the past decade have not been fully digested" (Almond 1950, 85). Consequently, "Perhaps the gravest general problem confronting policymakers is that of the instability of mass moods, and cyclical fluctuations which stand in the way of policy stability" (239).

Six years later, Almond restated his thesis, citing not only the instability of public moods but also other deficiencies of public opinion. He told an audience at the National War College, "For persons responsible for the making of security policy these *mood* impacts of the mass public have a highly irrational effect. Often public opinion is apathetic when it should be concerned, and panicky when it should be calm" (1956, 59).[4]

Expressions of concern about the instability of public opinion were not limited to such academic analysts as historian Bailey and political scientist Almond. George F. Kennan, a diplomat whose "long telegram" from Moscow in 1946 and subsequent "X" article in 1947 often have been depicted as the intellectual foundations of the American policy of containment, delivered a series of 1950 lectures that examined the bases, assumptions, and practices of American diplomacy. Kennan's diagnosis, like those of Tocqueville and Almond, focused broadly on American society rather than solely on public opinion. From a realist perspective on world affairs, Kennan raised some questions about the ability of a democratic society imbued with moralistic and legalistic values to conduct its external relations effectively. Using the metaphor of a dinosaur, Kennan vividly depicted his views on the inept ways in which democracies attempt to cope with their international environments:

But I sometimes wonder whether in this respect a democracy is not uncomfortably similar to one of those prehistoric monsters with a body as long as this room and a brain the size of a pin: he lies there in his comfortable primeval mud and pays little attention to his environment; he is slow to wrath—in fact, you practically have to whack his tail off to make him aware that his interests are being disturbed; but, once he grasps this, he lays about him with such blind determination that he not only destroys his adversary but largely wrecks his native habitat. (1951, 59)

Kennan recognized that it would be impossible to eliminate altogether the impact of public opinion, but his prescription, like those of Bailey and Almond, strongly emphasized giving foreign policy experts and the executive a greater degree of latitude in the conduct of policy:

Before this government can function effectively in foreign affairs, there will have to be a greater spirit of organization and discipline throughout it, a greater readiness to recognize and submit to constituted authority, a more courageous acceptance of the fact that power must be delegated and delegated power must be respected. I believe that there can be far greater concentration of authority within the operating branches of our Government without detriment to the essentials of democracy. (lecture on June 18, 1947, in Harlow and Maerz 1991, 214–15)[5]

Walter Lippmann, who by the 1950s had become America's most influential political columnist, delivered still another attack on public opinion, charging that democracy run amok had come to threaten the possibility of formulating and implementing effective foreign policies. During the interwar period, Lippmann had described the average citizen as indifferent and ill informed about the world and thus unable to play the role required by classical democratic theory. Moreover, Lippmann had repeatedly expressed doubts that the mass media could or would bridge the chasm between the public's stereotypes and international reality.

Three decades later, at the height of the Cold War, Lippmann had become even more alarmed about the prospects for democratic government because the "spirit of Jacobinism" had destroyed the proper balance between rulers and the ruled, resulting in "excesses of democracy" and "misrule by the people." While public opinion remained ignorant, in his view it had been transformed from a largely indifferent and inert body into an almost uncontrollable monster. "Where mass opinion dominates the government, there is a morbid derangement of the true functions of power. The derangement brings about the enfeeblement, verging on paralysis, of the capacity to govern." The consequences are no less than "the precipitate and catastrophic decline of Western society" (1955, 15). Tracing the roots of the problem to the need of democratic governments to pander to the public during World War I, Lippmann asserted that legislatures, representing the will of the public, had infringed seriously on the proper prerogatives of the executive, with disastrous consequences for the quality of foreign policy. Whereas his earlier analyses had emphasized the public's indifference and ignorance, by 1955 Lippmann had come to see public opinion as a virtually irresistible, highly irresponsible, and potentially catastrophic element in the conduct of foreign affairs:

> The unhappy truth is that the prevailing public opinion has been destructively wrong at the critical junctures. The people have impressed a critical veto upon the judgments of informed and responsible officials. They have compelled the government, which usually knew what would have been wiser, or was necessary, or what was more expedient, to be too late with too little, or too long with too much, too pacifist in peace and too bellicose in war, too neutralist or appeasing in negotiations or too intransigent. Mass opinion has acquired mounting power in this country. It has shown itself to be a dangerous master of decision when the stakes are life and death. (1955, 20)

Although Lippmann's book was intended to be a broad-ranging treatise on the philosophical foundations of all democratic governments rather than a commentary on the making of contemporary American foreign policy, it is somewhat ironic that his volume was published during the first Eisenhower administration, a period when executive dominance of foreign policy had perhaps reached its peak. A combination of personal popularity and impressive experience in international affairs provided Eisenhower with a good deal of latitude in the conduct of foreign and defense policy. Congressional challenges to the executive role in the conduct of foreign relations, in the form of the Bricker Amendment on treaty powers and Senator Joseph McCarthy's shotgun attacks on the State Department, the Foreign Service, the U.S. Army, General George Marshall, and Presidents Truman and Eisenhower, to name just a few of the more prominent targets, had recently been beaten back. Indeed, formal censure by his colleagues in 1954 effectively removed the power of the senator from Wisconsin to wreak havoc on American diplomacy. More generally, although Democrats regained control of Congress after the 1954 elections, the most vitriolic congressional attack on Eisenhower's foreign policies often came from right-wing Republicans. Although partisan differences certainly existed in congressional policy debates and votes, many disagreements of the period revolved around means, strategies, and tactics for achieving ends shared by most members on both sides of the aisle. (On this point, compare Wittkopf 1990 and Holsti and Rosenau 1984.) Moreover, it would be hard to find serious evidence that, during the Eisenhower years, public opinion was so significantly at variance with the main features of American external policies that it seriously hampered the White House's ability to conduct foreign relations. Few foreign policy issues of the Eisenhower era divided the public along primarily partisan lines (Campbell et al. 1964, 113–14; see also chap. 5). If the term *internationalist foreign policy consensus* was ever a valid description of the domestic bases of American foreign policy, it would appear to have been most applicable to the period between the traumas of the Korean and Vietnam Wars.

Many others contributed to the view that public opinion on foreign policy issues is highly volatile. By the mid-1960s, if not before, that conclusion had become a standard part of virtually all treatises and textbooks on the domestic sources of American foreign policy. Guided by Almond's hypothesis that superficial attitudes are "bound to be unstable since they are not anchored in a set of explicit values and means calculations or traditional compulsions" (1950, 69), studies directed at locating the sources of public volatility seemed to find the answer in the structure—or more precisely, in the lack of structure—of mass political beliefs.

Public Opinion Lacks Structure and Coherence

The growing volume of data on public opinion and voting behavior, as well as increasingly sophisticated surveys, statistical methodologies, and the advent of computers in social science research, enabled analysts not only to describe aggregate results and trends but also to delve into the structure of political beliefs.

Owing to immediate policy concerns about the U.S. role in the postwar era, many of the early studies were largely descriptive, focusing on attitudes toward such issues as participation in international organizations and alliances, the deployment of troops abroad, security commitments, foreign aid, and protectionism. Would the United States accept internationalist and cooperative policies to deal with these and other issues, or would it retreat into a more isolationist stance? The underlying premise was that a single internationalist-to-isolationist dimension would serve to structure foreign policy beliefs, much in the same way that a liberal-to-conservative dimension was assumed to underlie preferences on domestic issues.

Challenges to the notion that the public's political thinking had ideological underpinnings that gave rise to coherent and consistent issue voting emerged most prominently from studies of American voters and the bases of their electoral decisions (Lazarsfeld, Berelson, and Gaudet 1944; Berelson, Lazarsfeld, and McPhee 1954; Campbell et al. 1964). In a classic study based on evidence from the late 1950s and early 1960s, Philip Converse (1964) analyzed the correlations across responses to questions on domestic and foreign policy issues as well as between these two policy areas. Finding only very low correlations, he concluded that the political beliefs of the mass public lacked any "constraint" or underlying ideological consistency that might provide genuine structure or coherence to political thinking and to the act of voting. Converse's findings yielded little support for those who had argued that foreign policy attitudes constituted a special case because this issue area was remote from the daily concerns of the average citizen. In contrast to these findings about the general public, his analyses of elites—congressional candidates—revealed substantially higher correlations across responses to various domestic and foreign policy issues. Moreover, Converse found that both mass and elite attitudes on a given issue had short half-lives. Responses to a question in 1956 only modestly predicted answers to the same question two years later, much less in 1960. These findings led him to conclude that mass political beliefs are best described as "nonattitudes" (Converse 1970).

Although Converse's findings later became the center of an active debate, his was not a lone voice in the wilderness. His results contributed additional evidence in support of hypotheses developed by Almond and others about the absence of intellectual foundations for public moods and provided a plausible explanation for the putative volatility of public attitudes. More-over, Converse's findings were only one of the most widely quoted results emerging from the voting studies. Other students of electoral behavior came to essentially the same conclusions about the absence of structure, coherence, or persistence in the political beliefs of the mass public, especially in the area of for-eign affairs (W. Miller 1967). For most Americans, these scholars asserted, the bases of voting decisions did not lie in structured or ideological assessments and responses to policy issues. Campbell and his coauthors have offered a concise summary of the primary findings that emerged from the voting studies: "What psycholog-ical dimensions of voting are of greatest importance to the polit-ical system? Our discussion will focus on the low emotional in-volvement of the electorate in politics; its slight awareness of public affairs; its failure to think in structured, ideological terms; and its pervasive sense of attachment to one or the other of the two major parties" (1964, 280–81). Thus, whether analyzed as a respondent to Gallup or other surveys or as a voter, the average American citizen portrayed in study after study was a rather pale imitation of the informed and engaged citizen celebrated in clas-sical democratic theory and countless civic textbooks. Indeed, the average citizen was sometimes depicted as ignorant of, indiffer-ent about, and perhaps even a threat to the most fundamental tenets of democratic society (Prothro and Grigg 1960).

Thus, unlike the earlier analysts, who had focused on foreign policy attitudes as a special case, at least some of these studies of public opinion and voting behavior tended to regard the lack of information and structure on foreign policy issues as part of a broader problem—the gap between the ideal and actual Ameri-can citizen.

Public Opinion Has a Limited Impact on Foreign Policy

The most important reason for interest in public opinion on for-eign affairs arises from the assumption that in some ways and at least some of the time, public attitudes have an impact, for better or worse, on the conduct of the nation's external policy.

For students of foreign policy and international relations, the central questions were not merely whether one party or the other controlled the White House or Congress. The United States was armed with atomic weapons, as was its primary adversary after 1949, and was the political leader of a Western coalition attempting to contain the Soviet Union. The U.S. economy produced half of the world's goods and services soon after World War II, and, as the core country in a network of international institutions that was intended to prevent a replay of the beggar-thy-neighbor economics of the decade prior to World War II, the American impact on trade and financial issues was enormous. Even if Almond, Bailey, Kennan, Lippmann, and other critics did not always agree on specific U.S. policies and undertakings, these observers were united by the fear that the public would render ineffective foreign policy elites' efforts to provide enlightened global leadership in the quest for a more stable world order. These fears even appear to have provoked some prescriptive overreactions. For example, Bailey, a fervent "small d" democrat whose frequent jibes at "low blow Joe" McCarthy and other demagogues enlivened Bailey's enormously popular history classes at Stanford, nevertheless felt sufficiently alarmed about the public's potential impact to justify distinctly undemocratic leadership behavior: "Franklin Roosevelt repeatedly deceived the American people during the period before Pearl Harbor. . . . He was like the physician who must tell the patient lies for the patient's own good. . . . Because the masses are notoriously shortsighted and generally cannot see danger until it is at their throats, our statesmen are forced to deceive them into an awareness of their own long-run interests" (quoted in Shogan 1995, 278).

It is certainly not hard to find policymakers' statements avowing the importance of public opinion. In his August 21, 1858, debate with Stephen Douglas, Abraham Lincoln asserted, "Public sentiment is everything. With public sentiment nothing can fail; without it nothing can succeed" (Angle 1991, 128). In 1936, Secretary of State Cordell Hull stated, "Since the time when Thomas Jefferson insisted upon a 'decent respect to the opinions of mankind,' public opinion has controlled foreign policy in all democracies" (1936, 47). Almost all presidents and secretaries of state have made similar assertions at one time or another.

Such hyperbolic statements, depicting an unalloyed direct democracy or "bottom-up" model of government, are unlikely to withstand serious empirical scrutiny. Not the least limitation of assertions such as those by Lincoln and Hull is that they neglect the role of institutions that may shape, mobilize, transmit—and perhaps distort—public preferences. These institutions include the media, opinion leaders, interest groups, parties, and legislators. Furthermore, presidents and others in the executive branch are not merely passive receptors of public sentiments. Moreover, the impact of public opinion cannot be assessed merely by describing its content, and we should not assume that its impact is constant across administrations, circumstances, and issues. Policymakers may vary widely in their answers to some important questions: What is the appropriate role of public opinion in the formulation of foreign policy? Under what circumstances and for what issues should it play a greater or lesser role? What are the most appropriate indicators of public sentiments? The media? Interest groups? Prominent opinion leaders? Congress? Opinion surveys? What strategies should policymakers use to gain public support for policies? I shall return to these questions in chapter 7.

As we have seen, the driving force behind many of the analyses of public opinion during and after World War II was the fear that an ill-informed and emotional mass public would powerfully constrain the conduct of American diplomacy, establishing unwise limits on policymakers, creating unrealistic expectations about what is feasible in foreign affairs, and otherwise doing serious mischief to American diplomacy and, given the American role in the world after 1945, perhaps even to international stability (compare Lowi 1967 and Waltz 1967 on this point). In contrast to these fears, some analysts concluded that policymakers could not take very seriously an ill-informed and largely indifferent public, limiting its impact on policy. As a leading social psychologist stated, "A public opinion so impoverished can hardly have a major impact on foreign policy decisions" (H. Kelman 1965, 580). In line with this reasoning, a consensus in fact seemed to emerge by the mid-1960s on a third point: public opinion has little if any impact on foreign policy. The weight of the research evidence cast doubt on the potency of public opinion as the driving force behind or even a significant constraint on the making of foreign policy.

Bernard Cohen's (1973) research most directly attacked the proposition that the public significantly affected foreign policy or that it even established limits beyond which policymakers would not dare to venture. In a critical review of the literature, he argued that assertions about the constraining role of public opinion far outnumbered any empirical demonstration of that relationship. Indeed, he argued that the often-cited "limits" proposition was rarely if ever even put to a serious test. His interview study of the foreign policy bureaucracy indicated that State Department officials had a rather modest interest in public opinion, and to the extent that they even thought about the public, it was as an entity to be "educated" rather than as a lodestar by which to be guided in formulating and implementing foreign policy. As one State Department official told Cohen, "To hell with public opinion. . . . We should lead, and not follow" (62).

Elections are intended to provide an opportunity for the public to have an impact on policy. According to the "electoral retribution" model, officeholders will be sensitive to public opinion for fear of alienating voters to the point of losing office at the next election; vigilant voters will "throw the rascals out" if they fail to respond to public preferences. Virtually all the election studies found that there was so little issue-based voting as to raise serious questions about the classic views of accountability to the public on policy issues. As the authors of one of these studies noted, "The quality of the public's review of policy formation is that the electoral decision gives great freedom to those who must frame the policies of government" (Campbell et al. 1964, 282). Moreover, the evidence indicated that while public officials might find it prudent to respect their constituents' preferences on domestic issues, these officials felt largely free of such constraints on votes pertaining to foreign affairs. A classic study of the public-legislator relationship revealed that constituents' attitudes on foreign policy issues had less impact on members of the House of Representatives than did views on domestic issues (W. Miller and Stokes 1963). Research that focused on the presidency came to similar conclusions. The proposition that the president has "almost a free hand" in the conduct of foreign affairs received support from diverse studies (Lipset 1966; Caspary 1970; LaFeber 1977; Paterson 1979; Graebner 1983).

This period also witnessed a proliferation of case studies of key foreign policy decisions.[6] With some exceptions, however, these studies tended to make few references to the impact of public opinion.[7] But it is not always clear whether that is because public opinion was irrelevant as even a partial explanation for the decisions under analysis. Some alternative reasons for the omission might include the following: decision makers quietly anticipated public opinion without consciously considering it or might have been reluctant to state that they were acting in response to public pressures, preferring instead to ascribe their actions to broader values such as the "national interest"; public opinion was excluded from the research design and thus no effort was made to assess its impact; or disproportionate research attention to international crises—events that are usually characterized by short decision time—tended to exclude episodes in which decisions represent the culmination of a long and complex political process that may also play out in the domestic arena. All other things being equal, the more protracted the decision process, the more likely policymakers are to be subjected to the impact of public opinion through the activities of Congress, interest groups, the media, and opinion leaders. Finally, analyses of recent events must necessarily rely more on interviews of foreign policy officials than on archival research. To the extent that policymakers are biased toward attributing their decisions to "doing what is right" rather than to pressures or constraints from the public, such research might underemphasize the actual impact of public opinion. Presidents as diverse as Franklin Roosevelt and George W. Bush have shared a deep interest in polling data—and a determination to keep that interest secret.

These studies did not answer all of the questions about the public's impact on foreign policy processes and outcomes. For example, the realities of research access required Cohen to exclude White House personnel from his study and to focus on precisely those officials—State Department bureaucrats—who are most sheltered from the effects of elections and who thus might be somewhat freer to express and act on cavalier attitudes toward the average person. Nevertheless, the weight of the evidence cast significant doubt on the public's impact on policy. These findings should have assuaged those who shared Lippmann's fears that mass public opinion "has shown itself to be a dangerous master of decision when the stakes are life and death" (1955, 20).

Such results might also explain why interest in the topic, which had been so evident in the years immediately following the two world wars, had waned considerably. If the impact of public opinion on foreign policy ranges from little to none and from rarely to never, it robs the topic of significance and urgency. Students of voting behavior might continue to pursue research agendas directed at illuminating the sources, nature, representation, and impact of public opinion; these are, after all, some of the classic and enduring issues of democratic theory and governance. But there would be fewer compelling reasons for foreign policy analysts to invest much of their attention in these topics. It took another war—the longest, least successful, and ultimately least popular in American history—to rekindle interest in public opinion and foreign policy while stimulating a reexamination of the consensus about the volatility, lack of structure, and impotence of public opinion regarding foreign policy.

CHAPTER 3

Challenges to the Postwar Consensus

Just as World War II and fears of postwar isolationism among the mass public gave rise to concerns about public opinion and its impact on foreign policy, the war in Vietnam was the primary impetus for a renewed interest in the domestic sources of foreign policy. As the editor of a major 1965 symposium on public opinion and foreign policy put it, "The intense controversy in the United States over the struggle in Vietnam has dramatized anew the fact that the foreign policy of governments is more than simply a series of responses to international stimuli, that forces at work within a society can also contribute to the quality and content of its external behavior" (Rosenau 1967, 2). That conflict was also a major catalyst in stimulating a reexamination of the consensus, described in chapter 2, that had emerged during the two decades after World War II. Most broadly, many of those who had believed that a stronger executive hand on the tiller of foreign policy, relatively free from the whims and vagaries of public moods, best served both national interests and global stability came to reexamine their views in the light of the conflict in Southeast Asia. Indeed, influential columnist Walter Lippmann, who only a little more than a decade earlier had despaired of the tyranny of a feckless public opinion and had called for a stronger executive to counteract the general public, became a leading critic of the Johnson administration's Vietnam policy. Lippmann eventually even came to regard war protesters and draft card burners as more enlightened than the administration (Steel 1980, 571).

At a narrower level, some critics of U.S. policy became increasingly persuaded that the Gallup, Harris, and other commercial polls inadequately represented public attitudes toward the war by posing excessively restrictive and simplistic questions. For example, among the most widely asked questions was whether respondents supported or opposed current American policy in

UNIVERSITY
OF SHEFFIELD
LIBRARY

Vietnam. The critics complained that these polling organizations far less commonly employed more probing questions that offered respondents an opportunity to express their views about policy options other than those favored by the Johnson administration. Thus, in addition to generating secondary analyses of survey data relating to the war (Mueller 1973), the conflict in Southeast Asia stimulated independent surveys designed specifically to assess foreign policy opinions in greater depth than the typical survey conducted by Gallup or other major polling firms.

The first of these studies, the Verba-Stanford surveys, focused on specific aspects of American policy in Vietnam, including some options other than support for or opposition to the Johnson administration's actions. Sidney Verba and his colleagues in fact found support for the administration's Vietnam policy, but they also unearthed approval for such alternative policies as negotiating an end to the conflict (Verba et al. 1967; Verba and Brody 1970). The period since the Verba-Stanford polls has witnessed a proliferation of public opinion surveys with a foreign affairs focus, including surveys both of the general public and of opinion leaders.[1] As a consequence, we no longer depend completely on evidence generated by the major commercial polling organizations. Moreover, the independent surveys were often designed to deal with policy or theoretical concerns that can only imperfectly be probed by secondary analyses of the Gallup and other more general public opinion polls.

Thus, public opinion analysts, armed with growing central archives of data generated by major polling organizations as well as evidence produced by independent surveys, have begun to challenge important aspects of the consensus described in chapter 2.[2]

Is Public Opinion Really So Volatile?

William Caspary (1970) offered the first systematic challenge to Gabriel Almond's thesis that public opinion about international affairs is best characterized by volatile moods. Caspary took issue with Almond's (1950) heavy reliance on a single question in which respondents were asked to identify "the most important problem before the American people today." Analyzing a broader set of foreign policy questions led Caspary to conclude that "American public opinion is characterized by a *strong* and *stable* permissive mood" rather than by mindless volatility toward international involvement (1970, 546). While differing from Almond on the nature of public opinion, Caspary hardly characterized his findings as cause for celebration. Citing four years of combat in Vietnam as an example, Caspary concluded that the permissive public mood provided a blank check for foreign policy adventures rather than responsible support for international organizations, genuine foreign assistance, and basic defense measures.

A limitation of Caspary's analysis is that he included data for a period of only a little more than a decade ending in 1953. A longer perspective would nevertheless appear to support important aspects of his thesis while assuaging the fears of those who forecast public disenchantment with and a retreat from an active U.S. role in world affairs. Since 1942, Gallup, the Office of Public Opinion Research, the National Opinion Research Council, and several other organizations have asked the public whether it is better to take an active role in or to stay out of international affairs. The first survey found that 71 percent favored the internationalist option, whereas only 24 percent preferred withdrawal from world affairs. Responses to more than fifty surveys, summarized in figure 3.1, spanned six decades encompassing World War II; the onset of the nuclear age; the Cold War; two long costly wars in Asia and a short victorious one in the Persian Gulf region; crises in the Caribbean, the Taiwan Straits, Berlin, and the Middle East; several periods of warming relations between Moscow and Washington; the end of the Cold War and the disintegration of the Soviet Union; controversial interventions in Somalia, Haiti, Bosnia, Kosovo, and elsewhere; and the months following the terrorist attacks on New York and Washington in 2001.

Despite the almost unprecedented turbulence of this period and some variation in the precise wording used in the surveys, responses to these questions about the appropriate international stance of the United States have not been characterized by wild volatility. A modest decline in support for internationalism in 1947 coincided with worsening East-West relations, but at this low point approximately two-thirds of the public still favored an active American role, outnumbering the supporters of withdrawal by a margin of about five to two. The question was not posed between June 1965 and March 1973, apparently because survey organizations felt that the issue of the appropriate American stance toward international affairs had been settled in favor of an active role and therefore was no longer worth asking. Although the Vietnam War did in fact evoke calls for revisiting the

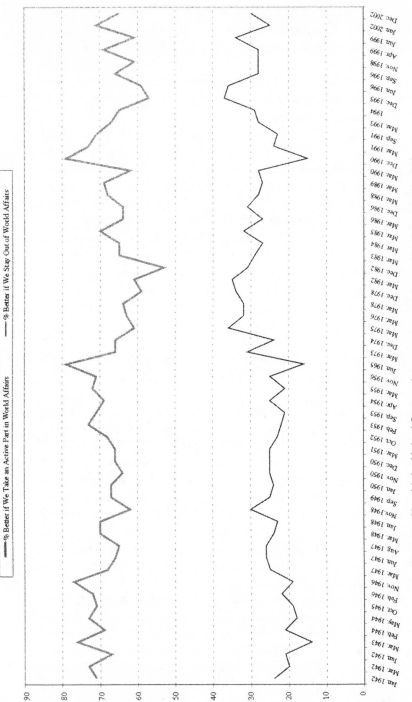

Fig. 3.1. Should the United States play an active role in world affairs, or should it stay out? (1942–2002)

issue—in his acceptance speech at the 1972 Democratic National Convention, George McGovern urged, "Come home, America"—even in the aftermath of that controversial conflict, those favoring the "stay out of world affairs" option never reached 40 percent, much less a majority. A number of critics have charged that excessive U.S. involvement abroad lay at the root of the 2001 terrorist attacks, but the public appears to reject that thesis. Seventy-one percent of respondents to the 2002 Chicago Council on Foreign Relations (CCFR) survey expressed a preference for an "active part" in world affairs, far outnumbering the 25 percent who would have the country "stay out." Throughout the period, no survey recorded more than 40 percent of the respondents stating that "it is better if we stay out of world affairs," and only two surveys found that fewer than 60 percent felt that "it is better if we take an active part in world affairs." Because an "active role in world affairs" can encompass a wide array of international undertakings, ranging from military interventions abroad and foreign aid programs to liberalizing the terms of international trade and coping with such worldwide public health issues as AIDS, it is important not to read too much into these data. They certainly should not be counted as evidence of a broad consensus or sustained support for specific foreign policies. Nevertheless, these findings suggest that at least the deepest concerns of some critics who feared an American return to isolationism after World War II or after the disintegration of the USSR and the end of the Cold War, including those cited in chapters 1 and 2, may have been somewhat overdrawn.

The indictment of public caprice was also dismissed in an analysis that absolved it from blame for foreign policy shortcomings during the Korean War. While agreeing that erratic governmental actions may indeed threaten international stability and peace, Kenneth N. Waltz attributed the "mixture of firmness and vacillation" in U.S. policy to leaders rather than to public pressures or fears of electoral retribution. Indeed, he concluded that whatever shortcomings it may have exhibited in the past, "the mass of the American people have learned to live with danger, to tolerate ambiguity, to accept setbacks, and to understand that victory is sometimes impossible or that it can only be gained at a price the wise would refrain from paying" (1967, 277, 279, 293; for an opposing view on the quality and impact of public opinion, see Rosenberg 1967, 151).

A fuller and more systematic analysis of public opinion toward the wars in Korea and Vietnam posed another challenge to the thesis of irrational mood swings in public attitudes. To be sure, public support for the American war effort in both conflicts eventually declined, but it did so in ways that seemed explicable and rational rather than random and mindless. More specifically, John E. Mueller (1973) found that increasing public opposition to both conflicts followed a pattern that matched a curve of rising battle deaths, suggesting that the public used an understandable, if simple, heuristic to assess American policy.

The most comprehensive challenge to the thesis that public opinion is volatile has emerged from a series of studies conducted by Benjamin Page and Robert Shapiro. Their evidence includes all questions that have been posed by major polling organizations, beginning with the inception of systematic surveys in the mid-1930s and extending through the 1980s. Of the more than six thousand questions included in these surveys, almost 20 percent have been asked at least twice, providing a substantial data set with which to assess the degree of stability or change in public attitudes. Employing a criterion of a difference of 6 percent from one survey to another to distinguish between continuity and change, Page and Shapiro found that public opinion in the aggregate is in fact characterized by a good deal of stability; moreover, this conclusion was equally valid for domestic and foreign policy issues (Shapiro and Page 1988; Page and Shapiro 1992). Most importantly, when attitude shifts took place, they seemed to be neither random nor completely removed from international realities. Rather, changes appeared to be "reasonable, events-driven" reactions to the real world, even if the factual information on which these changes were based was marginally adequate at best. Page and Shapiro concluded that

> virtually all the rapid shifts [in public opinion] we found were related to political and economic circumstances or to significant events which sensible citizens would take into account. In particular, most abrupt foreign policy changes took place in connection with wars, confrontations, or crises in which major changes in the actions of the United States or other nations quite naturally affect preferences about what policies to pursue. (1982, 34)[3]

A very similar conclusion about the importance of external events emerged from an analysis of opinion changes on both domestic and foreign policy during the period from the Kennedy administration through the Reagan administration (Mayer 1992, 274).

The sudden shifts in public attitudes highlighted by Almond and summarized in chapter 2 were also responses to wars, crises, and other dramatic international events, including Hitler's conquests during the spring of 1940, increasing Japanese-American tensions in the fall of 1941, the attack on Pearl Harbor, the end of World War II, the Czech coup in 1948, the Berlin Crisis of 1948–49, and the like. Almond, however, chose to interpret the, fluctuations as evidence of massive mood swings rooted in shallow opinions about the world rather than as reasonable responses to rapidly changing international conditions (1950, 70–80).

Because their analyses are based on aggregate responses rather than on panel studies in which the respondents in the sample are interviewed repeatedly, Page and Shapiro cannot address definitively one fundamental aspect of the debate about the volatility of public opinion: precisely what proportion of individuals in fact changed their minds on each question? For an issue on which the public divided evenly—50 percent in support of a particular policy and a like percentage in opposition—in each of two time periods, it is theoretically possible that all respondents switched positions. However, volatility approaching this magnitude seems highly unlikely because, as Page and Shapiro have shown, opinion changes tended to be in directions that make sense in terms of events.

The volatility thesis can be tested most directly and satisfactorily by individual-level rather than aggregate analyses of opinion data. Using alternative methods for correcting for measurement error, several studies have shown convincingly that at the individual level, mass foreign policy attitudes are every bit as stable as those on domestic issues (Achen 1975). These studies revealed an impressive level of stability during times of constancy in the international environment. A panel study also found very substantial stability in policy attitudes and international images even during the late 1980s, a period that witnessed rapid and dramatic changes in Soviet-American relations and other important aspects of international affairs (Peffley and Hurwitz 1992).

Similar conclusions supporting Page and Shapiro and casting doubt on the thesis of unstable and irrational public moods also have emerged from other studies. During the post-Vietnam era, variations in public support for the use of force are best explained by differences between two quite distinct situations: the use of force to coerce foreign policy restraint by others versus the use of force to influence or impose political changes within another state. The former goal consistently has received much stronger support than the latter (Jentleson 1992; Jentleson and Britton 1998; Eichenberg 2003).

An interesting variant of the "rational public" thesis stipulated that the public attempted to moderate American behavior toward the USSR by expressing preferences for a conciliatory stance from a hawkish administration (Reagan) while supporting more assertive policies when a dovish leader (Carter) controlled the White House (Nincic 1988, 1992). The Nincic thesis gained additional support from Mayer's assessment of opinion changes. During the Ford and Carter years (1974–81), the preponderance of opinion changes, including foreign policy issues, occurred in a conservative direction. In contrast, during the eight Reagan years that followed, the public moved in a liberal direction on thirteen of nineteen issues, including all of those involving international affairs (Mayer 1992, 120–21). To the extent that one can generalize from these studies to other periods or other aspects of foreign policy, they further challenge the Almond-Lippmann thesis of volatility in public attitudes; indeed, these findings turn that proposition on its head, identifying the public as a source of moderation and continuity rather than instability and unpredictability.[4]

It is important to emphasize that none of these challenges to the Almond-Lippmann thesis is based on some newly found evidence that the public is in fact well informed about international affairs. Surveys not only repeatedly reveal that the public has a very thin veneer of factual knowledge about politics, economics, and geography but also indicate that most Americans are poorly informed about the specifics of conflicts, treaties, negotiations with other nations, characteristics of weapons systems, foreign leaders, and the like. Indeed, a seven-nation study in 1994 revealed that the American public substantially trails those in Germany, Italy, France, Great Britain, and Canada in levels of political information; only Spain ranked behind the United States in this respect. The results were traced at least in part to Americans' heavy dependence on television rather than newspapers as sources of information (Dimock and Popkin 1996).[5]

Because the modest factual basis on which the mass public reacts to international affairs remains an unchallenged—and unchallengeable—fact, we are faced with a puzzle. If an often poorly informed general public does indeed react to international affairs in a stable and reasonable manner, and if opinion changes are driven by events rather than whimsy or emotion, what means permit the public to do so? Have publics undergone a "skills revolution" that permits them to exercise sound political judgment despite low levels of factual knowledge (Rosenau 1990; Yankelovich 1991; Kay 1992a)? Do they make effective use of certain heuristics or rules of thumb to organize even the modest levels of information that they possess? As discussed in chapter 2, a significant body of research evidence indicates that mass public attitudes lack the kind of ideological underpinnings that would provide some structure and coherence across specific issues and stability through time.

Do Public Attitudes Lack Structure and Coherence?

Philip Converse's (1964) chapter on mass belief systems is one of the most widely cited studies in the literature of American political science. In recent years, his research has also stimulated a plethora of studies that have, on the one hand, vigorously challenged his findings and, on the other, supported the main thrust of his conclusion that mass public attitudes lack ideological structure, whereas those of leaders are characterized by far greater coherence. Part of the debate is methodological, centering on the manner in which questions are framed, the clarity of questions, the degree to which the "unsure" respondents are prodded to state a position on issues, and similar aspects of research procedures. Did the evidentiary base include enough questions to support the conclusions? Did the analytical methods deal adequately with problems of measurement error? Did an analysis that examined correlations across specific public policy issues exhaust the possible structures that might be used to lend coherence to political thinking? These and other significant methodological questions about the Converse findings emerged from several studies (Achen 1975; Sullivan, Piereson, and Marcus 1978).

Another part of the controversy focuses on trends—specifically, on the durability of findings that, to a large degree, drew from evidence generated during the 1950s. This was a period of American economic, political, and military dominance in foreign affairs—the shock of the pioneering Soviet space capsule *Sputnik* notwithstanding—and the 1956 and 1960 elections took place while the United States was at peace during the interim between the Korean War armistice and escalation of the Vietnam conflict.

Domestically, the late 1950s and early 1960s were marked by relatively low inflation and unemployment, and despite the Montgomery bus boycott and Greensboro sit-ins, the full impact of the civil rights movement had yet to be felt. According to the critics, this period, both celebrated and condemned for marking the "end of ideology," is insufficiently representative for assessing the degree of ideological consistency among the general public. In support of that view, a number of analysts found that beginning with the Johnson-Goldwater election campaign of 1964, ideological consistency among the public did in fact increase (Nie and Anderson 1974; Nie, Verba, and Petrocik 1976). Some corroborating evidence also appeared to emerge from an assessment of public opinion polls on domestic and foreign policy issues from the late 1930s to 1967. Although there was generally a weak relationship between attitudes on domestic and international issues, the evidence also revealed a stronger correlation between them during the post-Eisenhower years (Hero 1969).

Those who claim to have found greater ideological consistency among the general public during the turbulent era of the late 1960s and 1970s have also encountered criticism. Are the claims of greater issue consistency really rooted in increasing ideological consciousness? Alternatively, do such claims merely result from the parroting of ideological rhetoric or from some methodological artifact? This is not the place to provide a blow-by-blow account of the many and varied answers to these and other questions on the issue, especially as excellent and detailed summaries of the vast literature are available elsewhere (P. Converse 1975; Kinder 1983; Kinder and Sears 1985; Sniderman and Tetlock 1986; Zaller 1992; Sniderman 1993). It will suffice to say that a consensus appears to be emerging that public responses to political issues are not adequately captured by the most familiar bipolar dimensions—liberal to conservative and internationalist to isolationist. If these dimensions constitute the standard by which to determine the existence of attitude structures, then mass public attitudes do indeed appear to lack coherence, although this may not be an insuperable barrier to making adequate sense of politics (Luttbeg and Gant 1985). Given that tentative conclusion, does the literature on international issues reveal anything else about organizing concepts that might tend some coherence to public attitudes on foreign affairs?

Although more recent research has yet to create a consensus on all aspects of the question, there does appear to be a considerable convergence of findings on two general points relating to belief structures. First, even though the general public may be rather poorly informed about the factual aspects of international affairs, attitudes about foreign affairs are in fact structured in moderately coherent ways. Indeed, low information and an ambiguous international environment may motivate rather than preclude the existence of some type of attitude structure. For example, the conception of humans as "cognitive misers" suggests that they may use a limited number of beliefs to make sense of a wide range of facts and events. Second, there is growing evidence that a single internationalist-to-isolationist dimension inadequately describes the structure of public opinion on international affairs.

In a study of the domestic sources of American foreign policy, Barry Hughes (1978, 30) was one of the first to note that internationalism encompasses two quite different perspectives, which he called *military internationalism* and *nonmilitary internationalism*. Soon thereafter, a study based on the first of the quadrennial CCFR surveys of both the general public and elites employed factor analyses and other methods to uncover three foreign policy outlooks described as *liberal internationalism, conservative internationalism,* and *noninternationalism* (Mandelbaum and Schneider 1979). A comparable trichotomy labeled the "three-headed eagle" emerged from early analyses of the data on opinion leaders generated by the Foreign Policy Leadership Project (FPLP) (Holsti 1979; Holsti and Rosenau 1979, 1984). These findings did not go unchallenged, however. Other observers have questioned the division of foreign policy attitudes into three types rather than three dimensions and have offered useful evidence in support of their critiques. William Chittick and Keith Billingsley (1989) undertook both original and secondary analyses that supported the case for dimensions rather than types for the adequate description of the foreign policy beliefs of both leaders and the mass public, and their findings have received other support (Bardes and Oldendick 1978; Oldendick and Bardes 1982; Chittick, Billingsley, and Travis 1990, 1995).

A major contribution to the debate about how best to describe foreign policy attitudes has come from Eugene Wittkopf's (1986, 1990) secondary analyses of the CCFR surveys of both leaders and the general public. His results, which parallel Barry Hughes's (1978) distinction between two kinds of internationalism, were developed inductively from the CCFR surveys conducted in 1974, 1978, 1982, and 1986. Wittkopf's work revealed that with a single exception, two dimensions are necessary to describe foreign policy attitudes: "support-oppose militant internationalism" (MI) and "support-oppose cooperative internationalism" (CI). Dichotomizing and crossing these dimensions yields four types of foreign policy belief systems, with the quadrants labeled *hard-liners* (support MI, oppose CI), *internationalists* (support both MI and CI), *accommodationists* (oppose MI, support CI), and *isolationists* (oppose both MI and CI). The MI/CI scheme also proved useful for characterizing respondents to the first post–Cold War CCFR survey, which occurred in 1994 (Wittkopf 1995; see also Chanley 1999).

More generally, methods of classification such as the MI/CI scheme that operate in terms of dimensions rather than types provide a good deal of conceptual freedom. For example, a critic might suggest that the fourfold MI/CI classification scheme is too simple or that it overemphasizes between-type differences while obscuring those among persons who are classified within any of the four cells; the latter point is a common criticism of typologies based on fourfold tables. Focusing on the two dimensions rather than on the four types permits us to escape from the limits of a two-by-two matrix. Thus, the MI/CI scheme could be expanded into a three-by-three matrix by making somewhat finer distinctions along both dimensions (for example, "strongly support," "neutral," "strongly oppose"). The types discussed here would then appear in the four corner cells, and additional descriptive labels would be developed for the other five types—for example, *indifferents* for those who are neutral on both dimensions. Moreover, when we think in terms of dimension rather than type, we are more likely to search for other dimensions that may enhance the analytical power of the scheme. The latter point is illustrated by Ronald Hinckley's (1992) classification scheme, which resembles Wittkopf's MI/CI but adds an important third dimension, unilateralism-multilateralism. Hinckley demonstrates the scheme's utility not only for classifying respondents to Cold War surveys but also for distinguishing adherents of competing schools of thought on the proper U.S. role and strategies during the interwar period. The importance of the unilateralism-multilateralism dimension also emerges from other studies, including Chittick, Billingsley, and Travis 1995.[6] Chapter 6 includes a further discussion of this dimension.

Strong support for Wittkopf's MI/CI scheme also has emerged from analyses of the FPLP data on American opinion leaders (Holsti and Rosenau 1990, 1993). Those studies put the MI/CI

scheme to a demanding test because of three major differences between the CCFR and FPLP data sets. First, the CCFR surveys
were undertaken at four-year intervals starting in 1974, whereas
the six FPLP studies followed two years later in each case. Moreover, the two sets of surveys have only a few questions in common.
Finally, the MI/CI scheme was developed largely from data on the
mass public, whereas the FPLP surveys focused solely on opinion
leaders.

Although the origins of the MI/CI scheme are strictly inductive,
the militant and cooperative internationalism dimensions correspond closely to the most venerable theoretical approaches to international relations, realism, and liberalism. Realism views conflict between nations as a natural state of affairs, either because of
human nature or because of the anarchic structure of the system,
rather than as an aberration that is subject to permanent amelio-
ration. Such realist concepts as security dilemma, relative capabilities, relative gains, and a zero-sum view of conflict are also basic
to the militant internationalism dimension.

Similar links exist between liberalism and the cooperative internationalism dimension. Although acknowledging the primacy
of the state as a self-interested actor, liberalism denies that conflict
is an immutable element of relations between nations. Liberalism
defines security in terms that are broader than the geopolitical-
military spheres and emphasizes the potential for cooperative relations among nations: institution-building to reduce uncertainty
and fears of perfidy as well as information costs; improved international education and communication to ameliorate fears and
antagonisms based on misinformation and misperception; and the
positive-sum possibilities of such activities as trade are but a few
of the ways liberals believe nations may jointly gain and thus mitigate, if not eliminate, the harshest features of international relations emphasized by the realists. In short, the CI dimension shares
important elements with the liberal school of international relations theory. These MI and CI dimensions also seem clearly related to other conceptualizations of American thought on foreign
affairs. For example, Thomas Hughes's (1980) distinction between the "security culture" and the "equity culture" in American
foreign policy and James Billington's (1987) categories of "realist-
conservatives" and "idealist-liberals" appear to parallel, if not
match exactly, the MI and CI dimensions. The MI/CI scheme has
been linked to broader American ideologies—cosmopolitan liberalism, nativism, and multiculturalism—in a study encompassing a

period of six decades beginning in 1930 (Citrin et al. 1994). The four types that emerge from the MI/CI scheme also bear more than a passing resemblance to the distinction between the Hamiltonian (internationalists), Wilsonian (accommodationists), Jeffersonian (isolationists), and Jacksonian (hard-liners) approaches to American foreign policy (Mead 2001).

Although the empirical and theoretical cases for measuring attitudes about both militant and cooperative internationalism rather than on a single isolationist-to-internationalist dimension seem quite strong, there is also some evidence that these two dimensions may not be sufficient to describe all contours of contemporary international opinions. As noted earlier, a number of studies have suggested a further distinction between unilateralism and multilateralism (Wittkopf 1986; Hinckley 1988; Chittick and Billingsley 1989; Russett 1990; Chittick, Billingsley, and Travis 1995; for a somewhat different formulation, see Russett and Shye 1993). It is not reasonable, moreover, to expect that any belief structure could encompass all possible aspects of foreign affairs, and there is indeed rather persuasive evidence that attitudes toward some rather important issues cut across the main dimensions identified previously. One such example is trade and protectionism, issues that are likely to become more rather than less important—and more contentious, to judge by the protests accompanying almost every major international meeting on global trade issues—during the post–Cold War era. Questions involving Israel and American policy toward that nation appear to form another cluster of attitudes that does not fit neatly into the MI/CI scheme. That is, the four types that emerge from that scheme—hard-liners, internationalists, isolationists, and accommodationists—do not differ significantly on either trade issues or U.S. policy toward Israel.

A somewhat different approach to the question of attitude structures emerges from several studies of the general public conducted by Jon Hurwitz and Mark Peffley (1987). In contrast to Philip Converse's search for a "horizontal" coherence that relies on correlations among attitudes toward various issues, Hurwitz and Peffley proposed and tested a hierarchically organized foreign policy belief structure in which specific policy preferences are derived from postures—militarism, anticommunism, and isolationism—that in turn are assumed to be constrained by a set of core values (morality of warfare, ethnocentrism) relating to the international community. These authors found that their survey respondents possessed such structures. Thus, a few rather general beliefs—attitudes toward militarism and a general preference for a "tough-minded" approach to international affairs—appear to have served as organizing devices that enabled subjects to respond in a reasonably coherent manner to a broad range of issues, including defense spending, nuclear arms policy, military involvement, policies toward the USSR, and international trade.

Once again, however, none of these studies challenges the overwhelming evidence on one important point: the American public is generally poorly informed about international affairs. Indeed, even the Persian Gulf War, the first international conflict to be telecast in real time, increased the normally low level of information among the general public by only a very modest amount (S. Bennett 1992). Rather, the evidence appears to suggest that even in the absence of much factual knowledge, members of the general public use some simple—perhaps even simplistic—cognitive shortcuts to make some sense of an increasingly complex world; a few salient criteria rather than complete information may serve as the bases of judgment. Even experts may well use such shortcuts to organize their attitudes. "Domino theory," "lessons of Munich," "lessons of Vietnam," and "my enemy's enemy is my friend" are among the shortcuts that have served—for better or worse—to guide the thinking of more than a few policymakers and their expert advisers. Stated differently, although lacking a deep reservoir of factual information, members of the mass public may act as "cognitive misers," employing a few superordinate beliefs to guide their thinking on a broad spectrum of international issues. Thus, people may organize their political worlds in richer and more diverse ways than Converse and his colleagues indicated (Conover and Feldman 1984).

Recent research clearly has yet to produce complete agreement on many important issues relating to the structure of the mass public's foreign policy beliefs. Nevertheless, the earlier consensus depicting public attitudes as lacking any real coherence has been challenged from many quarters and for many reasons. As a result of substantial empirical research, there is now a good deal of credible evidence suggesting that members of the mass public use various heuristics—although not necessarily the traditional liberal-to-conservative or internationalist-to-isolationist blueprints—for organizing their political thinking.

Is the Public Really Impotent?

Among the most important questions about public opinion are these: To what extent, on what kinds of issues, under what circumstances, and in what types of political systems, if any, does public opinion affect public policy? If public opinion is indeed impotent, that would reduce the reasons for studying it; the topic might be of interest to cognitive psychologists, but it would be largely irrelevant to students of foreign policy. If it has an influence, what are the means by which public attitudes become known so that they can have an impact on decision makers? These are also the most difficult questions to answer, for our ability to do so is not materially enhanced by the many technical improvements that have characterized public opinion research during the past half century: better sampling designs, greater attention to construction of questions, more sophisticated statistical models to analyze the data, and, of course, the widespread availability of computers that make possible complex analyses rarely attempted even a few decades ago. Not surprisingly, then, we have a good deal more systematic evidence describing the state of or trends in public opinion than detailing how it has affected the conduct of foreign affairs.

As noted in chapter 2, much of the evidence through the 1960s pointed toward the conclusion of public impotence in the process by which foreign policy is made. Even when there appeared to be some correspondence between public sentiments and foreign policy, not all analysts were prepared to accept the inference that the former had any independent impact on the latter. According to some of these observers, for example, any evidence of a correlation between public opinion and foreign policy merely serves to underscore the effectiveness of efforts by policymakers, aided and abetted by pliant print and electronic media, to manipulate the mass public into accepting the ruling elites' political or class-based interests.

There is certainly no shortage of evidence that most post–World War II presidents have followed Theodore Roosevelt in thinking that the White House is a "bully pulpit," whether it was used by Harry Truman to "scare the hell out of them" to gain support for aid to Greece and Turkey in 1947; by Dwight Eisenhower to warn against the dangers of "unwarranted influence, whether sought or unsought, by the military-industrial complex" in 1961; by Jimmy Carter to generate approbation for the Panama Canal

Treaties during the early months of his administration; by Ronald Reagan to drum up support for assistance to the contras in Nicaragua during the 1980s; by George Bush to rally support for a military intervention, followed by an air campaign and a ground war to force Iraq out of Kuwait in 1990–91; by Bill Clinton to gain passage of the North American Free Trade Agreement and General Agreement on Tariffs and Trade/World Trade Organization treaties; and by George W. Bush to gain public support for strong but unspecified measures against nations he called an "axis of evil" (Iran, Iraq, and North Korea) in his 2002 State of the Union address, followed by a vigorous campaign to rally support for military action against the Saddam Hussein regime in Iraq. It is also evident that all such presidential efforts to shape public opinion have not had equal success. At least one noted public opinion analyst has asserted that the relationship between leaders and the public has changed in the post-Vietnam era—"farewell to 'the President knows best'" (Yankelovich 1978). Although it remains to be demonstrated that the equation has been permanently altered, some recent evidence indicates that the public is both able and willing to express views that do not necessarily follow those of policymakers or opinion leaders (Clough 1994; Isaacs 1994, 1998).

The more difficult question concerns influence in the other direction. How much did public impatience lead the Carter administration to embark on an ill-fated effort to free American hostages held in Tehran in 1980; how much did public impatience lead the Reagan administration to withdraw U.S. Marines from Lebanon after a terrorist bombing had killed more than 240 of them in 1983? Was George Kennan (1993) correct in blaming media-generated public pressures for the first Bush administration's humanitarian intervention in Somalia shortly after the 1992 presidential election? (For a detailed rebuttal, see Strobel 1997.) Did President Kennedy genuinely believe that he would be impeached should he fail to force removal of Soviet missiles from Cuba, as he told his brother, or was he merely seeking to bolster decisions arrived at for reasons that had nothing to do with public opinion? Perhaps a more telling example from the Cuban missile crisis emerges from transcripts of a crucial White House meeting on October 27, 1962, the day before the crisis was resolved peacefully. It appears that Kennedy was prepared to accept a compromise solution that many of his top advisers strongly opposed—removal of American missiles in Turkey in exchange for withdrawal of the Soviet missiles in Cuba that had precipitated the Caribbean confrontation—rather than initiate a further escalation of the crisis, and that he would have done so in large part because it would have been hard to explain to the public why such a seemingly symmetrical arrangement had been rejected (Bundy and Blight 1987–88).

Some anecdotal evidence may also be suggestive, but it hardly offers irrefutable answers to these questions. Franklin D. Roosevelt was the first president to make extensive use of public opinion data, and he even specified to polling organizations exactly what questions he wanted to have posed to the public on a regular basis. Virtually all recent presidents have extensively used pollsters. John Kennedy's 1960 presidential campaign relied heavily on private polls conducted by Louis Harris, and after the election Kennedy made public opinion analysis a regular part of White House activities (Jacobs and Shapiro 1994a, 1995). Lyndon Johnson, who often carried survey results to show critics that he had strong public support for his policies, expanded the use of public and private polls, but he proved to be rather ineffective as an opinion leader (Altschuler 1986; Jacobs and Shapiro 1999). The process of institutionalizing and politicizing public opinion polling, not only for election purposes but also for making policy decisions, was even more fully advanced by the Nixon White House (Jacobs and Shapiro 1995). Moreover, whereas Nixon and his predecessors took considerable efforts to keep such polling activities secret, they have now become a well-known activity of every administration (Heith 1998; Murray and Howard 2002).

The Iraqi invasion of Kuwait in August 1990 stimulated an immense amount of public and private polling by a wide variety of sources, including almost nightly surveys commissioned by the government of Kuwait to determine, among other things, how the public reacted to various reasons for opposing Saddam Hussein's aggression: oil, restoration of Kuwait's preinvasion government, U.S. jobs, international norms, and Iraq's nuclear weapons aspirations. Although George H. W. Bush's administration made less extensive use of polling than did the Reagan White House, there is evidence that the government was not immune to the impact of public preferences. In recalling events of the period, General Norman Schwarzkopf wrote, "Washington was ready to overreact, as usual, to the slightest ripple in public opinion" (1992, 468). In their joint memoir, the George H. W. Bush and National Security Adviser Brent Scowcroft (1998) make no mention of public opinion but, as noted earlier, policymakers may be reluctant to acknowledge that they were influenced by polls. (For results of public polls before and during the Gulf War, see Mueller 1994.)

Bush and Scowcroft's silence in their memoir notwithstanding, a careful analysis of policy-making before and during the Gulf War, drawing not only on surveys but also on interviews with such key officials as the president and Secretary of Defense Richard Cheney, revealed that public opinion played an important role in American policy. Its influence was not so much in formulating the plans to go to war—Cheney asserted that "even if public opinion was against us, we were still going to go [to war]" (168)—but in the manner in which the policy was implemented. Two examples illustrate the many ways in which concerns with the public were reflected in policy: the last-minute talks with Foreign Minister Tariq Aziz of Iraq were intended to convey to the public that the administration was seriously pursuing negotiations with Baghdad; and the decision to call up National Guard and Reserve units was, according to Cheney, intended to "play a role in terms of helping us mobilize public opinion when it is time to go to war" (Sobel 2001, 159, 167, 173). Chapter 6 will discuss polls concerning the use of force in Afghanistan and Iraq during the months following the 9/11 terrorist attacks.

We have relatively few detailed accounts from public opinion analysts within the government about how their expertise and survey results were used in the policy process, but those that exist suggest that the mass public is not viewed merely as an essentially shapeless lump that can readily be molded through public relations activities and compliant media to meet the immediate policy needs of the administration (H. Cantril 1967; Beal and Hinckley 1984; Hinckley 1992). Hadley Cantril, who undertook public opinion analyses for Presidents Roosevelt, Eisenhower, and Kennedy, summarized his experience: "I want to emphasize that no claim is made here that the [public opinion] data and suggestions that Lambert [a drug company heir who financed Cantril's polls] and I provided the President [Roosevelt] were crucial to his decisions. But actions taken were certainly very often completely consistent with our recommendations" (1967, 42).

Although the evidence describing public attitudes still far outstrips—both in quality and quantity—that on the causal links between mass opinions and foreign policy, research in recent years has begun to cast some doubt on the earlier thesis of public impotence. In addition to anecdotal evidence, two classes of studies have challenged the proposition that the processes by which

foreign policy is made are essentially impervious to public influence: quantitative-correlational analyses and intensive case
studies.

Several quantitative studies have challenged some important
foundations of the theory that, at least on foreign and defense policy, the public is impotent. One element of that proposition is that
policymakers are relatively free agents on foreign policy questions
because these issues pose few dangers of electoral retribution by
voters. Elections are said to be decided by domestic questions,
especially those sometimes described as "pocketbook" or "bread-
and-butter" issues, because international affairs are so far removed from the average voter's concerns and information. For example, Dwight Eisenhower's landslide victory at the height of the
Korean War in 1952, giving Republicans control of the White
House for the first time in two decades, was described by Warren
E. Miller in a way that discounted the effects of foreign policy:
"Coming up to 1956 and 1960, we can be sure of no more than that
public opinion on foreign policy matters constituted a thin veneer
on the basic structure of the vote decision" (1967, 229).

That conclusion about the distinction between domestic and
foreign policy in voting behavior has been challenged by John H.
Aldrich, John L. Sullivan, and Eugene Borgida on the grounds that
"there has been no theoretically plausible account of attitude formation and salience that would explain why attitudes on domestic
issues—as opposed to foreign policy issues—should be so acces-
sible and so likely to affect voting behavior" (1989, 125). These authors' systematic study of presidential campaigns between 1952
and 1984 revealed that in five of the nine elections during that period (1952, 1964, 1972, 1980, and 1984), foreign policy issues had
"large effects." Or, as the authors put it, when presidential candidates devote campaign time and other scarce resources to articu-
lating their positions and debating questions of external policy,
they are "acting reasonably, because voters do in fact respond to
their appeals. The candidates are waltzing before a reasonably
alert audience that appreciates their grace. Also, given a choice,
the public votes for the candidate who waltzes best" (Aldrich, Sullivan, and Borgida 1989, 136; Zaller 2004).

Research on voting behavior also has emphasized the importance of retrospective evaluations of performance on voter
choices among candidates, especially when one of them is an incumbent (Fiorina 1981; Abramson, Aldrich, and Rohde 1990).
Because voters are perceived as punishing incumbent candidates

or parties for foreign policy failures (for example, the Iran hostage episode and the failed rescue mission damaged President Carter's reelection campaign) or rewarding incumbents for successes (for example, victory over Iraq in the Persian Gulf War brought President Bush's approval ratings to the highest level— 89 percent—ever recorded up to that point), decisions by foreign policy leaders may be made in anticipation of public reactions and the probabilities of success or failure (Zaller 1992; Stimson, MacKuen, and Erikson 1994, 1995; Foyle 1999).

The electoral retribution hypothesis received a different kind of test in a study of American policy toward China during the three decades following establishment of Mao Tse-tung's government in 1949. Leonard A. Kusnitz (1984) found that, with few exceptions, the correspondence between public preferences and U.S. policy toward China was remarkably high. Policy sometimes led opinion, and opinion at other times led policy, but on the whole the two remained in harmony. These findings are explained by issue visibility, partisan differences, and the nonrandom changes of opinion, which combined to create the belief among policymakers that the possibility of electoral retribution required them to pay close attention to public opinion on the China issue.

Two other studies also seem to cast some doubt on the universal validity of Warren E. Miller and Donald E. Stokes's (1963) classic finding that public attitudes on foreign policy questions have far less impact on members of Congress than domestic issues do (Bartels 1991; Hartley and Russett 1992). A careful analysis of voting on Pentagon appropriations at the beginning of the Reagan administration's defense buildup revealed that "public opinion was a powerful force for policy change in the realm of defense spending in the first year of the Reagan administration. Moreover, the impact of constituency opinion appears to have been remarkably broad-based, influencing all sorts of representatives across a wide spectrum of specific defense spending issues" (Bartels 1991, 467; see also Russett, Hartley, and Murray 1994). Another study of defense spending revealed a strong reciprocal connection between public inputs—preferences for "more" or "less" spending for the Pentagon—and policy outputs (Wlezien 1996).

Finally, two major studies have measured the congruence between changes in public preferences and a broad range of policies over extended periods. The first, an analysis of public opinion and policy outcomes spanning 1960–74 revealed that in almost two-thirds of 222 cases, policy outcomes corresponded to public preferences. The consistency was especially high (92 percent) on foreign policy issues. The author offered three possible explanations for his findings: foreign policy issues permit more decision making by the executive, are likely to be the object of less attention and influence by organized interest groups, and are especially susceptible to manipulation by elites (Monroe 1979). A follow-up study revealed that policy outcomes were consistent with public preferences in 55 percent of the cases during 1980–93, a decline from 63 percent in 1960–79. But once again the level of consistency was higher (67 percent) for foreign policy decisions than for those in other issue areas (Monroe 1998). A second study of the opinion-policy relationship covered an even longer time span—1935 to 1979—that included 357 significant changes of public preferences. These data also revealed a high degree of congruence between opinions and policy, with little difference in this respect between domestic (70 percent) and foreign policy (62 percent) issues (Page and Shapiro 1983).

Although anecdotal and correlational analyses can make useful contributions toward understanding the public opinion–foreign policy relationship, they are not an entirely satisfactory substitute for intensive case studies that could shed more direct light on how, if at all, public opinion enters into and influences the policy-making process. It is not wholly sufficient to describe the state of or trends in public opinion on an issue immediately before or during foreign policy decisions because a finding that major decisions seemed to be correlated with public preferences does not establish, by itself, a causal link: "not even time-series analysis can provide a magic bullet that will kill all the demons of causal ambiguity" (Page 1994, 27). For example, policymakers might be responding solely to pressures and constraints from the international system, precisely as realist theorists insist that they should, without any significant attention to public sentiments on the issue, even if those attitudes are highly congruent with those of policy-making officials. If international events are sufficiently dramatic and unambiguous in their implications—for example, the Japanese attack on Pearl Harbor or the terrorist attacks on the World Trade Center and Pentagon—leaders and the general public may react similarly, but this would not demonstrate that the latter affected the former. Alternatively, the direction of causality might run from policymakers to the public rather than vice versa, as depicted by critics who describe the public as the targets of public relations efforts by American elites (Ginsberg

1988; Herman and Chomsky 1988; Margolis and Mauser 1989; Jacobs and Shapiro 2000).

When opinion change precedes shifts in policy, the latter interpretation loses potency. However, we could not rule out still another possibility: the administration manipulates events; the events, now a part of the information available to the public, result in changes of opinion about the issue in question followed by policy changes that are congruent with public opinion. A somewhat related variant of this sequence is the "rally round the president" hypothesis, according to which the executive may manipulate the public indirectly by first undertaking external initiatives and then responding to the resulting events abroad in a manner calculated to increase his popularity with domestic constituents (Brody and Shapiro 1989; Marra, Ostrom, and Simon 1990; Hugick and Gallup 1991; Lian and Oneal 1993). But the "rally" effect is generally of moderate magnitude and depends on whether elites are united on the issue. It is a dicey reelection strategy, as Jimmy Carter (who launched the effort to rescue American hostages in Tehran in 1980) and George H. W. Bush (who received only 37 percent of the popular vote a little more than a year after the Gulf War) might attest. Moreover, a careful analysis of post–World War II presidents found no evidence to support the diversionary thesis that an administration might use force abroad to enhance public support at home (Foyle 1999, 283), but others have come to somewhat different conclusions (Lowi 1985). Finally, one of the understudied questions is whether adversaries abroad have initiated crises during election years on the belief that Washington's reactions might be constrained by the distractions of domestic politics. If and when Russian archives on the issues are opened, it would be interesting to determine the extent to which the Berlin blockade (1948) and the invasions of Hungary (1956), Czechoslovakia (1968), and Afghanistan (1979–80), for example, might have been affected by the Kremlin's calculations that presidential elections in the United States made the timing of aggressive action especially propitious.

Among the more difficult cases in which to assess causality are those dealing with public opinion as a possible constraint on action. During the 1980s, the Reagan administration undertook a massive public relations campaign to generate public support for assistance to contra rebels in Nicaragua, but careful analyses of surveys on the issue indicated that a majority of the public consistently opposed American military involvement in Central

America (Parry and Kornbluh 1988; Sobel 1989, 1993, 2001; Hinckley 1992). Would the Reagan Administration have intervened more directly or massively in Nicaragua and El Salvador in the absence of such public attitudes? Unambiguous evidence about the causes of contemporary nonevents is, to understate the case, rather hard to come by. Intensive case studies involving archival research, elite interviews, or both appear to be the only way to address such questions, although even this approach is not wholly free from potential problems of inference. Does an absence of documentary references to public opinion indicate a lack of interest by policymakers in public sentiments? Alternatively, was attention to public attitudes so deeply ingrained into their working habits that it was unnecessary to refer explicitly to it? A participant in the deliberations that led to the 1986 bombing of Libya recalled that public opinion was never discussed or brought up, but "it was clearly in the air," and "everyone knew what polls [their private ones] showed" about bombing a nation supporting terrorism. (Hinckley 1995). Even if frequent discussions and analyses of public views on the issue occurred, the inference to be drawn from that fact may not always be wholly self-evident. Are we to conclude from these deliberations that public attitudes played a significant role in policy decisions, or does the evidence merely reveal a desire on the part of officials to be on record as seriously having taken public sentiments into account?

These examples do not imply that we are limited to simple, one-directional models of the links between the public and policymakers; a number of more complex alternatives have been put forward (Rosenau 1961; Graber 1968; B. Hughes 1978; Russett 1990; Hinckley 1992; Zaller 1992; Stimson, MacKuen, and Erikson 1995; Powlick and Katz 1998; Entman and Herbst 2000). Moreover, a full analysis of the opinion-policy links would often require explorations into many aspects of the domestic political process, including the role of parties and candidates in raising issues, the impact of interest groups, the role of the media, the manner in which opinions form and circulate in the body politic, and the level of elite competition, just to mention a few salient aspects of the process. The literature on each of these topics is enormous.[7]

V. O. Key's definition of public opinion as "those opinions held by private persons which governments find it prudent to heed" (1961, 14) provides an especially appropriate introduction to any causal analysis of the opinion-policy link. He also pointed to the central research task: "If one is to know what opinions governments heed, one must know the inner thoughts of presidents, congressmen, and other officials" (14). Consequently, to develop and test competing hypotheses about opinion-policy linkages, there are no satisfactory alternatives to carefully crafted case studies employing interviews and, if possible, archival research designed to uncover how, if at all, decision makers perceive public opinion; feel themselves motivated or constrained by it; factor it into their identification and assessment of policy options; and otherwise take it into account when selecting a course of action, including a decision not to act.[8]

Although the literature systematically addressing these questions is dwarfed by the number of studies that describe the state of public opinion, several examples illustrate this type of research. The availability of substantial collections of documents relating to the 1914 European crisis enabled Richard Fagen to study top German leaders' uses and assessments of public opinion during the weeks leading up to World War I. The kaiser and other leaders in Berlin regarded public opinion as "hard goods" capable of being assessed in the same manner as military or economic capabilities. Although public opinion meant different things to different leaders, it was perceived as "an active, initiating, coercive, reified, and even personified force" (Fagen 1960, 457). For German decision makers, public opinion played four important roles during the six weeks prior to the outbreak of a general war: (1) adding a national dimension to governmental positions, (2) defining national limits of tolerance, (3) excusing actions of others, and (4) excusing one's own actions.

Doris Graber undertook an intensive study of four decisions during the early years of American history: John Adams's decision to renew negotiations with France in 1800, the Louisiana Purchase during the first Jefferson administration, James Madison's policies leading up to the War of 1812, and the enunciation of the Monroe Doctrine in 1823. Despite differences in personality, ideology, and other attributes among the four presidents, Graber found that in each case public opinion was "an important factor in decision making, but by no means the most important single factor" (1968, 318).

A study on the making of foreign policy about a century later came to a rather different conclusion. Robert Hilderbrand (1981) was unable to discover that public opinion had any significant impact on foreign policy during the quarter century

(1897–1921) encompassing the McKinley, Roosevelt, Taft, and Wilson administrations. To the extent that public opinion entered into executive discussions, it did so only after policy decisions had already been made. Other students of the Wilson presidency have come to somewhat different conclusions about his interest in and sensitivity to public opinion (Turner 1957; Cornwell 1959). Still different findings emerged from an analysis of public opinion and foreign policy from the period leading up to World War II through President Truman's March 1947 speech to Congress requesting aid to Greece and Turkey. Michael Leigh (1976) tested two approaches to the foreign policy process: the traditional democratic model that public opinion constrains American policymakers versus the radical model that manipulation of the public in favor of predetermined policy choices not only takes place but invariably succeeds. His findings validated neither the traditional nor the radical model.

Striking evidence that public opinion significantly affects policy emerged from a study of four cases of U.S. arms control policy—international control of atomic energy, the Limited Test Ban Treaty of 1963, the SALT I/Antiballistic Missile Treaties, and the SALT II Treaty—spanning every administration between Presidents Truman and Reagan. Thomas Graham (1989) used a research design that included an analysis of more than five hundred public opinion surveys and an examination of primary source materials to determine whether correlations between public opinion and policy decisions were causal or spurious. The evidence indicated that public opinion had at least some impact on decisions at all stages of the policy process, including agenda setting, arms control negotiations, the treaty ratification process, and implementation of the agreement. Moreover, the impact varied directly with the level of public support for a policy—that is, whether it reached the level of *majority* (50 to 59 percent), *consensus* (60 to 69 percent), *preponderant* (70 to 79 percent), or *virtually unanimous* (80 percent or more).

A detailed analysis of four episodes during the Eisenhower administration—the "New Look" defense policy, the decision not to intervene in Indochina following the military disaster suffered by France at Dien Bien Phu, the Quemoy-Matsu confrontation with China, and the reaction to the pioneering Soviet space capsule *Sputnik*—drew heavily on archival research. These cases, supplemented by briefer analyses of all post–World War II presidents, were used to test realist, Wilsonian liberal, and "beliefs" models of the role of public opinion in the policy process. The beliefs model, based on an individual's normative beliefs about the proper role of public opinion and practical beliefs about the importance of public support in the success of foreign policy undertakings, proved best able to explain the role of public opinion in the policy process (Foyle 1999).

Studies of the opinion-policy links are not limited to cases in which sufficient time has passed to permit full examination of the relevant archives. Philip Powlick's analysis of the role of public opinion in U.S. decisions on the Lebanon intervention during the first Reagan administration relied almost entirely on interviews with policy officials. Whereas public opinion influenced many midlevel officials and a few higher ones—for example, Caspar Weinberger—it had little impact on others, including President Reagan, Robert McFarlane, and George Shultz.[9] Powlick concluded that public opinion formed the basis of several recommendations to pull the marines out of Lebanon several months after a terrorist attack killed more than 240 American servicemen; public opinion also helped to ensure that most officials and members of Congress would warmly receive the decision to withdraw. However, President Reagan's decision to withdraw apparently was less influenced by public opinion than by the kinds of external considerations to which realists would assign top priority in decision making. Public opinion was thus only one of several factors that came together to bring about the evacuation from Beirut in February 1984. Another study of policy-making in the Reagan administration came to a somewhat different conclusion. In searching for the sources of Reagan's transformation from a Cold War hawk who had blamed the USSR—an "evil empire"—for all international problems to a president who came to describe his Soviet counterpart as "my friend," Fischer (1997) concluded that public opinion played little if any role.

Powlick's conclusions regarding the Lebanon intervention may, however, have understated the impact of public opinion on those at the top levels of the government. According to another official in the administration, Ronald Hinckley, the president and McFarlane constantly had public opinion information fed to them. Reagan received his from pollster Richard Wirthlin, whereas McFarlane was briefed on public opinion by his crisis management center team. Hinckley concludes that the Lebanon episode (as well as the later decision to bomb Libya in response to suspected terrorist activities in 1986) illustrates officials' tendency to discount public opinion when explaining their decisions "because it is not consciously on the table when the decision is made, but it has been in the mind of the decision maker for some time" (Hinckley 1995).

Because most of the relevant archives have yet to be opened, Richard Sobel's (2001) study of public opinion in four U.S. interventions abroad—the Vietnam War, aid to the contras in Nicaragua, the Gulf War, and the civil war in Bosnia—relied heavily on interviews. The key policy officials whom Sobel interviewed included former President George H. W. Bush, four secretaries of defense, and three secretaries of state. Sobel concluded that "public opinion has constrained the U.S. foreign policy decision-making process over the last generation," but its impact varied in the four cases (240). For example, the controversial issue of aid to Nicaraguan contras yielded somewhat mixed results. Although the public consistently opposed aid, Congress was willing to provide assistance to the rebels but did so in far more limited amounts and restricted form than the Reagan administration had requested. Several key members of Congress denied that their votes had been cast in direct response to public preferences within their districts, but under questioning they admitted sounding out their constituents' opinions and voting their own minds when they found evidence of public indifference. Administration officials also attempted to ignore public opposition. Nevertheless, public opinion did constrain more aggressive intervention in Nicaragua. Despite his deserved reputation as the "great communicator," Reagan's inability to win over the public to his view was one of his major political defeats, and it probably forced him to rely on the proceeds of illegal arms sales to Iran to fund the contras (Sobel 1993, 2001).

Lawrence Jacobs and Robert Shapiro have been engaged in the most ambitious analyses of the public opinion–policy link. Their many studies have ranged across several administrations between those of John F. Kennedy and Bill Clinton. Through archival research the authors identified the polling data—generated both internally and by such organizations as Gallup and Harris—available to the president and his advisers (Jacobs and Shapiro 1994a, 1995, 1995–96, 1999, 2000). In addition to consulting archival data, Jacobs and Shapiro interviewed top White House personnel as well as those engaged in conducting the surveys.

Taken as a whole, these studies clearly point to mixed conclusions about the impact of public opinion on foreign policy and seem to suggest that public opinion's effects may have intensified during recent decades. This tentative conclusion also receives some support from interview studies of foreign policy officials. Although the bureaucrats interviewed by Powlick (1991, 1995) were not notably more sanguine about the public and its ability to contribute constructively to foreign policy than were those interviewed in similar research by Bernard Cohen (1973) more than two decades earlier, these leaders were more inclined to accept the legitimacy of a public contribution to the policy process and consequently tended to avoid policy options perceived as likely to engender public opposition. In contrast, Graham's (1989) study of U.S. arms control policies found little change over time because his research revealed that public opinion has played an important role in such decisions in all administrations since President Truman's. This, then, is one of the many areas in which contradictory findings exist. This mixed assessment and call for additional research is consistent with that of an extensive recent review of the opinion-policy link across a wide range of issues: "although policy will tend to follow public opinion more often than not, there is sufficiently wide variation in the extent of responsiveness across different issues and at different points in time to warrant increased scholarly attention to examining the institutional and political sources of variation" (Manza and Cook 2002, 657–58).

Some salient features of American public opinion can be illustrated in more detail by examining responses to some of the most important foreign policy issues that have confronted the United States since World War II. First, I will focus on questions rooted in the Cold War, notably assessments of the Soviet Union (Russia since 1991) and, much more briefly, of China. I will then examine responses to a broader set of questions that have lost none of their importance since the end of the Cold War—namely, the appropriate goals for American foreign policy.

Public Opinion on the Soviet Union and Russia

On February 27, 1946, Arthur Vandenberg asked his colleagues in the Senate, "What is Russia up to now?" Few questions have so persistently engendered debate within the United States after the end of World War II as those concerning the Soviet Union, its foreign policies, and the appropriate American approaches for dealing with the USSR. In his famous 1946 "long telegram" and in an essay on "The Sources of Soviet Conduct" a year later, George F. Kennan wrote that Soviet foreign policy was driven largely by internal forces, including the need for real or imagined external enemies; at least in the short run, therefore, American offers of friendship and cooperation were likely to prove fruitless. Kennan's diagnosis of Soviet international behavior and his prescription of a "long-term, patient but firm and vigilant containment of Russian expansive tendencies" (1947, 575) were enormously influential in providing an intellectual framework for American policy toward Stalin's Russia but did not end the debate about Soviet foreign policy or the best means for dealing with the USSR.

The debate has often been stimulated by external events. The Berlin blockade; the invasion of South Korea; the death of Stalin; the invasions of Hungary, Czechoslovakia, and Afghanistan; *Sputnik;* the Cuban missile crisis; and the activities that constituted the high point of détente in 1972–73 are some of the more dramatic episodes that have intensified interest in the question. Almost as often, the debate has been aroused by American domestic politics, especially presidential election campaigns. In 1952, the concept of containment came under attack from some Republicans, notably John Foster Dulles, as too "static." Later events demonstrated clearly that its putative replacement—"roll back" of the Iron Curtain—was campaign rhetoric rather than policy. To disarm critics in the right wing of his own party in 1976, President Ford let it be known that *détente* was no longer a part of the White House working vocabulary. Four years later, the soon-to-be-nominated Ronald Reagan blamed the USSR for all international problems, and during the subsequent campaign he attacked arms control and détente as the causes of the "worst decade in American history" (House 1980, 1).

American interest in these questions has recently been enhanced by external and internal developments. After 1985, Mikhail Gorbachev provided the Soviet Union with a style of leadership that seemed light-years removed from that of most previous Soviet leaders. He was certainly a far cry from the dour, reclusive Stalin, the mercurial Nikita Khrushchev, or the aged, doddering trio of Leonid Brezhnev, Yuri Andropov, and Konstantin Chernenko, who preceded Gorbachev in the Kremlin; even those most skeptical about the significance or permanence of glasnost or perestroika agreed that Gorbachev possessed political and public relations skills unmatched in Soviet history. At the same time, the American president who excoriated the Soviet Union as an "evil empire" in 1983 was within five years meeting regularly with

Gorbachev and describing him as a friend. Relations between the superpowers continued to improve during the early 1990s, reaching a level of cooperation not witnessed since World War II; in 1990 and 1991, the two countries joined forces at the United Nations Security Council to pass a series of resolutions aimed at compelling Iraq to reverse its invasion of Kuwait.

The disintegration of the Soviet Union at the end of 1991 coincided with the effective end of Gorbachev's political career and the emergence of Boris Yeltsin as the Kremlin leader. Expectations that Yeltsin would preside over a continuing process of democratization and liberalization proved overly optimistic. Although reelected president in 1996, Yeltsin was plagued by a plethora of domestic problems, including a rebellion in Chechnya, ill health, and suspicions of alcoholism. Yeltsin stepped aside in 2000 in favor of his handpicked successor, Vladimir Putin. Bloody repression in Chechnya by Russian armed forces; the North Atlantic Treaty Organization's war against Serbia, a traditional Russian ally, and eastward expansion; and differences over the American plan to deploy a national missile defense system roiled relations between Washington and Moscow. These differences appeared to have been pushed aside, at least temporarily, by the 2001 terrorist attacks on New York and Washington, which dramatically resurrected cooperation between the two countries, but the differences reemerged on the question of how best to deal with charges that Iraq had failed to divest itself of weapons of mass destruction, as required by several United Nations resolutions.

During the more than half century between the onset of World War II and the dissolution of the Soviet Union at the end of 1991, the Gallup and other polling organizations provided an immense amount of survey data on questions relating to superpower relations. Aside from the Soviet Union's obvious importance for American foreign relations, there is also evidence that attitudes toward the USSR have played a central role in organizing public attitudes toward a wide array of international issues (Herrmann 1986; Holsti 1988; Hurwitz and Peffley 1990; Murray 1996). The disintegration of the USSR has not wholly extinguished debates about how best to manage relations between Washington and Moscow. Thus, the combination of ample data and the salience of these issues provides a good opportunity to assess several competing theories of public opinion.[10]

Two of the theories have been described earlier. The Almond-Lippmann thesis stipulates that public reactions to world affairs are characterized by volatility and little if any relationship to international realities. An alternative interpretation describes mass public reactions as rational and events-driven. A third theory, developed largely to deal with the Cold War period, depicts the American public quite differently, although not necessarily in a more flattering light than the Almond-Lippmann thesis. Rather than focusing on volatility and mood cycles that have a random or negative correlation with the real world, this theory emphasizes certain continuities in public opinion, with special attention to a putative American propensity toward a Manichaean worldview. The public is depicted as imbued with a frontier mentality for which the appropriate metaphor is the cowboy movie, with its "white hats" and "black hats" and a concomitant absence of multidimensional characters, simplistic plots, violent shoot-outs as the characteristic mode of conflict resolution, and the inevitable triumph of the good guys over the villains. According to this thesis, Americans have regarded communism as the great evil and the Soviets as its black-hatted agents. To the extent that public opinion has been a factor in American foreign policy, it has buttressed and perhaps even cast into concrete the great constant in Washington's post–World War II diplomacy: a reflexive anti-Soviet policy that was allegedly so often out of touch with reality that it served neither the national interest nor the prospects for peace, stability, and justice.

There are at least two broad variants of this third theory. According to one, public opinion is the victim in that it was manipulated into a hard-line anti-Soviet position by the ruling class and its faithful handmaidens in the media and other key institutions. Because public opinion has little autonomous life of its own, it is also of limited relevance in any effort to understand American foreign and defense policies. This viewpoint may be found in several revisionist histories of the Cold War (for example, Kolko and Kolko 1972). A second version locates irrational anti-Soviet sentiments in certain widely shared values, beliefs, and attitudes about the world that are central features of American culture. For example, in analyzing the cultural bases of American foreign policy, Robert Dallek has written of an "unthinking anticommunism" that serves several nonrational needs, providing, among other things, "a convenient excuse for not facing up to troubling domestic concerns" (1983, xvii, xviii). The ample data on the Soviet Union and the successor Russian regime provide an opportunity to assess, if not put to a definitive test, these quite distinctive depictions of American public opinion. Responses to questions about the Soviet Union/Russia and appropriate American policies for dealing with Moscow provide the evidence for this purpose.

Soviet-American Cooperation

Almost from the moment that the United States entered World War II, various polling organizations started asking the public to appraise the prospects for relations between Washington and Moscow after the fighting ended. While the wording of the questions varied, all of them focused on the probability that the Soviets could be trusted to continue cooperation with the United States into the postwar period as envisaged, for example, by President Roosevelt's plan for collaboration among the "Four Policemen"—Britain, China, the USSR, and the United States—to maintain peace.

During World War II, the American public was offered a good deal of information that sustained hopes of good Soviet-American relations. Most public pronouncements by policymakers were optimistic on this score. One example will illustrate the extent to which the Roosevelt administration attempted to portray the USSR in favorable terms. During the summer and fall of 1941, survey evidence revealed a lack of public enthusiasm for aid to Russia, which had recently been invaded by its erstwhile German ally. Opposition was especially strong among American religious groups. Roosevelt mounted a strong campaign to disarm the critics by asserting that the Soviet constitution guaranteed freedom of conscience and worship (Dallek 1979). Such books as *Mission to Moscow* by former Ambassador Joseph Davies (1941) and *One World* by Wendell Willkie (1943), the 1940 Republican presidential nominee, also depicted the Soviet Union in highly favorable terms. Many wartime movies, including the film version of *Mission to Moscow,* were similarly upbeat. To be sure, some skeptics remained, but the information available to the public stressed the Soviets' important military role in defeating the Nazi regime and the wartime cooperation among the Allies while deemphasizing the nature of Stalin's regime and the possibilities that there might be strong divergences of interests or competing and perhaps incompatible preferences about the nature of the postwar international order.

Of the many wartime surveys that touched on the prospects

for postwar collaboration between Washington and Moscow, not a single one yielded a plurality that answered the question in the negative (table 3.1). A peak in trust was reached in the wake of the 1945 Yalta Conference, which Roosevelt reported had re-

TABLE 3.1.   "Can Russia Be Trusted to Cooperate with the United States?" 1942–49

Dates		Number of Surveys	Yes (%)	No (%)	Key Events
1942:	Jan.–June	4	41	34	Moscow Conference: U.S., USSR, U.K.
	July–Dec.	6	49	26	(Aug.)
1943:	Jan.–June	3	46	30	Soviet victory at battle of Stalingrad (Jan.)
					Soviets dissolve Comintern (May)
	July–Dec.	3	49	25	Tehran Conference: U.S., USSR, U.K. (Nov.)
1944:	Jan.–June	2	45	30	Allied invasion of France (June)
	July–Dec.	2	47	36	Soviets allow Germany to crush Warsaw uprising (Aug.–Oct.)
1945:	Jan.–June	2	50	35	Yalta Conference: U.S., USSR, U.K. (Feb.)
					UN Conference at San Francisco (April)
					German surrender (May)
	July–Dec.	5	46	38	Potsdam Conference: U.S., USSR, U.K. (July)
					USSR declaration of war against Japan (Aug.)
					Japanese surrender (Aug.)
1946:	Jan.–June	6	36	48	Dispute over laggard Soviet withdrawal from Iran (Jan.)
					Stalin speech on "inevitability of war" (Feb.)
	July–Dec.	4	35	50	Molotov attack on U.S. at UN (Nov.)
1947:	Jan.–June	3	28	59	Truman Doctrine: Aid to Greece and Turkey (Mar.)
					Marshall Plan speech on aid to Europe (June)
	July–Dec.	2	19	70	Soviet Union creates Cominform (Oct.)
1948:	Jan.–June	1	25	63	Communist coup in Czechoslovakia (Feb.)
					Berlin blockade initiated (June)
	July–Dec.	2	18	73	Soviet Union vetoes Berlin compromise proposal in UN (Oct.)
1949:	Jan.–June	4	21	67	Berlin blockade lifted (May)
	July–Dec.	3	21	68	First Soviet atomic bomb test announced (Sept.)

Source: Survey data from National Opinion Research Center (NORC), Gallup Organization, and Office of Public Opinion Research. Reported percentages are averages of the "yes" and "no" responses for each six-month period.

Note: Several NORC questions in 1947–49 asked, "Can the Russians be trusted to meet us halfway?"

solved a number of outstanding issues among the United States, Britain, and USSR; at that time, the affirmative responses outnumbered the negative ones by a margin of almost two to one: 55 percent to 31 percent. Another Gallup poll revealed almost identical results immediately after the Soviet Union joined the war against Japan, as Stalin had promised at Yalta.

From these high points, a steady if irregular erosion of public trust in Soviet cooperation occurred, coinciding with a potential crisis revolving around the laggard withdrawal of Soviet wartime occupation troops from northern Iran in 1946 as well as the failure of various foreign ministers' conferences to resolve such issues as peace treaties for Germany and Austria. Yet as late as December 1946, nineteen months after the German surrender, a Gallup survey revealed that a 43 percent plurality of the public remained optimistic on the question of Soviet cooperation with the United States. Within less than three years—a period that witnessed consolidation of the Soviets' hegemonic position in Eastern Europe, the coup that brought a communist government to power in Czechoslovakia, and the Berlin blockade—those who responded that the Soviets could be trusted to be cooperative had shrunk to a small minority.

The "cooperation" question was rarely used after 1950, but two decades later, Harris surveys began regularly posing a somewhat similar question that asked Americans to assess the prospects for Soviet-American agreements "to help keep the peace." The results appear quite consistent with actual international developments. In July 1968, those who felt that agreements were possible outnumbered the naysayers by 12 percent, but following the Soviet invasion of Czechoslovakia in August, the number of optimists fell from 49 to 34 percent. Public opinion also reflected the developing détente between the superpowers. Strong majorities, reaching a peak of 60 percent in 1973, answered that it was possible for the superpowers to reach such agreements. By the time Harris stopped asking the question in 1975, détente had been subjected to a number of strains, including a major confrontation between Washington and Moscow during the Yom Kippur War of October 1973; concomitantly, positive responses concerning the prospects for U.S.-USSR agreements dropped to 45 percent.

Although strictly comparable data are more limited for the Gorbachev period, there were many indications of increasing optimism about cooperation between the superpowers. A 1988 survey found that only 19 percent of the respondents felt that improving relations between the two nations "will *not* lead to any lasting, fundamental changes." In contrast, 57 percent stated that the changes will be fundamental and lasting, "though the two countries will never be allies," and a surprisingly high 23 percent predicted that "one day" they would indeed be allies (*Americans Talk Security* 1988, 64). By the end of 1989, when asked to look ahead to the end of the millennium, two-thirds of the respondents agreed with the statement that "The Soviet Union and West will be living peacefully together" (De Stefano 1990). Finally, when the "cooperation" question was posed again in 1990, after the pathbreaking Intermediate-Range Nuclear Forces Treaty and other agreements between the superpowers as well as well-publicized summit conferences between Soviet and American leaders, those events were reflected in the overwhelmingly optimistic responses to a Gallup survey on the question.

Several post–Cold War Gallup surveys have asked whether Russia is an ally, friendly but not an ally, unfriendly but not an enemy, or an enemy. The results reveal a good deal of ambivalence about the most appropriate term for describing the U.S.-Russian relationship, but a survey just prior to the Russian presidential election won by Vladimir Putin in 2000 indicated some optimism on this score. Although few respondents were willing to depict Russia as an ally (12 percent) or enemy (11 percent), most of the others selected the friendly (49 percent) rather than unfriendly (22 percent) option (G. Gallup Jr. 2000, 175). Similar results have emerged from three NBC/*Wall Street Journal* surveys since the mid-1990s. Americans are somewhat more inclined to think of their erstwhile Cold War rival as an ally rather than as an adversary, although not by overwhelming margins. The responses were 56 to 35 percent in favor of the "ally" designation in 1995, 48 to 28 percent a year later, and little changed in a 2002 survey undertaken seven months after the terrorist attacks (52 to 26 percent).

Soviet/Russian Foreign Policy Objectives

Since World War II, polling organizations have frequently asked the public whether Soviet foreign policy goals are expansionist or defensive. The immediate postwar era, 1946–53, witnessed a steady erosion of the cooperation that had marked wartime relations between Moscow and Washington, the start of the Cold War, the Korean War, and the death of Joseph Stalin. After 1976, the U.S.-Soviet relationship was marked by the collapse of détente, an accelerated arms race, rapid turnover among Kremlin leaders, the beginnings of dramatically better relations between the superpowers, and, at the end of 1991, the disintegration of the USSR.

Survey data from the first period reveal a rather steady decline—from 29 to 12 percent between 1946 and 1949—in the proportion of Americans who believed that the Soviet Union was merely acting defensively by "building up protection against being attacked in another war." The invasion of South Korea in 1950, widely assumed to have had at least tacit Soviet support, further reduced to a minority of less than one in ten those who believed that the Kremlin was acting out of defensive motives.[11]

After a lapse of more than a quarter century, a similar question was again posed regularly but with a more diverse set of response options. As was the case during the earlier period, the results appear to have been at least moderately sensitive to the course of international events. Whereas in October 1979 only 18 percent of the respondents believed that the Soviet Union was willing to risk war in a quest for global domination, that figure more than doubled to 39 percent within four months, an interval highlighted by the Soviet invasion of Afghanistan. Conversely, the later 1980s saw a steady decline in the proportion of the public that believed that the USSR would use any means, not excluding war, to achieve essentially unlimited international goals. By January 1988 an Americans Talk Security survey revealed that a majority (54 percent) of Americans attributed defensive motives to the Kremlin, whereas a Roper poll at the same time indicated that fewer than half of respondents (44 percent) believed that global domination was "Russia's primary objective in world affairs." By the end of the year, almost two-thirds of the registered voters polled by the Americans Talk Security project attributed defensive motives to Soviet foreign policy. The trend toward a more benign view of Soviet/Russian foreign policy motives continued into the early 1990s, with a steady increase in those who believed that self-defense was the driving motive behind Moscow's external policy. By the end of the decade, the public was quite evenly divided about whether "Russia poses a significant military threat to the United States today." Indeed, an April 1999 Gallup poll found that whereas 48 percent perceived a significant military threat, exactly the same number disagreed. The issue was not a partisan one, as Republican, Democratic, and independent responses were virtually identical (G. Gallup Jr. 1999, 183). Despite Russia's assistance during the months following the 9/11 attacks, concern for its internal stability does not rank high among perceived threats. More than four-fifths of Americans asserted, in responses to the 2002 CCFR survey, that the United States has "a vital interest" in Russia. However, only about a quarter of respondents also rated the possibility of political turmoil in that country as a "critical" threat to American interests.

General Assessments of the Soviet Union and Russia

When asked for general assessments of the Soviet Union, aggregate responses from the American public reveal considerable shifts in response to international developments rather than a consistently negative image (fig. 3.2). During the 1950s, at the height of the Cold War, the ratings were overwhelmingly negative, but they tended to moderate somewhat thereafter. Not surprisingly, a survey undertaken in December 1956, immediately after the Soviet invasion crushed the Hungarian rebellion, found that only 2 percent of Americans had a favorable view of the USSR. Within the next ten years, relations between the superpowers had witnessed both crises, such as those involving American U-2 spy flights over Soviet territory and the introduction of Soviet offensive missiles into Cuba, and cooperation on arms control, including such agreements as the Limited Test Ban Treaty and the Nuclear Nonproliferation Treaty. Concomitantly, American appraisals of the USSR, while still negative on balance, improved considerably. By the early 1970s, the peak of the Nixon-Kissinger period of détente that was characterized by agreements on arms (SALT I) and in other areas as well as pronouncements from the White House that the Cold War was over, well under half of the public expressed unfavorable judgments of the Soviet Union; only 30 percent did so in response to a March 1973 Gallup poll. Public assessments of the USSR similarly reflected the erosion of détente during the remainder of the decade.

After the invasion of Afghanistan at the end of 1979 and the destruction in 1983 of Korean Airlines flight 007 as it strayed over Soviet territory, unfavorable ratings of the USSR increased sharply, reaching levels not seen since the 1950s. Another shift in sentiment began during the second Reagan administration, after Mikhail Gorbachev assumed leadership in Moscow. By 1987 two surveys reported that fewer than half of the respondents had an unfavorable opinion of the USSR. For the next four years, public assessments continued to improve, although with some irregularity.

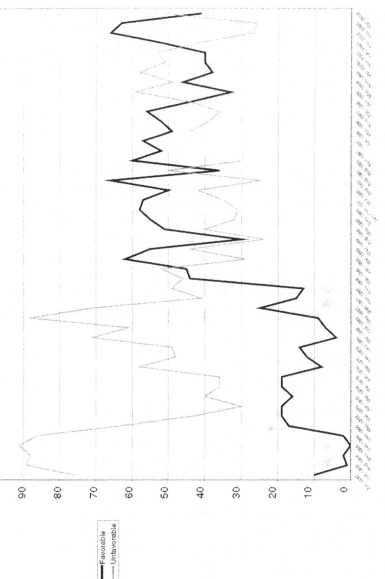

Fig. 3.2. General evaluations of the Soviet Union and Russia, 1947–2003. (Data from Gallup Organization except NORC [April 1994]), General Social Survey [March 1974, March 1975, March 1997], ABC/Washington Post [February and March 1989], Los Angeles Times [May 1987], ORC [November 1987], CBS/New York Times [September 1987, May 1989])

President Gorbachev's crackdown on Lithuania and Latvia in 1991 resulted in some decline. More dramatically, a Gallup survey taken the day after hard-line communist coup plotters had deposed Gorbachev in August 1991 found that favorable appraisals had dropped by 30 percent from levels found in a poll taken a few days earlier, but support rebounded after the coup's failure.

Despite the turbulent course of Russian politics and governance during the post-Soviet period, evaluations of that country remained favorable by a margin of three to two in early 1994. Gallup surveys in 1996 and 1997 revealed majorities with a positive assessment of Russia, but the next three years witnessed growing disenchantment in public appraisals of that country. Two surveys in 2000 found that only 40 percent of respondents had a favorable view of Russia, whereas small majorities held the opposite view. A year earlier, Republicans, Democrats, and independents had identical favorable ratings of Russia (46 percent), but minor partisan differences emerged by 2000, with Republicans very slightly more inclined toward a negative view.

The 9/11 terrorist attacks on the World Trade Center and the Pentagon elicited prompt Russian expressions of sympathy and offers of assistance in support of the military campaign against al Qaeda and Afghanistan's Taliban regime. The public responded to these developments with significantly more favorable assessments of Russia. Whereas only a bare majority (52 percent) rated Russia favorably in early 2001 (nine months prior to the attacks on New York and Washington), that figure rose to 66 percent a year later. The solid majority (63 percent to 26 percent) of those holding a favorable view of Russia in February 2003 fell sharply within a month—a period of well-publicized differences between Washington and Moscow on how best to deal with charges that Iraq was developing and maintaining weapons of mass destruction, in violation of the terms that ended the first Gulf War in 1991.

Assessments of Soviet and Russian Leaders

Until the 1980s, polling organizations rarely asked the American public to evaluate individual Soviet leaders. Even Stalin's death in 1953 did not elicit probes about its implications for Soviet-American relations or for assessments of his successors. This apparent lack of interest on the part of polling organizations in specific Soviet leaders changed dramatically with Mikhail Gorbachev's accession to leadership in 1985. Indeed, the frequency with which pollsters asked the public to assess Gorbachev—the question was posed at least thirty-four times between 1985 and 1991—may have been a good indicator of his manifest public relations skills. Although the results reveal a considerable range of responses, in part from inconsistency in the wording or context of questions, one rather remarkable constant runs through the results for the entire six-year period: not a single survey found that as much as 40 percent of the public expressed a negative opinion of the Soviet leader. During his last three years in office, Gorbachev had an average favorable rating of more than 70 percent. By 1988, those with a favorable view of Gorbachev typically outnumbered his detractors by margins of two, three, or even four to one. A 1988 Harris survey found that the Soviet leader had a 76 percent positive rating, twenty points higher than that accorded to President Reagan during his final months in office. Just prior to Gorbachev's retirement when the Soviet Union disintegrated at the end of 1991, 80 percent of the public appraised the Soviet leader in favorable terms. These results confirmed that the Soviet leader enjoyed a higher degree of popularity in most Western nations, including the United States, than in his own country.

His manifest domestic political difficulties notwithstanding, the American public continued to express support for Russian President Boris Yeltsin. A remarkably small proportion of the public had not heard of him—in three Gallup surveys, those who failed to do so numbered fewer than 5 percent—and American support for Yeltsin had widespread public approval, reaching 62 percent in 1993 (G. Gallup Jr. 1993, 54; 1994, 15). Perhaps these figures also reflected a feeling that, whatever his shortcomings, Yeltsin was preferable to those who might replace him as Russian leader. As Yeltsin's domestic problems multiplied and his health seemed to decline, his support in this country also eroded. By April 1999, those favoring support for the beleaguered Russian leader outnumbered those opposing support by the slim margin of 48 percent to 42 percent.

Yeltsin's successor, Vladimir Putin, was largely unknown to most Americans. Following his election in 2000, fewer than one in five respondents could identify Putin as president of Russia, but that was still almost ten times the number who could identify the longtime prime minister of Canada, Jean Chretien (G. Gallup Jr. 2000, 175).

Arms Control

In addition to survey data regarding public attitudes about the Soviet Union, there is ample information about several aspects of

U.S. policy toward the USSR. Support for arms control, both for general proposals and specific agreements, has been one of the constants in American public opinion since the 1950s. The SALT II agreement is the only exception to this generalization. A massive public relations campaign against the treaty, led by the conservative Committee on the Present Danger, sustained by the manufactured "Cuban brigade crisis," and brought to a climax by the Soviet invasion of Afghanistan, combined to erode early public support for the treaty. Even in the face of these events, a Gallup survey conducted early in 1980, immediately after the invasion of Afghanistan, found that supporters of the agreement outnumbered its critics by a slim margin of 30 to 27 percent, but several Roper polls found declining support for the treaty during the remainder of that election year.

Except for SALT II, the public has strongly endorsed proposals for several kinds of agreements on nuclear weapons: to stop testing them, to place limits on their numbers, and to freeze nuclear arsenals. Even before President Reagan's proposal at the 1986 Reykjavik summit meeting with Gorbachev that all offensive strategic weapons be destroyed within a decade, a plan along these lines gained support from a plurality of respondents in a 1981 Gallup poll. The Intermediate-Range Nuclear Forces Treaty received overwhelming support, as did various START agreements to reduce offensive nuclear weapons. No doubt the latter measures gained some support because they were endorsed by a popular president — Ronald Reagan — whose harsh anti–arms control rhetoric during the 1980 election campaign endowed him with the public image of a leader who would not rush into unfavorable agreements or otherwise be hoodwinked in superpower negotiations. But support of a popular president does not appear to explain fully the consistent public support for arms control; indeed, it does not even appear to be a necessary condition. Repeated polls and state-level referenda, only one of which failed, revealed widespread support for a nuclear freeze during the early 1980s even though President Reagan repeatedly denounced the proposals.

Confrontation or Accommodation?

During a five-year period (1948–53) encompassing the Truman administration and the first year of the Eisenhower administration, the National Opinion Research Center asked the public,

"Do you think the United States should be more willing to compromise with Russia, or is our present policy about right, or should we be even firmer than we are today?" According to their responses, the proportion of Americans who felt that Washington should adopt a more accommodating stance toward the Soviet Union never exceeded one in ten. In contrast, a policy of greater firmness consistently garnered support from majorities ranging between 53 and 66 percent of the respondents. The inauguration of the Eisenhower administration in 1953, the death of Stalin six weeks later, and the Korean armistice that summer did not significantly affect responses to this question.

After a hiatus of more than a decade, a somewhat comparable question was included in a 1964 Free-Cantril survey. Although this poll took place in the aftermath of the Cuban missile crisis — a period that included the Limited Test Ban Treaty, the "Hot Line" agreement, and generally less confrontational relations between Moscow and Washington than had been the case during the turbulent years between the 1958 Berlin "deadline crisis" and the Caribbean confrontation in 1962 — a substantial 61 percent of the respondents agreed that the United States should "take a firmer stand" in its dealings with the Kremlin. However, there were definite limits on what a "firmer stand" should entail; for example, the same survey found that only 20 percent favored "rolling back the Iron Curtain."

Sixteen years later, in the wake of the Soviet invasion of Afghanistan, two-thirds of those taking part in a CBS/*New York Times* poll also felt that the United States should "get tougher." During the Reagan years, however, every survey, save one taken immediately after the Soviet destruction of Korean Airlines Flight 007, revealed that Americans preferred trying "harder to reduce tensions with the Russians" to a more confrontational policy. By 1987 the tension-reduction option had become the preferred choice by a margin of well over two to one. Even though some support continued for a policy of "getting tougher," within a year the ratio in favor of reducing tensions increased to almost three to one. A year later, respondents who felt that President George H. W. Bush should do more to help the Soviet Union "deal with social and political changes taking place there" outnumbered by more than four to one those who stated that he was already doing too much (*Americans Talk Security* 1988, 141).

The President's Handling of Relations with the
USSR and Russia

Just before gaining the Republican presidential nomination in
1980, Ronald Reagan asserted in a long interview with the *Wall
Street Journal* that the Soviets were the sole source of all international problems (House 1980, 1). Although he was elected in a
landslide later that fall, some survey evidence from the Reagan
era suggests that most Americans rejected such a Manichaean diagnosis of world problems. When asked three times during the
1980s to respond to the proposition that "the U.S. has to accept
some of the blame for the tension that has plagued U.S.-Soviet
relations in recent years," three-fourths or more of the public
agreed each time. That three surveys undertaken by different organizations—*Time* magazine, the Public Affairs Foundation, and
Americans Talk Security—over more than five years yielded almost identical results lends greater credence to the data. Respondents to a 1988 survey also agreed by a margin of two to one
that "the U.S. often blames the Soviet Union for troubles in other
countries that are really caused by poverty, hunger, political cor-
ruption and repression" (*Americans Talk Security* 1988, 57).
These figures would also seem to cast some doubt on the thesis
that a moralistic and hypocritical American public is incapable of
transcending a simplistic black/white assessment of world affairs.
    Questions about presidential performance have long been a
staple item in opinion surveys, but, before the Reagan era, only the
Harris poll regularly asked the public to assess the president's
handling of relations with the USSR. Evidence from the Nixon
years reveals that respondents were generally divided on the question until the blossoming of détente. In mid-1972, the public gave
Nixon a positive rating by a margin of 68 to 25 percent, and six
months later the margin of approval had swelled to an even more
favorable 70 to 22 percent. The Yom Kippur War, which raised such
questions as "What did the Soviets know about the impending
Egyptian attack on Israel, and when did they know it?" saw a sharp
decline in the approval ratings to 55 percent, but they remained favorable, on balance, until 1975. The first survey of the Carter years,
during his honeymoon period and at a time of highly visible White
House support for human rights in the USSR, revealed that a plurality approved of his Soviet policies, but his rating fell steadily, if
irregularly, from that point on. A low point was reached late in
1979, when only 22 percent supported his handling of relations

with the Kremlin, and that figure had scarcely improved on the eve of the presidential election thirteen months later.

Although many Americans apparently disagreed with Reagan's 1980 diagnosis that the Russians were behind all international problems, they nevertheless gave the president relatively good marks for his policies toward the USSR. The data also offer a valuable lesson in caution about using survey data. In this case the lesson centers on systematic differences between results produced by various polling organizations. In some cases, differences between surveys are quite dramatic. For example, whereas in 1984 (a presidential election year) nine Harris polls found an average net rating for Reagan's Soviet policies of -18 percent, the comparable figure from five Gallup surveys was 6 percent. Three other polls by ABC, the *Washington Post,* and CBS/*New York Times* yielded results almost identical to those from the Gallup organization. These differences notwithstanding, it appears clear that Reagan generally received public approbation for his policies toward the USSR. Indeed, aside from the consistently negative ratings that emerged from Harris surveys, only four others out of more than one hundred found a plurality or majority that disapproved of Reagan's Soviet policies.

The data also indicate that after the honeymoon period in 1981, Reagan's strongest approval ratings on Soviet policy tended to come during his second term, years that were marked by regular meetings with Mikhail Gorbachev, progress on arms control, and a general easing of tensions between the superpowers. Because this was also a period when Reagan's overall performance rating scores tended to suffer—for example, he experienced the sharpest drop on record when it was revealed that his administration had been selling arms to the fundamentalist Islamic regime in Iran and using the receipts to fund the Nicaraguan contras despite (or perhaps because) the Bolin Amendments prohibited doing so—the evidence is especially revealing. By mid-1988, a Harris survey found that the president's high approval ratings on Soviet policy (67 percent) and his performance at the Moscow summit meeting far outstripped his overall popularity (54 percent). This suggests at least two interpretations linking public opinion to foreign policy that are not mutually exclusive.

Reagan was driven to seek a rapprochement with the Soviets in part to bolster his popularity ratings and perhaps his standing in history.

Whether or not bearbaiting was good domestic politics in 1980, by 1985, when Gorbachev assumed Soviet leadership, the domestic climate of opinion had shifted sufficiently to make dancing with the bear a more attractive option.[12]

Strong public approval for policies of seeking accommodation with the USSR extended into and swelled during the first Bush administration; for example, Bush's performance rating increased sharply after he announced that he would meet with Gorbachev at Malta. Bill Clinton's overall performance ratings were generally rather lukewarm, but his dealings with Russia have received greater public approval; in October 1993, those supporting his policies outnumbered the critics by a margin of 54 to 25 percent, with the remainder expressing no opinion (G. Gallup Jr. 1993, 175). Questions about presidential performance in dealing with Russian-American relations have rarely been posed since then, apparently another indicator of Russia's declining importance in the conduct of U.S. foreign affairs.

China

Compared to surveys on the Soviet Union/Russia, questions about China have been asked much less frequently. The reason can probably be found in the acrimonious relationship between Washington and Beijing for much of the Cold War. Asking the public about China or Sino-American relations probably seemed like an exercise in documenting the obvious. Although some Americans, including Republican foreign policy expert John Foster Dulles, called for establishing diplomatic relations after the communist regime took power in 1949, China's military intervention in the Korean War in November 1950 and the resulting two and half years of war ended any serious discussion of that option for two decades. President Nixon's trip to China in 1972, culminating in the Shanghai Communiqué, in which the United States accepted the Beijing regime as the legitimate Chinese government, initiated a process that culminated in full diplomatic relations between the two countries by the end of the decade.

Gallup polls asked for public assessments of China only three times prior to the 1980s—in 1967, 1976, and 1979—but since that time, questions about China have been posed more regularly. The results, summarized in figure 3.3, reveal some striking fluctuations

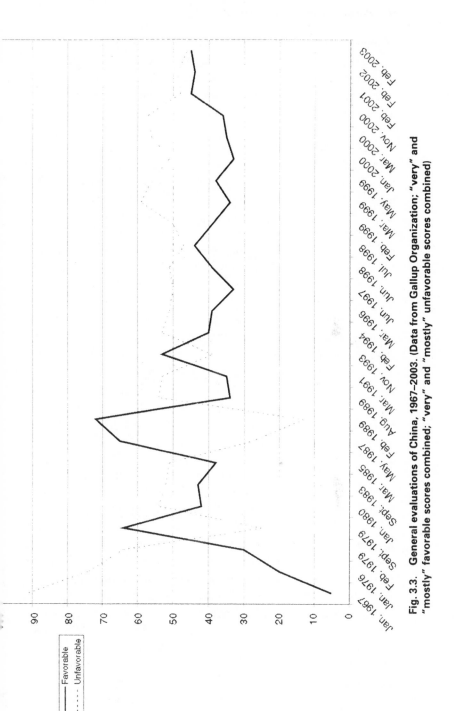

Fig. 3.3. General evaluations of China, 1967–2003. (Data from Gallup Organization; "very" and "mostly" favorable scores combined; "very" and "mostly" unfavorable scores combined)

in public sentiment.[13] Starting from a very low base—in 1967, only one in twenty respondents expressed a favorable assessment of China—there has been a very uneven long-term trend toward a somewhat more positive evaluation. As with evaluations of the Soviet Union, important events have played a major role in how the public has reacted (see table 3.1 and figure 3.2). The opening of diplomatic relations, increased trade between the two countries, and evidence of some post-Mao reforms in China were reflected in public assessments. In May 1987, almost two-thirds of the respondents judged China in "very" or "somewhat" favorable terms. Less than two years later, the comparable figure was 72 percent, although only one-sixth of those selected the "very favorable" option. The violent government crackdown in June 1989 against the Tiananmen Square protesters, some scenes of which were covered by U.S. television, resulted in a precipitous decline in public appraisals of China—the 72 percent favorable ratings of February 1989 fell by more than half to only 34 percent, while a majority (54 percent) reported holding an unfavorable view. Since that time, only one Gallup survey, taken in November 1993, found that those with a favorable appraisal of China outnumbered those with a negative assessment. The most recent surveys have revealed, however, that the margin between those expressing favorable and unfavorable opinions of the Beijing regime is narrowing. By February 2003, the latter held a barely distinguishable edge of 46 percent to 45 percent.

Public assessments of China, in short, have been marked first by a sharp increase in positive views through the 1980s, followed by considerable ambivalence during and since the 1990s. Even among those with a favorable appraisal of that country, a great majority prefer the "mostly favorable" to the "very favorable" response option; in the Gallup surveys reported in figure 3.3, only three times did the former option even reach double digits, and it did so only once after the Tiananmen Square episode. In the absence of a core of strongly held positive views of China and its post-Mao reforms, even less dramatic actions than the Tiananmen Square crackdown against those calling for greater democracy, toleration, and adherence to the rule of law have cast doubts among many Americans about the Beijing regime.

Of the other questions that polling organizations have asked about China, the most interesting are those focusing on questions of human rights and trade. Specifically, should the expansion of trade between the two countries be made contingent on China meeting certain standards of human rights? This question of "link-age" was at the core of debates on the appropriate trade status for China during the Reagan, Bush, and Clinton administrations. Al-though Bill Clinton argued for linkage while criticizing incumbent George H. W. Bush's China policy during the 1992 presidential campaign, Clinton ultimately joined those advocating permanent normalization of China's trade status and eliminating the annual review of human rights in that country. Proponents of that posi-tion, including Henry Kissinger and other notable realists, were vocal supporters of the thesis that relations with China were too important to be held hostage to American preferences about Bei-jing's domestic institutions and practices; in any case, these ob-servers argued, there was in reality no trade-off to be faced be-cause expanding trade relations is the best vehicle for promoting political reform.

Trade is one of the few issues on which cleavages cut across rather than along party lines, a point that will be developed more fully in chapter 5. Nowhere has this been clearer than on trade with China. Within the Republican Party, its strong business consti-tuents ("Wall Street Republicans") have staunchly supported expanding commercial relations, citing opportunities for selling goods and services to an ambitious modernizing country with a market of 1.2 billion people. In contrast, the "Main Street Repub-licans," including its strong religious right constituency, have ques-tioned the wisdom and morality of trading with a country that can-not be trusted to honor the human rights of its own citizens; in this view, trade is a snare and delusion because it will in fact strengthen an adversary rather than opening it up to liberalizing influences. The Democratic Party is no more united on the issue. Many Dem-ocrats accept the thesis that greater contacts with the West, includ-ing trade, will work in the long run to erode authoritarian controls over China's economy and political life. In contrast, the strong labor, human rights, and environmental Democratic constituencies point to low wages, alleged use of slave labor in some industries, in-tolerance of political dissidence, and poor environmental practices as powerful reasons to link trade to domestic reform in China.

The Gallup and NBC/*Wall Street Journal* surveys posed two questions about the trade/human rights linkage several times during the 1990s. The results, presented in table 3.2, indicate that the public is somewhat more inclined to accept the prolinkage view, though not by overwhelming majorities. Moreover, the mar-gin in favor of taking China's human rights record into account eroded considerably during the decade. The figures in table 3.2 also indicate that the wording of the question is important. Version A (NBC/*Wall Street Journal*), which mentions human rights in China but not U.S. economic interests, yielded majorities in favor of taking the state of human rights into consideration. The Gallup wording of the question (Version B) specifically mentions the possibility that a policy of linkage could "hurt U.S. economic interests." The result was a much more even division of opinion with only the barest of pluralities supporting linkage in the 1998 and 1999 surveys. Thus, although recent presidents of both parties have been strong proponents of lifting restrictions on expanding trade with China, divisions within the public more closely reflect those in Congress and among important interest groups.

Goals for American Foreign Policy

Although much of the data cited to this point suggests significant changes in public opinion relating to the USSR and Russia, especially during and after the Gorbachev era, some significant

TABLE 3.2.   China: Human Rights and Trade, 1993–99 (in percentages)

	December 1993	March 1994	May 1994	June 1994
A. *Which of the following comes closer to your point of view?*				
We should maintain good relations with China despite disagreements we might have with its human rights policies.	29	31	40	42
We should demand that China improve its human rights policies if China wants to continue to enjoy its current trade status with the U.S.	65	61	51	50
Neither/not sure	6	8	9	9

	October 1997	June 1998	May 1999	
B. *Which of the following comes closer to your view?*				
The United States should link human rights issues in China with U.S.–China trade policy, even if doing so hurts U.S. economic interests.	55	47	46	
The United States should not link human rights issues in China with U.S.–China trade policy because doing so might hurt U.S. economic interests.	36	45	45	
No opinion	9	8	9	

Source: Item A: NBC/*Wall Street Journal* surveys; Item B: Gallup Organization.

continuities also exist. Since 1974 the eight CCFR surveys have included a cluster of items asking respondents to rate the importance of various foreign policy goals. A few of the same items appeared in a 2001 Gallup survey. In the wake of the attacks on the destroyer *Cole,* the U.S. embassy in Kenya, and New York and Washington, it is scarcely surprising that "combating international terrorism" ranked at or near the most important foreign policy goals for the public in the two most recent CCFR studies. Other results of the 2002 CCFR survey, conducted ten months after the terrorist attacks, will be presented and discussed in more detail in chapter 6.

The data summarized in table 3.3a reveal that during the 1990s the general public gave very high priority to defending the country's economic interests. This does not, however, constitute a post–Cold War change of priorities. Protecting the jobs of American workers has ranked as the top goal in all but three of the surveys, and it just barely missed doing so in 1974 as well; in 1998 it ranked second to stopping the flow of illegal drugs into the United States, as it had done four years earlier. The question was omitted from the Gallup survey, but even in the absence of hard evidence there is every reason to believe that job protection increased rather than declined in importance, especially in light of the recession that began in 2001. Energy security also has consistently been accorded a "very important" rating by more than 60 percent of the public. Two surveys during the 1990s also saw an increase in the number of respondents who rated "protecting the interests of American business abroad" as a top priority.

In contrast to the urgency accorded to protecting economic interests—and despite occasional charges that the American public has been obsessed with Cold War concerns—such goals as "containing communism" and "matching Soviet military power" have ranked at the top of the foreign policy agenda in none of the surveys, not even in those conducted prior to disintegration of the USSR. Indeed, the public has consistently been at least as concerned about arms control and preventing nuclear proliferation. A more general military/security goal, "maintaining superior military power world wide," ranked tenth among the sixteen goals rated by those taking part in the 1994 CCFR survey. Despite persistent Republican charges that the Clinton administration had permitted a dangerous erosion of military capabilities, this goal moved up only three places four years later. Even after the September 11 terrorist attacks, it ranked only seventh in the 2002 CCFR survey.

TABLE 3.3a. **The Importance of American Foreign Policy Goals: Assessments by the General Public in the CCFR Surveys, 1974–2002 (percentage of "very important" ratings)**

"For each [foreign policy goal], please say whether you think that it should be a very important foreign policy goal of the United States, a somewhat important foreign policy goal, or not an important goal at all."

	1974	1978	1982	1986	1990	1994	1998	2002
World-order security issues								
Preventing the spread of nuclear weapons	—	—	—	—	84	82	82	90
Combating international terrorism	—	—	—	—	—	—	79	91
Strengthening the United Nations	46	47	48	46	52	51	45	57
Protecting weaker nations against aggression	28	34	34	32	32	24	32	41
Worldwide arms control	64	64	64	69	68	—	—	—
Strengthening international law and institutions	—	—	—	—	—	—	—	43
World-order economic and environmental issues								
Combating world hunger	61	59	58	63	—	56	62	61
Improving the global environment	—	—	—	—	73	58	53	66
Helping to improve the standard of living in less developed countries	39	35	35	37	33	22	29	30
Safeguarding against global financial instability	—	—	—	—	—	—	—	54
U.S. economic interest issues								
Stopping the flow of illegal drugs into the U.S.	—	—	—	—	—	89	81	81
Protecting the jobs of American workers	74	78	77	78	84	83	80	85
Securing adequate supplies of energy	75	78	70	69	76	62	64	75
Controlling and reducing illegal immigration	—	—	—	—	—	72	55	70
Reducing the U.S. trade deficit with foreign countries	—	—	—	62	70	59	50	51
Protecting the interests of American business abroad	39	45	44	43	46	52	—	49
U.S. values and institutions issues								
Promoting and defending human rights in other countries	—	39	43	42	40	34	39	41
Promoting market economics abroad	—	—	—	—	—	—	34	36
Helping to bring a democratic form of government to other nations	28	26	29	30	28	25	29	34

TABLE 3.3a.—Continued

	1974	1978	1982	1986	1990	1994	1998	2002
Cold War/security issues								
Maintaining superior military								
power worldwide	—	—	—	—	—	50	59	68
Defending our allies' security	33	50	50	56	43	41	44	57
Containing communism	54	60	59	57	42	—	—	—
Matching Soviet military power	—	—	49	53	40	—	—	—

Source: Rielly 1975. See also Rielly 1979, 1983, 1987, 1991, 1995, 1999; and Bouton and Page 2002.

Another Cold War concern, "defending our allies' security," appeared among the top three goals only after the Cold War had ended. This concern's high ranking in 1990 reflected events surrounding the Iraqi invasion of Kuwait and perhaps the fact that the United States and Soviet Union were on the same side rather than adversaries in that conflict, thereby eliminating the risk of a major confrontation between them. In 1994 and 1998, the goal of protecting allies received its lowest ratings since 1978, but the 2002 survey revealed a heightened sense of urgency for the security of allies as well over half of the respondents gave it a "very important" rating. A more general security concern, "protecting weaker nations against aggression," received a high rating only in 1990, when Iraqi forces still occupied Kuwait. The prospect of an open-ended commitment to protect unspecified countries clearly gained less support than did fulfilling obligations to allies.

It is harder to measure long-term trends on some issues because there are no Cold War baselines against which to compare responses to the most recent CCFR surveys. Stopping the flow of illegal drugs ranked among the top three foreign policy goals in the 1990s and it remained a high priority in 2002. Concern about illegal immigration declined from its position as the fourth-highest goal in 1994. Nevertheless, 55 percent of the public still rated stopping illegal immigration as "very important" four years later, and the recession and terrorist attacks perpetrated primarily by Saudis heightened concern for that goal.

Finally, the public has rarely expressed much enthusiasm for promoting American values and institutions abroad. Although the first Bush administration and the Clinton administration placed the expansion of democracy high on their foreign policy agendas, at least rhetorically, the public seems unpersuaded. With a single exception, efforts to promote human rights or democratic forms of government abroad have ranked among the least important foreign policy goals. "Promoting and defending human rights in other countries" as a foreign policy goal never received a "very important" rating from even half of either group, not even in 1990, when there were reports of widespread human rights violations by Iraqi invasion forces in Kuwait. Even though many communist and other authoritarian regimes collapsed in the late 1980s and early 1990s, few respondents expressed much interest in "helping to bring a democratic form of government to other nations." Indeed, that goal consistently ranked among the lowest throughout the almost three decades covered by the eight surveys. The difficulties of achieving success, especially in countries lacking any tradition of democratic institutions, probably contributed to these ratings. There is also compelling evidence that a "pretty prudent public" may support interventions abroad to cope with aggression but is much less enthusiastic about efforts to reform governments. (Jentleson 1992; Jentleson and Britton 1998; Nincic 1997). Perhaps abuse of the term *democracy* by American officials when referring to friendly tyrants—for example, when President Reagan compared the Nicaraguan contras to the American founding fathers or when other presidents toasted the Shah of Iran or Ferdinand Marcos of the Philippines in glowing terms as "friends of democracy"—has also made the public somewhat cynical about America's ability to export democracy.

The Gallup Organization also used a small cluster of items on foreign policy goals in surveys conducted in 2001 and 2003. Because the wording of several items varied somewhat from those in the eight Chicago Council surveys—for example, "building democracies in other countries" [Gallup] versus "helping to bring a democratic form of government to other nations" [CCFR]—the responses are presented separately in table 3.3b, from which two general conclusions emerge. Despite wording differences, the results of the Gallup and CCFR studies are quite similar and they reveal more continuity than change. Moreover, although the Gallup results yielded some variations in the importance attached to the goals, the rank orderings of the eight goals that appeared in both surveys are identical.

Conclusion

It would clearly be overstating the results summarized here to conclude that the public was generally correct in its opinions about the Soviet Union and Russia, if only because with respect to such critical questions as Stalin's intentions—or, indeed, those of his successors—it is often impossible to identify the "correct" answer. That observation is no less valid for China. Nevertheless, it is possible to draw some tentative conclusions that would appear to shed light on the three theories identified earlier.

Despite considerable volatility in responses to those questions, the first major conclusion is that aggregate opinions tend to reflect events and trends in the real world. When shifts take place, they appear to be neither random nor systematically out of touch with international realities, as suggested by Almond (1950) and Lippmann (1955) at the height of the Cold War. Second, the findings do not appear to offer a great deal of support for the thesis that the public has been wedded to a reflexive and unyielding hostility toward the USSR or China. Nor did such Cold War goals as containment or matching Soviet military power dominate assessment of U.S. foreign policy goals. To the contrary, substantial numbers of Americans appear to have yearned for good relations between the superpowers and, when given reasonable pretexts for doing so, Americans expressed opinions to that effect. This is not evident only in data from the World War II period, when the common war effort against Nazi Germany provided a clear mutuality of interests; it is also apparent in evidence from the détente of the

TABLE 3.3b. The Importance of American Foreign Policy Goals: Assessments by the General Public in Gallup Surveys, 2001 and 2003 (percentage of "very important" ratings)

"I'm going to read a list of possible foreign policy goals that the United States might have. For each one please say whether you think it should be a very important foreign policy goal of the United States, a somewhat important goal, not too important a goal, or not an important goal at all."

	Feb. 1–4, 2001	Feb. 3–6, 2003
Preventing future acts of international terrorism	—	87
Preventing the spread of nuclear weapons/weapons of mass destruction	82	82
Securing adequate supplies of energy	79	68
Defending our allies' security	62	60
Maintaining superior military power worldwide	59	56
Promoting and defending human rights in other countries	51	50
Protecting weaker nations against foreign aggression	39	40
Helping to improve the standard of living of less-developed nations	40	35
Building democracy in other countries	32	29

Source: Gallup Poll Social Series: World Affairs (2003), 9, 10.

early 1970s as well as the "détente II" that began in the mid-1980s. Evaluations of China also seem to reflect developments in that country and in relations between Beijing and Washington. Most dramatically, the violent crackdown against prodemocracy demonstrators in Tiananmen Square arrested and reversed a long period of increasingly favorable assessments of China. In short, the survey data summarized here would seem to offer greater support for theories that depict the public as rational and events-driven than for the competing theses.

Finally, the evidence that the public reacted to what the Soviets did rather than who they were during the Cold War suggests how the masses are likely to assess Russia as the post–Cold War era is well into its second decade. Evidence of genuine success in movements toward democratization and economic liberalization, agreements on control of nuclear weapons and arms sales, and cooperation in antiterrorism policies should reverse a trend that saw the consistently favorable assessments of the early 1990s decline fairly steadily through 2000. By 2003, positive appraisals of Russia were near an all-time high just before the final acts of the Iraq issue were played out. At that point, open differences between the George W. Bush and Putin administrations were reflected in public appraisals of Russia. Although relatively few Americans have much knowledge of politics, personalities, and parties within the republics of the former USSR, wariness borne in part of an appreciation of the difficulties of creating democratic institutions in these countries is likely to persist. Moreover, support for any major U.S. aid program is likely to remain lukewarm, but that is part of a general skepticism about foreign aid—the public would also reduce assistance to such allies as Israel and Egypt—rather than an expression of displeasure targeted specifically against Moscow (Rielly 1999, 21).

Conversely, any campaign by Moscow to reconstitute the Russian empire by force, especially should such efforts be directed against the newly independent countries on Russia's western frontier—most notably Latvia, Lithuania, Estonia, Moldova, Belarus, and Ukraine—would almost surely accelerate negative appraisals of Russia and revive fears of its foreign policy goals. Similarly, a Chinese invasion of Taiwan would almost certainly create a major crisis in Sino-American relations. Although public support for using the American military to protect Taiwan is quite limited (see table 4.4), an invasion of that island would no doubt resolve the current public ambivalence about China and could well result in unfavorable assessments similar to those of the 1970s or earlier. Repeated Russian uses of force against internal groups, most notably in a brutal civil war in Chechnya during 1995–96 and again since 1999, has elicited considerable criticism from many American opinion leaders, most of whom rejected the thesis put forward by former President Yeltsin and President Putin that the rebels are merely terrorists (Sestanovich 2001). The attacks on the World Trade Center and Washington in 2001 clearly put concerns with the plight of Chechins on the back burner of American attention. The events of September 11 also muted Washington officials' criticism of human rights violations in Russia and elsewhere in the former Soviet Union. Priority has been given to the fact that Russia, Tajikistan, and Uzbekistan pledged to cooperate in the American war effort against the Taliban regime in Afghanistan and even provided some basing rights for U.S. forces. Similarly, Washington has agreed with Beijing's assertion that dissidents in western China are in fact terrorists. As long as Russia and China are perceived as cooperating in the war on terrorists, that belief is likely to dominate American assessments of those countries.

It should, of course, be borne in mind that Russian foreign policies do not exist in a vacuum; like those of all countries, they are at least in part reactions to those of others. To the extent that American actions are wholly indifferent to Russian vital interests—in keeping with the realist dictum that the strong (the United States) do what they have the power to do, and the weak (Russia) accept what they have to accept—leaders in Moscow and the Russian public are not forever likely to see much benefit in close cooperation with the United States. Some of the same voices that have warned of China as a probable future threat to U.S. interests have also been most dismissive of any Russian assertions of its vital interests. Many of the strongest Bush administration cheerleaders in the media, including Charles Krauthammer, William Safire, and the *Wall Street Journal,* have consistently urged the United States to regard Russian expressions of its interests as nothing more than the whining of Cold War losers. This and related issues will be revisited in chapter 6.

CHAPTER 4

Opinion Leaders

Until the post-Vietnam era, one of the glaring gaps in public opinion research was the neglect of opinion leaders. Indeed, most analysts have assumed that opinion leaders serve as a critical link between policymakers and the general public—that is, the public receives its cues about politics through opinion leaders (see, for example, E. Katz and Lazarsfeld 1955; E. Katz 1957; Neuman 1986; Powlick and Katz 1998). Although this premise has recently been challenged on the grounds that the public can and does get its information directly from the media, only in a pure bottom-up model of direct democracy would the distinction between the general public and opinion leaders appear to be superfluous. All other approaches to government—from theories that view the United States as a pluralist democracy to those that depict it as a pseudodemocracy ruled by self-perpetuating elites who seek to use foreign policy as an instrument of narrow class-based interests—recognize the disproportionate influence of some citizens (Devine 1970). Moreover, at least since Almond's seminal study, *The American People and Foreign Policy* (1950), it has been customary to distinguish between various strata of the public. With a few exceptions, the polity has been depicted as a pyramid, with decision makers at the apex. Typically, a further distinction has been drawn between a small coterie of opinion leaders, a somewhat larger group comprising the informed public, and a large base of the general or uninformed public, although the precise terms and shape of the distribution among strata may vary from study to study (compare Kriesberg 1949; Almond 1950; Rosenau 1961; Genco 1984; Neuman 1986). Despite a general consensus on a stratified conception of the American polity, with a few exceptions (Rosenau 1963), until the late 1970s there was a paucity of systematic evidence about the political beliefs of opinion leaders. On occasion, the Gallup Organization has surveyed samples of biographees in *Who's Who in America*—for example, in a 1941 poll on whether the United States should join a general international organization after the war or in a 1953 survey on tariffs—but these have typically been one-shot studies that are of limited value, especially for purposes of assessing trends.

Three reasons may explain the puzzling neglect of opinion leaders in survey research. The realist perspective on international affairs that dominated most of the period since World War II primarily emphasizes the imperative arising from the international system and the manner with which decision makers cope with these systemic threats and opportunities. Other domestic political actors, including opinion leaders, rarely enter into the analysis except perhaps as residual categories to explain the nation's deviations from rational choices in international affairs. From this perspective, sufficient reasons rarely exist to survey elites with a view to uncovering how they might differ from the general public.

The prior question of identifying "opinion leaders" is also among the possible barriers to this type of research. There is, of course, an extensive debate on the precise definition of who U.S. leaders are; if a consensus on that question were a prerequisite for elite surveys, they would never be undertaken. Those designing leadership studies have typically bypassed the broader question and selected subjects in one of two ways: (1) by identifying key roles and then surveying a sample of the persons filling them, or (2) by identifying groups thought to be logical sources of opinion leaders and then drawing samples from directories of such persons. The first method might survey a sample of persons holding key offices in business, government, media, or other organizations. The latter approach might draw samples from *Who's Who in America, Who's Who in American Politics,* and similar directories; subscribers to the journals *International Security* or *Foreign Affairs;* or students at the National War College. Some studies have combined these sampling designs.

Still another area of disagreement that might have constrained leadership surveys centers on the ability to use a selected stratum of the data from national probability samples for studying elites; if one can do so validly, there is little reason to incur the very substantial costs of separate surveys. To oversimplify somewhat, the contending views can be reduced to two positions on the adequacy of respondents' education levels as a surrogate measure of leadership status. Considerable evidence certainly exists that international attitudes are strongly related to levels of education. The affirmative view on this issue was presented in a prognosis of how public opinion research is likely to develop during the next half century.

> The mathematics and economics of surveys make them most cost-effective for assessing large, undifferentiated populations, i.e., mass publics. And until you get to a handful of individuals at the very top, you don't learn much from studying "elites" — they seem to be just like better educated people in the general population. These two generalizations suggest no major shift in our attention. The same is true in totalitarian countries (and, I suspect, poor countries). (Davis 1987, S178–79)

Although the question is far from settled, at this point the proponents of the opposite viewpoint would appear to have at least an equally plausible case. A number of studies have found that, by itself, the level of educational attainment is an inadequate yardstick for identifying opinion leaders (Neuman 1986). Extensive analyses of the 1968, 1980, and 1984 National Election Studies and the first three Chicago Council on Foreign Relations (CCFR) surveys by Jon Krosnick and Catherine Carnot (1988) indicate that education is an insufficient indicator of the attentive foreign policy public, much less of foreign policy opinion leadership. Their findings reveal little support for the hypothesis that the "foreign-policy-attentive public" is composed simply of highly educated persons who are concerned with all aspects of public policy. An earlier study also cast doubt on the sufficiency of education as a measure of leadership (Rogers, Stuhler, and Koenig 1967).

Despite these possible impediments to survey research on leaders, the past several decades have seen a substantial number of projects directed specifically at the foreign policy beliefs of this group. As I noted in chapter 3, the Vietnam War was a catalyst in provoking challenges to the Almond-Lippmann consensus about public opinion. In the same way, it is not purely coincidental that systematic surveys on the views of opinion leaders followed on the heels of the controversial conflict in Southeast Asia. There was a widespread sense that the Vietnam War was a major watershed in American foreign policy because the bitter debates on that conflict had fractured, if not permanently shattered, the post–World War II consensus among both leaders and the general public on the fundamental axioms underlying U.S. policy for a quarter century.

Indeed, the two most extensive elite surveys originated in the mid-1970s as a direct consequence of the post-Vietnam debates on the proper future course of American foreign relations. As a result of these concerns, Secretary of State Henry Kissinger is reported to have asked the CCFR to undertake the first of its surveys, including samples of both the general public and leaders, in 1974. The CCFR subsequently has conducted similar surveys at four-year intervals (Rielly 1975, 1979, 1983, 1987, 1991, 1995, 1999; Bouton and Page 2002). The Foreign Policy Leadership Project (FPLP), which focuses on opinion leaders, was initiated in 1976 to explore in depth the ways in which leaders interpreted the Vietnam experience, including diagnoses of the causes of American failure in that costly undertaking, prescriptions about lessons that should be learned from the conflict, and predictions about the domestic and international consequences of the war. FPLP surveys were also undertaken at four-year intervals (Holsti and Rosenau 1984, 1990, 1993, 1998; Holsti 2001).

In addition to the CCFR and FPLP surveys, a number of one-time studies of American elites have occurred. Some of them have included leaders in a broad spectrum of occupations. Others have focused on more specific groups, including business and military leaders and general officers.[1] Several features of the samples in these studies are summarized in table 4.1.[2]

The General Public and Leaders:
The Content of Foreign Policy Beliefs

Interest in opinion leaders arises from the hypothesis that in at least some respects they may differ systematically from the general public. If they do not, then there is indeed no reason to go to the very considerable effort and expense that is required to undertake surveys on their foreign policy views. The remainder of this chapter will explore this question by comparing the general public and opinion leaders with respect first to the content of their foreign policy beliefs and subsequently to the ways in which those beliefs are organized or structured. The analyses that follow will compare the content of foreign policy beliefs among leaders and the general public at the aggregate level. This approach does not assume, however, that either leaders or the public constitute a homogeneous group. Chapter 5 will undertake analyses that disaggregate data for both groups with a view to identifying some of the background correlates of views on foreign policy.

U.S. Role in the World

Data presented earlier revealed that for six decades—more specifically, since less than one year after the attack on Pearl Harbor that brought the United States into World War II—a majority of the general public has favored an "active role" for the United States in world affairs; not a single survey during that period has shown a ratio of less than three to two in favor of internationalism (see figure 3.1). By the late 1980s, a period marked by dramatically improving relations between Washington and Moscow, that margin had increased to more than two to one. The end of the Cold War did not bring about a dramatic reorientation of public attitudes in this respect. A 1991 National Opinion Research Center survey revealed that almost three-fourths of the public favored an active American role in the world. Two years later, when it had become clear that the disintegration of the Soviet Union did not necessarily mean an end to troubling conflicts abroad, support for an internationalist American role remained quite high: 67 percent favored that position, compared to only 28 percent who preferred to "stay out of world affairs." Even continuing controversies over the appropriate American role in peacekeeping operations, such as those in Somalia, Haiti, and Bosnia, had little impact on the strong majority (61 to 28 percent) favoring "an active part in world affairs" during the turbulent weeks leading up to the 1998 congressional elections (Rielly 1999, 4).[3] The terrorist attacks of 2001 gave rise to sharply increased public interest in foreign affairs, and by June 2002, support for an active U.S. international role increased to 71 percent, the highest figure since the period surrounding the Gulf War in 1991.

Although comparable evidence about leaders' preferences is less extensive and is heavily concentrated in the post-Vietnam era, most of it indicates that elites outstrip the general public in supporting active involvement in international affairs. The CCFR surveys, conducted every four years since 1974, have posed the question directly to the general public and to a smaller sample of elites starting in 1978. Because the surveys of the two groups were conducted at the same time by the same polling organization and using identically worded questions, the results provide

TABLE 4.1. A Description of Samples in Some Surveys of Leaders on Foreign Policy and Defense Issues, 1974–2002

Survey Name	Year	Sample Size	Sample designed to include these groups									
			POL	MIL	BUS	MED	FPX	STD	LAB	CLE	ED	WOM
CCFR	1974	328	+	0	+	+	+	+	+	+	+	0
CCFR	1978	366	+	0	+	+	+	+	+	+	+	0
CCFR	1982	341	+	0	+	+	+	+	+	+	+	0
CCFR	1986	343	+	0	+	+	+	+	+	+	+	0
CCFR	1990	377	+	0	+	+	+	+	+	+	+	0
CCFR	1994	383	+	0	+	+	+	+	+	+	+	0
CCFR	1998	379	+	0	+	+	+	+	+	+	+	0
CCFR	2002	397	+	0	+	+	+	+	+	+	+	0
FPLP	1976	2,282	+	+	+	+	+	+	+	+	+	+
FPLP	1980	2,502	+	+	+	+	+	+	+	+	+	+
FPLP	1984	2,515	+	+	+	+	+	+	+	+	+	+
FPLP	1988	2,226	+	+	+	+	+	+	+	+	+	+
FPLP	1992	2,312	+	+	+	+	+	+	+	+	+	+
FPLP	1996	2,141	+	+	+	+	+	+	+	+	+	+

			POL	MIL	BUS	MED	FPX	STD	LAB	CLE	ED	WOM
Barton	1971/72	593	+	+	+	0	+	0	0	0	0	0
Russett & Hanson	1973	1,188	0	+	+	+	0	+	0	0	0	0
Kinnard	1974	173	0	+	0	0	0	0	0	0	0	0
Sussman	1976	2,469*	+	+	+	0	+	0	0	0	+	+
Chittick et al.	1984/85	506**	+	0	0	0	0	+	+	0	0	0
Koopman et al.	1986	604	0	+	+	+	0	0	0	0	+	0
Times Mirror	1993	649	+	+	+	+	+	+	+	+	+	0
Pew	1997	591	+	+	+	+	+	+	+	+	+	0
TISS	1998/99	2,132	+	+	+	+	+	+	+	+	+	+

Key: POL (political leaders), MIL (military), BUS (business), MED (media), FPX (foreign policy experts), STD (State Department/Foreign Service), LAB (labor), CLE (clergy), ED (education), WOM (women)

CCFR (Chicago Council on Foreign Relations), FPLP (Foreign Policy Leadership Project), TISS (Triangle Institute for Security Studies)

+ = Group targeted in sampling design

0 = Group not targeted in sampling design (but persons in these groups may appear in the sample by virtue of other affiliations). For example, women are included in the CCFR and several other surveys because of their membership in one or more occupational groups)

* Also included farm leaders, black leaders, youth at elite universities

** "Foreign policy elites": government officials and those in nongovernmental organizations

an excellent basis for comparing leaders and the general public with respect to preferred roles for the United States.

The results of these CCFR surveys reveal strong and consistent differences between leaders and the general public. During the twenty-eight years covered by the eight CCFR surveys, the general public preferred an active American international role rather than withdrawal from world affairs by margins ranging from a high of 71 to 25 percent (2002) to a low of 53 to 35 percent (1982). The latter figures constitute the smallest margin in favor of internationalism in any of the more than fifty surveys since 1942 in which some variant of that question has been posed.

In contrast, leaders taking part in the 1978–2002 CCFR studies have been virtually unanimous in judging that it is better for the United States to "take an active part in world affairs"; that option never failed to gain the support of fewer than 96 percent of respondents. Indeed, it is hard to find any other significant question about foreign policy that has yielded such one-sided results. However, because it reduces international involvement to only two broad options, this question is too general to provide much insight into how the two groups appraise U.S. policies on specific issues and undertakings abroad. Nor does it reveal how they might react when confronted with trade-offs or with the costs of active involvement in world affairs, especially when the price is paid in the coin of American casualties. Moreover, even those favoring an "active role" can differ on crucial questions of implementation. Unilateralists prefer that the United States go it alone, unbridled by the need to consult, coordinate, and cooperate with other countries. In contrast, multilateralists favor acting and sharing the burdens with others, even if doing so requires some compromises. Thus, we need to turn to appraisals of specific international threats and then to preferences of both the general public and opinion leaders on more specific issues such as globalization, trade and protectionism, foreign aid, deployment of troops abroad, and foreign policy goals.

Threats to Vital U.S. Interests

Although the disintegration of the USSR at the end of 1991 brought the Cold War to an end, most Americans continue to perceive a world that poses a plethora of threats to vital U.S. interests. The CCFR studies asked both the general public and leaders to assess such threats. The 1998 and 2002 surveys pre-

sented respondents with much broader menus than had been the
case in 1990 and 1994 (table 4.2).

Compared to leaders, the public has been consistently more
apprehensive about external threats; that was the case with all
thirteen items presented in 1998 and all but two of them in the
survey four years later. Solid majorities in both groups rated terrorism, chemical and biological weapons, nuclear proliferation,
the Arab-Israeli conflict, weapons of mass destruction in Iraq, Islamic fundamentalism, and the conflict between India and Pakistan as "critical" threats. Increasing apprehension about China
was especially evident among leaders in 1998, fewer than one in
six of whom had expressed such concerns as recently as eight
years earlier, but those fears fell somewhat by 2002.

In contrast to the areas of agreement between the general
public and leaders, several of which are linked, directly or indirectly, to the 9/11 attacks, wide gaps exist on appraisals of other
threats. Economic issues stand out in this respect even though
they do not rival in perceived severity such threats as terrorism,
proliferation of weapons of mass destruction, or regional conflicts that might involve countries with nuclear arsenals. Although
concern for economic competition from abroad abated somewhat in 2002 among both the public and leaders, without exception the former expressed a greater degree of concern about
threats arising from globalization, immigrants and refugees, and
financial crises abroad. Although perceived economic threats
stemming from competitors abroad have declined substantially
among leaders, especially compared to the views that they held in
1990, members of the general public are less persuaded on that
score. In 2002, the gaps between the two groups were quite large
with respect to competition from Japan (24 percent) and low-wage
countries (also 24 percent) and somewhat smaller in the case of
Europe (4 percent). In a similar vein, public concern for such social and environmental issues as global warming, AIDS and other
epidemics, and world population growth far outdistanced that of
opinion leaders. Even among the threats judged to be less critical,
including civil wars in Africa and Russian military power, the gaps
between leaders and the general public are quite wide.

Public expressions of strong concerns about terrorism, origi-
nating both at home and abroad, began long before the September 11, 2001, attacks (the impact of which will be discussed more
fully in chapter 6) (Kuzma 2000). Indeed, compared to leaders,
the members of the general public expressed a greater degree of

TABLE 4.2. Threats to Vital U.S. Interests: Assessments by the General Public and Leaders in the CCFR Surveys, 1990–2002 (percent "critical" ratings)

	1990 Public	1990 Leaders	1994 Public	1994 Leaders	1998 Public	1998 Leaders	2002 Public	2002 Leaders
International terrorism	—	—	69	33	84	61	91	83
Chemical and biological weapons	—	—	—	—	76	64	86	67
Iraq developing weapons of mass destruction	—	—	—	—	—	—	86	72
The possibility of unfriendly countries becoming nuclear powers	—	—	72	61	75	67	85	72
AIDS, ebola virus, and other potential epidemics	—	—	—	—	72	34	68	48
Military conflict between Israel and its Arab neighbors	—	—	—	—	—	—	67	73
Islamic fundamentalism	—	—	33	39	38	31	61	61
Large number of immigrants and refugees coming into the U.S.	—	—	72	31	55	18	60	14
The development of China as a world power	40	16	57	46	57	56	56	47
Tensions between India and Pakistan	—	—	—	—	—	—	54	61
Global warming	—	—	—	—	43	27	46	28
World population growth	—	—	—	—	—	—	44	25
Economic competition from low-wage countries	—	—	—	—	40	16	31	7
Globalization	—	—	—	—	—	—	29	22
Economic competition from Japan	60	63	62	21	45	14	29	5
Political turmoil in Russia	—	—	—	—	—	—	27	26
Financial crises in other countries	—	—	—	—	—	—	25	14
Military power of Russia[a]	33	20	32	16	34	19	23	7
Economic competition from Europe	30	41	27	11	24	16	13	9
Regional ethnic conflict	—	—	—	—	34	26	—	—

Source: Rielly 1991; see also Rielly 1995, 1999; CCFR survey, June 2002; and Bouton and Page 2002.

[a]Soviet Union in 1990

concern about international terrorism as a threat to vital American interests in each of the three most recent CCFR studies. A 1997 Pew survey also revealed that leaders in all occupational groups as well as the general public rated the danger for "foreign-sponsored terrorists" as far greater than either the danger posed by foreign military power or the danger posed by domestic terrorists (Pew 1997, 66, 95).

Trade and Protectionism

The Vietnam era coincided with a period of relative economic decline for the United States. The most visible symptoms included worsening trade balances and eroding confidence in the dollar. The "Nixon economic shock" of August 1971, effectively ending the Bretton Woods monetary regime established at the end of World War II, symbolized the declining U.S. international economic position. During the preceding quarter century, polling organizations only infrequently posed questions about trade and protectionism. Several points emerge from a half dozen Gallup surveys taken between 1947 and 1962 that asked about trade issues. Only one-third to half of the respondents were familiar with such issues as the 1947 Geneva agreement to lower tariffs and the Reciprocal Trade Agreement. Among those who knew of these agreements, proponents of reducing tariffs outnumbered the protectionists by substantial margins. For example, of those who were familiar with President Kennedy's trade program, 58 percent supported lower tariffs, whereas only 9 percent wanted to raise them. The comparable figures among all respondents were 38 percent and 15 percent, respectively. The lone Gallup survey of opinion leaders, conducted in 1953, revealed that supporters of the Reciprocal Trade Agreement outnumbered opponents by a margin of 67 percent to 11 percent; moreover, at least three-fifths of the leaders in every occupational category favored that agreement (G. H. Gallup 1972, 505, 695, 1151, 1155, 1760). As trade and other international economic issues took on added significance, however, survey evidence about public and elite attitudes toward them mounted.

The final decade of the twentieth century witnessed important steps toward a globalized economy featuring lowered trade barriers, creation of such trade organizations as the North American Free Trade Agreement (NAFTA) (a controversial pact bringing Mexico, Canada, and the United States into a free-trade zone) and the World Trade Organization (WTO) vastly expanded international markets in currencies and securities and movement of production facilities from high production cost to low cost areas. With the disintegration of the Soviet Union, the United States emerged as the world's predominant military power. America's position as the leading economic power is equally evident, in part because countries that earlier seemed poised to challenge the U.S. position — notably Japan, Germany, and the Soviet Union — suffered serious economic setbacks during the 1990s, whereas the United States enjoyed an extended period of high employment, low inflation, and rising stock markets (at least until the recession that began in early 2001) and a steadily widening gap between the most and least affluent sectors of society.

When asked in the 1998 CCFR survey to assess globalization, "especially the increasing connection of our economy with others around the world," 54 percent of the public judged it to be "mostly good," whereas only 20 percent responded "mostly bad." Four years later, the comparable figures were 56 percent and 27 percent. Respondents with a favorable verdict on globalization also held internationalist views on other aspects of foreign affairs, including an active part for the United States in world affairs, participation in United Nations peacekeeping forces, repaying its back dues to that organization, foreign aid, and maintenance of the commitment to the North Atlantic Treaty Organization (NATO) (Rielly 1999, 22). Support for globalization has consistently been stronger among leaders who, by margins of 87 to 12 percent (1998) and 85 to 12 percent (2002), judged it favorably.

Broad support for globalization notwithstanding, there is also evidence of public disquiet. As a result of worries about such issues as the trade deficit and job losses, "concern about international economic matters as perceived foreign policy problems stands out in this survey over any previous study" (Rielly 1999, 19). The public has not shared leaders' view that threats arising from international economic competition have declined sharply and has consistently ranked "protecting the job of American workers" at or near the top of the foreign policy agenda (table 3.3a). The seven most recent CCFR surveys asked both the general public and leaders whether they "sympathize more with those who want to eliminate tariffs or those who think such tariffs are necessary" (table 4.3). The results reveal a wide gap between the two groups, with a steady majority of the general public supporting tariffs through the 1990 survey. Four years later, in the midst of energetic efforts by the White House and many congressional leaders in both political parties to gain approval of the treaty incorporating the Uruguay Round of the General Agreement on Tariffs and Trade and creation of the WTO, support for tariffs fell below 50 percent; however, proponents of such trade barriers still outnumbered those who would eliminate them by 48 percent to 32 percent, and the margin in favor of tariffs remained in double digits in 1998 (49 to 32 percent) and 2002 (50 to 38 percent). Efforts to identify the sources of support for protectionism have yielded mixed results. Contrary to the widespread belief that protectionism is confined largely to union members and blue-collar workers, the 1994 CCFR survey revealed that retention of tariffs actually received slightly higher than average approval from the college-educated and those with incomes above fifty thousand dollars per year (Rielly 1995, 29–30). However, a more recent study found that support for free trade rises steadily with increasing income. Fifty-three percent of respondents with incomes under twenty thousand dollars supported free trade, whereas 76 percent of those with incomes above fifty thousand dollars did so (Kohut 2001, 8).

In contrast, some increase had occurred in support for protectionism among leaders during the dozen years ending in 1990, but that position was espoused by no more than one-third of those taking part in any of the CCFR surveys. By 1994, only one leader in five wanted to retain tariffs, but that figure increased to 34 percent four years later. However, wording of the CCFR question may have affected the results because respondents were not offered such options as "maintain tariffs at current levels" or "reduce but do not eliminate tariffs." The most recent CCFR survey, conducted in 2002, also posed another question to gauge views on trade in somewhat greater depth. Respondents were asked whether their views on free trade were conditioned on government programs to assist those who lose their jobs. Interestingly, when given that response option, the yawning gap between leaders and the general public when the issue is framed more simply— as either support for or opposition to tariffs—virtually disappeared. About seven out of every ten respondents in both groups asserted, "I favor free trade and I believe that it is necessary for the government to have programs to help workers who lose their jobs." In contrast, fewer than 10 percent in either group expressed outright opposition to free trade. Before concluding that these results indicate an emerging consensus on trade and

TABLE 4.3. Opinions on Trade, Protectionism, and Trade Organizations: The General Public and Leaders, 1978–2002

	Date	Survey	Tariffs are necessary (%) General public	Leaders
"Generally, would you say you sympathize more with those who want to *eliminate* tariffs or those who think such tariffs are *necessary*?"	1978	CCFR	57	23
	1982	CCFR	57	28
	1986	CCFR	53	29
	1990	CCFR	54	33
	1994	CCFR	48	20
	1998	CCFR	49	34
	2002	CCFR	50	—

	Date	Survey	Each option (%)	
Which of the following three options comes closest to your point of view?	2002	CCFR		
I favor free trade and I believe that it is necessary for the government to have programs to help workers who lose their jobs			73	70
I favor free trade and I believe that it is not necessary for the government to have programs to help workers who lose their jobs			16	21
I do not favor free trade			9	8
Not sure/decline			2	1

	Date	Survey	Agree strongly or agree somewhat (%)	
Please indicate how strongly you agree or disagree with . . .				
"Erecting trade barriers against foreign goods to protect American industries and jobs"	1984	FPLP	—	24
	1988	FPLP	—	16
	1992	FPLP	—	21
	1996	FPLP	—	22
"Opening negotiations for a free-trade zone with Mexico"	1992	FPLP	—	84
"Creating a free-trade zone with Canada"	1992	FPLP	—	95

	Date	Survey	Favor NAFTA (%)	
Favor or oppose the North American Free Trade Agreement	1993	T-M	46	89
	1993	Gallup[a]	38	—
	1994	CCFR[b]	50	86
	1996	FPLP	—	80
	1997	Pew	47	—
Signing the GATT trade agreement and joining the World Trade Organization (WTO)	1996	FPLP	—	80

Note: CCFR: Chicago Council on Foreign Relations surveys; FPLP: Foreign Policy Leadership Project surveys; T-M: Times Mirror survey, "America's Place in the World."

[a]Average of "favor" NAFTA responses in four surveys conducted in August, September, early November, and mid-November. The average "oppose" and "no opinion" responses in these surveys were 43 percent and 19 percent, respectively.

[b]Respondents who rated NAFTA as "mostly good" for the U.S. economy.

globalization, however, it would be necessary to probe further the kinds of government programs that are deemed acceptable to cope with job losses.

Opposition to protectionism also emerges from a question posed four times between 1984 and 1996 to larger samples of leaders in the FPLP surveys. Even though the question was phrased in a manner that explicitly incorporates the most widely used argument for protectionism—"erecting trade barriers against foreign goods to protect American industries and jobs"— fewer than one leader in four expressed either strong or moderate agreement with such a policy in any of the four surveys, and by 1996, opponents of trade barriers outnumbered proponents by a margin of 77 to 22 percent.

Finally, assessments of NAFTA, which narrowly passed Congress in December 1993, and the WTO provide further evidence of attitudes on trade. Leaders taking part in surveys conducted by three organizations across a three-year period expressed overwhelming support for NAFTA. The WTO received comparable support in the 1996 FPLP study, but that survey was undertaken well before WTO meetings in Seattle and Washington, D.C., that provoked sometimes violent demonstrations. These protests against various facets of globalization at recent international trade and finance meetings also suggest that discontent with policies aimed at reducing, if not eliminating, various barriers to the flow of goods and services is not limited to union members and other traditional proponents of protectionism. In contrast, the public was much more evenly divided on NAFTA, with opponents slightly outnumbering supporters until 1994, when the CCFR poll found that NAFTA was judged as "mostly a good thing for the U.S. economy." But the latter survey was undertaken just before the financial crisis triggered by devaluation of the Mexican peso. Thus, the wide gap between the general public and leaders spans general attitudes toward tariffs as well as such specific undertakings as NAFTA.

Economic and Technical Aid

Strong majorities among the general public favored such early post–World War II foreign aid undertakings as the European Recovery Program (commonly known as the Marshall Plan); a November 1948 Gallup survey found that the public supported the plan by a margin of 65 to 13 percent. During the past two decades, however, international economic and technical assistance programs have fallen into public disfavor. They often rank as the most popular candidates for reduced budget allocations, although there is also evidence that this negative view of foreign aid is grounded in widespread misconceptions about the actual level of U.S. spending for assistance abroad. According to the results emerging from a survey conducted in 1995, "A strong majority says that the United States is spending too much on foreign aid. But this attitude is based on the assumption that the United States is spending vastly more than it is in fact. Asked what an 'appropriate' amount would be, the median level proposed is five times the present spending level" (Kull 1995c, 3; Kull and Destler 1999, 125).

The eight CCFR surveys conducted between 1974 and 2002 again provide directly comparable evidence about support for such programs among leaders and the general public. When asked, "On the whole, do you favor or oppose our giving economic aid to other nations for purposes of economic development and technical assistance?" the general public was generally quite evenly divided on the question, with support for such programs ranging between 45 percent (1990 and 1994) and 53 percent (1986). In 1998, supporters of foreign aid narrowly outnumbered opponents by 47 percent to 45 percent. A plurality of respondents favored keeping the same level of assistance to Africa, Russia, Poland, Israel, and Egypt but also preferred reducing rather than increasing aid to those countries. College graduates, liberals, travelers abroad, and those with higher incomes have been the strongest supporters of foreign aid (Rielly 1999). One consequence of the 9/11 attacks was that public support for foreign aid as an instrument against terrorists increased quite sharply (PIPA 2002b).

A comparison of public attitudes with those of opinion leaders reveals a dramatic gap, as leaders have consistently expressed strong approval of economic assistance. In none of the CCFR surveys through 1990 did fewer than 90 percent of the leaders express support for foreign aid when asked the same question as was asked of the general public. In 1998, the public-leader gap topped 40 percent—88 percent approval among leaders and 47 percent among the general public. Among leaders, business executives (24 percent) and members of Congress (19 percent) expressed the weakest support for foreign aid (Rielly 1995, 31).

A related question asked opinion leaders taking part in the six FPLP surveys whether they would support economic aid to poorer countries "even if it means higher prices at home." After an equal division between supporters and opponents on the question in 1976, moderate majorities of respondents in the subsequent five surveys have favored such assistance.

Military Assistance

Since the outbreak of the Korean War, a very substantial part of American foreign aid programs has consisted of various forms of military assistance. Of the $390 billion devoted to various U.S. foreign assistance programs during the Cold War years between 1946 and 1991, about $146 billion consisted of military aid (U.S. Department of Commerce 1994, 816). In comparison to the level of support for economic development and technical aid, neither leaders nor the general public have expressed as much enthusiasm for military assistance programs. The CCFR surveys asked leaders and the general public whether they supported or opposed foreign military aid, providing an opportunity to compare the sentiments of the two groups. Even though the question explicitly stated that "by military aid I mean arms and equipment but not troops," support among the general public for such assistance was never especially strong. After reaching a peak in 1986, when one-third of the respondents expressed approval, support fell to less than one-fourth of the public four years later. By 1998, military aid ranked as the favorite target of budgetary cutbacks, a position maintained in 2002.

In contrast, strong majorities of leaders supported military aid through 1986; the gap between the general public and leaders on this issue exceeded 30 percent in each of the CCFR surveys to that point. Between 1986 and 1990, support for these programs also fell sharply among leaders, no doubt reflecting such dramatic events as the demolition of the Berlin Wall and, more generally, the end of the Cold War. The illicit sale of arms to Iran, the receipts of which were used to fund the Nicaraguan contra rebels, may also have contributed to doubts about military assistance programs. By 1994 leaders and the general public were in complete agreement on military aid; those favoring a cutback outnumbered proponents of expanded military aid by 64 percent among both groups (Rielly 1995, 12). The comparable figures in 1998 revealed continued support for reducing military assistance, with net (decrease minus expand) scores of 47 percent and 48 percent, respectively (Rielly 1999, 9). In 2002 military aid maintained its position as the least favored government program, with net support for cutting back such assistance at 36 percent among the general public and at 32 percent among opinion leaders. The six FPLP surveys posed a related question, asking leaders to assess one of the arguments used by opponents of military aid programs—that they "will eventually draw the United States into unnecessary wars." That critique of military assistance has never gained the support of a majority among opinion leaders. Forty-two percent agreed with it in 1984, but by 1992 the level of support had dropped to 36 percent, where it remained four years later.

U.S. Troops Abroad

The deployment of troops abroad has been among the most controversial aspects of American foreign policy almost since the beginning of the republic. A public controversy was sparked during the War of 1812 when militia units refused to invade Canada on the grounds that fighting for the "common defense" could be done only on American soil.[4] During the Mexican-American War, young Congressman Abraham Lincoln mercilessly hectored the Polk administration with "spot resolutions," demanding to know the exact location of the bloodshed that allegedly justified the American invasion of Mexico. Even before World War II, numerous deployments of U.S. troops abroad had occurred without declarations of war—for example, to quell the Philippine insurrection after the Spanish-American War and to pursue Pancho Villa in Mexico during the Wilson administration. The issue became even more visible with the expanded American international role after 1945. During one of his wartime meetings with Winston Churchill, Franklin Roosevelt told the British prime minister that the public would force the U.S. leader to withdraw all troops from Europe within two years after the end of the conflict. Roosevelt's prognosis, which did not take into account the deterioration of East-West relations over such issues as the fate of Poland and other Eastern European countries, the status of Berlin, and the other disputes that contributed to the Cold War, proved to be wrong. Nevertheless, the overseas deployment of troops rarely has been free of controversy. Symbolizing the controversy were the contentious debates about the obligations entailed in the NATO Treaty; the constitutionality and wisdom of the War Powers Resolution of 1973, a congressional effort to restrict the president's ability unilaterally to send troops into combat or into situations that might entail combat; and the extremely close congressional vote on authorizing the use of force to expel Iraq from Kuwait. The most recent controversy centered on whether the George W. Bush administration could launch a war to topple the Saddam Hussein regime without congressional approval, which, in fact, was granted in the fall of 2002.

Each of the CCFR surveys asked leaders and the general public to indicate whether they favored or opposed the use of U.S. troops in various hypothetical situations, including five that involved an enemy invasion of American friends or allies: Western Europe, South Korea, Taiwan, Israel, and Saudi Arabia. A very similar question was included in a 1993 Times Mirror survey on "America's Place in the World," the Pew Research Center survey four years later, and the most recent FPLP study. At the time of these surveys, the results of which are presented in table 4.4, U.S. troops were already stationed in Western Europe, Saudi Arabia, and South Korea.[5] The results have varied substantially by geographical area. The only case in which majorities among the general public consistently approved of such action by Washington concerned a hypothetical Soviet or Russian invasion of Western Europe. Much of the public presumably was aware that U.S. troops were already stationed in Germany and thus would almost surely be involved if Western Europe were attacked. Although Poland had recently joined NATO, in 1998 less than one-third of the public expressed similar approval in support of the Warsaw government. However, if the question included the phrase "as part of a multilateral force," a clear majority favored U.S. action in support of Poland.[6]

In 1990, while American forces were being deployed in the Persian Gulf area after Iraq's invasion of Kuwait, a slight majority of those surveyed also approved using U.S. troops if Iraq invaded Saudi Arabia; this attitude remained little changed through 1997, long after most of the troops that had been engaged in Operations Desert Storm and Desert Shield had been withdrawn, but by 1998 that approval fell below 50 percent, where it remained even after a small increase in 2002. In contrast, questions in 1982 and 1986 about protecting Saudi Arabia from a revolutionary Islamic regime in Iran yielded minimal support, even though few Americans had a great deal of affection for the Tehran government. Although Israel has never asked for aid in the form of American soldiers, Saddam Hussein's frequent and vocal threats, combined with Scud missile attacks against that

TABLE 4.4.   Opinions on Use and Stationing of U.S. Troops Abroad: The General Public and Leaders, 1976–2002 (in percentages)

	Date	Survey	General public	Leaders
Would yo.. favor or oppose the use of U.S. troops if:				
Soviet troops invaded Western Europe	1978	CCFR	54	92
	1982	CCFR	65	92
	1986	CCFR	68	93
	1990	CCFR	58	87
Russia invaded Western Europe	1994	CCFR	54	91
	1996	FPLP	—	88
Russia invaded Poland	1998	CCFR	28	58
North Korea invaded South Korea	1978	CCFR	21	45
	1982	CCFR	22	50
	1986	CCFR	24	64
	1990	CCFR	44	57
	1993	T-M	31	69
	1994	CCFR	39	82
	1996	FPLP	—	63
	1997	Pew	35	77
	1998	CCFR	30	74
	2002	CCFR	36	82
Arab forces invaded Israel	1978	CCFR	22	31
	1982	CCFR	30	47
	1986	CCFR	33	57
	1990	CCFR	43	70
	1993	T-M	45	67
	1994	CCFR	42	72
	1996	FPLP	—	61
	1997	Pew	45	74
	1998	CCFR	38	69
	2002	CCFR	48	77
Iran invaded Saudi Arabia	1982	CCFR	25	54
	1986	CCFR	26	—
Iraq invaded Saudi Arabia	1990	CCFR	52	89
	1993	T-M	53	74
	1994	CCFR	52	84
	1996	FPLP	—	78
	1997	Pew	54	86
	1998	CCFR	46	79
	2002	CCFR	48	82
If the Mexican government was about to	1993	T-M	41	23
fall because of revolution or civil war	1997	Pew	43	25
China invaded Taiwan	1978	CCFR	20	18
	1982	CCFR	18	15
	1986	CCFR	19	—
	1996	FPLP	—	40
	1998	CCFR	27	51
	2002	CCFR	32	52

TABLE 4.4.—*Continued*

	Date	Survey	General public	Leaders
People in Cuba attempted to overthrow the Castro dictatorship	1994	CCFR	44	18
	1996	FPLP	—	15
	1998	CCFR	38	18
Serbian forces killed large numbers of ethnic Albanians in Kosovo	1998	CCFR	36	54

Please indicate how strongly you agree or disagree with . . .			Agree strongly or agree somewhat (%)	
Stationing American troops abroad encourages other countries to let us do their fighting for them	1976	FPLP	—	60
	1980	FPLP	—	54
	1984	FPLP	—	63
	1988	FPLP	—	66
	1992	FPLP	—	65
	1996	FPLP	—	58

Note: CCFR = Chicago Council on Foreign Relations surveys; FPLP = Foreign Policy Leadership Project surveys; T-M = Times Mirror survey; Pew = Pew Research Center for the People and the Press surveys.

country during the Persian Gulf crisis, also appear to have resulted in a sharp increase among those favoring assistance to Israel. That support persisted into 1997, and it rose rather sharply between 1998 and 2002.

Finally, the United States has had several security commitments in Asia, but the public generally has been less willing to use troops in that area. Although American armed forces have long been stationed in South Korea, at no time during the past quarter century has a majority expressed support for using U.S. troops to defend South Korea against another attack from North Korea. The use of American forces in response to an invasion of Taiwan by China gained even less approval. However, in the face of recent Chinese threats against Taiwan, public attitudes may be undergoing some changes. The 2002 CCFR study found that public support for using U.S. troops to aid Taiwan had risen to 32 percent, and a 1999 survey revealed that the general public was prepared to accept quite high American casualties if required to defend Taiwan (Feaver and Gelpi 1999).

Although public support for sending troops to assist South Korea, Israeli, Saudi Arabia, and Taiwan increased marginally in 2002, in none of the hypothetical scenarios did a majority approve such deployments. In contrast, leaders have consistently been more willing to use American troops in the hypothetical situations described previously, with two notable exceptions, both involving the Western Hemisphere; whereas only 18 percent of leaders would send American troops to Cuba if people on that island attempted to overthrow the Castro dictatorship, more than twice as many among the general public would approve a deployment of U.S. forces in such circumstances. Similarly, members of the general public expressed substantially stronger support than did leaders for deploying armed forces in case a revolution or civil war threatened the fall of the Mexican government. Differences between the two groups on the uses of troops abroad were typically quite large, ranging from 9 percent to more than 40 percent.

An FPLP survey item posed the issue of troops abroad in a somewhat different and more general way. Instead of focusing on reactions to using U.S. troops in specific hypothetical conflicts, this question asked leaders to appraise the general critique that "stationing American troops abroad encourages other countries to let us do their fighting for them." Consistent majorities of those taking part in these six leadership surveys, reaching a peak of 66 percent in 1996, expressed agreement with this proposition. Thus, it appears that while leaders are generally predisposed to come to the aid of key friends and allies under siege, they are also wary of more general commitments, especially to countries that may be willing to turn the conflict over to the United States because they are unable or unwilling to make a full commitment to self-defense. No doubt these views at least in part represent a lingering residue of the war in Vietnam.

Post–Cold War United Nations and NATO peacekeeping activities have generated controversies centering on two points: Under what circumstances should U.S. forces be included in peacekeeping forces, and under whose command should they be permitted to serve? Former Senator Robert Dole's proposed Peace Powers Resolution would have restricted the president's ability to deploy American forces in international peacekeeping efforts, and the 1994 Republican Contract with America would also have limited the circumstances under which U.S. forces might serve under foreign commanders. These controversies notwithstanding, a multitude of surveys during the 1990s revealed broad if not unconditional public support, ranging between 57 percent and 91 percent, for U.S. participation in peacekeeping activities, especially if the United States votes in the Security Council to take part (Kull and Destler 1999, 98; Rielly 1999, 25). It is, of course, inconceivable that the United States could be forced against its will to join any such undertaking because it can use its veto in the Security Council. The Program on International Policy Attitudes, CCFR, and FPLP surveys also indicate that neither opinion leaders nor the general public would balk at having American peacekeeping forces serve under foreign commanders appointed by the United Nations or NATO (Kull and Destler 1999, 109–11; Rielly 1995, 8).

In that climate of controversy, proposals to send troops to Bosnia stimulated vigorous debates about the feasibility and desirability of American intervention, the proper role of public opinion in policy-making, and the meaning of survey data on the Bosnia issues (Newport 1995; Saad 1995; Saad and Newport 1995; Sobel 1995, 2001; Kull 1995–96; Rosner 1995–96; Sobel and Shiraev 2003). Proponents of intervention acknowledged the lack of public enthusiasm for deploying U.S. troops but asserted that it was imperative for the United States to assume a leadership role in maintaining a tolerable world order (A. Schlesinger 1995). Emphasizing that American interests rather than values should govern foreign policy, opponents of intervention attacked President Clinton for "applying the standards of Mother Teresa to U.S. foreign policy" (Mandelbaum 1996, 18). Among leaders, support for using NATO forces, including U.S. troops, for peacekeeping in Bosnia was exceptionally strong, ranging between 63 percent among business leaders to well over 80 percent among foreign affairs experts, security specialists, academics, union leaders, and congressional staffers (Pew 1997, 72). Surveys of the general public revealed persisting and stable opinions on several points: A solid majority believed that solution of the Bosnia issue was a "very important" or "somewhat important" foreign policy goal, an equally large proportion of the public asserted that Congress must approve any military involvement, and although few Americans believed that unilateral intervention in Bosnia was either a moral obligation or in the national interest, there was moderately strong support for deploying U.S. troops as part of a United Nations peacekeeping force. These opinions remained relatively stable after President Clinton's decisions to send American forces into Bosnia as part of a multinational effort to enforce the 1995 Dayton peace accord. Whether public support for the Bosnia or the later Kosovo War and peacekeeping undertakings would have collapsed were they to have resulted in even moderate casualties—a proposition that, fortunately, was not put to a test—remains uncertain. Survey evidence on this point depends on the manner in which the question is posed (compare Saad 1995 with Kull 1995b). More generally, the issue of casualties lies at the heart of controversies about post–Cold War undertakings.

Questions about the willingness of the public in democracies to accept combat deaths predate the end of the Cold War. Catastrophic losses during World War I are often linked to French and British unwillingness to confront Hitler's Germany through most of the 1930s, and some historians have faulted American military strategy during World War II as excessively driven by aversion to casualties (Kennedy 1999). A leading critic of U.S. policy in Vietnam, George Ball, warned in 1965 that the conflict could not be won because the public would not accept large casualties: "Producing a chart that correlated public opinion with American casualties in Korea, Ball predicted that the American public would not support a long and protracted war" (Clifford 1991, 412). A study of the Korean and Vietnam Wars indeed revealed a strong inverse relationship between public support and combat deaths (Mueller 1973). More broadly, Luttwak (1994) has argued that postindustrial societies, including the United States, are afflicted by casualty aversion arising from small families, thus preventing such societies from effectively playing the role of great powers. The U.S. response to the 1993 ambush of eighteen Rangers in Mogadishu is often cited as proof that the U.S. public cannot accept the almost inevitable costs of military operations abroad. Indeed, Somali faction leader Mohamed Farah Aideed reportedly told U.S. Ambassador Robert Oakley, "We have studied Vietnam and Lebanon and know how to get rid of Americans, by killing them so that public opinion will put an end to things" (quoted in Blechman and Wittes 1999, 5).

These episodes seemingly provide a rich base of evidence supporting those who assert, whether with satisfaction or dismay, that a long history of public casualty aversion has a powerful constraining grip on policy decisions. Most commentaries on the 1999 NATO air war against Yugoslavia asserted that public opinion had created a virtually insurmountable barrier against the introduction of ground troops to protect Kosovars from ethnic cleansing by the Milosevic regime in Belgrade because NATO troop deployments would surely entail costs—casualties—that Western publics were unwilling to tolerate. The strategy of flying beyond the reach of Serbian air defense systems, even if the less precise high-altitude bombing campaign increased collateral deaths among civilians, was also linked to the public's alleged unwillingness to countenance the loss of pilots.

The most compelling evidence of public sensitivity to casualties during the post–Cold War era emerges from a massive study that encompasses American threats or the use of military force between 1992 and 2000, including responses to events in Bosnia, Yugoslavia, North Korea, Haiti, Somalia, Rwanda, Afghanistan/ Sudan, and Serbia/Kosovo. The findings, based on 1,374 surveys, reveal that the public is indeed very sensitive to the use of "troops" and to any mention of civilian or military casualties (Eichenberg 2002).

Yet some evidence also indicates that this depiction of public casualty aversion may be overdrawn. A study covering an extended period of American history reveals that the public will accept high casualties, as during World War II, to achieve goals that are deemed to be both desirable and feasible (E. Larson 1996). Even controversial post–Cold War interventions have evoked public responses that cast some doubt on the conventional wisdom. The initial reaction to the Mogadishu ambush was to stay the course and seek to punish the perpetrators rather than withdraw. When confronted with a hypothetical scenario involving one hundred U.S. fatalities in Bosnia, a plurality of respondents (37 percent) wanted to "bring in reinforcement," another 26 percent preferred to "strike back," and 10 percent wanted to "stay the course" (Kull and Destler 1999; see also Logan 1996). Finally, a 1999 survey of the general public, civilian leaders, and military elites revealed that the last two groups were actually less willing than the general public to accept casualties in a series of six hypothetical scenarios, including "to prevent widespread 'ethnic cleansing' in Kosovo." According to Peter D. Feaver and Christopher Gelpi, "The public can distinguish between suffering defeat and suffering casualties" (1999, B3). Although this evidence does not suggest that the public is indifferent to combat fatalities, especially in undertakings for which the administration is unable or unwilling to demonstrate that U.S. participation is desirable (because of a compelling link to vital national interests) and feasible (there is a reasonable prospect for success), it does raise questions about the alleged iron law of the post–Cold War national security policy: public insistence on casualty-free operations.

The evidence reviewed here suggests that sensitivity to casualties may depend significantly on the circumstances. U.S. casualties rose as a result of the successful 1944 invasion of France, but because it represented a vital step in the defeat of Hitler's Germany, support for the war effort did not decline. Public support for the Korean and Vietnam Wars did fall as casualties rose, but in these instances the passing of time also raised increasing doubts about ultimate victory in either conflict. Although public support for military operations in Afghanistan remained exceptionally high during the months following the terrorist attacks in 2001, it fell from an average of 89 percent to 68 percent when the questions mentioned casualties. Yet even the latter figure suggests that if the goal is perceived as desirable, the public is prepared to accept some loss of life. Post 9/11 surveys suggest less support (71 percent) for military operations against Iraq, especially if casualties are mentioned (43 percent) (Eichenberg 2002, table 6). The low level of U.S. and British battle deaths in the 2003 invasion of Iraq would initially appear to rule out use of that undertaking as a crucial test of the impact of casualties on public support for military interventions abroad. But Bush administration predictions about the postwar situation in Iraq proved to be far too optimistic. Not only were the United Nations and International Red Cross headquarters in Baghdad bombed with a high loss of life, but by the end of October 2003, postwar deaths among U.S. military personnel exceeded those incurred in the war itself. At the same time, Gallup polls showed steady decline in public support. By early October, a solid majority of Americans—58 percent—judged that things are going "very badly" or "moderately badly" for the United States in Iraq, and 40 percent said that America "made a mistake in sending troops to Iraq" (Gallup, October 14, 2003, 1–2). These and other postwar Gallup surveys did not ask direct questions concerning casualties, but it seems reasonable to assume that almost daily news of military deaths have contributed significantly to the growing disaffection with U.S. policy.

The data summarized here reveal a consistent pattern of substantially higher support by leaders for various aspects of internationalism, in the form not only of stronger approval for an "active part in world affairs" but also of greater support for liberal trade policies, economic and military assistance, and deployment or use of American troops abroad. The evidence also indicates that both leaders and the general public distinguish between various types of international policies and undertakings and that these distinctions appear to reflect events and developments in the international arena.

Foreign Policy Goals

Results from the CCFR and Gallup surveys presented in chapter 3 indicated that the general public has tended to give top priority to goals that promote American economic interests (tables 3a and 3b). Protecting the jobs of American workers ranked as the number one goal in all but three of the CCFR surveys of the general public, and it just barely missed doing so in 1974 as well; in 2002 it ranked a close third behind only combating terrorism and preventing nuclear proliferation. Energy security also has consistently been accorded a high ranking, and the 1990 survey saw a sharp increase in the number of respondents who rated "protecting the interests of American business abroad" as a "very important" foreign policy goal, but assessments have declined since then. In contrast, despite occasional charges that the American public has been obsessed with Cold War concerns, such goals as "containing communism" and "matching Soviet military power" have ranked at the top of the foreign policy agenda in none of the CCFR surveys. A more general post–Cold War goal—"maintaining superior military power worldwide"—ranked only tenth among respondents to the 1994 CCFR survey and rose only slightly in 2002. Moreover, another Cold War goal, "defending our allies' security," did not appear among the top three until after the Cold War had ended.

The "goals" questions also were posed to leaders in all eight CCFR studies, although some variations occurred at times in the specific items presented to the two groups. Many of the same questions appeared in the six FPLP questionnaires and the 1999 Triangle Institute for Security Studies (TISS) survey as well. These studies thus provide assessments of a wide range of possible foreign policy goals in fifteen surveys of leaders conducted over the 1974–2002 period. Aside from a shared judgment that energy security is "very important," other goals accorded the highest rating by leaders revealed a somewhat different and broader set of priorities than those similarly rated by the general public. The differences are generally consistent with the proposition that leaders are more internationally oriented. Thus, their most highly ranked goals in the FPLP and CCFR surveys have usually included such world-order issues as arms control; "fostering international cooperation to solve common problems, such as food, inflation and energy"; "improving the global environment"; and "combating world hunger." Eliminating hunger also was accorded a high priority by the general public in surveys prior to 1990, when the question was dropped. By 1994 it ranked only eighth among the sixteen foreign policy goals in the general public's judgment.[7] In contrast to the views of the general public, leaders in three of the CCFR surveys (1978, 1982, 1986) accorded high priority to "defending our allies' security"; after declining in importance in 1990, this concern rebounded in leaders' judgment to rank as the third-most-important goal (behind only preventing nuclear proliferation and energy) in 1994 and to tie for third in 1998 (trailing only preventing nuclear proliferation and combating international terrorism). Four years later it ranked fourth with 55 percent "very important" ratings.

Conversely, the CCFR surveys found that the general public consistently appraised the goals of "strengthening the United Nations" as more important than leaders did; indeed, in 2002 well over half of the general public respondents accorded this goal the top rating, whereas only 28 percent of leaders did so. What might at first glance appear to be an anomaly is perhaps consistent with the rest of the data. Although the evidence does not permit the proposition to be tested beyond all doubt, it is possible that many among the general public view a stronger United Nations as an alternative to unilateral American interventions and other international undertakings or at least as a way of sharing the risks and burdens of such activities. That hypothesis suggests that a pro–United Nations attitude may in fact be consistent with a public yearning for a less unilateral leadership role for the United States. This question and others arising from the 2002 CCFR survey will be examined in more detail in chapter 6. Support for the United Nations among leaders increased sharply in the 1990 CCFR and 1992 FPLP surveys (probably as a result of Security Council activities in the wake of Iraq's invasion of Kuwait in August 1990) before dropping in 1994, when only one-third of the leaders taking part in the CCFR survey rated "strengthening the United Nations" as a "very important" foreign policy goal. That assessment was little changed in 1998, when 32 percent of the leaders gave that goal the top rating.

There are, finally, some broad similarities in the less highly rated goal priorities of the general public and leaders. Such Cold War goals as containment or "matching Soviet military power" failed to dominate the rankings of either group. Neither leaders nor the general public exhibited a great deal of fervor for promoting U.S. values and institutions abroad. "Promoting and defending human rights in other countries" as a foreign policy goal only once received a "very important" rating from even half of either group; the exception was the public appraisal of that goal in 1990. Even in the wake of the collapse of many communist and other authoritarian regimes in the late 1980s and early 1990s, few respondents, whether among the elite or the general public, expressed much interest in "helping to bring a democratic form of government to other nations." Indeed, that goal consistently ranked among the lowest in the priorities of both leaders and the public. Other studies offer rather compelling evidence that interventions abroad for the purpose of promoting internal political changes have quite limited public support (Jentleson 1992; Nincic 1997; Jentleson and Britton 1998; Eichenberg 2003). Among some leaders, especially those who describe themselves as "realists," exporting democracy and "nation building" are anathema. As noted in chapter 3, the public also appears to appreciate the difficulties of transplanting U.S. institutions abroad and may have become a bit cynical about the "friendly tyrants" who have been welcomed in Washington as supporters of democracy.[8]

In summary, the generalization that leaders outstrip the general public in their support for a broad range of internationalist policies and undertaking seems well supported by the evidence. However, an important limitation of the findings bears repeating. Survey data on leadership attitudes before the 1970s are at best very sketchy and certainly are not sufficient to permit the types of comparisons that have been possible for the period since the end of the Vietnam War.

The General Public and Leaders: The Structure of Foreign Policy Beliefs

As shown in chapter 3, the earlier consensus that public attitudes lack coherence and structure has been challenged from a variety of perspectives. A growing body of evidence suggests that some organizing concepts and heuristics enable even a poorly informed general public to make some sense of the blooming, buzzing confusion that characterizes contemporary foreign affairs.

Debates on the structure—or lack thereof—of political attitudes among the general public continue. However, there is somewhat greater consensus on the proposition that elite political beliefs are in fact more highly structured than those of the general public. Whereas evidence from studies of the general public on this point is mixed, elite studies have rarely failed to uncover some coherence and structure. Consequently, the debates tend to focus on the best ways of describing the structures rather than on their existence (compare Mandelbaum and Schneider 1979; Wittkopf 1990; Hinckley 1992; Chittick and Billingsley 1989; Chittick, Billingsley, and Travis 1995; Herrmann and Keller 2004).

Perhaps more importantly, comparative studies generally have found a higher degree of belief structure among leaders. Philip E. Converse's (1964) widely cited study found that the political beliefs of congressional candidates had a much higher degree of coherence or "constraint" than those of the general public as measured by higher correlations—0.25 versus 0.10—among items. A parallel analysis of panelists in the National Election Studies and National Convention Delegate Studies provided additional strong evidence on this score.

> Overall, political party elites have a vastly more constrained and stable set of political preferences—in terms of the traditional liberal-conservative dimension—than does the mass public, a conclusion that applies whether the test is a demanding one based on opinions about policy issues or a less stringent one based on appraisals of socio-political groups and prominent political actors. (Jennings 1992, 419)

This section addresses two related questions about the structure of elite foreign policy beliefs. First, to what extent do they resemble those of the general public? More specifically, a scheme based on a distinction between militant internationalism and cooperative internationalism was found to have provided a powerful means of describing the structure of public attitudes (Wittkopf 1990, 1995). Are the attitudes of leaders similarly organized?

The dramatic events since the late 1980s, marking the end of the Cold War, have given rise to a second and related question to be addressed here. Inasmuch as a preponderance of the evidence on public opinion and international affairs was generated by research during the period between the end of World War II and the demolition of the Berlin Wall—that is, the Cold War era—how can we be sure that our findings are not severely time and context bound? For example, is it possible that the salience, intensity, and endurance of the Cold War gave rise to only temporary organizing devices or heuristics for structuring beliefs about international affairs? Were the threats posed by the Soviet Union and the possibility of a Soviet-American nuclear war of such significance that they provided a powerful but evanescent degree of coherence and structure to attitudes on foreign affairs? Stated differently, are research findings that drew almost exclusively on more than four decades of the Cold War sufficiently robust to survive a period of unprecedented international change? Because attitudes toward the Soviet Union and the possibility of nuclear war with that nation played a central role in structuring U.S. foreign policy beliefs during the Cold War, what are the consequences of Soviet disintegration and a dramatic transformation of relations between the United States and the successor states of the former USSR?[9]

According to one line of reasoning, the end of the Cold War should result in fundamental changes in the structure of foreign policy belief systems. Evidence summarized in the first three chapters indicates that major events—notably World War I, World War II, and the Vietnam War—have not only had a significant impact on public opinion but have even affected the ways in which public opinion analysts have approached the subject of public opinion and foreign policy. One can make a reasonable argument that, taken together, the monumental events of the past decade and a half—including but not limited to the USSR's liberalization and subsequent disintegration, vast political change in Eastern Europe, the two wars against Iraq, the Russian and Japanese economic crises, China's increasing importance in the world economy, major steps toward the economic unification of Western Europe, and the 2001 terrorist attacks—represent international changes of a magnitude that could be expected to effect fundamental changes in ways of thinking about international affairs.

An alternative line of reasoning suggests that the end of the Cold War may have changed opinions about specific countries and issues but that the fundamental structure of opinions has remained intact. This view is grounded in the assumption that basic orientations toward international affairs, reflected, for example, in the persisting debates between realists and liberals, preceded the Cold War, transcended the specific issues of that era, and will survive its demise. Hence, although it would scarcely be surprising to find that opinions about onetime adversaries or specific issues may have changed, it does not automatically follow that more fundamental ways of thinking about the nature of international politics have also done so.

These questions will be addressed by analyzing data from a series of nationwide surveys of American opinion leaders. The

FPLP has conducted such surveys by means of a mailed questionnaire in March of every fourth year between 1976 and 1996. The sample for each survey, representing leaders in a wide range of occupations—including politics, business, the military, the media, the State Department and Foreign Service, labor unions, churches, academia, law and health care—was drawn in part from such standard sources as *Who's Who in America, Who's Who of American Women, Who's Who in American Politics,* and the *State Department Directory.* Others were included by virtue of their positions in specific institutions—for example, membership in the current class at the National War College, chief editorial writers of newspapers with circulations of one hundred thousand or more, and labor union officers. (For a more precise description of the FPLP samples, see table 4.1.) Each of the six surveys brought forth completed questionnaires from more than twenty-one hundred opinion leaders. The most recent survey, undertaken in March 1996, yielded responses to a sixteen-page questionnaire on domestic and foreign policy issues from 2,141 opinion leaders for a return rate of 54 percent. The analyses that follow will focus on the 1992 and 1996 data because they are the first generated since the end of the Cold War.

A series of studies of public opinion on foreign affairs by Wittkopf (1990), described briefly in chapter 3, has demonstrated that attitudes toward two dimensions—support or oppose militant internationalism (MI) and cooperative internationalism (CI)—provide an effective way of describing the belief structures of both elites and the mass publics. Dichotomizing and crossing these two dimensions yields four types, with quadrants labeled *hard-liners* (support MI, oppose CI), *accommodationists* (oppose MI, support CI), *internationalists* (support both MI and CI), and *isolationists* (oppose both MI and CI). Analyses of the 1976, 1980, 1984, and 1988 FPLP surveys revealed that the MI/CI scheme effectively describes core elements of leaders' beliefs about international affairs. Respondents' placements in the four quadrants defined by the MI and CI dimensions provided a powerful predictor of attitudes toward a broad array of international issues (Holsti and Rosenau 1990, 1993).

In the first four FPLP surveys, the militant internationalism scale focused on two core elements: attitudes toward the USSR or communism and the use of force. Responses to seven questions from the 1976–88 FPLP surveys represent various dimensions of an MI orientation, with an emphasis on a conflictual world in which the USSR and its expansionist policies represent a major threat to the United States; the necessity of being prepared to use force, including by the Central Intelligence Agency, to cope with the threats; the dangerous consequences, as postulated by the domino theory, of failing to meet international challenges; and a zero-sum view of the Cold War conflict.

Although the validity of longitudinal analyses is materially enhanced by using precisely the same wording each time a question is posed, altered global realities required four changes in the 1992 and 1996 versions of the militant internationalism scale. *Russia* replaced *Soviet Union* in one question. The wording in two questions on the domino theory and on U.S. obligations to cope with aggression was altered by using the terms *aggressor nations* and *expansionist power* in lieu of *communism*. Finally, a proposition that seems quite central to a MI perspective — "Rather than simply countering our opponent's thrusts, it is necessary to strike at the heart of the opponent's power" (J. Schlesinger 1975, 25) — replaced an item opposing better relations with the USSR. Owing to these changes, any direct comparison of overall support for an MI perspective in 1992 and 1996 relative to the four previous FPLP surveys may be somewhat problematical. The specific questionnaire items that constituted the MI scale are as follows.

There is considerable validity in the "domino theory" that when one nation falls to communism, others nearby will soon follow a similar path. (1976–88 surveys)

There is considerable validity in the "domino theory" that when one nation falls to aggressor nations, others nearby will soon follow a similar path. (1992 and 1996 surveys)

Any communist victory is a defeat for America's national interest. (All surveys)

The Soviet Union is generally expansionist rather than defensive in its foreign policy goals. (1976–88 surveys)

Russia is generally expansionist rather than defensive in its foreign policy goals. (1992 and 1996 surveys)

There is nothing wrong with using the CIA to try to undermine hostile governments. (All surveys)

The United States should take all steps including the use of force to prevent the spread of communism. (1976–88 surveys)

The United States should take all steps including the use of

force to prevent aggression by any expansionist power.
(1992 and 1996 surveys)

Containing communism (as a foreign policy goal). (All surveys)

It is not in our interest to have better relations with the Soviet Union because we are getting less than we are giving to them. (1976–88 surveys)

Rather than simply countering our opponent's thrusts, it is necessary to strike at the heart of the opponent's power. (1992 and 1996 surveys)

Leaders taking part in the six FPLP leadership studies generally have been almost evenly divided in their support for militant internationalism, although there have been some sharp changes in responses to specific items. Not surprisingly, varying majorities attributed expansionist motives to Soviet foreign policy in the 1976, 1980, 1984, and 1988 surveys, whereas by 1992 and 1996, strong majorities exceeding 60 percent of the leaders denied that Russian foreign policy goals were thus motivated. Another notable shift took place in response to the proposition that "the United States should take all steps including the use of force to prevent the spread of communism." A majority of leaders taking part in the first four surveys (1976–88) expressed their disagreement with that policy prescription. However, when the item was reworded in 1992 to reflect the end of the Cold War—"The United States should take all steps including the use of force to prevent *aggression by any expansionist power*"—support increased sharply, as more than 70 percent of the respondents agreed. Although those responses no doubt reflected reactions to the Iraqi invasion of Kuwait, even four years later that proposition gained approval from a still-strong majority of 59 percent. Thus, the respondents' willingness to accept international security undertakings rose when such commitments were broader than containing communism. This evidence would appear to provide another challenge to the thesis, discussed in chapter 3, that Americans have been imbued with an unalterable anticommunism that borders on the obsessive.

The seven items on the CI scale emphasize international cooperation and institutions; world-order and "North-South" issues, including hunger and the standard of living in less developed nations; arms control; and foreign aid. The specific questions that constituted the cooperative internationalism scale in all six FPLP surveys are as follows.

It is vital to enlist the cooperation of the United Nations in settling international disputes.

The United States should give economic aid to poorer countries even if it means higher prices at home.

Helping to improve the standard of living in less developed countries (as a foreign policy goal).

Worldwide arms control (as a foreign policy goal).

Combating world hunger (as a foreign policy goal).

Strengthening the United Nations (as a foreign policy goal).

Fostering international cooperation to solve common problems, such as food, inflation, and energy (as a foreign policy goal).

Whereas changed international realities seemed to mandate alterations in the wording of some MI items, this was not true of those in the CI scale; the items and their wording have remained precisely the same in all six FPLP surveys. Responses to these items have shown a very modest trend toward greater support of CI during the twelve-year period covered by the first four FPLP surveys and a somewhat sharper increase in this respect in 1992. The latter change was entirely the consequence of a striking shift toward more favorable attitudes regarding the United Nations. The direction and magnitude of these opinion changes no doubt reflect the events surrounding the Persian Gulf War and the ability of the United States, with the cooperation of the Soviet Union and the acquiescence of China, to lead the Security Council toward action to force Iraq out of Kuwait. Responses to questions on the United Nations offset moderately declining support, sometimes labeled "compassion fatigue," for three items that have a significant Third World focus: global hunger, foreign aid, and the standard of living in less developed countries. In 1996, support for the CI items fell somewhat, to the pre-1992 levels. Majorities ranging between 58 percent and 88 percent supported six of the seven items; the lone exception, economic aid, garnered approval from 40 percent of the respondents.

Despite these changes, correlations among responses to the seven questions on the 1992 MI scale are uniformly positive, as they have been in all of the leadership surveys. The correlation coefficients across the six FPLP surveys averaged .37 and ranged from a low of .10 to a high of .66. Although the average interitem correlation declined in 1992 and 1996, Cronbach's alpha, a measure of the reliability of a scale, remained above the conventional requirement that it reach the .70 level. The interitem correlations for the CI scale have also been uniformly positive, ranging from .12 to .67, and have scaled well. In the six FPLP surveys, Cronbach's alpha coefficients have never fallen below .77. The premise that the two scales are measuring different dimensions of internationalism is supported by the fact that correlations of responses to the items on the MI scale versus those on the CI scale were negative in each of the six FPLP studies.

To classify respondents into four groups, a score of 0.00 was used as the cutting point on both scales for each of the six surveys.[10] Whereas those opposing MI have slightly outnumbered the supporters since 1984, there has been a moderate trend toward increasing support for cooperative internationalism. Table 4.5, depicting the distribution of hard-liners, isolationists, internationalists, and accommodationists, confirms that the latter two

TABLE 4.5.   The Distribution of Hard-Liners, Internationalists, Isolationists, and Accommodationists in the 1976–96 FPLP Surveys

Militant Internationalism	Cooperative Internationalism			
	Oppose (%)		Support (%)	
	Hard-liners		Internationalists	
Support	1976	20	1976	30
	1980	20	1980	33
	1984	17	1984	25
	1988	16	1988	25
	1992	9	1992	33
	1996	13	1996	29
	Isolationists		Accommodationists	
Oppose	1976	8	1976	42
	1980	7	1980	41
	1984	7	1984	51
	1988	8	1988	52
	1992	5	1992	53
	1996	10	1996	48

Reliability:

	Militant Internationalism		Cooperative Internationalism	
Year	Mean correlation	alpha	Mean correlation	alpha
1976	.41	.83	.35	.79
1980	.41	.83	.35	.79
1984	.43	.84	.35	.79
1988	.45	.86	.36	.80
1992	.28	.73	.33	.77
1996	.26	.71	.40	.81

groups—leaders with a favorable stance toward CI—outnumber the other two. In the 1984, 1988, and 1992 studies, accommodationists constituted a slight majority of the entire sample, but they fell to 48 percent in the most recent survey. The most discernible change in 1992 was the increased number of internationalists, mostly at the expense of the hard-liners and, to a lesser degree, the isolationists. The 1992 results were probably affected by the recently concluded and successful Gulf War, and by 1996 the distribution of respondents very closely resembled that of eight years earlier. Moreover, changes in the items constituting the MI scale in the post–Cold War era—the 1992 and 1996 surveys—may also have affected these results. In any case, neither the distribution of leaders in the MI/CI classification scheme for 1992 and 1996 nor a comparison of that distribution with those of earlier surveys will suffice to establish its adequacy for depicting the structure of attitudes toward international affairs. Although analyses of earlier FPLP surveys revealed that leaders in the four groups consistently and systematically varied in their responses to other issues, for reasons discussed previously it remains to be demonstrated that patterns and relationships that existed during the Cold War era have survived its demise.

The durability of the MI/CI classification scheme can be tested by exploring how leaders taking part in the two post–Cold War surveys responded to a broad range of questions about international affairs, including beliefs about the current structure of the international system, approaches to peace, future threats to U.S. national security, U.S. roles and interests, the Persian Gulf War, and perceived sources of change in the USSR and Eastern Europe. Some of these issues were included in either the 1992 or 1996 surveys but not both.[11]

The Structure of the Post–Cold War International System

The military preponderance of American- and Soviet-led blocs— that is, a bipolar international system at the strategic level—was a dominating feature of the Cold War era. When asked to describe the contemporary international system, almost 90 percent of respondents to the 1992 leadership survey agreed that it was multipolar. A 10 percent range of responses across the four groups defined by the MI/CI classification scheme is statistically significant, but that difference pales in comparison to the striking convergence of views on the structure of the system. Although

Russia remains a highly armed nuclear power, the sea change in attitudes is reflected in the fact that fewer than 3 percent of the opinion leaders viewed the system as bipolar. Nor did the thesis that the disintegration of the USSR has created a "unipolar moment" in which only the United States has the means and, therefore, the responsibility to create and maintain international stability gain much support among leaders taking part in the 1992 survey (Krauthammer 1990–91); only 8 percent of the respondents asserted that "unipolar" best describes the post–Cold War international system.

Approaches to Peace

Opinion leaders were asked to evaluate the effectiveness of a broad array of approaches to peace (table 4.6). Responses to these questions in both the 1992 and 1996 surveys reveal a sharp increase in the number of those who rated "military superiority of the United States" as a "very effective" approach to peace. Nevertheless, striking and consistent differences also occurred among leaders in the four groups. More importantly, the differences offer very substantial support for the MI/CI classification scheme. "Military superiority of the United States" was the only approach to peace that generated strong support from the hard-liners, and leaders in this group offered very negative assessments of three approaches strongly identified with their opposites (accommodationists): arms control, narrowing the gap between rich and poor nations, and strengthening the United Nations and other international organizations. The internationalists favored prescriptions that are consistent with a group defined as supporting both MI and CI. Specifically, they awarded high effectiveness ratings to two approaches that fit well with MI: U.S. military superiority and collective security through alliances. The internationalists were also inclined to support approaches to peace that are associated with cooperative internationalism: trade, technical cooperation, and economic interdependence and better international communication and understanding.

The isolationists, defined as those opposing both MI and CI, would not be expected to express a great deal of support for any of the prescriptions listed in table 4.6. The data are fully consistent with that expectation. None of the four varied approaches favored by their opposites—the internationalists—elicited much enthusiasm among the isolationists, although in 1996 half of them rated

TABLE 4.6. Assessments of Approaches to Peace by Opinion Leaders in 1992 and 1996: Isolationists, Hard-Liners, Accommodationists, and Internationalists

How effective do you consider each of the following as an approach to world peace? Please indicate your assessment.

Very effective (%)

	All Respondents		Isolationists		Hard-Liners		Accommodationists		Internationalists	
	1992	1996	1992	1996	1992	1996	1992	1996	1992	1996
Trade, technical cooperation, and economic interdependence	50	43	31	34	29	21	56	49	48	45
Better communication and understanding among peoples and nations	45	47	22	29	24	22	49	53	49	54
Collective security through alliances	41	40	18	26	31	32	37	39	53	49
Arms control	33	25	18	12	10	5	38	31	33	28
Military superiority of the U.S.	32	51	39	50	67	78	12	34	53	66
Narrowing the gap between rich and poor nations	30	26	8	11	6	4	42	38	22	19
Strengthening the UN and other international organizations	30	21	1	4	3	2	39	30	28	20
Political efforts to achieve a balance of power within regions and between great powers	20	18	10	9	11	9	22	21	22	21

N: 1992 = 2,312; 1996 = 2,141
Note: Differences among groups significant at the .001 level for all items in 1992 and 1996.

"military superiority of the United States" as very effective, and they were even more skeptical of the other three approaches favored by the internationalists. Finally, the MI/CI classification scheme suggests that the accommodationists' responses should be the mirror image of those elicited from the hard-liners. That is precisely the case. The latter emphasized the effectiveness of military superiority while scorning the value of arms control, a narrowing of the rich nation/poor nation gap, and international organizations. In contrast, among the four groups, the accommodationists were the least enthusiastic about the efficacy of military superiority, and by a very substantial margin they accorded the highest rating to four approaches to peace that incorporate a strong element of international cooperation: economic interdependence, arms control, narrowing the economic gap between nations, and international organization. A fifth cooperative approach, better international communication, drew equally high ratings from the internationalists and accommodationists. In summary, in both 1992 and 1996, the pattern of favored prescriptions for peace reveals striking differences that are wholly consistent with the MI and CI scales used to define the four groups.

U.S. International Interests and Roles

Much of the foreign policy debate since the early 1990s has focused on the proper U.S. role in a world transformed by the disintegration of the Soviet Union and the end of the Cold War. When asked to assess American interests and roles in the post–Cold War international system, opinion leaders offered little support for an indiscriminate retrenchment into isolationism. Four propositions in the two post–Cold War FPLP surveys that probed for various aspects of isolationism received rather limited support. Only about a third of the respondents agreed that the United States should "concentrate more on our own national problems," and an even smaller proportion supported the view that vital U.S. interests are limited to the industrial democracies and nations in this hemisphere. Propositions indicating that U.S. international interests are limited to questions of peace and stability and that Third World conflict cannot jeopardize those interests gained the agreement of even fewer respondents. The isolationists and hard-liners were generally more supportive of a more restricted conception of the appropriate definition of vital national interests than were members of the other two groups. Although differences among the four groups are statistically significant, in no case did a major-

ity of the respondents support any of the four items described earlier. In contrast, a slight majority of 54 percent agreed that the
United States could best promote democratic development by
solving its own problems; once again, the isolationists and hard-
liners were significantly more supportive than the internationalists and accommodationists. Finally, in both 1992 and 1996, at least
80 percent of the leaders in all groups supported a key element of
the Weinberger Doctrine: "Before the United States commits
combat forces abroad, there must be reasonable assurance of support by the American people."

Two other questions focus on the type of international role
that the United States should play. In 1992, a slight majority (57
percent) agreed that "America's conception of its leadership role
must be scaled down," but four years later dictum garnered approval from only 42 percent. In both studies, differences among
the four MI/CI groups were very large, and as expected, the
strongest support came from the accommodationists and isolationists, whereas there was far less agreement among the internationalists and hard-liners. A related item in the 1992 survey—
"Although its power is greater relative to other countries, the
United States is no superpower and it ought not to act as if it
is"—yielded a very similar pattern of responses. Fewer than two-
fifths of the leaders agreed with this assessment, but about half of
the accommodationists did so, far outstripping the internationalists (26 percent) and hard-liners (18 percent) in this respect.

Finally, two questions with strong realpolitik overtones addressed the appropriate goals for the projection of American
power abroad. The leadership sample divided almost evenly in
1992 in its preferences if faced with a trade-off between supporting international stability and self-determination movements, but
fewer than one leader in five favored intervention in the domestic affairs of other countries in support of a more democratic
world order. Four years later, the latter proposition gained the
support of only 10 percent of the opinion leaders. As one would
expect, the hard-liners and internationalists consistently expressed significantly stronger support for both propositions than
did leaders in the other two groups, but even these groups' enthusiasm was very limited.

The Persian Gulf War of 1991

Operation Desert Storm to drive invading Iraqi armed forces out
of Kuwait in 1991 constituted the most significant U.S. military

undertaking abroad between the war in Vietnam and the intervention in Afghanistan after the terrorist attacks of 2001. Some half million members of the American armed forces led a successful anti-Iraq coalition of twenty-six nations, including Russia. Although the Soviet Union had been an important supporter of the Baghdad regime prior to the disintegration of the USSR, and although Moscow and Washington did not agree on all aspects of the effort to drive Iraq out of Kuwait, the Gulf War provided dramatic evidence that the dominant East-West cleavage of the Cold War era had indeed gone by the boards. Two clusters of questions permitted those taking part in the 1992 leadership survey to record their policy preferences during and after the war and to assess its consequences.

Much of the policy debate ignited by the Iraqi invasion of Kuwait centered on the relative merits of initiating military operations against the Baghdad regime versus relying on economic sanctions to force Iraq out of Kuwait; relatively fewer participants in those debates questioned whether the United States should even have become involved in the issue. When asked which of these options they had preferred prior to the start of Desert Storm in mid-January 1991, those favoring the immediate use of force outnumbered the advocates of giving economic sanctions a longer time to work by a margin of about three to two, and only 5 percent opposed getting involved at all (table 4.7). Respondents were also asked about their policy preferences after the war. Despite the overwhelming defeat of Iraqi armed forces and the relatively light U.S. casualties, the overall increase in support for the use of force was a rather modest 5 percent, and there was an almost equal increase in the number of those who opposed any U.S. involvement.

Responses to the Persian Gulf War should provide an especially salient test of the MI/CI scheme because the two primary policy options in the debate about how to deal with Iraq's invasion of Kuwait are closely linked to MI (use force) and CI (rely on the effectiveness of economic sanctions imposed by a substantial part of the world community). Differences across the four groups are very substantial and are consistent with expectations based on the MI/CI scheme. The hard-liners and internationalists are defined as supporting MI, and in fact they overwhelmingly favored the use of force; the former did so in somewhat greater proportions than the latter. Accommodationists favor CI, and they were by a substantial margin the strongest advocates of giving sanctions more time to effect an Iraqi withdrawal from Kuwait.

TABLE 4.7. Policy Preferences before and after the Persian Gulf War among Opinion Leaders in 1992: Isolationists, Hard-Liners, Accommodationists, and Internationalists

People differed over President Bush's decision to start the war against Iraq. Some felt he was right to use military force right away. Others felt he should have given economic sanctions a longer time to work. Still others opposed getting involved at all. Please indicate which position comes closest to your own feelings, both before the U.S. launched military operations on January 16, 1991, and retrospectively after the war ended.

			Checking each option (%)		
	All Respondents (N = 2,312)	Isolationists (N = 120)	Hard-Liners (N = 216)	Accommodationists (N = 1,222)	Internationalists (N = 754)
Before the start of the Gulf War					
I tended to favor using force right away	56	67	86	37	75
I tended to favor giving sanctions a longer time to work	38	23	10	54	22
I tended to oppose getting involved at all	5	10	4	7	2
Not sure	1	1	*	2	1
Retrospectively after the war					
I tended to favor using force right away	61	66	89	44	83
I tended to favor giving sanctions a longer time to work	27	17	5	40	13
I tended to oppose getting involved at all	8	13	4	12	2
Not sure	4	4	2	5	3

Note: Differences both before and after the war significant at the .001 level.
*Less than 0.5 percent.

Isolationists support neither militant nor cooperative internationalism. In this instance, they preferred the use of force to economic sanctions, but they were also the strongest advocates of not getting involved at all.

The opinion leaders were also asked to express agreement or disagreement with ten judgments—five favorable and five unfavorable—of the Persian Gulf War (table 4.8). Each of the five positive judgments received agreement from a majority of the respondents. Four out of five leaders agreed that the war increased U.S. influence and that cooperation with the Soviet Union during the war would enhance the prospects for creating a new world order. Smaller majorities supported assessments that the war was a great U.S. victory, provided leverage for a settlement of other Middle Eastern issues, and "put the Vietnam War behind us." Support for the five unfavorable consequences ranged from 39 percent who felt that the funds spent in the war should have been spent at home to 21 percent who feared that the war would breed overconfidence in the U.S. ability to cope with future foreign threats.

Responses to the Gulf War items by leaders in the four groups provide another example of strong support for the MI/CI scheme. Four of the five favorable consequences received significantly stronger support from hard-liners and internationalists; the item on Soviet-American cooperation yielded a more ambiguous pattern of responses. Conversely, four of the five unfavorable consequences elicited the strongest support from accommodationists and isolationists; as one would expect, the fifth, concerning fears of unwarranted U.S. overconfidence in dealing with future threats, received the strongest support from hard-liners and internationalists. Four of the same items appeared in the 1996 survey and yielded a very similar pattern of responses. Hard-liners and internationalists most strongly agreed that the Gulf War was a great victory, put the Vietnam War behind us, and increased U.S. influence in the world. In contrast, whereas only a minority of leaders stated that the conflict spent money that could better have been used at home, accommodationists and isolationists were significantly more likely to agree. One additional question—that the war should have resulted in the removal from power of Saddam Hussein—elicited support from all four groups, most strongly from the hard-liners (84 percent) and internationalists (78 percent) and somewhat less enthusiastically from the accommodationists and isolationists (63 percent each). Differences among four groups were statistically significant on all of these questions.

TABLE 4.8. Assessments of the Persian Gulf War by Opinion Leaders in 1992: Isolationists, Hard-Liners, Accommodationists, and Internationalists

Here are some assessments of the Persian Gulf War. Please indicate how strongly you agree or disagree with each statement.

	Agree strongly + Agree somewhat (%)				
	All Respondents (N = 2,312)	Isolationists (N = 120)	Hard-Liners (N = 216)	Accommodationists (N = 1,222)	Internationalists (N = 754)
It increased the influence of the United States with other nations	80	79	89	72	90
Soviet-American cooperation before and during the war helped to establish firmer foundations for a new world order	80	73	75	77	86
It was a great victory for the United States	60	57	83	45	78
It has given the United States the leverage needed to gain settlement of other Middle Eastern issues such as the Arab-Israeli conflict	58	44	62	52	70
It put the Vietnam War behind us	55	47	69	44	68
The U.S. spent money abroad that needed to be spent at home	39	31	17	55	22
Too many Iraqis were killed	38	24	10	56	19
The U.S. will be too ready to use military force and go to war again	36	32	13	50	22
It increased frustration and hatred in the Middle East and will bring more violence and terrorism	33	30	20	42	22
The U.S. will be too confident and drop its guard against foreign threats	21	14	37	14	29

Note: Differences among groups significant at the .001 level for all items.

Sources of Change in the USSR and Eastern Europe

Referring to developments in Eastern Europe and the Soviet Union that culminated in destruction of the Berlin Wall, columnist George Will described 1989 as the "most startling, interesting, promising and consequential year, ever" (1989, 90). No doubt that judgment could be challenged, if only because events of the next several years were hardly less intriguing—or less widely predicted by either practitioners or scholarly specialists on Eastern Europe and the Soviet Union.[12]

The 1992 leadership survey, which followed the disintegration of the USSR by only three months, asked respondents to evaluate eight possible explanations for the monumental changes in the Soviet Union and Eastern Europe. The results reveal a pattern of very strong agreement on internal causes and much greater disagreement on external explanations for change. Virtually all respondents, irrespective of their placement in the MI/CI classification scheme, agreed that Soviet internal weakness (97 percent), communism's failure to provide a satisfactory standard of living (95 percent), and Mikhail Gorbachev's reformist policies (92 percent) contributed importantly to the unprecedented changes. A somewhat smaller proportion of opinion leaders (69 percent) agreed that "the desire on the part of the people in the Soviet Union and Eastern Europe to get rid of governments that rule by force" was an important reason for change.

Questions relating to external forces' impact on the Soviet Union and Eastern Europe gave rise to much sharper intergroup differences. The defining characteristics of the four MI/CI groups would suggest that compared to the isolationists and accommodationists—the two groups opposing MI—the hard-liners and internationalists should be more inclined to credit external sources for transformation of the USSR and Eastern Europe. That expectation is supported amply by the data. A preponderance of leaders in all four groups (74 percent) agreed that the Western media contributed importantly to change, with modestly stronger support from the two groups supporting militant internationalism. The same pattern, although with much stronger intergroup differences, emerged on the role of Western defense policies in general and more specifically on the "military build-up by the United States during the Reagan years." The latter question divided the leadership almost evenly, as 48 percent expressed their agreement with it. However, intergroup differences were huge and in the direction predicted by the MI/CI scheme. Whereas three-fourths of the hard-liners and two-thirds of the internationalists agreed that the American military buildup had contributed to changes in the Soviet Union and Eastern Europe, only about half of the isolationists and one-third of the accommodationists expressed the same judgment. Finally, the proposition that the election of a Polish Pope in 1978 could have stimulated change received relatively little support (20 percent), but differences among groups were significant and in the predicted direction in that hard-liners and internationalists were most inclined to agree.

Two competing lines of reasoning presented at the outset of this section hinged on the extent to which the end of the Cold War has altered the structure of beliefs about international affairs. The first predicted that the dramatic events culminating in the disintegration of the USSR would affect the structure of foreign policy beliefs, whereas the second emphasized the likelihood of continuity in belief structures. On balance, evidence from the 1992 and 1996 leadership surveys indicates that positions on MI and CI, yielding four distinct types of belief systems, continue to provide an effective way of depicting opinion leaders' attitude structures on a broad range of issues. From one perspective, this may seem an anomaly in the light of the unprecedented international changes in recent years. From another viewpoint, this finding is less surprising. The MI and CI dimensions correspond closely to the most venerable theories of international relations, realism and liberalism. Inasmuch as the debates between these schools of thought predate the Cold War, it is perhaps not so surprising that, in the main, the MI/CI scheme has continued to identify important elements in the structure of thinking about international affairs.

It must also be acknowledged, however, that the MI/CI scheme is not sufficient to encompass all important aspects of foreign relations. The most notable example of this failure concerns trade-related issues. As mentioned earlier, only a small proportion of leaders rated "economic competition from Japan and Europe" as a major future threat to American security. Several other questions reveal that the pattern of responses is poorly predicted by placement in the four quadrants of the MI/CI scheme. Fewer than one-fourth of the opinion leaders agreed with a proposal to erect "trade barriers against foreign goods to protect American industries and jobs," and only among those in one group—unexpectedly, the internationalists—did support reach as high as 30 percent. And when asked to choose between two economic growth scenarios—Japan grows at a 6.5 percent annual rate and the United States at 2.5 percent or Japan grows at 1.1 percent per year and the United States at 1 percent—57 percent of the entire sample preferred the former option even though the latter scenario would ensure that the Japanese could never catch up with the United States. This is interesting evidence for the debate among proponents of relative gains versus absolute gains as the driving force in foreign affairs; most leaders apparently prefer a better outcome for both countries even if that would enable Japan to close the economic gap with the United States. For present purposes, the more important point is that leaders in all four groups favored the high-growth scenario and that differences among the groups were rather narrow and not statistically significant. Although the MI/CI scheme does not adequately predict responses to trade and protectionism, this does not represent a post–Cold War change in the structure of foreign policy beliefs. Evidence from earlier FPLP surveys revealed that neither the MI/CI scheme nor such otherwise powerful variables as party and ideology effectively predicted positions on international trade (Holsti and Rosenau 1990).

Third, the 1992 and 1996 survey evidence demonstrates that a high level of agreement on structural aspects of the international system does not necessarily predict responses to other issues, whether broad ones such as the most effective approaches to peace or narrower questions such as how best to cope with Iraq's invasion of Kuwait. A central axiom of realist theories is that systemic structures severely constrain, if not dictate, foreign policy choices. However true this may be at the most abstract level—not even superpowers can be totally oblivious to the international environment—this is also a fundamental weakness of structural realism. Realism appropriately points to survival and security as core goals but beyond this does not tell us about the other values and preferences that can affect the selection of goals, strategies, and tactics. An overwhelming majority of American leaders believe that the contemporary international system is multipolar, but by itself, multipolarity does not dictate that major powers must or must not adopt specific international roles, rank foreign policy goals (beyond survival) in a certain order, or pursue or abstain from specific undertakings. Hard-liners usually placed the greatest emphasis on the military dimensions of security, whereas accommodationists were most inclined to focus on international organizations and Third World development issues. These represent quite different policy stances, but it is not possible to derive either approach directly and unambiguously from perceptions about the structure of the international system or to judge their relative merits merely by references to the logic of multipolarity.

A fourth point that emerges from this analysis is that the most contentious and divisive issues revolve around MI rather than CI. Several reasons come to mind. At least 70 percent of the leadership sample has supported CI since 1976, and that figure has increased since the end of the Cold War—that is, roughly three-quarters of respondents are classified as either accommodationists or internationalists (table 4.5). Conversely, the hard-liners and internationalists—those who support militant internationalism—have constituted a minority of fewer than one leader in three. To the extent that one can draw broader conclusions from these figures, they suggest that it may be easier to build domestic coalitions for undertakings abroad that have a tenor of CI rather than MI. The probability of high casualties is also greater in the latter than the former case. This reasoning may offer at least a partial explanation for the broad support behind the 1992 Operation Restore Hope in Somalia (at least until broadening the initial scope of the humanitarian mission into an exercise in nation building led to American casualties), in contrast to the decidedly more lukewarm enthusiasm for military intervention to restore peace in Bosnia. These issues will be raised again in chapter 6, with some attention to both the pre– and post–September 11 evidence.

The Structure of Leaders' Beliefs: Domestic and Foreign Policy

Still another question about belief structures is the relationship between attitudes on domestic and foreign policy issues. Are preferences on domestic issues systematically linked to those international ones, or are the two areas largely independent of each other? As on many questions relating to public opinion, the evidence is mixed. Much of it is derived from analyses generated either by panel studies of the electorate or Gallup and other surveys of the general public. Comparable data about opinion leaders are in much shorter supply.

At first glance it appears that virtually all the findings point toward the conclusion that attitudes about issues in the domestic and international arenas are independent rather than systematically linked. In their study of the 1948 election, Bernard R. Berelson, Paul F. Lazarsfeld, and William N. McPhee found a limited correlation between domestic "position [economic] issues" and either civil rights or foreign policy "style issues." "The dilemma is that the two contemporary axes of liberalism-conservatism, the one economic-class and the other ethnic-international, vary independently of each other. . . . To know, for example, that someone supported the New Deal on economic issues provided no indication of his international or civil rights opinions" (1954, 197–98). Similar findings emerged from several other studies of the electorate. Angus Campbell and his colleagues reported, "Across our sample as a whole in 1956 there was no relationship between scale positions of individuals on the domestic and foreign attitudinal dimensions" (1964, 113). Partisanship characterized responses to domestic issues but not to foreign policy issues. V. O. Key uncovered a similar pattern. Assessing the relationship between internationalism—a willingness to tolerate international involvement—and domestic liberalism, he concluded, "The lines of cleavage in the two policy areas did not coincide" (1961, 158). Philip Converse's (1964) previously cited analysis of belief systems among elites and the general public reported correlations among responses by both groups to domestic and foreign policy issues. He came to the same conclusion. Among the general public, the degree of policy consistency— whether on domestic issues, foreign policy issues, or across the two issue areas—was quite low.

For my present purposes, the more directly relevant question concerns the degree of consistency of views across domestic and foreign policy issues among persons in leadership positions. Compared to data for the general public, evidence about elite attitudes is much scantier. Many findings point toward greater ideological consistency among leaders, and the usual explanations are located in different levels of education and awareness of the issue content associated with such terms as *liberal* and *conservative*. Gabriel Almond's pioneering study, *The American People and Foreign Policy,* asserted the existence of a broad consensus among elites that cut across the two issue areas:

> More basically, this foreign policy consensus is founded upon a consensus of fundamental attitudes and ideologies that may be described in two dimensions—values and means. The advocates of the American foreign consensus are, in general, agreed that the primary aims of American policy, both do-

mestic and foreign, should turn on a reconciliation of individual freedom and mass welfare of a primarily material kind. (1950, 150)

Although Almond did not present systematic survey evidence to buttress his findings on this score, most analysts have tended to agree at least with the point that, compared to the general public, elites are more likely to hold policy positions that are consistent — that is, that their beliefs are held together by some underlying ideological principles. Bruce M. Russett and Elizabeth Hanson surveyed military officers and business leaders and had access to Allen H. Barton's (1974–75) data from a broader spectrum of elites. Russett and Hanson found "dovish [international] and liberal [domestic] attitudes consistently together on the one hand, and conservative [domestic] and hawkish [international] attitudes regularly together on the other" (1975, 138). Similar results emerged from an analysis of a 1984 survey of American opinion leaders as well as from a panel study of American elites (Holsti and Rosenau 1988; Murray 1996).

Despite the indications of a greater propensity for consistency among elites than among the general public, conclusions on this score should be drawn with some caution because contradictory evidence also exists. For example, Norman R. Luttbeg (1968) found no substantial difference between elites and the general public with respect to the structure of their beliefs, a conclusion supported by Eugene R. Wittkopf's (1990) reanalysis of the CCFR surveys. Also, the base of evidence from which tentative conclusions about leadership beliefs may be adduced is rather limited, especially when compared to the mountains of data on the opinions of the general public. Finally, not all elite studies deal with both domestic and foreign policy issues. For example, the CCFR surveys and the first two FPLP surveys are devoid of questions on domestic policy.

The analysis that follows is based on data from the four most recent FPLP surveys; unfortunately, the 1976 and 1980 studies did not include enough domestic issue items to be included in this analysis. The 1984–96 studies encompass three strikingly different international settings, especially in the range of relations between Washington and Moscow. The 1984 survey took place at the height of "Cold War II," when vitriolic rhetoric and arms racing had long since overtaken any manifestations of détente. Only four years later, President Reagan and Chairman Gorbachev were meeting regularly, had signed an unprecedented arms control agreement eliminating an entire class of weapons, and referred to each other as friends rather than as leaders of "evil empires." Startling as the changes between 1984 and 1988 were, they paled in comparison with those of the next four years, which witnessed the end not only of the Cold War but also of the Soviet Union. By 1996 it had become clear that many of the more optimistic scenarios positing warming relations between reformist, democratic, market-oriented Russia and the United States were at best premature. Indeed, it took the 2001 terrorist attacks on New York and Washington to generate a substantial degree of cooperation between Russia and the United States. To summarize very briefly, then, the four surveys spanned the Cold War, the transition from confrontation to cooperation, and the early post–Cold War era. Any findings that persist through such dramatic changes would appear to be very robust indeed.

As a first step toward classifying respondents, scales were created for economic and social issues. The six items for each scale had to meet two criteria: (1) the questions had to appear in each of the four FPLP surveys since 1984; and (2) the questions had to meet several standards for forming a reliable scale. The first criterion excluded several questions that appeared in the later surveys but not in 1984, including items about AIDS testing, the balanced budget amendment, and term limitations for elected officials, all of which scaled well. The 1999 TISS survey also included some of the items on domestic issues.

Table 4.9 summarizes responses for each of the twelve issues in 1984, 1988, 1992, 1996, and 1999. The economic issues scale includes items on taxation, tuition tax credits, regulation, defense spending, and income redistribution; those in the social issues scale focus on several of the most controversial and emotion-laden issues of recent years: school busing, abortion, school prayer, gay rights, the death penalty, and the Equal Rights Amendment (which was replaced in 1999 by an item on the proper workplace for mothers). Virtually all of these issues appear to have played a prominent role in recent elections.

Aggregate responses to these dozen questions reveal a greater degree of stability than change over the fifteen-year period in question. Support for reducing the defense budget increased from 58 percent in 1984 to 75 percent eight years later—a change that no doubt reflects the end of the Cold War—and then declined again in 1996 and 1999; by then it had become

TABLE 4.9. Economic and Social Issues Scales: Surveys of U.S. Opinion Leaders, 1984–99

This question asks you to indicate your position on certain domestic issues. Please indicate how strongly you agree or disagree with each statement.

	Agree strongly + Agree somewhat (%)					
	1984 (N = 2,515)	1988 (N = 2,226)	1992 (N = 2,312)	1996 (N = 2,141)	1999 (N = 1,231)
Economic Issues Scale					
Reducing the federal budget deficit by raising taxes	67	67	66	50	76
Relaxing environmental regulation to stimulate economic growth*	28	16	21	28	23
Providing tuition tax credits to parents who send children to private or parochial schools*	37	35	40	42	45
Reducing the defense budget in order to increase the federal education budget	58	61	75	53	44
Easing restrictions on the construction of nuclear power plants*	39	37	46	38	33
Redistributing income from the wealthy to the poor through taxation and subsidies	43	42	45	41	39
Social Issues Scale					
Busing children in order to achieve school integration	37	39	37	33	32
Leaving abortion decisions to women and their doctors	81	81	79	82	76
Reviving the Equal Rights Amendment	55	54	52	49	—
Encouraging mothers to stay at home with their children rather than working outside the home*	—	—	—	—	46
Permitting prayer in public schools*	38	40	44	47	51
Barring homosexuals from teaching in public schools*	37	33	28	25	23
Banning the death penalty	33	35	33	34	30

Source: Foreign Policy Leadership Project surveys, 1984–96; Triangle Institute for Security Studies survey, 1999.

Note: For items without an asterisk, "agree" responses scored as "liberal" and "disagree" responses scored as "conservative." Reverse scoring used for items with an asterisk.

clear that neither the end of the Cold War nor the victorious Persian Gulf War had ushered in a period of peace and stability. Despite interim fluctuations, questions on two economic issues relating to the environment gave rise to very limited change between 1984 and 1999. The proposition that environmental regulation should be relaxed to stimulate economic growth never stirred much enthusiasm among opinion leaders, even in 1992, when the country was slipping into recession. Slightly more respondents—but never a majority—favored easing restrictions on the construction of nuclear power plants. Responses to the six social issues were even more stable. For four issues—school busing, abortion, the Equal Rights Amendment, and the death penalty—the changes were negligible. Support for school prayer increased by 13 percent, and there was a 14 percent decline among those who favored banning homosexual teachers from public schools.

Correlations among the six items on the economic issues scale were uniformly positive for all four surveys, averaging .31, and those for the social issues scale were also positive in all instances, with a somewhat higher average correlation coefficient of .35. For both scales, Cronbach's alpha ranged between .70 and .78, thus meeting or exceeding the conventional criterion of acceptable scale reliability.

The classification scheme for domestic issues assumes that respondents may have policy preferences on economic issues that do not necessarily correspond ideologically to those on social issues and, therefore, that it is useful to distinguish between them. The terms *liberal* and *conservative* have varied sufficiently in meaning so that their contemporary content cannot be considered self-evident. The present analysis incorporates the following defining premises. With respect to economic issues, liberals were assumed to favor

> an active role for government in regulating the economy;
> an active role for government in regulating activities that may threaten the environment;
> taxation for purposes of income redistribution while opposing tax policies that provide benefits primarily to the more affluent.

On social issues, liberals were assumed to favor

an active role for government in promoting the interests of those who have traditionally been at a disadvantage owing to race, class, gender, or other attributes;

a ban on the death penalty, at least in part because it has been inflicted disproportionately on some traditionally disadvantaged groups.

Conservatives were assumed to favor the following positions on economic issues:

removing or reducing governmental restrictions on economic activity;

reducing taxes;

a large defense budget to ensure a strong national defense.

On social issues, conservatives were assumed to oppose

an active role for government in attempting to legislate equality between classes, sexes, races, and other groups;

an active role for government in support of those who challenge "traditional values."

These premises are incorporated into scoring responses to the twelve items that constitute the domestic issue scales. Agreement with seven of them was scored as "liberal," whereas agreement with the other five (identified by an asterisk in table 4.9) was rated as a "conservative" answer.[13] Each respondent then received two scores, the first based on summed responses to the six economic issues and the second derived from preferences on the six social issues. A cutting point of 0.00 was used for each of the scales.[14] Respondents who scored on the "liberal" side of both the economic and social scales are classified as *liberals,* and those who were on the "conservative" side with respect to both economic and social issues are designated as *conservatives.* Respondents with a liberal position on economic issues and conservative preferences on social issues are labeled *populists.* The final group—those who favored a conservative position on economic issues and a liberal stance on social issues—are the *libertarians.*[15]

According to these criteria, leaders taking part in these four surveys were distributed in the following manner.

Liberals (leaders who were liberal on both the social and economic and issue scales) constituted 45 percent of those taking part in the 1984 survey. The comparable figures for the next three surveys were 48, 47, and 45 percent, respectively.

Conservatives (conservative on both scales) accounted for 33 percent of the 1984 leadership sample. Their numbers fell to 28 percent in 1988 and to 27 percent four years later but rose to 35 in 1996.

Populists (conservative on the social issues scale and liberal on the economic issues scale) made up 15 percent of leaders in the 1984 study. That group increased to 17 percent four years later and to 19 percent in 1992 before falling to 11 percent in the latest survey.

Libertarians (liberals on social issues and conservatives on economic issues) constituted 7 percent of the entire leadership sample in each of the first three surveys and rose to 9 percent in 1996.

Several points emerge from the distribution of respondents. First, of the two underlying dimensions, the social issues appear to be more divisive than the economic ones. Second, although the liberals and conservatives constitute a strong majority of the entire leadership sample, there are enough populists and libertarians to support the premise that a single ideological scale is not sufficient to capture preferences on both economic and social issues. Liberals and conservatives combined to account for 78 percent of the total in 1984, declined slightly in the next two surveys, and increased to 80 percent in 1996. The populist group increased between 1984 and 1992, mostly at the expense of the conservatives, but then fell sharply four years later. The libertarians—social liberals and economic conservatives—have consistently constituted the smallest of the four groups.

Domestic and Foreign Policy Beliefs, 1984–1996

We can get a summary assessment of the extent to which positions on domestic and foreign policy are related by combining the classification schemes for the two types of issues in the four leadership surveys under consideration (table 4.10). The distributions indicate that there is a rather strong correspondence, a conclusion supported by the summary statistic phi, which ranges from

TABLE 4.10. Relationship between Domestic Issues Typology (Liberals, Conservatives, Populists, Libertarians) and Militant and Cooperative Internationalism (Accommodationists, Internationalists, Hard-Liners, Isolationists) among U.S. Opinion Leaders, 1984–96 (in percentages)

Economic Issues

Social Issues: Liberal

Liberal — Liberals	1984	1988	1992	1996
Accommodationists	79	79	79	73
Isolationists	6	6	3	7
Internationalists	12	12	16	10
Hard-liners	3	3	2	1

Conservative — Libertarians	1984	1988	1992	1996
Accommodationists	46	44	43	46
Isolationists	10	10	8	13
Internationalists	30	31	40	31
Hard-liners	14	16	9	10

Social Issues: Conservative

Liberal — Populists	1984	1988	1992	1996
Accommodationists	44	40	44	40
Isolationists	8	8	5	10
Internationalists	34	38	44	42
Hard-liners	15	15	7	8

Conservative — Conservatives	1984	1988	1992	1996
Accommodationists	16	14	16	19
Isolationists	7	9	8	13
Internationalists	39	37	51	37
Hard-liners	38	40	25	32

Note: Phi for 1984 = .60; 1988 = .61; 1992 = .56; 1996 = .55

.55 to .61. A strong and consistent majority of domestic liberals are also foreign policy accommodationists—that is, they support CI and oppose MI. Conversely, almost equal proportions of the domestic conservatives are either foreign policy hard-liners or internationalists, the two groups that favor MI. With respect to foreign policy issues, the populists and libertarians are quite similar; both are predominantly accommodationists and internationalists. These are the two groups that favor CI. One possible interpretation is that although both populists and libertarians favor CI, their reasons for doing so differ. The former (economic liberals) may support CI because they prefer government spending for domestic rather than defense purposes and thus less enthusiastic about MI; perhaps the latter (economic conservatives) do so because they oppose the type of "big government" that almost invariably attends wars, crises, confrontations, and extensive commitments abroad.

For a more detailed picture of the relationship between domestic and foreign policy preferences, table 4.11 presents responses by leaders in the four MI/CI groups to a wide range of domestic issues, including seven that were not used to create the domestic issues scales (see table 4.9). The results reveal strong and consistent differences among the four groups defined by their foreign policy views, although in a few cases the statistical significance of intergroup differences is less compelling than the commonalities. Erecting trade barriers and legalizing drugs gained very limited support among any of the four groups. Interestingly, two of the most incendiary issues of recent years, abortion and gun control, gave rise to overwhelming majorities. More than 80 percent of the leaders favored leaving abortion decisions to women and their physicians, a position that gained the support of no less than three-fifths of any group. A comparable majority favored strict control of handgun sales, although on this issue a small majority of the hard-liners disagreed.

An obvious question that emerges from these findings is whether some more fundamental overarching beliefs link views on domestic and foreign policy beliefs. If there are, these might be somewhat comparable to but broader than the "core values" that Jon Hurwitz and Mark Peffley (1987) identified on their hierarchical model of foreign policy attitudes. At best, the FPLP data lend themselves to speculation rather than any definitive answers. One candidate might be the degree to which one believes in carrots (incentives) or sticks (penalties) as the most effective means of influence and social control. Does this simple proposition explain, at least in part, the links among hard-line attitudes toward foreign affairs (the primacy of military force, deterrent threats, and so on), conservatism on social issues (belief in the efficacy of capital punishment, support for the use of state power to enforce certain standards of conduct), and conservatism on economic issues (support for high defense budgets, reliance on markets to mete out penalties and rewards)?

Conversely, do comparable links exist among an accommodationist view on foreign affairs (support for foreign aid and other forms of rewards, emphasis on issues that lend themselves to bargaining and negotiation), liberalism on social issues (support for state incentives to reduce or eliminate differences in opportunities and perhaps outcomes as well), and economic liberalism (preferences for redistributive policies, restrictions on the penalties arising from market forces)? Obviously, this is at best highly speculative.

Conclusion

Despite fears expressed during the past six decades by presidents and other top leaders, the evidence presented in chapter 3 indicates that even in the wake of the disastrous Vietnam War, the American public has not retreated into an indiscriminate isolationism. A more specific question, for which the evidence presented here is certainly not conclusive, is whether Americans have adopted a stance that will accept international undertakings only as long as they involve no casualties (see, for example, Luttwak 1994; Friedman 1995; A. Schlesinger 1995; for more detailed analyses, see E. Larson 1996; Eichenberg 2003). As noted earlier, proponents of this thesis point to the 1993 decision to withdraw U.S. forces from Somalia almost immediately after eighteen troops were killed in a firefight as well as to the decision not to land forces in Haiti after a dockside demonstration suggested that there might be some resistance to the landing. Opponents point to the Persian Gulf War to buttress their argument that casualties will be accepted for undertakings that have clear goals. The distinction drawn by Bruce W. Jentleson (1992) between the use of force to restrain aggressor states, as in the Gulf War, and to impose internal political changes within another state, as in Somalia and Haiti, seems relevant to this debate. He found that the public support is higher in the former than the latter cases. Evidence

TABLE 4.11. Domestic Policy Preferences: Isolationists, Hard-Liners, Accommodationists, and Internationalists in the 1996 FPLP Survey of U.S. Opinion Leaders

This question asks you to indicate your position on certain domestic issues. Please indicate how strongly you agree or disagree with each statement.

	All Respondents (N = 2,141)	Isolationists (N = 217)	Hard-Liners (N = 288)	Accommodationists (N = 1,020)	Internationalists (N = 616)
Busing children in order to achieve school integration	34	19	8	49	25
Reducing federal budget deficits by raising taxes	50	42	22	66	40
Relaxing environmental regulation to stimulate economic growth	28	37	61	13	34
Providing tuition tax credits to parents who send children to private or parochial schools	42	46	71	29	48
Leaving abortion decisions to women and their doctors	82	82	60	89	80
Reviving the Equal Rights Amendment	49	42	15	61	47
Permitting prayer in public schools	46	47	73	18	39
Erecting trade barriers against foreign goods to protect American industries and jobs	22	20	27	16	31

Reducing the defense budget in order to increase the federal education budget	54	44	14	72	45
Barring homosexuals from teaching in public schools	25	30	54	11	32
Restricting the number of terms elected officials may serve	52	51	71	41	60
Easing restrictions on the construction of nuclear power plants	38	43	64	27	42
Redistributing income from the wealthy to the poor through taxation and subsidies	41	29	11	58	31
Banning the death penalty	34	20	9	51	21
Adding a balanced budget amendment to the Constitution	44	53	70	29	58
Requiring that applicants for marriage licenses, insurance policies, and some jobs be tested for AIDS	61	63	74	49	73
Legalizing drugs such as cocaine in order to reduce drug-related crimes	28	32	21	35	20
Reducing the growth of spending for Medicare and Medicaid	67	75	84	61	69
Placing stringent controls on the sale of handguns	82	75	48	93	91

Note: Differences among groups significant at the .001 level for all items.

from another series of surveys suggests that the public is not unequivocally set against the use of force, even in such civil wars as Somalia, Bosnia, and Haiti (Kull and Ramsay 1993a, 1994a, 1994b).

However, the data summarized in this chapter provide additional support for the proposition that in comparison to the general public, leaders have been consistently more inclined to support an active international role for the United States. This conclusion appears to be valid both at the most general level and across a wide variety of more specific issues.

The policy implications of these divergences between leaders and the general public depend in substantial part on one's conception of the American polity and the role that public opinion plays in that political system. I will explore this question further in chapter 7. Suffice it to say for now that if one assumes that top officials and opinion leaders will have an overwhelming influence in shaping the primary features of American foreign policy and that the general public will have little or no influence and will play a role primarily as the target of elite manipulation, the evidence suggests that the United States will continue to pursue an internationalist foreign policy, broadly defined. In that case, the debates are likely to center on how the United States participates in global affairs: the hard-liners and accommodationists will put forward quite different blueprints in answer to that question and will express sharply different preferences about the appropriate means to be employed. If, however, public preferences play a significant role in shaping at least the broad contours of American foreign policy, the policy debates may also include discussion of the extent that the United States should play an active international role as opposed to focusing on issues that have a direct domestic impact. Although there is little indication of a wholesale rush "back to the womb," the evidence does suggest that, compared to leaders, the general public is somewhat less enthusiastic about some important aspects of foreign affairs, including trade liberalization, immigration, foreign aid, and deployment of troops to areas outside traditional U.S. interests. In that eventuality, some aspects of the debates are likely to pit the internationalist vision of America's proper role in the world against that espoused by the isolationists.

Although the evidence on the structural features of foreign policy attitudes is somewhat less conclusive, there appears to be some convergence in the ways that leaders and the general public think about international affairs. The data summarized previously suggest that two dimensions of internationalism—the militant and cooperative versions—capture a good deal, although surely not all, of the variance. The convergence of attitudes on domestic and foreign policy issues also suggests at least a moderate degree of ideological coherence in leaders' political beliefs. This will be welcome news for critics on both the right and left who lament what they believe to be an excessive pragmatism and disregard for ideological principles in American politics. Others may be less certain that the erosion of crosscutting cleavages augurs well for the tenor and content of political debates.

Finally, these findings bring up questions about the sources and correlates of foreign policy attitudes among both the general public and opinion leaders. I will turn to these questions in chapter 5.

CHAPTER 5

Sources of Foreign Policy Attitudes

During the mid-1980s, three perceptive analysts of American foreign policy, one of whom later served as National Security Adviser to President Clinton, asserted, "For two decades, the making of American foreign policy has been growing far more political—or more precisely, far more partisan and ideological" (Destler, Gelb, and Lake 1984, 13). Although their observation was not specifically focused on or limited to public opinion, it brings up a number of interesting questions related to the sources of public attitudes. First, in pointing to partisanship and ideology, did these authors properly locate the main fault lines on the American political landscape? More specifically, do party and ideology reinforce each other as sources of foreign policy attitudes, or are they, as in some earlier periods of American history, essentially independent of each other? Is it even possible that they create crosscutting cleavages? Second, are there other sources of foreign policy attitudes that compete with or perhaps even supersede the impact of partisanship and ideology? Extensive post-Vietnam debates have identified some other prominent candidates, most notably generation and gender, as potent sources of foreign policy attitudes.

Third, are the demographic sources of foreign policy attitudes stable across issues? Across time? These questions are essentially variants of a broader one encountered in the first three chapters. Those who hold that an ill-informed public possesses little more than "nonattitudes" about politics—and especially about world affairs—would expect the demographic correlates of attitudes to be weak and unstable. If much of the public responds to foreign affairs in an almost random manner and if their reactions to such issues are anchored in little more than the mood of the moment, then one would not expect to find powerful and enduring correlations between demographic attributes and foreign policy attitudes. The alternative view is that the public may effectively use simple—or even simplistic—guidelines to help make some sense of the complex and remote actors, issues, and events that constitute foreign affairs. Do such permanent or relatively stable background characteristics as gender, generation, education, and race play any significant role in that process? Other attributes, including party and ideological preferences, are more easily subject to change but, if I. M. Destler, Leslie Gelb, and Anthony Lake are correct, the impact of these attributes has increased. Which, if any, of these factors has been consistently related to ways of thinking about foreign policy?

The final question concerns how the end of the Cold War may have affected the sources of foreign policy attitudes. The era of systematic public opinion polling was scarcely a decade old when an era of confrontation, punctuated by periodic crises, superseded the wartime cooperation between Washington and Moscow. The vast bulk of the data, theories, hypotheses, and analyses of public opinion derive from the more than four decades of the Cold War. Given the central role of Soviet-American relations, not only in global affairs but also in shaping foreign policy attitudes, how can we be sure that the theories and findings generated during the decades prior to the disintegration of the Soviet Union are sufficiently robust to survive into the post–Cold War era? For example, even if Destler, Gelb, and Lake were correct in identifying partisanship and ideology as the primary sources of cleavages of foreign policy during the early years of the Reagan administration, is it possible that their diagnosis is no longer valid as we are fully in the second decade after the Cold War? After all, Ronald Reagan, a highly partisan and ideological president, underwent an almost complete reversal in attitudes about the USSR during his presidency, as did the general public.[1] Because many of the deepest partisan cleavages of the 1970s and 1980s centered on strategies and tactics for dealing with Moscow and related Cold War issues, could the disintegration of the Soviet Union have also brought about a significant erosion of partisan and ideological stances on foreign affairs?

This chapter will explore these questions and examine some relevant evidence from both the general public and opinion leaders. In addition to reviewing findings that emerged from research during the Cold War, we will examine at least some evidence from the period since the end of that conflict. Reactions to one event will receive special attention: the Persian Gulf War, the culmination of events precipitated by Iraq's August 2, 1990, invasion of Kuwait, has been described as the "mother of all polling events" (Mueller 1994, xiv). It may well have been the subject of more public opinion surveys than any prior episode of comparable duration.[2] Because it was a victorious undertaking that took place over a relatively short period and resulted in relatively light U.S. casualties, the Gulf War avoided at least three of the characteristics that ultimately ignited widespread public opposition to the conflict in Vietnam. These reasons, combined with the unambiguous nature of Iraq's action and the character of its leaders, suggest that the Gulf War should be a strong candidate for the "rally round the flag" phenomenon. If, in fact, vast numbers of Americans, irrespective of party, ideology, and other attributes, rallied behind the administration, the impact of background characteristics would be suppressed rather than heightened.[3] Conversely, any demographic correlates of foreign policy attitudes that persisted in these circumstances would be especially significant. The impact of the tragic terrorist attacks on New York and Washington and the subsequent war against Iraq will be assessed separately in chapter 6.

The pages that follow will begin with the impact of party, followed by ideology, generation, gender, education, region, and race. Surveys have not always probed for each of these respondent attributes; thus, the evidence is not equally plentiful for each of them.

Political Party

The General Public

Two generalizations about American politics, if valid, would lead to the expectation that party affiliation is at best weakly linked to foreign policy attitudes. The first is that the two major parties are broad coalitions that cut across rather than between ideological orientations or other major sources of beliefs. The second stipulates that, however divided Americans may be on domestic questions, bipartisanship rather than partisanship is the rule on foreign policy issues. "Politics stops at the water's edge" has been a favorite slogan of countless orators on the hustings as well as presidents who seek to stifle criticism of their policies from members of the other political party.

Whether these generalizations were ever an even moderately

accurate depiction of the foreign policy process over any period is open to question. It would be hard to deny that partisan differences colored debates on issues as diverse as responses to the wars arising from the French Revolution, the tariff issue at various times during the nineteenth and early twentieth centuries, and the question of American participation in the League of Nations. Conversely, deliberate efforts by the Roosevelt administration to develop a bipartisan coalition in support of American membership in the United Nations were highly successful, and the Hull-Dulles agreement assured that the United Nations would not become a partisan issue in the 1944 presidential election. As a result of these efforts, the United Nations Treaty won Senate approval the following year by an overwhelming vote of eighty-nine to two. During the early post–World War II years, bipartisan cooperation between the White House and Congress on many issues related to Europe made possible such initiatives as aid to Greece and Turkey (the Truman Doctrine), the Marshall Plan, and the North Atlantic Treaty Organization (NATO).[4] Each of these striking departures from traditional American foreign policies had rather solid public support. Agreement among prominent leaders of the two major parties no doubt contributed to the fact that, among the general public, Democrats and Republicans differed little with respect to these and other major internationalist foreign policy undertakings. For example, a 1946 Gallup survey revealed that 72 percent of respondents in both political parties favored an "active" international role for the United States, and the 1947 program of aid to Greece and Turkey also received identical levels of approval from Democrats and Republicans (table 5.1).

Issues relating to the Far East tended to be more contentious and placed greater strains on bipartisan cooperation, especially after the Truman-MacArthur confrontation during the first year of the Korean War. The president's decision to dismiss MacArthur, culminating a dispute that reflected some fundamental differences about civil-military relations as well as the appropriate conduct of the Korean War, was not popular among Democrats (opposed 53 to 30 percent), independents (51 to 30 percent), or (especially) Republicans (72 to 17 percent).[5] But even on most issues related to Asia, survey data revealed limited partisan differences. For example, the decision to resist aggression in Korea, the move to aid the Chinese government in Taiwan, and a proposal to send American forces to Indochina as the French effort there was collapsing found Republicans and Democrats about equally supportive or critical.

To be sure, by 1952, American participation in the Korean War — "Harry Truman's War," as critics often called it — had lost far more support among Republicans than among Democrats, but sharp partisan divisions on foreign and defense policy did not persist into the Eisenhower years. Even though the defense budget had become a controversial issue in 1960, with charges from Senator John F. Kennedy and other prominent Democrats

TABLE 5.1.   Partisanship on Selected Foreign and Defense Policy Issues: The General Public, 1946–63

Date	Issue[a]	Response	Republican	Democrat	Independent
			Responses by Party Affiliation (%)[b]		
February 1946	Role U.S. should play in world affairs	Active	72	72	NR
		Stay out	23	22	NR
March 1947	Aid to Greece (Truman Doctrine)	Approve	56	56	NR
		Disapprove	31	32	NR
April 1948	Should U.S. and all European Marshall Plan nations join in a permanent military alliance?	Yes	66	68	57
		No	22	16	29
July 1948	Evaluation of U.S. policy toward Soviet Union	Too soft	73	70	NR
		Too tough	3	4	NR
		About right	14	14	NR
February 1950	Defense budget	Too much	16	12	18
		Too little	22	25	24
		About right	46	46	40
July 1950	Send military supplies to Chiang Kai-shek government on Taiwan	Should	48	50	NR
		Should not	39	32	NR
July 1951	Send U.S. troops to Europe or keep them at home to defend the Americas	Europe	53	61	49
		At home	39	30	38
May 1954	Send U.S. troops to Indochina	Approve	18	22	17
		Disapprove	76	70	72
June 1955	Should the U.S. and Russia work out a trade agreement?	Should	55	57	54
		Should not	33	27	29
December 1956	Approve foreign aid to help stop communism	Yes	59	58	58
		No	28	28	28
January 1963	Foreign aid	For	54	59	61
		Against	35	28	28

Source: Gallup Organization surveys.
[a]Summary statement of the issue rather than the exact wording of the question asked.
[b]Excludes "no opinion," "not sure," and "don't know" responses.
NR = Not reported.

that a complacent Eisenhower administration had permitted a dangerous "missile gap" to develop, a Gallup poll revealed that differences attributable to party loyalties were relatively modest. Although more Democrats (24 percent) than Republicans (15 percent) asserted that the Pentagon was receiving "too little" in the Eisenhower budget, far more respondents in both political parties judged defense spending to be "about right." Even foreign aid programs received approximately similar levels of support from adherents of the major political parties. Republican nominee Barry Goldwater's 1964 attacks on the "eastern establishment" that had provided an important base for bipartisanship in foreign and defense policy issues and his campaign theme that the GOP should offer voters a "choice, not an echo," proved to be insufficiently persuasive to avert a landslide electoral loss. The absence of strong partisan cleavages extended into the early years of the Vietnam War, as majorities within both parties expressed strong support for the Johnson administration's policies.[6]

For two decades spanning the Truman, Eisenhower, Kennedy, and early Johnson administrations, then, whatever differences divided the American public on foreign policy issues rarely fell along a cleavage defined by partisan loyalties. Writing in the 1970s, Barry Hughes concluded that the "evidence points overwhelmingly to insignificant party differences in the general population" on most foreign policy issues (1978, 128). Indeed, before Vietnam, the distribution of attitudes among supporters of the two major parties was sufficiently similar that the self-identified independents usually stood on one side or another of the Democrats and Republicans rather than between them.

The period since the end of the Vietnam War has witnessed the emergence of striking partisan differences on a broad range of issues relating to foreign and defense policy. The very concept of bipartisanship came under increased attacks from several quarters; by 1979 a leading Republican senator called for its termination and for a return to a frankly partisan foreign policy. At the same time, efforts by several administrations to create a foreign policy consensus fell short of enduring success. The Nixon-Kissinger campaign to create a post-Vietnam foreign policy consensus grounded in détente with the Soviet Union ultimately failed. Attempts by the Carter administration to achieve the same goal through an emphasis on human rights and by the first Reagan administration to create a consensus around a more assertive and confrontational stance toward the Soviet Union were equally unavailing in the longer run.

During the years immediately following the 1975 evacuation of the last Americans from Saigon, pollsters generally concentrated on such domestic issues as inflation, unemployment, and crime because they seemed to be of the most immediate concern to much of the public. Even the controversial question of how the United States should respond to the civil war in Angola did not elicit a probe from the Gallup organization. Data on foreign policy attitudes became more plentiful during the 1980s, however, and reveal clearly that sharp and persistent partisan differences characterized most issues related to the Cold War (table 5.2). Defense budget increases initiated by President Carter and escalated by President Reagan, the intervention in Lebanon, the proper U.S. role in the civil wars in Central America, and proposals to place economic sanctions on South Africa were among the controversial issues that gave rise to very substantial differences between Republicans and Democrats. The bifurcation along partisan lines was sufficiently great that, unlike during the pre-Vietnam period, responses of political independents typically fell between those of Democrats and Republicans.

Toward the end of the 1980s, however, the evidence also reveals some diminution of partisan differences on questions linked most closely to Soviet-American relations. A sense of diminishing threat from the USSR, shared by members of both major parties, no doubt reflected the emergence of "détente II" during the period following Mikhail Gorbachev's accession to power in the Kremlin and coinciding with Ronald Reagan's second presidential term. By the time Reagan left the White House in 1989, almost half of Republicans assessed the Soviet Union as no more than a "minor threat," and 60 percent of Democrats responded in a like manner. In light of a rather strong Republican tendency toward skepticism regarding the Kremlin during the Reagan years, it is perhaps more than a little ironic that, four months after disintegration of the USSR, Republicans outstripped Democrats by a margin of 64 to 46 percent in supporting assistance to the former Soviet Union. Indeed, the proposed aid package received the highest approval from various groups often more closely associated with the GOP than the Democrats: white, male, higher-income college graduates (G. Gallup Jr. 1992, 71–72).

Several Gallup surveys since the early 1990s yielded evidence of both partisan differences and bipartisan convergence. When

TABLE 5.2. Partisanship on Selected Foreign and Defense Policy Issues: The General Public, 1977–2003

Date/Poll	Issue[a]	Response	Responses by Party Affiliation (%)[b]		
			Republican	Democrat	Independent
June 1977	Withdrawal of U.S. troops from South Korea	Favor	32	47	36
		Oppose	51	30	41
March 1982	Defense budget	Too much	18	43	39
		Too little	27	16	18
		About right	46	32	36
October 1983	A mistake to send marines to Lebanon?	Yes, mistake	36	61	50
		No	53	29	36
January 1985	Defense budget	Too much	29	60	49
		Too little	15	7	10
		About right	49	27	35
May 1985	Trade embargo against Nicaragua	Approve	65	26	45
		Disapprove	16	58	38
March 1986	Should the U.S. provide an aid package to the contras in Nicaragua?	Should	44	29	34
		Should not	44	60	51
July 1991	Decision to remove economic sanctions against South Africa	Approve	56	35	45
		Disapprove	22	39	31
April 1992	Plan to join other nations in providing various types of aid to former Soviet Union	Favor	64	46	50
		Oppose	33	50	45
July 1993	Should immigration be kept at its present level, increased, or decreased?	Present level	26	33	23
		Increased	4	7	9
		Decreased	69	59	65
October 1995	The job the UN is doing in solving problems it has had to face	Good	33	45	32
		Poor	55	41	51

Date	Item	Response			
December 1995	Presence of U.S. troops in Bosnia	Approve	30	57	36
		Disapprove	67	37	58
June 1999	Presence of U.S. ground troops, with troops from other countries, in a Kosovo peacekeeping force	Favor	57	73	65
		Oppose	15	12	14
July 2000	Build a missile defense system	Favor	63	51	47
		Oppose	N/R	N/R	N/R
October 2000	Reestablish diplomatic relations with Cuba	Favor	50	61	54
		Oppose	N/R	N/R	N/R
January 2002	Military action to end Saddam Hussein's rule in Iraq	Favor	78	58	62
		Oppose	14	28	28
April 2003	Do you think that in the future the U.S. should:	Feel more free to use force without UN authorization	48	24	38
		Not feel more free to use force without UN authorization	49	74	58
September 2003	U.S. decision to use military force against Iraq	Right decision	85	43	63
		Wrong decision	9	50	33
September 2003	Give up some control over military decisions to get other nations to provide troops for Iraq	Yes	37	63	53
		No	57	29	42

Source: Gallup Organization surveys, except the final four items are from Pew Research Center survey in 2002 and three PIPA surveys in 2003.

[a] Summary statement of the issue rather than the exact wording of the question asked.

[b] Excludes "no opinion," "not sure," and "don't know" responses.

N/R: Not reported.

asked, "Should immigration be kept at the present level, increased, or decreased?" substantial majorities in both parties preferred the decreasing immigration. California voters' overwhelming approval in 1994 of Proposition 187, which was supported by Republican candidates for the governorship and the U.S. Senate and opposed by their Democratic counterparts, also suggests the emergence of a bipartisan agreement on a restrictive immigration policy. Further evidence on this point emerged from the 1994 Chicago Council on Foreign Relations (CCFR) survey: the general public ranked "controlling and reducing illegal immigration" as the fourth-most-important foreign policy goal, with almost three-fourths of the respondents rating it "very important" (Rielly 1995, 15).

Employment of U.S. troops abroad yielded sharp partisan differences, with approval from 30 percent of the Republicans and almost twice as many Democrats. In contrast, American participation in peacekeeping operations in a Serbian region of the former Yugoslavia—Kosovo—found a 16 percent partisan gap but, more importantly, majority support from both Republicans and Democrats. Three additional issues also yielded overall support among members of both major parties and large partisan gaps: building a missile defense system, reestablishing diplomatic relations with Cuba, and using military action to remove Saddam Hussein from power in Iraq. Even after the invasion of Iraq had achieved this goal, the question of using force without United Nations authorization remained a source of sharp partisan differences, with Republicans evenly divided on the issues and Democrats opposed by a margin of three to one.

For reasons cited earlier, the Persian Gulf War in 1991 provides a good opportunity to determine the extent to which partisan foreign policy differences among the general public have persisted or dissolved in the post–Cold War period. The naked Iraqi aggression against Kuwait, Saddam Hussein's well-deserved reputation for exceptional brutality, and the absence of a risk that the crisis would turn into a dangerous confrontation between Washington and Moscow would be expected to increase the prospects for bipartisan support of American policies. Table 5.3 reports the results from a very small sample of the many Gallup surveys on the situation in the Persian Gulf area undertaken before the initiation of the American air war on Iraq, during the conflict, and in its aftermath. Excluded are all the many questions that mentioned President George H. W. Bush by name: for example, "Do you approve of the way George Bush is handling the current situation in the Middle East involving Kuwait?" (January 6, 1991; see G. Gallup Jr. 1991). Such questions could be expected to inflate partisan divisions among the public; in fact, they did so by about 10 percent compared to similar questions in which the president was not named.

The evidence indicates that, although the Bush administration enjoyed a high degree of overall public support for its Persian Gulf policies—notably with respect to the decision to initiate a war within hours after the January 15, 1991, deadline for Iraqi

TABLE 5.3.   Attitudes on Selected Issues Relating to the Persian Gulf Conflict, before, during, and after the War: The Impact of Party

Date	Question	All	Repub-licans	Demo-crats	Indepen-dents
Prewar surveys					
Jan. 13, 1991	Do you think the United States made a mistake in sending troops to Saudi Arabia, or not? [% yes]	29	18	39	30
Jan. 13, 1991	Which of the following comes closest to your opinion? Favor: withdraw; sanctions; war. [% initiate a war]	50	62	40	52
Wartime surveys					
Jan. 20, 1991	Do you approve or disapprove of the U.S. decision to go to war in order to drive the Iraqis out of Kuwait? [% approve]	80	91	70	80
Jan. 26, 1991	Do you favor or oppose using tactical nuclear weapons against Iraq if it might save the lives of U.S. troops? [% favor]	45	46	45	46
Jan. 26, 1991	Would you favor or oppose a law to ban peace demonstrations while U.S. troops are fighting overseas? [% favor]	31	31	37	26
Feb. 17, 1991	Do you favor or oppose the U.S. use of tactical nuclear weapons in the Persian Gulf War? [% favor]	28	31	30	25
Postwar surveys					
July 14, 1991	All in all, was the current situation in the Mideast involving Iraq and Kuwait worth going to war over, or not? [% yes]	66	80	54	64
July 21, 1991	Looking back, do you approve or disapprove of the U.S. decision last January to go to war with Iraq in order to drive the Iraqis out of Kuwait? [% approve]	78	91	67	74

Source: Gallup Organization surveys. The typical survey was spread out over a 3–4 day period. The first column reports the final date of the survey.

withdrawal from Kuwait had expired—rather substantial partisan differences may nevertheless be found in survey responses before, during, and after the conflict.[7] Only three of the questions in table 5.3, two of them dealing with the possible use of nuclear weapons, failed to yield significant differences. Strong majorities within both parties opposed the use of tactical nuclear weapons against Iraq, although nearly half of both Democrats and Republicans were willing to do so "if it might save the lives of U.S. troops." A proposition to ban peace demonstrations during the conflict found favor from only about one-third of the respondents, with only a moderate gap between members of the two major parties. Each of the remaining questions gave rise to substantial differences ranging from 21 to 26 percent. Moreover, these cleavages were not bridged as a consequence of the successful military campaign to drive Iraqi forces out of Kuwait.

Although some degree of disenchantment with the war effort emerged later in the year—apparently as the result of Saddam Hussein's ability to stay in power and to attack with impunity the Shiite and Kurdish minorities within Iraq—public assessments several months after the cease-fire found that the overall approval of American actions was distributed very unevenly across parties. Stated differently, the longer-term consequences of the Persian Gulf conflict did not appear to have included a lasting, bipartisan post–Cold War foreign policy consensus among the general public. It remains to be seen whether comparable cleavages have divided opinion leaders.

Opinion Leaders

As noted earlier, compared to the vast collections of systematic data on the general public, information on opinion leaders for the decades prior to the Vietnam War is in relatively short supply. The available evidence, some of it including indirect indicators, would seem to point to two conclusions.

First, partisan differences among leaders probably exceeded those found among the general public. To be sure, debates and votes on some of the most important foreign policy issues in Congress—including but not limited to the United Nations Treaty, Truman Doctrine, Marshall Plan, and NATO—tended not to follow strictly partisan lines. The Truman and Eisenhower administrations worked fairly effectively on many foreign policy issues with Congresses dominated by the opposition party during periods of divided government in 1947–49 and 1955–61. Indeed, Eisenhower faced more consistent and vocal opposition from right-wing members of the GOP—for example, from Senators William Knowland, Joseph McCarthy, William Jenner, and John Bricker—during the years of Republican control of Congress (1953–55) than from Democrats. A classic study of executive-legislative relations during this period found that the president was typically better able to get congressional support on foreign policy than on domestic issues (Wildavsky 1966). Even debates during the election campaigns that gave rise to changes in control of the White House in 1953 and 1961 focused more on implementation and administration of American foreign and defense policies than on the principles underlying such basic policies as containment, deterrence, alliance membership, economic and military assistance programs, and the like.

Conversely, evidence of partisan differences among leaders is also available. A study of party leaders and followers during the 1950s revealed that partisan gaps on several international questions were greater among the former than the latter (McCloskey, Hoffmann, and O'Hara 1960). Similarly, an analysis of congressional voting on all foreign policy issues, rather than just the most consequential ones cited earlier, also found evidence of partisanship, especially after the Korean War (Wittkopf 1990). Finally, the occasional Gallup special surveys of *Who's Who in America* biographees suggest some partisan differences on such issues as the Bricker Amendment to restrict executive treaty-making powers and on the admission of communist China to the United Nations. The latter issue gave rise to an especially wide partisan gap, as half of the Democrats favored bringing the Beijing regime into the world organizations, whereas only 20 percent of Republicans did so.[8]

The second major conclusion is that partisan cleavages among leaders widened considerably during the 1970s and 1980s. Since the end of the Vietnam War, systematic data about the foreign policy attitudes of opinion leaders have become much more plentiful. Most of the evidence provides considerable support for Destler, Gelb, and Lake's observation, cited at the beginning of this chapter, about the growing partisan chasm on foreign policy issues during the post-Vietnam era. This point emerges clearly, for example, from studies of business and military leaders as well as secondary analyses of the small elite samples in the quadrennial CCFR surveys (Russett and Hanson 1975; Wittkopf 1990).

The Foreign Policy Leadership Project (FPLP) surveys, extending from 1976 through 1996, also found quite striking differences among Republicans, Democrats, and independents on a wide range of foreign policy issues. When respondents to each of the surveys are classified as *hard-liners, isolationists, internationalists,* or *accommodationists,* a clear and consistent pattern of partisan differences emerges (table 5.4). In each survey, more than 60 percent of Republicans are either hard-liners or internationalists, the two groups that expressed support for militant internationalism. Equally substantial majorities among the Democrats were accommodationists, a group defined as opposing militant internationalism while supporting cooperative internationalism. The end of the Cold War witnessed some movement among Republicans away from hard-line and internationalist positions and toward an isolationist one. In contrast, the positions of Democrats remained relatively stable over the twenty-year period in question, although the number of internationalists increased with the end of the Cold War. Perhaps the only point of strong agreement among these leaders is that few of them—whether Repub-

TABLE 5.4.   The Relationship between Party and Foreign Policy Orientations among American Opinion Leaders, 1976–96

Of the leaders who identify themselves as . . .	Year	The percentage whose foreign policy attitudes classify them as . . .			
		Hard-liners	Isola-tionists	Interna-tionalists	Accomoda-tionists
Republicans	1976	34	7	39	21
	1980	34	7	43	17
	1984	34	6	40	20
	1988	34	7	40	20
	1992	17	6	52	25
	1996	26	13	37	24
Democrats	1976	9	7	22	62
	1980	9	7	25	60
	1984	6	6	14	74
	1988	4	7	13	76
	1992	3	3	19	75
	1996	3	6	24	67
Independents	1976	21	8	33	38
	1980	20	6	34	40
	1984	12	8	25	54
	1988	13	8	24	55
	1992	9	7	29	55
	1996	11	10	28	51

Note: Phi for 1976 = .55; 1980 = .61; 1984 = .60; 1988 = .63; 1992 = .54; 1996 = .42.

licans, Democrats, or independents — are isolationists. The correlation between party and foreign policy orientation remained consistently high, never falling below .40 in any of the surveys.

We can gain a more detailed view of how the end of the Cold War has affected the impact of political party by examining the pattern of responses to several clusters of questions, including some about the Gulf War, in the 1992 and 1996 FPLP surveys. I noted in chapter 4 that almost 90 percent of opinion leaders believed that the post–Cold War international system is multipolar rather than bipolar or unipolar. The very slight 2 percentage point difference between Republicans and Democrats on this issue pales in comparison to the striking convergence of views across party lines.

The End of the Cold War

Predictions about the consequences arising from the end of the Cold War provide further insight into leadership views of the international system.[9] Four major themes emerge from the data. The first is a rather widespread agreement that many fundamental features of international relations will persist into the post–Cold War era. An overwhelming majority of opinion leaders (93 percent), irrespective of party identification, believed that greater international cooperation rather than unilateral action will be necessary to deter and resist aggression. Because international cooperation in the form of alliance systems was a crucial feature of the Cold War period, this judgment does not necessarily represent a perception of fundamental systemic change.

Responses to other items reinforce the point that a majority of opinion leaders anticipated continuity rather than revolutionary change in international relations. For example, more than two-thirds agreed that nations will continue to adhere to traditional definitions of their national interests; barely over one-third of respondents believed that any sort of world government is likely to be established, even within the next half century; and a comparable minority predicted that loyalty to nation-states will decline because they are decreasingly able to meet citizens' demands. The leadership group as a whole was almost evenly divided on the proposition that "the collapse of the Soviet Union and the unwillingness of the United States to deal with its budget deficit are likely to accord ever greater influence to the United Nations and other international organizations." Democrats were somewhat more likely than Republicans to foresee changes on each of these questions, but the differences, although statistically significant in several cases, were generally rather moderate—in the range of 5 to 11 percent.

A second theme, on the prospects for international stability, is addressed by two items. The questions ask whether we are entering a period of fragmentation and disorder arising from, first, weakening support for governments and, second, exploding nationalist sentiments. Both questions gave rise to sharp divisions within the entire leadership sample, although not necessarily along partisan lines. Compared to Republicans, Democrats were somewhat more pessimistic on both questions, but once again the differences are of a very modest magnitude.

A third pair of questions focuses on the agenda of critical international issues. Very strong majorities of Democrats (73 percent) and Republicans (69 percent), without significant partisan differences, agreed that "nonstrategic issues such as pollution, the drug trade, migrations, and AIDS are likely to replace military concerns on the world's agenda." Somewhat greater disagreement, with a 10 percent partisan gap, emerged on the prospects for neglect and increasing impoverishment of the Third World as a consequence of vanishing Cold War rivalries in that part of the world. Whereas a slight majority of Democrats agreed that this dismal scenario was likely to occur, slightly more than two-fifths of the Republicans did so.

Finally, responses to two items with strong military overtones reveal very strong partisan differences. The proposition that military threats are no longer effective elicited agreement from 52 percent of Democrats but from only one Republican in five. A slim majority of Democrats also agreed that the United States, as the dominant power, can channel the direction of change toward a "new world order"; the comparable figure among Republicans was almost four out of five. These results are wholly consistent with the finding (table 5.4) that Republicans and Democrats have strikingly different orientations toward the military dimensions of international affairs.

The data to this point indicate that Democrats and Republicans tend to have rather similar views on the nature of the post–Cold War international system, even though the former are somewhat more likely than the latter to predict fundamental changes. In contrast, the most significant partisan differences arise from questions about military issues and the U.S. role in the system.

Approaches to Peace

As for the perceived effectiveness of various approaches to peace, opinion leaders in the 1992 and 1996 surveys were offered a broad array of options. The items in this cluster of questions (table 4.5) span the full range of views from a basic realpolitik perspective (military superiority, balance of power) to key aspects of traditional liberal positions (trade, international organizations, better international communication and understanding, arms control).

Some elements of bipartisan agreement emerge from the responses to this cluster of items. Two approaches that have usually found favor among liberals—trade and technical cooperation and enhanced international communication—were rated as "very effective" by 43 percent and 47 percent of the leaders, respectively. "Better communication and understanding among peoples" was rated first and second by Democrats (53 percent) and Republicans (42 percent), and trade was ranked as the second-most-effective path to peace by Democrats (48 percent) and as fourth-highest by Republicans (36 percent). Nevertheless, the differences were statistically significant in both cases. The 1994 congressional votes on the General Agreement on Tariffs and Trade/World Trade Organization (GATT/WTO) agreement provide some further evidence that, among leaders, trade issues cut across rather than along party lines. In the Senate, Democrats and Republicans recorded favorable votes in identical proportions—76 percent. In the House of Representatives, 68 percent of GOP members supported the agreement, as did 65 percent of the Democrats.

In contrast, the most striking example of partisan discord is the different assessments accorded to "American military superiority" by members of the two major parties. More than 70 percent of Republicans rated military superiority as a "very effective" approach to peace, and it was by a considerable margin their preferred approach. In dramatic contrast, Democrats as a group rated military superiority as only the fifth-most-promising strategy for peace, with only 35 percent giving it a "very effective" rating. Another partisan divergence of views arose from assessments of the effectiveness of narrowing the gap between rich and poor nations. In contrast to the 39 percent of Democrats who gave this approach the highest rating, only 11 percent of Republicans did so. Two of the traditional instruments of foreign policy, collective security through alliances and balance-of-power politics, received rather different assessments. Forty percent of the leaders in the

1996 survey rated the former as "very effective," whereas fewer than one in seven expressed the same judgment about policies directed at achieving a balance of power. Partisan differences were significant only in the latter case.

In summary, these responses generally fall along lines that are familiar to theorists of international relations. Republicans accorded their highest rating to an approach with a strong realpolitik flavor, whereas Democrats favored liberal strategies for peace. The primary point of convergence across party lines was the lukewarm appraisal of collective security, an approach that failed to rank among the top two by members of either major party. These results are also consistent with the finding that most Republicans can be classified as internationalists or hard-liners, whereas Democrats are predominantly accommodationists.

Implications for U.S. Foreign Policy

When asked to explore the implications for U.S. policies of the end of the Cold War and the collapse of the Soviet empire, it is clear that few opinion leaders believe that the appropriate answer is a significant retrenchment from international activism toward isolationism. The proposition that the United States should limit its involvement in world affairs to military undertakings for peace and stability was rejected by an overwhelming bipartisan majority, garnering the assent of fewer than one respondent in six in 1992 and fewer than one-quarter of the leaders four years later. Nor was there much support for the self-centered approach represented by columnist Patrick Buchanan's call for a new foreign policy that "puts America first, and second and third as well" (1990, 82). Given Buchanan's status as a perennial Republican presidential candidate, at least until his decision to run as an independent in 2000, it is perhaps not surprising that members of the GOP recorded a significantly higher level of agreement with his prescription, although only about one-third of that group agreed in 1992; even fewer Democrats (14 percent) did so. The comparable figures in 1996 were 46 percent and 16 percent, respectively. There was also declining support for a proposition with at least some isolationist overtones: because America's allies are now capable of defending themselves, the United States can focus its attention on domestic issues rather than external threats to its well-being. Half of the Republicans and two-thirds of the Democrats agreed in 1992, but by 1996 partisan differences had completely disappeared, as 45 percent of leaders in each party agreed.

A second major point of convergence across party lines emerged on two propositions to expand the nation's foreign policy agenda to give greater emphasis to economic and social issues, including hunger and poverty. Although support among Democrats outstripped that among Republicans at a statistically significant level in both 1992 and 1996, these differences are less salient than the much more important agreement with these propositions by well over 80 percent of opinion leaders in both political parties. The 1992 FPLP survey was completed months before the George H. W. Bush administration launched Operation Restore Hope to distribute relief supplies to Somalia. Although that undertaking drew heavy criticism in Congress after the Mogadishu firefight that resulted in the deaths of eighteen U.S. Rangers, overwhelming support for U.S. leadership of international coalitions to deal with poverty and hunger persisted into 1996.

Points of strong partisan differences emerge, not surprisingly, on questions about the role of the military in the post–Cold War era. Given their sanguine appraisal of U.S. military superiority as an approach to peace, it is not surprising that Republicans strongly (87 percent) supported the maintenance of substantial military forces and rejected by a comparable majority of 83 to 16 percent the view that the United States and other countries should "cede some of their sovereignty to strengthen the powers of the United Nations and other international organizations." The Democrats also supported maintenance of strong armed forces, though by a less substantial margin of 58 to 41 percent. Democrats were much more closely divided on the issue of ceding some sovereignty, opposing it by only 50 to 48 percent.

U.S. Roles and Interests

Responses to questions about U.S. roles and interests indicate once again that most opinion leaders reject an indiscriminate retreat to isolationism as an appropriate reaction to the end of the Cold War. In 1992 both Republicans (57 percent) and Democrats (56 percent) agreed that "the best way to encourage democratic development in the Third World is for the United States to solve its own problems"; the comparable figures in 1996 were 58 percent and 47 percent, respectively. But four additional questions yielded strong majorities in opposition to various isolationist positions.

Specifically, relatively few leaders in either party expressed agreement with the following propositions:

> We shouldn't think so much in international terms but concentrate more on our own national problems (34 percent agreed in 1992; 29 percent agreed in 1996).
>
> Vital interests of the United States are largely confined to Western Europe, Japan, and the Americas (29 percent agreed in 1992; 27 percent agreed in 1996).
>
> The United States should only be involved in world affairs to the extent that its military power is needed to maintain international peace and stability (15 percent agreed in 1992; 25 percent agreed in 1996).
>
> Third World conflict cannot jeopardize vital American interests (14 percent agreed in 1992; 18 percent agreed in 1996).

Except on the last issue, concerning the irrelevance of Third World conflicts, partisan differences were statistically significant. Although in each case Republican leaders were more inclined to support the restrictive view of U.S. interests, the more important point is that none of these propositions commanded the support of much more than one-third of Republican or Democratic opinion leaders in either 1992 or 1996.

Although both Republicans and Democrats spurn an American retreat to isolationism and a narrow, self-regarding definition of the national interest, this agreement does not extend to the type of role that the United States should play in the international system. When asked in 1992 whether the United States should scale down its leadership position, Republicans overwhelmingly responded in the negative, whereas more than two-thirds of the Democrats agreed. The closely related proposition that the country should quit acting like a superpower elicited little agreement (22 percent) among Republicans while splitting Democrats almost evenly. By 1996 the partisan gap on whether the United States should scale down its leadership role had virtually disappeared, however. Forty-two percent of the entire leadership sample approved of a reduced U.S. role, and the gap between members of the two major political parties shrank to a nonsignificant 4 percent. No doubt part (but certainly not all) of the change can be traced to control of the White House. In 1992, when George H. W. Bush sat in the Oval Office, few Republicans supported a reduced role for the United States, but support for that position had increased somewhat by 1996, when Bill Clinton was president. Conversely, the Democratic support for a smaller American international role dropped from a strong majority to 42 percent during that four-year interval.

Foreign Policy Goals

A more specific perspective on policy preferences emerges from responses to a cluster of questions asking for an assessment of American foreign policy goals. These questions, cited earlier in chapters 3 (tables 3.3a and 3.3b) and 4, provide an opportunity to assess trends in foreign policy concerns as well as the level of elite partisan differences across a broad array of Cold War and post–Cold War concerns, including world-order security issues, global economic and environmental issues, and U.S. economic and value issues. Table 5.5 summarizes the overall "very important" ratings for each goal over two decades and reports the extent to which Republican and Democratic opinion leaders differed. The discussion that follows focuses on the two FPLP surveys undertaken since the end of the Cold War.

At first glance it appears that the data provide support for the thesis of declining importance attached to some important aspects of foreign affairs, especially when the 1992 and 1996 responses are compared. However, a longer-term perspective indicates that in several cases the 1992 results may represent an anomaly. For example, the importance attached to strengthening the United Nations reached an exceptionally high level in that year, no doubt because the Gulf War was conducted under the formal authorization of several Security Council resolutions. Support for strengthening the United Nations declined quite sharply in 1996 but reached a level that was quite typical of the four surveys conducted prior to the end of the Cold War. A similar pattern emerged on several other questions, including arms control and protecting weaker nations from aggression. The latter goal received higher-than-normal support in 1992 as a result of the successful liberation of Kuwait a year earlier.

The evidence in table 5.5 also suggests a declining sense of urgency among leaders about other foreign policy goals, especially those clustered under the heading of "world-order economic and environmental issues." The end of the Cold War has coincided with an especially sharp decline in the importance attributed to

TABLE 5.5. The Importance of American Foreign Policy Goals Rated by Leaders in the FPLP Surveys, 1976–96: Assessments of Importance and Partisan Gaps

Here is a list of possible foreign policy goals that the United States might have. Please indicate how much importance should be attached to each goal.

"Very important" ratings, entire leadership sample (%)
[Partisan gaps: % Republican VI ratings minus % Democrat VI ratings]

	1976	1980	1984	1988	1992	1996
World-order security issues						
Preventing the spread of nuclear weapons	—	—	—	—	87 [-1]	83 [-5]
Strengthening the United Nations	25 [-11]	32 [-13]	27 [-13]	27 [-8]	44 [-12]	26 [-27]
Protecting weaker nations against aggression	18 [0]	24 [3]	—	—	28 [3]	18 [-8]
Worldwide arms control	66 [-9]	55 [-21]	71 [-21]	68 [-15]	73 [-11]	60 [-16]
Keeping peace in the world	70 [-6]	76 [-7]	—	—	—	—
Maintaining a balance of power among nations	44 [-7]	57 [3]	44 [10]	—	—	—
World-order economic and environmental issues						
Combating world hunger	50 [-13]	51 [-18]	56 [-16]	57 [-16]	55 [-14]	36 [-28]
Improving the global environment	—	48 [-19]	54 [-20]	69 [-19]	66 [-19]	46 [-37]
Helping to improve the standard of living in less developed countries	38 [-12]	43 [-11]	59 [-17]	51 [-19]	43 [-17]	28 [-19]
Worldwide population control	—	47 [-9]	55 [-8]	55 [-12]	—	—
Fostering international cooperation to solve common problems such as food, inflation, and energy	70 [-15]	73 [-11]	66 [-19]	70 [-20]	71 [-15]	56 [-30]
Helping to solve world inflation	49 [-3]	—	45 [-7]	47 [-7]	—	—
Averting financial crises arising from Third World debt						

U.S. economic interest issues

Issue						
Stopping the flow of illegal drugs into the U.S.	—	—	—	—	—	—
Protecting the jobs of American workers	30 [3]	30 [2]	—	36 [4]	32 [5]	58 [18]
Securing adequate supplies of energy	72 [8]	78 [8]	85 [3]	76 [2]	68 [7]	29 [-2]
Controlling and reducing illegal immigration	—	—	—	—	—	53 [15]
Reducing the U.S. trade deficit with foreign countries	—	—	—	64 [0]	49 [11]	33 [26]
Protecting the interests of American business abroad	14 [11]	20 [17]	23 [19]	—	24 [13]	20 [14]
Keeping up the value of the dollar	—	64 [8]	—	—	—	—

U.S. values and institutions issues

Issue						
Promoting and defending human rights in other countries	6 [5]	28 [-12]	34 [-19]	39 [-12]	39 [-10]	23 [-22]
Promoting market economies abroad	—	10 [12]	—	—	—	—
Helping to bring a democratic form of government to other nations	7 [0]	10 [-1]	18 [1]	25 [8]	23 [0]	15 [-8]

Cold War/security issues

Issue						
Maintaining superior military power worldwide	—	—	—	—	—	40 [34]
Defending our allies' security	37 [8]	44 [11]	48 [13]	51 [8]	34 [13]	36 [4]
Containing communism	39 [34]	42 [17]	39 [30]	36 [34]	12 [12]	15 [15]
Matching Soviet/Russian military power	—	—	41 [23]	33 [18]	18 [14]	—
Promoting and defending our own security	85 [9]	90 [5]	84 [14]	—	—	—
Strengthening countries who are friendly toward us	23 [10]	38 [8]	—	—	—	—

Note: Gaps exceeding 6 percent are significant at the .001 level.

combating hunger, improving the standard of living in less developed countries (LDCs), the global environment, and international economic cooperation. Moreover, the 1996 responses to these goals are not merely a drop from abnormally high levels in 1992 but are part of a longer-term trend of "compassion fatigue."

Among goals encompassing U.S. economic interests, energy security continues to be regarded as very important by most respondents, but only small numbers of respondents have regarded two others—protecting jobs and the interests of American business abroad—as of great urgency. Drug trafficking and illegal immigration did not appear in surveys prior to 1996, precluding any assessment of trends. Security goals that formed the core of American foreign policy during the Cold War did not evoke a great deal of urgency in 1996, but with one exception, these results do not represent a sharp shift from earlier surveys. Even during the Cold War, "containing communism" never achieved the status of a superordinate goal among opinion leaders—it peaked in 1980 when 42 percent of the respondents rated it as "very important"—but not surprisingly, it has ranked as the least important goal since the end of the Cold War. Nor have opinion leaders taking part in the FPLP surveys ascribed much importance to promoting such American values as human rights and democracy abroad. During the Cold War, efforts to support human rights and democracy other than at the rhetorical level risked alienating some allies— "friendly tyrants"—as well as escalating tensions with adversaries. Yet there is scant evidence that the end of the Cold War has been widely perceived as providing a low-risk environment for elevating human rights and democracy promotion toward the top of America's foreign policy agenda.

The partisan gaps in table 5.5 offer only modest evidence that the end of the Cold War has resurrected a foreign policy consensus among opinion leaders. Bipartisan agreement on the importance of preventing the spread of nuclear weapons is diluted somewhat by the substantial gap—16 percent—on the importance of "worldwide arms control." There are also rather muted differences between Republicans and Democrats on several of the less highly rated goals: defending allies, protecting weaker nations, protecting the jobs of American workers, and helping to bring a democratic form of government to other countries.

In contrast, substantial partisan gaps emerged on many other issues. World-order security issues gave rise to significant differences, with Democrats attributing considerably greater importance to these goals. A similar pattern, though with even greater partisan differences averaging almost 30 percent in 1996, characterizes responses to such goals as combating hunger, improving the standard of living in LDCs, improving the environment, and fostering international economic cooperation. Conversely, compared to Democratic leaders, Republicans typically attributed greater importance to American economic interests and security goals. Just as Republicans gave a higher priority to matching Soviet military power during the Cold War, in 1996 they were far more enthusiastic than Democrats about "maintaining superior military power worldwide." Finally, as noted earlier, promoting American values abroad has gained a great deal of support in none of the FPLP surveys, but as overall support for human rights has declined, reaching a new low in 1996, the gap between Republicans and Democrats widened.

International Interventions and Commitments

Nine items in the 1992 and 1996 leadership surveys focus on specific U.S. international commitments and undertakings. The data indicate bipartisan agreement on several of them. In 1992, two-thirds of the opinion leaders endorsed the proposition that the "U.S. has a moral obligation to prevent the destruction of the state of Israel," and four years later that support had risen to almost three-fourths of the respondents; this is the only international commitment that elicited stronger Democratic (71 percent and 78 percent) than Republican (63 percent and 71 percent) support. Even before Harry Truman's recognition of Israel within hours of its 1948 declaration of statehood, members of the American Jewish community tended to support the Democratic Party. Although some visible Jewish leaders subsequently have become outspoken conservative Republicans—Norman Podhoretz and his *Commentary* magazine provide a prominent example—strong support for Israel among Democratic opinion leaders is not very surprising. Even Democrats who criticize other American security undertakings abroad (as table 5.4 shows, most Democrats have been accommodationists since the mid-1980s) may point to the fact that, unlike some other allies, Israel is a democratic country that has shown a willingness to defend itself without requesting that U.S. troops be deployed there. Four years later, a modest majority of opinion leaders also favored protecting Taiwan from invasion, with Republicans expressing slightly stronger support.

Finally, the general proposition that the United States should not hesitate to intrude in the domestic affairs of other countries in support of a "democratic world order" gained approval from fewer than one-quarter of adherents to either political party in 1992, and by 1996 agreement with that dictum had dropped to less than 10 percent.

Responses to questions about four additional security commitments and undertakings yielded quite divergent results. Preservation of NATO despite the disintegration of the USSR and the Warsaw Pact received strong bipartisan support in 1992, as did a question four years later about the expansion that brought Hungary, Poland, and the Czech Republic into NATO. In addition, fewer than 40 percent of opinion leaders in either party favored withdrawing all U.S. troops from Japan. But a proposal to maintain an American military presence in the Middle East to protect oil fields gave rise to powerful partisan cleavages. In both 1992 and 1996, the FPLP leadership sample was divided almost equally between supporters and opponents, but by margins of 28 percent and 20 percent, respectively, Republicans expressed far greater enthusiasm than did Democrats. The deployment of U.S. troops to Haiti also found leaders in the two major parties on opposite sides, as 60 percent of Democrats expressed approval and only 42 percent of Republicans did so.

Finally, two additional items with a strong realpolitik tenor also brought forth very large partisan gaps. Well over 60 percent of Republicans agreed in both 1992 and 1996 that "there is nothing wrong with using the CIA to try to undermine hostile governments," but only 28 percent of Democrats supported that strategy in 1992, and 35 percent did so four years later. The proposition that "the United States may have to support some dictators because they are friendly toward us" yielded a similar pattern of responses. Whereas fewer than four Democrats in ten expressed agreement in either FPLP survey, a strong majority of Republicans approved of U.S. support for such "friendly tyrants."

Trade

Although partisan cleavages are evident in most of the evidence reviewed previously, some exceptions exist. Striking agreement among Democrats, Republicans, and independent opinion leaders on trade-related issues represents an island of harmony in an ocean of partisan discord (table 5.6). A majority of respondents

TABLE 5.6. Attitudes on Trade Issues among Opinion Leaders in the 1996 FPLP Survey: The Effects of Party (in percentages)

	Reported Responses	All Respondents (N = 2,242)[a]	Republicans (N = 746)	Democrats (N = 800)	Independents (N = 448)
Erecting trade barriers against foreign goods to protect American industries and jobs	Agree	22	21	21	23
Granting most-favored-nation trade status to China	Agree	46	48	46	46
Signing NAFTA with Canada and Mexico	Agree	80	80	81	79
Signing the GATT trade agreement and joining the WTO	Agree	80	77	84	80
Using the threat of protectionism to open Japanese and European markets to U.S. goods	Agree	72	74	72	71
Economic rivalries among nations [as a cause of war]	Very serious	36	33	38	36
Economic competition from Europe [as a national security threat]	Very serious	4	3	5	3
Economic competition from Japan [as a national security threat]	Very serious	7	7	7	6
Protecting the jobs of American workers [as a foreign policy goal]	Very important	29	28	30	28
Protecting the interests of American business abroad [as a foreign policy goal]*	Very important	20	28	14	17

[a]Includes 248 who did not express a party preference.
*Differences among groups significant at the .001 level.

opposed erecting trade barriers; rated protecting jobs and the interests of American businesses abroad as foreign policy goals of limited importance; and approved major steps toward trade liberalization, including the North American Free Trade Agreement, GATT, and the WTO agreements. The grant of most-favored-nation trade status to China divided opinion leaders almost evenly, but the cleavages cut across rather than along party lines. Only two of the items in table 5.6 gave rise to statistically significant differences—the WTO and protection for U.S. businesses abroad—but these differences seem less compelling than the fact that more than three-fourths of leaders in both parties favored membership in the WTO and fewer than a third felt that it was "very important" to protect businesses abroad. Finally, bipartisan agreement on trade liberalization appears to arise from the widespread belief, shared by Republicans, Democrats, and independents, that economic competition, whether from Europe or Japan, does not constitute a threat to the United States. It should be noted that the absence of partisan divisions on trade issues represents continuity rather than change in the views of opinion leaders. As in 1996, trade has consistently stood out as one of the few areas of agreement in previous FPLP surveys.

These results indicate that although evidence of a bipartisan consensus may be found on such general questions as the structure of the post–Cold War international system or trade issues, agreement does not necessarily extend to more specific policy-oriented areas, including the appropriate post–Cold War roles for the United States and the priorities that should be attached to various international goals. Substantial majorities among both Republicans and Democrats may oppose an undiscriminating retreat into an isolationist role for the country, but there is considerable disagreement on what kind of international role is most appropriate as well as on strategies and means for pursuing U.S. interests abroad. These differences also extend to the types of international undertakings and interventions that Republicans and Democrats are prepared to endorse. More generally, Republicans tend to favor a leadership role consistent with American superpower status, whereas Democrats are more supportive of a U.S. role as a "normal nation" that pursues its interests in conjunction with others, including through the United Nations. Stated somewhat differently, members of the GOP appear more inclined to favor unilateral action in the pursuit of national interests, whereas multilateralism finds stronger support among Democrats. The issue of multilateral versus unilateral approaches to foreign affairs will be revisited in chapter 6.

Ideology

The data reviewed to this point support Destler, Gelb, and Lake's lament about the increasingly partisan nature of the making of foreign policy, but the other part of their diagnosis—the role of ideology—has yet to be explored. Some anecdotal evidence would seem to suggest that for several decades each of the two major parties has become ideologically less diverse as the GOP has moved sharply toward the right and the Democrats to the left; it includes the presidential nominees in recent campaigns, the defections of some prominent conservative Democrats to the Republican party—Strom Thurmond, John Connally, Phil Gramm, Richard Shelby, and Ben Nighthorse Campbell are some of the more visible switchers—and the growing use of such candidate litmus tests as positions on taxes or abortion.

The 1994 congressional elections appear to provide further evidence of this trend. Indeed, there is some evidence that ideology may even dominate partisanship. In the early 1980s, the Republican chairman of the Senate Foreign Relations Committee, Charles Percy of Illinois, called for a revival of bipartisanship in the making of foreign policy (Percy 1981–82). Not long thereafter, Percy was defeated in his bid for reelection, in part because conservative Republicans such as his Foreign Relations Committee colleague Jesse Helms (a Republican from North Carolina), hoping to purge the GOP of moderates, supported Percy's liberal Democratic opponent, Paul Simon; that support included substantial financial aid from Helms's fund-raising Congressional Club. Can these tendencies toward increasing ideological cleavages also be found in public attitudes toward foreign policy issues and in the views of opinion leaders?

The General Public

Eugene R. Wittkopf's extensive secondary analyses of the CCFR surveys examined the relative potency of party and ideology on foreign policy attitudes. He concluded that the latter tends to dominate the former: "Compared with ideology as a source of the divisions that so often seem to have plagued recent American foreign policy, partisanship is again shown to be the less important factor"

(1990, 48). More specifically, he found that liberals tend to have an accommodationist orientation toward foreign affairs, supporting cooperative internationalism while opposing militant internationalism. In contrast, conservatives typically take precisely the opposite positions and thus are hard-liners. He further found that political moderates are likely to be internationalists owing to their support for both varieties of internationalism (46). The potency of ideology remained fairly stable through the 1974–86 period covered by the first four CCFR surveys. Similar findings about the powerful impact of ideology on public attitudes emerge from the Americans Talk Security and Americans Talk Issues surveys initiated prior to the 1988 presidential campaign and continuing into the mid-1990s (*Americans Talk Security* 1987–90; *Americans Talk Issues* 1991–94). Finally, an analysis of the 1994 CCFR survey confirms again that party and ideology remain powerful correlates of foreign policy beliefs, with the sharpest polarization between liberal Democrats and conservative Republicans. However, a somewhat more complex pattern also may be emerging; when partisanship was held constant, the most liberal and conservative respondents were the only political groups with strong isolationist tendencies (Wittkopf 1995, 14).

The Gallup surveys on the Persian Gulf War provide an opportunity to assess the impact of ideology following the end of the Cold War. As I demonstrated earlier, responses to these questions revealed that strong partisan differences emerged on virtually all questions posed before, during, and after the 1991 war (table 5.3). When responses to the same questions are reported on the basis of the respondents' ideology, the results strongly resemble those on the impact of political party. In brief, conservatives were uniformly more supportive of U.S. policy, including the decision to initiate hostilities after the January 15, 1991, deadline passed without an Iraqi withdrawal from Kuwait. Whereas on January 13 almost 60 percent of conservatives favored going to war instead of relying on sanctions or withdrawing from the conflict, fewer than half of the liberals supported that policy option. Once the air war had begun, approval from the conservatives outstripped that of liberals by 16 percent, and approximately similar gaps emerged from three questions asking for an appraisal of U.S. policy toward Iraq several months after the fighting had ended. The two questions relating to the use of tactical nuclear weapons against Iraq gave rise to minuscule partisan differences; the ideological chasm on these questions was similarly insignifi-

cant. In short, the data suggest a convergence of partisan and ideological positions on the Persian Gulf War, with Republicans and
conservatives providing the strongest support for U.S. policies.

Opinion Leaders

Evidence reviewed in chapter 4 indicates that, compared to the
general public, opinion leaders are more likely to think about
public affairs in coherent ideological terms. For example, the consistently strong correlations between attitudes on domestic and
on foreign policy issues would appear to indicate the existence of
coherent underlying ideological beliefs. The questions to be addressed here concern the relationship between partisanship and
ideology: How do they interact? Does one dominate the other?
Has the end of the Cold War significantly altered the relationship? Data from the six FPLP surveys conducted between 1976
and 1996 will be examined to provide answers to these questions.

Respondents to the FPLP surveys were asked not only to identify preferences among political parties but also to locate themselves on a standard seven-point ideological scale, the end points
of which were "far left" and "far right." Because so few respondents placed themselves in the two extreme positions on the
scale, "far left" and "far right" were combined with the adjoining
categories of "very liberal" and "very conservative," thereby collapsing a seven-point ideology scale into five categories.

When party preferences of opinion leaders are cross-tabulated
against ideological self-placement, the strong relationship between the two attributes clearly emerges (table 5.7). Members of
the GOP are overwhelmingly conservatives, and a vast majority
of Democrats identify themselves as liberals. Indeed, conservative Democrats and liberal Republicans appear to represent endangered species. Moreover, the relationship between party and
ideology, as measured by the correlation between them, steadily
strengthened during the twenty-year span of the six FPLP surveys. The end of the Cold War witnessed no erosion of the trend
toward increasing confluence of party and ideology among opinion leaders.

The distribution of opinion leaders in table 5.7 does not, however, provide any clues about the relative potency of partisanship
and ideological positions. An initial answer may be obtained by
examining how leaders of all combinations of party identification
and ideological preference are distributed across four foreign

policy orientations—hard-liners, isolationists, internationalists, and accommodationists (table 5.8). As was true of the general public, ideological preferences dominate party identification among leaders taking part in the 1992 and 1996 FPLP surveys. The same was also true of the previous four FPLP surveys. Irrespective of party loyalties, liberals are overwhelmingly in the two groups that support cooperative internationalism—accommodationists and internationalists. Conservatives, however, are almost equally likely to be found among the two groups—hard-liners and internationalists—that support militant internationalism. Although there are relatively few cross-pressured leaders (liberal Republicans and conservative Democrats), their foreign policy orientations are revealing; they tend to resemble the orientations

TABLE 5.7.   The Relationship between Party and Ideology among American Opinion Leaders, 1976–99

Of the leaders who identify themselves as . . .	Year	The percentage who also identify themselves as . . .				
		VL	SL	Mod	SC	VC
Republicans	1976	1	5	23	58	13
	1980	0	4	20	60	17
	1984	—[a]	2	18	63	18
	1988	—[a]	3	18	57	22
	1992	1	2	18	64	15
	1996	1	3	18	56	22
	1999	1	3	16	55	25
Democrats	1976	20	46	23	10	1
	1980	12	49	27	12	1
	1984	15	50	27	8	1
	1988	18	51	24	6	—[a]
	1992	19	50	23	7	—[a]
	1996	18	50	26	5	1
	1999	15	38	32	13	2
Independents	1976	7	24	33	30	6
	1980	6	20	34	34	6
	1984	5	23	39	29	3
	1988	5	20	38	32	4
	1992	3	21	45	28	2
	1996	2	21	45	27	4
	1999	5	19	41	30	5

Source: Foreign Policy Leadership Project surveys, 1976–96; Triangle Institute of Security Studies survey, 1999.

Note: Phi for 1976 = .64; 1980 = .67; 1984 = .70; 1988 = .72; 1992 = .75; 1996 = .75; 1999 = .64.

Key: VL = very liberal; SL = somewhat liberal; Mod = moderate; SC = somewhat conservative; VC = very conservative.

[a]Fewer than 0.5 percent.

TABLE 5.8. Ideology, Party, and Foreign Policy Orientations in the 1992 and 1996 FPLP Surveys

Ideology	Party	N 1992	N 1996	Hard-Liners 1992	Hard-Liners 1996	Isolationists 1992	Isolationists 1996	Internationalists 1992	Internationalists 1996	Accommodationists 1992	Accommodationists 1996
Very liberal	Republican	4	5	0%	0%	0%	0%	0%	0%	100%	100%
	Independent	18	10	0	0	0	0	0	0	100	100
	Democrat	171	146	1	1	0	2	4	15	95	82
Somewhat liberal	Republican	17	22	6	0	12	0	41	18	41	82
	Independent	120	93	4	5	3	3	19	22	73	70
	Democrat	444	396	1	—a	3	6	14	20	82	73
Moderate	Republican	129	135	5	11	2	16	53	35	40	38
	Independent	263	199	5	7	9	10	28	28	58	55
	Democrat	202	209	6	2	4	11	33	36	57	52
Somewhat conservative	Republican	457	416	17	26	7	11	54	42	23	21
	Independent	164	121	18	16	6	16	41	36	35	33
	Democrat	61	40	15	28	5	10	41	28	39	35
Very conservative	Republican	105	160	31	45	10	18	50	28	10	10
	Independent	14	18	43	61	0	11	50	22	7	6
	Democrat	2	4	50	50	0	0	50	50	0	0

Note: Row totals may not equal 100 because of rounding error. Phi = .57 (1992) and .57 (1996).
aFewer than 0.5%.

of their ideological brethren far more than they resemble the orientations of those with whom they share a party identification. Among the "very liberal" opinion leaders, only two respondents in 1992 and one in 1996 (all Democrats) are classified as hard-liners; conversely, only a few of the "very conservative" leaders taking part in the 1992 survey had an accommodationist foreign policy orientation.

Finally, a more extensive multivariate analysis that includes all 182 questions in the 1996 FPLP survey confirms that ideological self-identifications outweigh partisan loyalties. More specifically, two-way analyses of variance revealed that ideological differences alone were significant at the .001 level on 46 percent of the questions, including both domestic and foreign policy issues. The comparable figures for party alone, both ideology and party, and neither ideology nor party were 2 percent, 32 percent, and 20 percent, respectively. The last category—questions for which neither ideology nor party are sources of significant differences—includes virtually all of the trade issues.

In summary, then, the Destler, Gelb, and Lake diagnosis, although published two decades ago and well before the end of the Cold War, has lost none of its validity. Partisan and ideological differences continue to characterize the foreign policy attitudes of the general public and, to an even greater extent, those of opinion leaders.

Generation

A generational interpretation of American foreign policy views appears to offer an attractive way to account for periodic shifts in public attitudes on foreign affairs. It seems to provide an explanation for the long-term cycles in which public moods have been described as swinging between internationalism and isolationism at intervals of approximately a generation in length throughout the history of the republic (Klingberg 1952, 1979, 1983; Holmes 1985). It is also consonant with the observation that members of each generation view the world in the light of the critical events that marked their coming to maturity.

Although generational analyses of American foreign policy received an impetus from domestic divisions arising from the Vietnam War, these interpretations antedated that conflict. Some years earlier, Karl Mannheim suggested that generation is one of the most important factors shaping social beliefs and action:

The fact of belonging to the same class, and that of belonging to the same generation or age group, have this in common, that both endow the individual with a common location in the social and historical process, and thereby limit
them to a specific range of experience, predisposing them
for a certain characteristic mode of thought and experience,
and a characteristic type of historically relevant action.
(1952, 291)

His thesis is especially germane for analyses of public opinion
and foreign policy because it posits explicit linkages between age
and lessons of history.

Mannheim's injunction has not gone unheeded. In recent
decades, the concept of generation has played a central role in
analyses ranging from the political right in interwar Finland to a
proposed new paradigm for the entire course of American history and from the Sino-Soviet conflict to the political views of
American students. Even turmoil in Poland before the collapse of
its communist regime has been explained by reference to generational differences (Rintala 1962; S. Taylor and Wood 1966; Lipset
and Ladd 1971; Huntington 1974; Spivak 1981a, b). And, as befits
its growing prominence in social research, the concept also has
spawned a critical literature and several controversies (Spitzer
1973). Finally, interest in the characteristics of the so-called Generation X has also stimulated speculation and analysis from a
generational perspective (Strauss and Howe 1991; Howe and
Strauss 1992).

American involvement in Vietnam and the resulting domestic
conflict generated a good deal of speculation about generational
differences and, more specifically, about the divergent lessons that
Americans of different ages have drawn from the most salient foreign policy episodes they have experienced. *Generation gap* has
thus joined those other famous gaps—*bomber, missile,* and *credi-
bility*—in the vocabulary of many foreign policy analysts. The most
visible lines of cleavage quite often have been described as falling
between persons whose views were shaped by events leading up to
World War II on the one hand and those whose outlook was
molded by the war in Southeast Asia on the other (Gergen and
Back 1965; Bobrow and Cutler 1967; Cutler 1970; S. Kelman 1970;
Allison 1970–71; Handberg 1972–73; Roskin 1974; Russett 1975;
Knight 1977). The interpretation that links post-Vietnam dissensus
on matters of foreign policy to the lessons that each generation has

adduced from dramatic and traumatic episodes was summarized by former White House National Security Adviser Zbigniew Brzezinski:

> There is a tendency in America to be traumatized by international difficulties. The generation of the Nineteen-forties was always thinking about the failure of the League of Nations. I'm talking about leadership groups now. The leadership of the sixties was always thinking about Munich. Now there is a generation worried by Vietnam, with consequences of self-imposed paralysis, which is likely to be costlier in the long run.[10]

To be more specific, the "Munich generation versus Vietnam generation" thesis usually takes some variant of the following line of reasoning. Those who experienced the bitter fruits of appeasement and American isolationism during the 1930s tended to identify British and French concessions to Hitler at the 1938 Munich Conference as the paradigmatic example of how not to deal with expansionist totalitarian regimes. When faced after World War II with the Soviet occupation of Eastern Europe, the absence of any liberalization within the USSR, as well as periodic crises in Berlin and elsewhere, persons of this generation were prepared to support an active American foreign policy to meet challenges from the Soviet Union and its satellites.

In contrast, according to this thesis, persons of a more recent generation—for whom World War II and its genesis as well as the origins of the Cold War are merely distant historical events rather than episodes experienced firsthand—are more likely to look to the war in Southeast Asia as a source of guidance on the proper and improper conduct of foreign relations. According to this description of contemporary American society, then, what the parents regarded as indispensable commitments to maintain a viable world order, their offspring view as indiscriminate (if not incriminating) undertakings against ill-defined, often phantom threats that have no intimate connection to legitimate American interests, let alone the propagation or preservation of democratic values and institutions abroad.[11] Unencumbered by the memories and ideological baggage accumulated during World War II and the Cold War, the Vietnam generation is sometimes described as concerned with the physical safety not only of the nation but also of this fragile "spaceship Earth"; as ready to give up the hide-

bound political shibboleths of their elders in favor of a more enlightened worldview; as eager to renounce a materialistic lifestyle
that eats up a disproportionate share of the world's resources in
favor of simpler pleasures; and as inclined to respond to the
sound of falling dominoes with a bored, "So what?" To some, this
is a harbinger of better days to come, and to others it is no doubt
profoundly threatening.

This is, of course, a vastly oversimplified summary of a rather
complex line of reasoning. Nevertheless, even if it is something of
a caricature, it does capture some central elements of the thesis
that in important respects the cleavages on foreign policy issues
in this country represent a confrontation of two distinct worldviews, each rooted in and sustained by the experiences of different generations.

The generational thesis, if valid, has some important implications for the conduct of American foreign policy because it
suggests that members of the "Vietnam generation," as they
achieved positions of leadership and influence, brought to their
roles an intellectual baggage radically different from that of the
leaders they were replacing. Under these circumstances, moreover, the prognosis is that as the next generation of leaders replaces those currently in positions of influence, a new consensus
reflecting the sensibilities of the younger group will emerge.[12] It
is frequently asserted that this has been especially true of military
leaders who served as junior officers in Vietnam. Thus, the core of
the "Powell Doctrine"—which resembles the Weinberger Doctrine discussed in chapter 1—about the conditions under which
U.S. military forces could appropriately be deployed overseas is
said to have been forged in Vietnam during Powell's service in
that war. George H. W. Bush was almost certainly the last president with military service during World War II, and Bill Clinton
was the first born after the end of that conflict. Furthermore, persons who had reached voting age at the time of the Munich Conference reached retirement age during the 1980s.

Although it is too early to present conclusive evidence, the
generational thesis also leads to speculation about the future impact of the terrorist attacks on New York and Washington in
2001. Pearl Harbor represented the defining event of the World
War II generation—Senator Arthur Vandenberg was one of
many for whom it marked the bankruptcy of isolationism—and
Vietnam led many people to question the validity of post–World
War II international commitments. Will the terrorist attacks have

a similar impact on the unilateralist worldviews of not only George W. Bush but also of the generation that came to age at the dawn of the new millennium? Chapter 6 will consider this question in more detail.

The General Public

However theoretically plausible the generational interpretation of foreign policy differences may be, it is not unambiguously supported by empirical evidence. Both survey and voting data suggest that, at least within the general public, cleavages do not fall quite so neatly along age lines. Thus, the popular image of a dovish or isolationist generation of students demonstrating on college campuses in the midst of the Vietnam War to protest against the excessive foreign policy commitments of their elders provides a skewed, if not inaccurate, picture of American society. The generational interpretation of positions on U.S. policy in Vietnam received little support from surveys conducted during the decade before the 1973 Paris agreement that was to have ended the war. Indeed, these surveys revealed that, compared to their elders, the younger respondents were usually more inclined to support American policy in Southeast Asia as well as to oppose withdrawal from Vietnam (P. Converse and Schuman 1970; Erskine 1970; Mueller 1973; Lunch and Sperlich 1979). More-over, the allegedly dovish younger generation provided stronger support than other age groups for the decidedly hawkish George Wallace–Curtis LeMay ticket in the 1968 presidential election. More generally, a broad-scale study of American public opinion during the final three decades of the Cold War found little evidence of a generational basis for changes in public opinion about world affairs. Specifically addressing the "Munich versus Vietnam generation" thesis, William G. Mayer (1992, 166–67) concluded, "If the experience of the last three decades is any guide to the future, the destiny of détente and the 'new world order' depends considerably more on the kinds of external events and conditions that cause intracohort change than on the workings of generational replacement."

Public opinion surveys of the post-Vietnam period also reveal few, if any, striking age-based differences on foreign and defense issues. Even when small differences appear, they do not consistently fit the pattern implied by the "Munich versus Vietnam generation" thesis. For example, a 1975 Gallup survey asked whether the United States should continue a policy of protecting other nations against communist takeovers. There were virtually no differences in levels of support among the three youngest age groups: eighteen to twenty-four, twenty-five to twenty-nine, and thirty to forty-nine. In each case, about four respondents out of seven agreed that containment should be maintained. In contrast, respondents over age fifty expressed somewhat more, rather than less, skepticism: only 47 percent of them supported that policy. Later surveys dealing with such controversial Cold War issues as the proper level of defense spending and the appropriate American role in Central American civil wars also failed to reveal any sharp age-based discontinuities.

Finally, the end of the Cold War has not significantly widened systematic generational differences on foreign policy issues. Questions concerning U.S. involvement in Bosnia yielded quite similar responses from the various age groups, with some exceptions: proposed American air strikes against Bosnian Serbs failed to win approval of respondents in any age group, but the gap between supporters and opponents of such military action was widest among the oldest ones (G. Gallup Jr. 1993). By 1995, the oldest respondents were most inclined to assess the level of American involvement in Bosnia as too great (Saad 1995). A plurality of Americans supported lifting economic sanctions against South Africa after Nelson Mandela was released from jail (G. Gallup Jr. 1991), and a strong majority favored reducing immigration (G. Gallup Jr. 1993). Age-based differences on both questions were negligible.

Evidence from other studies also reveals mixed results. An analysis based on the first CCFR survey found that the under-thirty age group was almost evenly divided between "liberal internationalists" (30 percent), "conservative internationalists" (32 percent), and "noninternationalists" (38 percent). Indeed, compared to the thirty-to-sixty-four and over-sixty-four age groups, those of the youngest generation were the most evenly divided among these three categories (Mandelbaum and Schneider 1979).[13] Conversely, a fuller analysis of the first four CCFR surveys did uncover some generational differences. Wittkopf (1990, 42–44) found that members of the oldest age group tended to be hard-liners in their foreign policy orientations, whereas the youngest group was more inclined toward an accommodationist stance. Responses to the 1994 CCFR survey revealed, however, that significant generational differences did not survive multivariate analyses that included other sociode-mographic variables (Wittkopf 1995, 14).

An especially interesting study from a generational perspective analyzed the analogies used to depict the situation in the Persian Gulf following Iraq's invasion of Kuwait: World War II, in which Saddam Hussein's Iraq is viewed as playing an unremittingly expansionist role similar to Hitler's Germany; and the Vietnam War, in which an initial small commitment runs the risk of years of conflict without a clear outcome (Schuman and Rieger 1992). After being asked to assess the relevance of the two analogies, respondents were asked, "Which of the two comparisons do you think best fits the Middle East situation with Iraq—the comparison to Hitler and Germany in the 1930s or the comparison to Vietnam in the 1960s?" The results revealed significant generational effect on the choice of analogy before the start of the war against Iraq, with older respondents more likely to choose the Hitler comparison, even when education, race, gender, and region were controlled, whereas the younger ones were more inclined to select the Vietnam analogy. That relationship faded considerably, however, after the war began. The analysis further found that the choice between the Hitler and Vietnam analogies was strongly correlated, both before and during the war, with support for or opposition to U.S. military action against Iraq. Despite the significant relationship between age and the choice of analogies, however, the results also indicated a very modest relationship between generation and support for policy choices before and during the conflict. The authors conclude,

> We have demonstrated the influence of generational experience in directing attention to one historical analogy or another—and also its limitation in influencing support for policy choices. Rather than past experience controlling the present, the present controlled the past, as most Americans of all generations came to accept the analogy to World War II—an analogy that justified massive military action against an enemy that was almost unknown a few months earlier. (Schuman and Rieger 1992, 325)

The widespread propensity to use familiar analogies also emerges from a 1993 Gallup survey. Respondents were asked whether the conflict in Bosnia was more like the Vietnam War or the Persian Gulf conflict. Presumably, the outstanding difference between the two events was that the former was a protracted and failed American undertaking, whereas the latter resulted in a quick victory. By a margin of 57 to 34 percent respondents in the eighteen-to-twenty-nine age group chose the Persian Gulf analogy, whereas those aged fifty and higher (all of whom had reached adulthood before the American pullout from Saigon in 1975) were split evenly on the choice between the two historical analogies. However, these generational differences in choice of analogy did not translate into consistently different policy preferences on Bosnia. Another Gallup survey less than three weeks later did indeed find that the youngest age groups were most inclined to judge a Clinton plan for Bosnia involvement as "about right" (49 percent), whereas only about a third of the older respondents came to a similar judgment. But when the question was posed two weeks later, in this instance without reference to President Clinton, generational differences in judgments about the appropriate level of U.S. involvement in Bosnia virtually disappeared.[14]

The extensive surveys on the Persian Gulf War provide a further opportunity to assess the impact of age on a major post–Cold War undertaking as well as to confirm the results of Howard Schuman and Cheryl Rieger's study. Gallup surveys placed respondents into three groups based on age: eighteen to twenty-nine, thirty to forty-nine, and fifty and over. (The questions are described in table 5.3.) The cutting points for these groups do not coincide very precisely with crucial events experienced during formative years, as posited by some generational hypotheses. The youngest, born in the years 1962–73, clearly constitute a post-Vietnam generation. Those in the middle group were born between 1942 and 1961; thus, only the older members of this cohort might be considered members of the Vietnam generation. The oldest group, born before 1942, would include some respondents of the World War II generation but would not be limited to them.

The results of these Persian Gulf War surveys fail to provide a great deal of support for a generational interpretation of foreign policy preferences. Perhaps the results reflect, at least in part, the imperfect correspondence between age groups and the "critical" events that are central to some generational explanations. With a single exception, the variance of responses across the three age groups is less than 10 percent. Moreover, respondents in the thirty-to-forty-nine group, which includes the Vietnam generation, in fact tended to be slightly more rather than less supportive of U.S. policy, including the decision to launch a war against Iraq. Eighty-five percent of that age group approved of "the U.S. decision to go to war in order to drive the Iraqis out of Kuwait," whereas 74 percent of those aged fifty or older did so.

Opinion Leaders

Although evidence for a generational interpretation of the general public is at best mixed, perhaps the search for age-based cleavages is more fruitfully pursued among opinion leaders. At least some advocates of the generational perspective suggest that, irrespective of its relevance for the general public, it accurately describes the cleavages among elites, actual and emerging (Allison 1970–71). The Vietnam protests among the young were more often found at the "elite" universities—Stanford, Harvard, Berkeley, and the like—than at state and community colleges or in noneducational settings. There is evidence, moreover, that the generational hypothesis appears to fare best when applied to such specific groups as political activists or protesters (Jennings 1987). Some anecdotal evidence would also seem to raise questions even about a generational interpretation of elites, however. As is well known, Bill Clinton was among those on university campuses who voiced strong opposition to American policy in Vietnam, and by a combination of educational deferments and a high number in the draft lottery, he avoided being called to military service in that conflict. But many of Clinton's most visible and outspoken critics—among them, Senators Phil Gramm and Trent Lott, House Speaker Newt Gingrich, columnists George Will and Patrick Buchanan, and President George W. Bush—also sat out the war by various means, including pursuing postgraduate education during the years they were eligible for military service. In short, membership in the same generation and at least one important shared experience during their formative years did not stamp these leaders with similar worldviews.

The six FPLP surveys will again provide evidence about opinion leaders. To assess the effects of age on foreign policy attitudes, the division of respondents into age groups was based on two premises. Three wars in which the United States had been involved since 1941 were assumed to provide significant benchmarks. The "Munich versus Vietnam generation" thesis also identifies two of these wars as watershed points in American thinking about external affairs. The second premise is that late adolescence and young adulthood may have special significance. Because that period encompasses for many the beginning of eligibility for military service, consciousness of and interest in foreign affairs may be enhanced when prospects for personal involvement hinge on the outcome of foreign policy undertakings. More generally, those years in the life cycle have often been identified as especially crucial in the formation and development of political beliefs.[15]

Following this reasoning, three cutting points—1923–24, 1932–33, and 1940–41—divided the respondents into four groups. Even the youngest of the World War II generation—those born in 1923—had reached the age of eighteen when the attack on Pearl Harbor brought the United States into World War II. By the end of that war, they would have been likely, if otherwise eligible, to have experienced military service. But even those who were not on active military duty could scarcely have lived through the war without being cognizant of it. Leaders born between 1924 and 1932 would at least have reached the age of twenty-one during the Korean War. The older among them would also have been young adults during World War II, but for this group the Korean War would presumably have been an especially salient experience. Persons born between 1933 and 1940 would, if inducted into the armed forces, most likely have served during the period following the Korean armistice of 1953 and before the rapid escalation of the Vietnam conflict in 1965. Hence, this group is labeled the *interim generation*. Those born between 1940 and 1954 have been designated the *Vietnam generation*. Even the oldest persons in this group would have been only thirteen years old when the fighting in Korea ended. For them, "the war" almost certainly refers to the Vietnam conflict. For the 1992 and 1996 surveys, an additional cutting point (1954–55) was added, and those born after 1954 were designated as members of the *post-Vietnam generation*.

Evidence from the FPLP surveys provides rather limited support for the generational thesis. The relationship between the age groups described above and the four foreign policy orientations—hard-liners, internationalists, isolationists, and accommodationists—has been consistently quite weak.[16] More detailed analyses, summarizing appraisals of four possible U.S. foreign policy goals, can provide further insight into the strengths and limitations of the generational perspective. Two of them—"containing communism"

206 Public Opinion and American Foreign Policy

and "defending our allies' security"—are quintessential Cold War goals, whereas the other two address nonstrategic military concerns: "helping to improve the standard of living in less developed countries" and "strengthening the United Nations."

Assessments of containment as a foreign policy goal resulted in only minor differences among the generational groups. Variations in ratings of that goal during the six surveys over the 1976–96 period clearly reflected the nature of relations between Washington and Moscow; by 1996, fewer than one leader in seven rated containment as "very important." Generational differences within any single survey were quite muted, however, and the correlations (phi) between appraisals of containment and generation never reached .10 in any of the surveys. Moreover, even these minor variations did not fall into a consistent pattern: members of the World War II generation were by a very thin margin strongest supporters of containment in several surveys, including that in 1996, but in 1984 their "very important" ratings lagged behind those of the other groups, again by a very scant margin. Nor did appraisals of "defending our allies' security" yield much support for the generational thesis. The end of the Cold War was reflected in the declining urgency attributed to either containment or the defense of allies by respondents in all age groups.

The other two goals did yield significant generational differences as well as a tendency for members of the oldest generation to accord the highest ratings to both development assistance for helping to improve the standard of living in the Third World and strengthening the United Nations. These differences also may reflect generational experiences; both the creation of the United Nations and the initiation of aid to LDCs (for example, President Truman's Point Four program, first announced in his 1949 inaugural address) took place during the early years of the World War II generation. In 1996, 40 percent of that age group rated assistance to LDCs as a "very important" foreign policy goal (down sharply from 60 percent four years earlier), and 62 percent judged strengthening the United Nations in similar terms. However, members of the Vietnam and post-Vietnam generations were apparently least enthusiastic about these goals for U.S. foreign policy: their "very important" ratings failed to exceed 25 percent for either goal.

The word *apparently* is used advisedly here. Before accepting any evidence of generation gaps as definitive, it behooves us to consider whether the age groups in elite surveys also differ significantly with respect to other possible explanations for variations in their responses. To assess conclusively the impact of age on foreign policy attitudes, each of the generational groups should be as similar as possible with respect to other background attributes that might serve as competing explanations. For several reasons this is not true of the FPLP samples. Occupational differences offer a case in point. The sociology of occupations is such that prominence or leadership positions tend to come earlier in some professions or institutions than in others. For example, business executives typically do not reach the top levels of management before an age (mid- to late fifties) at which many senior military officials, even those who achieved flag rank, have already retired. The suspicion that responses to the four issues discussed here may not fully reflect the impact of age is supported by multivariate analyses. Occupational differences are highly significant for all four questions, whereas those for generations fail to reach statistical significance for the two Cold War issues, containment and defending allies.[17]

This point can be further illustrated by expressions of policy preferences for dealing with Iraq's 1990 invasion of Kuwait. The 1992 FPLP survey asked respondents whether they favored using force, relying on economic sanctions, or staying out of the conflict in the Persian Gulf region. As table 4.7 shows, opinion leaders expressed an overall preference, both before and after the war, for using force against Iraq rather than giving economic sanctions more time to work. Their responses also indicate rather sharp differences between the Vietnam and post-Vietnam generations. Before January 15, 1991, 62 percent of the Vietnam generation's opinion leaders favored using force right away, but only 38 percent of those in the post-Vietnam generation expressed support for that option. This gap narrowed only slightly when leaders were asked about their policy preferences after the war had ended. Support for the use of force increased to 69 percent for those in the Vietnam generation and to 50 percent for the members of the post-Vietnam age group. But these age-based differences once again melt away when occupation is introduced into the analysis. The reasons are not hard to find. Military officers account for more than 20 percent of the Vietnam generation elites—indeed, more than 88 percent of the military officers taking part in the 1992 FPLP survey were within that age group—but constitute fewer than 4 percent of the youngest, post-Vietnam generation. Conversely, the post-Vietnam age group included a significantly higher proportion of labor leaders, State Department officials, and media leaders. These results are not atypical. Multivariate analyses of the FPLP surveys have generally reduced rather than enhanced the impact of age on responses to most issues.[18]

In summary, there is little evidence presented here to sustain the hopes—or fears—that the inevitable replacement of one generation by its successor will give rise to significant changes in public or elite attitudes toward foreign affairs. These attitudes may well change over any extended period of time, as they have in recent years on a number of central Cold War issues, but generational differences may not be the most fruitful place to begin the search for the dynamics of change.

Gender

One of the pioneers of public opinion research wrote almost a half century ago that "more women than men seem to be ignorant of or apathetic to foreign policy issues" (Almond 1950, 121). More than thirty years later, Donald Regan, President Reagan's hapless chief of staff, offered similar observations about women being more interested in shopping than in foreign affairs. But the ignorance-apathy thesis is not the only such stereotype. A strong and systematic correlation between gender and attitudes toward the use of force is often alleged but is much less frequently supported with systematic evidence, although recent research has begun to provide some support.

Although such stereotypes may still be found in the literature, there are also signs that serious interest in the impact of gender on politics has grown substantially in recent years (see, for example, Beckman and D'Amico 1994; Brandes 1994; D'Amico and Beckman 1995; Eichenberg 2003; Nincic and Nincic 2002). In the United States, the term *gender gap* entered the mainstream political vocabulary only after the Reagan presidential election of 1980. One obvious reason for enhanced attention is that women are playing a more important, if not yet equal, leadership role in politics. Margaret Thatcher was England's longest-serving twentieth-century prime minister, and women have led governments in countries as diverse as Sri Lanka, Norway, Finland, Israel, Canada, New Zealand, France, Poland, Iceland, the Philippines, Pakistan, Nicaragua, Yugoslavia, Turkey, and India; women comprise at least 30 percent of national legislators in fourteen countries (Inter-Parliamentary Union 2003, 1). At the same time, there is a growing sense among students and observers of political behavior that much of the received wisdom, such as the stereotypes just cited, merits serious empirical examination. However, the interest in and literature about gender politics has not necessarily yielded a consensus. With respect to public opinion, for example, differences exist on such basic questions as the following:

1. Is there a gender gap? Or, more precisely, which issues give rise to consistent and substantial differences between men and women? There is some evidence of a systematic gender gap. For example, Philip Converse found substantial gender differences and that "'Rambo' themes come very disproportionately from males" (1987b, 61). According to Sandra Baxter and Marjorie Lansing (1980), war/peace concerns are an exception to the general rule that men and women agree on most issues, and a study by David Fite, Marc Genest, and Clyde Wilcox (1990) identified gender as among the most important demographic predictors of foreign policy attitudes. Lisa Catherine Olga Brandes (1994) also found large, stable, and significant gender gaps on security policy attitudes in the United States and Great Britain throughout the period since the end of World War II. A broad examination of survey data led Robert Y. Shapiro and Harpreet Mahajan (1986) to conclude that systematic gender differences also emerge from "compassion" issues and those involving regulation and protection. Wittkopf's (1990, 1995) analyses of the CCFR data during the 1970s and 1980s found some gender-based differences along both the militant internationalist and cooperative internationalist dimensions, but that was no longer the case in 1994, when gender was combined with other background variables. A multivariate study of U.S. interventions in Korea, Vietnam (in 1966 and 1972), and Iraq (both Desert Shield in 1990 and Desert Storm in 1991) revealed not only significantly greater support for these undertakings by men in all five cases but also stronger approval for tougher military action in the three cases in which respondents were offered multiple options about the preferred strategy (Nincic and Nincic 2002). The most comprehensive analysis of gender effects during the post–Cold War era found that women were generally less supportive of defense spending or the use of force abroad. The purpose for the use of force also affected the gender gap; for example, it narrowed in cases of humanitarian interventions (Eichenberg 2003). The gender gap on defense spending appears with great consistency, but there have been occasions

when women were stronger advocates of budget allocations for the Pentagon. One of them occurred in the wake of the terrorist attacks of 9/11. Whereas in January 2001 more men (53 percent to 42 percent) had rated strengthening the military as a "top priority," a year later the gender gap remained at 11 percent, but support among women was higher by a margin of 57 to 46 percent (Pew 2002b, 3).

Conversely, Pamela Johnston Conover (1988) has argued that "feminism," an ideological predisposition toward a certain stance on women's issues, overshadows gender in explaining beliefs and values. A number of Americans Talk Security (1988) surveys also cast some doubt on stereotypical views of gender differences. Women consistently expressed more skeptical opinions about the USSR than did men. Although women were more inclined to describe themselves as "doves," men offered more support on all five arms control items by an average margin of 6 percent; expressed more trust in the USSR on six of seven items (6 percent); assessed Mikhail Gorbachev more favorably on eight items (9 percent); had more benign views of Soviet motives on six of nine items (3 percent); assessed relations between the superpowers more favorably on ten of thirteen items (5 percent); and expressed a more optimistic view on the likelihood of nuclear war (10 percent). In the only exception to this pattern, women were more critical on three items relating to the impact of defense spending (6 percent).[19]

2. Have gender differences widened or narrowed during recent years? There appeared to be somewhat greater agreement on this issue, at least through the mid-1980s, as the evidence seemed to indicate that the gender gap was in fact widening (Baxter and Lansing 1980; Klein 1984; Shapiro and Mahajan 1986). The 9/11 terrorist attacks resulted in narrowing gender differences on a number of defense issues, but subsequent surveys on the Iraq issue reversed that trend, revealing once again some striking differences between men and women on questions revolving around the use of force abroad. The March 2003 invasion of Iraq is a good case in point. A Gallup survey during the first week of the war found a strong majority (72 percent) in favor of the attack, but support was considerably greater among men (78 percent) than among women (66 percent) (Jeffrey Jones 2003a).

3. To the extent that there is a gender gap, is it the result of changing attitudes and behavior among women? Conversely,

does the gender gap arise as a result, for example, of growing conservatism and identification with the Republican Party among men? According to Barbara Ehrenreich (1984), the gender gap will increase because a growing number of women will defect from conservative positions on three broad classes of issues — "peace, environmental protection, and social justice" — that correspond almost exactly with those on which Shapiro and Mahajan (1986) found evidence of significant gender differences. Conversely, Daniel Wirls (1986) proposed a male-oriented explanation of emerging gender differences on the same classes of issues, arguing that the differences have developed because of growing conservatism and Republicanism among men rather than a movement to the political left by women. Similar interpretations may be found in works by Louis Boyce (1985) and Karen M. Kaufmann and John R. Petrocik (1999), but in the latter study the results for defense and military questions were weaker and less stable. Richard C. Eichenberg (2003) also found that changes in support for defense spending among men tended to determine the size of the gender gap on the issue.

4. Are gender differences more pronounced among the general public or among leaders? Vicky Randall (1982) and Ehrenreich (1984) indicate that gender differences are widest among the most highly educated. Conversely, six elite surveys undertaken between 1976 and 1996 found relatively limited evidence of such differences on foreign policy issues (Holsti and Rosenau 1981, 1995).

Despite the growing interest in questions surrounding the gender gap hypothesis, studies to date have yet to yield a solid consensus except perhaps on the fact that the gap has been a consistent feature of recent U.S. presidential elections. The differences are all the more striking because, with the exception of Neil Nevitte and Roger Gibbins (1987), who undertook surveys of both Canadian and American students, and Brandes's (1994) study in the United States and Great Britain, most of the others are focused on a single country (the United States) and cover a relatively short span of time.

The General Public

Most of the findings on gender-based differences reflect results since the early 1980s. Thus they span the late Cold War years, the disintegration of the USSR, and the conflicts of the post–Cold War era, including the 9/11 attacks and the 2003 invasion of Iraq.

First, the differences between women and men are quite limited on some important issues, including Soviet international motives during the Cold War (39 percent of men and an equal percent of women judged it to be "world domination"), the impact of eliminating all nuclear weapons (46 percent of both women and men believed it would make no difference, and 22 percent of both groups stated that it would reduce the chances of a war with the USSR), the appropriate criteria and levels of defense spending (62 percent of men and 58 percent of women agreed that the United States should spend whatever is necessary rather than only what we can afford), assessments of U.S. participation in the Bosnian war (46 percent of men and 51 percent of women judged it to be "about right," and 30 percent of each group thought it was "too much"), proposals to send twenty thousand U.S. troops to Bosnia (opposed by more than two-thirds of both women and men), immigration (more than 60 percent of both men and women felt it should be reduced), and economic competition as "more of a threat to our nation's future than communism" ever was (45 percent of men and 44 percent of women agreed). Finally, after the government in Kuwait arrested several Iraqi agents and charged them with plotting the assassination of President George H. W. Bush, a June 1993 Gallup poll asked whether the United States should have Saddam Hussein assassinated to remove him from power. Women were very slightly more inclined to support that option (54 percent to 53 percent).[20]

A second conclusion is that moderate gender differences characterized assessments of the Soviet threat: women regarded it as more serious than men did. Third, substantial gender gaps have appeared on a number of issues.

> President Reagan's military policies in Central America received the approval of a slight majority of men but only 38 percent of women (*Americans Talk Security* 1988, no. 5).
>
> The Strategic Defense Initiative ("Star Wars") program was approved by 61 percent of men and only 42 percent of women (*Americans Talk Security* 1988, no. 6). After the 2001 terrorist attacks, however, slightly more women (51 percent) than men (47 percent) came to favor building a missile defense system (Kohut 2002, 13).

The proposition that "the United States has a special moral responsibility to help the disadvantaged of the world even if this means putting off some spending on our own domestic problems" was supported by only 35 percent of men and an even smaller 26 percent of women (*Americans Talk Security* 1988, no. 8).

The Bush administration's decision to lift economic sanctions on South Africa in 1991 gained the support of more than half of the men but only 37 percent of the women (G. Gallup Jr. 1991).

A proposal for U.S. air strikes against Bosnian forces attacking Muslim towns was favored by only 44 percent of men and 28 percent of women (G. Gallup Jr. 1993).

While 67 percent of men favored reestablishing relations with Cuba, only 46 percent of women did so (G. Gallup Jr. 2000).

An Americans Talk Security survey during the waning days of the Cold War provides additional evidence about the impact of gender. Respondents were asked to assess the severity of several potential national security threats. The results reveal rather modest gender differences on most issues. Women tended to see somewhat greater dangers in drug trafficking, domestic threats, and U.S. meddling in conflicts abroad. Most notably, women expressed strikingly greater concern about Soviet aggression and that country's military strength relative to the United States. The results in table 5.9, which further distinguish respondents by age, also reveal that older women—those aged forty or more—were consistently the most apprehensive among the four gender-age groups. On balance, however, men and women agreed far more than they disagreed on the more and less severe threats to national security.

The 1991 Persian Gulf War provides still another opportunity to assess gender differences. Responses to Gallup surveys conducted before, during, and after the war reveal the existence of a quite considerable gender gap prior to the initiation of the war when the January 15 deadline for the Iraqi evacuation of Kuwait expired (the questions are listed in table 5.3). In contrast to the strong male support for the George H. W. Bush administration's policies, women were almost evenly divided on most issues. When the war began, there was a tendency for opinions to converge, with a notable gain in support for U.S. policies among women.

When asked a hypothetical question about the use of tactical nuclear weapons "if it might save the lives of American troops," by a very narrow margin of 46 to 44 percent women expressed greater approval for that option, but when the same question was posed three weeks later without the clause about saving lives, support fell among women (to 25 percent) even more than among men, one-third of whom favored using such weapons.

Although men continued to be somewhat more supportive of the Gulf War undertaking, postwar assessments also revealed a

TABLE 5.9. Assessments of Threats to U.S. National Security in 1988: The Impact of Gender and Age

I would like to get your assessment of some of the national security threats (and other challenges) the United States will face in the next five years or so. Please tell me whether [*threat*] poses an extremely serious, very serious, somewhat serious, or not very serious threat to our country's national security interests.

		Extremely serious + Very serious (%)			
		Men		Women	
Threat	All Respondents	Under 40	40 and over	Under 40	40 and over
International drug trafficking	87	78	89	87	93
The spread of nuclear weapons to Third World countries	81	83	89	83	78
Terrorist activities around the world	79	80	76	77	83
Damaging our environment from things like air and water pollution or the heating of the earth's atmosphere known as the greenhouse effect	77	72	77	76	81
Domestic problems like unemployment, homelessness, and crime	73	68	68	71	83
The undermining of our constitutional government	59	59	59	56	61
The economic competition from countries like Japan and West Germany	55	53	57	44	65
Unnecessary U.S. involvement in conflicts around the world	52	48	49	53	56
Soviet aggression around the world	50	47	43	52	57
An increase in Soviet military strength relative to the United States	50	41	49	56	55
The spread of religious fanaticism in Third World countries	36	29	40	33	41

Source: Data from *Americans Talk Security* 1988, 93–103.

relatively small gender gap. When asked, "Do you approve or disapprove of the way George [H. W.] Bush has handled the situation in Iraq since the war in the Persian Gulf ended?" responses among women and men were identical—63 percent approved. Strong majorities also gave an affirmative answer to the question, "All in all, was the current situation in the Mideast involving Iraq and Kuwait worth going to war over?" In this case, however, men were somewhat more inclined to answer affirmatively—by a margin of 71 to 62 percent.

The evidence reviewed here neither wholly refutes nor strongly confirms the gender gap thesis. Women consistently expressed less support for such American interventions as assistance to the contras in Nicaragua or the invasion of Iraq to force Saddam Hussein's forces out of Kuwait, but women were no less willing to have the United States involved in efforts to end the civil war in Bosnia. Perhaps the latter undertaking appeared more attractive because its primary goal could be portrayed as a largely humanitarian project to prevent "ethnic cleansing" and the related horrors of that conflict. It is less clear, moreover, that the roots of women's attitudes on interventions lie in an aversion to the use of force. To be sure, a huge gender gap existed on proposals to initiate air strikes against Bosnian Serbs who were shelling Muslim cities, but women were no less prepared than men to use tactical nuclear weapons to reduce U.S. casualties in Operation Desert Storm or to remove Saddam Hussein from power by assassination. Nor did women express more empathetic attitudes toward U.S. Cold War adversaries or greater support for foreign assistance to poorer countries. And despite some evidence that gender and age combined to affect assessments of threats to national security, the more impressive pattern that emerges from the data in table 5.9 is the striking similarity in rankings of threats by men and women, whatever their ages.

Opinion Leaders

The six FPLP surveys of opinion leaders undertaken between 1976 and 1996 provide modest evidence of strong and persistent gender gaps on foreign policy issues. The militant/cooperative internationalism (MI/CI) classification scheme was shown earlier to be strongly related to party and ideology. In contrast, the distribution of men and women in the MI/CI scheme consistently yielded very low correlations.[21] More generally, evidence of a gender gap in these studies can be summarized briefly.

Women consistently expressed a greater degree of concern for protecting the environment. There has been some narrowing of gender differences on these issues, a trend that arises largely from men catching up with women rather than from a declining environmental sensitivity among women. At least on this cluster of issues, the results run counter to the previously cited hypothesis that the gender gap arises from a change in men's attitudes—specifically, that it is the result of men having moved toward more conservative positions during the 1980s.

As shown earlier, compared to the general public, opinion leaders are significantly less protectionist on trade issues, which were also among the few that did not divide opinion leaders along partisan lines (table 5.6). In contrast, consistent gender differences did emerge from the 1996 FPLP survey items on the same issues. Specifically, on nine of the ten items in table 5.10, women expressed somewhat more skeptical attitudes toward trade, its impact, and efforts to reduce restrictions on the flow of goods and services across national frontiers. These findings stand up fairly well even when responses are controlled for ideology; gender differences remain significant for all but three of the items: the use of threats against Japan and Europe on trade issues, economic rivalries as a cause of war, and the importance of protecting business interests abroad. These results do not limn a portrait of women as ardent protectionists but reveal a more consistent pattern of gender differences than is the case on many issues. The 18 percent gaps on the related questions about desirability of erecting trade barriers and job protection as a foreign policy goal stand out as especially significant. Trade policy is one of the few issues on which there are neither strong partisan nor ideological differences, and thus the strong gender gap on this issue stands out rather sharply.

Women tended to be more wary of America's Cold War adversaries—both China and the Soviet Union—a finding that survived even when the data were subjected to multivariate analyses. This wariness and skepticism about the USSR was no less evident during the Gorbachev years as the Cold War was winding down and after disintegration of the USSR.

Hypotheses about a greater sensitivity among women to international "compassion issues" such as combating world hunger or providing Third World development assistance received very little support from the FPLP data.

Perhaps the most consistent finding was a greater skepticism among women about foreign entanglements, including but not limited to military interventions abroad. The evidence suggests that the gender gap arises less from a general aversion to the use of force and more from greater doubts about commitments and interventions that might entangle the United States in undertakings abroad. This orientation manifested itself in a number of specific ways in which women differed from men, including less support for American responsibility for the defense of allies or commitments to specific nations and a more skeptical attitude toward

TABLE 5.10.   Attitudes on Trade Issues among Opinion Leaders in the 1996 FPLP Survey: The Impact of Gender (in percentages)

	Reported Responses	All Respondents ($N = 2{,}141$)	Men ($N = 1{,}736$)	Women ($N = 340$)
Erecting trade barriers against foreign goods to protect American industries and jobs*	Agree	22	19	37
Granting most-favored-nation trade status to China*	Agree	46	49	34
Signing NAFTA with Canada and Mexico*	Agree	80	81	71
Signing the GATT trade agreement and joining the WTO	Agree	80	81	74
Using the threat of protectionism to open Japanese and European markets to U.S. goods	Agree	72	73	66
Economic rivalries among nations [as a cause of war]	Very serious	36	34	44
Economic competition from Europe [as a national security threat]*	Very serious	4	3	8
Economic competition from Japan [as a national security threat]*	Very serious	7	6	13
Protecting the jobs of American workers [as a foreign policy goal]*	Very important	29	26	44
Protecting the interests of American business abroad [as a foreign policy goal]	Very important	19	19	21

*Differences among groups significant at the .001 level even when controlling for ideology.

both military and economic assistance programs abroad. Women were also more inclined than men to favor imposition of economic sanctions; because economic sanctions reduce or eliminate trade, aid, and related interactions with the target country, choice of that policy instrument can be viewed not only as a less violent alternative to war but also as a form of withdrawal from foreign entanglement. Thus, although women differed little from men in placement in the MI/CI scheme—specifically, there was no evidence of women being disproportionately in the isolationist quadrant of that scheme—they did express less support for various forms of American involvement abroad.

One significant reason for a skeptical view of internationalist undertakings is that they might lead to confrontations, crises, and conflict among major powers. Because the end of the Cold War and disintegration of the Soviet Union substantially reduced those risks, these events might also have affected the nature and magnitude of gender differences. A brief examination of some data from the 1992 and 1996 FPLP surveys on the Gulf War will offer some clues about whether these differences are in fact widening or narrowing.

Unlike most Middle East confrontations of the previous four decades, the conflict arising from Iraq's invasion of Kuwait did not carry the risk of an escalating crisis between Washington and Moscow. Moreover, when President George H. W. Bush ended the short military campaign after Iraqi forces had been expelled from Kuwait, American casualties had been lower than even the most optimistic projections. The reduced risks of a confrontation with the USSR and low casualties might have been expected to narrow gender differences on the war but did not do so. When asked about their policy preferences before the start of the war, male opinion leaders favored the immediate use of force over giving economic sanctions more time to work by a margin of 58 to 37 percent; only 5 percent opposed getting involved at all. Policy preferences among women were significantly different: a plurality of 48 percent favored the economic sanctions option, whereas only 41 percent supported the immediate use of force and 11 percent opposed any American involvement.

The successful end of the war against Iraq increased retrospective support for the use-of-force option but also slightly widened the gender gap. Whereas 64 percent of the men preferred the force option after the war, only 45 percent of the women did so. Moreover, by a margin of 16 to 7 percent, women outstripped men in opposing any involvement at all in the conflict. These significant gender differences persisted even when responses were controlled for ideology. That is, within each ideological group (very liberal, somewhat liberal, moderate, somewhat conservative, very conservative), women were less enthusiastic about the immediate use of force against Iraq.

A cluster of questions asking opinion leaders to assess the consequences of the Persian Gulf War provides additional evidence of a gender gap and the reasons for it. The first five items in table 5.11 emphasize various positive outcomes of the war, and the next five focus on less favorable ones. Majorities among male opinion leaders agreed with each of the favorable assessments and rejected the negative ones. In striking contrast, women were significantly less inclined to agree that the conflict increased U.S. influence in general or more specifically in the Middle East, and a majority rejected the judgment that the war "was a great victory for the United States." The largest gender difference emerged on the proposition that "the United States spent money abroad that needed to be spent at home." Women were also far more prone to agree that too many Iraqis had been killed in the war and to express the fear that the conflict had increased the prospects for violence and terrorism in the Middle East. It is again noteworthy that while each of the items in table 5.11 gave rise to significant ideological differences, in six cases the gender differences persisted even after multivariate analyses had controlled for ideology.

Several Gulf War items were repeated four years later, and a new one—on ending the war with Saddam Hussein still in power—was added. The responses bear a striking resemblance to those of the previous survey as women persisted in taking a less triumphalist view of the war. In light of the George W. Bush administration's repeated threats to launch a war against Iraq to remove Saddam from power, culminating in the 2003 invasion of Iraq, it is noteworthy that both men and women regretted the elder President Bush's decision in 1991 to end the war while the regime in Baghdad remained intact.

Some further evidence of a gender gap emerges on several questions in the 1996 FPLP survey about American commitments and undertakings abroad. Opinion leaders split sharply along gender lines on ten of these questions. Almost 40 percent of the women agreed that "we shouldn't think so much in international terms but concentrate more on our own national problems," whereas just over a quarter of the men (27 percent) expressed support for this proposition. These gender differences also manifested themselves in levels of approval for several items related to international commitments and undertakings.

America's conception of its leadership role must be scaled down (men: 40 percent; women: 49 percent).

The United States spends too much on military aid to other nations (men: 55 percent; women: 73 percent).

The United States has a moral obligation to prevent the destruction of the state of Israel (men: 75 percent; women: 65 percent).

Sending U.S. peacekeeping troops to Haiti (men: 61 percent; women: 52 percent).

TABLE 5.11.   Assessments of the Persian Gulf War: The Impact of Gender

Here are some assessments of the Persian Gulf War. Please indicate how strongly you agree or disagree with each statement.

| | Agree Strongly + Agree Somewhat (%) | | | |
| | 1992 | | 1996 | |
	Men	Women	Men	Women
It increased the influence of the United States with other nations	82	66*	84	58*
Soviet-American cooperation before and during the war helped to establish firmer foundations for a new world order	80	76	—	—
It was a great victory for the United States	62	43*	67	43*
It has given the U.S. the leverage needed to gain settlement of other Middle Eastern issues such as the Arab-Israeli conflict	60	46*	—	—
It put the Vietnam War behind us	56	48	47	38
The U.S. spent money abroad that needed to be spent at home	37	58*	22	50*
Too many Iraqis were killed	37	47*	—	—
The U.S. will be too ready to use military force and go to war again	35	43	—	—
It increased frustration and hatred in the Middle East and will bring more violence and terrorism	31	44*	—	—
The U.S. will be too confident and drop its guard against foreign threats	21	19	—	—
The U.S. should have continued the war until Saddam Hussein was removed from power	—	—	72	65

*Gender differences significant at the .001 level. Differences are significant after controlling for ideology.

The United States spends too much on economic aid to other nations (men: 28 percent; women: 47 percent).

The United States has a moral obligation to prevent the military conquest of Taiwan (men: 59 percent; women: 44 percent).

Military aid programs will eventually draw the United States into unnecessary war (men: 32 percent; women: 58 percent).

Our allies are perfectly capable of defending themselves and they can afford it, thus allowing the United States to focus on internal rather than external threats to its well-being (men: 41 percent; women: 52 percent).

The United States is the world's only superpower and must thus become involved in any region when political instability is jeopardized (men: 29 percent; women: 17 percent).

This pattern of responses is especially significant because, unlike many of the gender differences that have emerged from the FPLP surveys, they did not disappear when the responses were controlled for ideology.

In contrast to this evidence of a gender gap, two additional items that advocate at least some retrenchment of U.S. international commitments gained the support of majorities among both men and women without significant differences between the two groups. These questions focus on deploying troops abroad and serving as a model for democratic development in the Third World by solving domestic problems. In addition, huge majorities among both groups rejected the proposition that "the United States should not hesitate to intrude upon the domestic affairs of other countries in order to establish and preserve a more democratic world order."

Finally, a cluster of questions asking opinion leaders to evaluate a series of potential threats to U.S. national security may be especially telling because it offers a varied menu, including several threats that are at least in part residues from the Cold War (nuclear weapons in the former Soviet Union and the Third World, Russian military power, China as a world power, and Middle East conflicts), two environmental issues, potential dangers with a strong post–Cold War flavor (drugs, population, the rich nation–poor nation gap, economic competition, immigration, and mass migrations), two others that took on greater significance after 9/11 (international terrorism and Islamic fundamentalism), two domestic issues, and one that addresses the possibility that this country will meddle in conflicts that are "none of our business." Judgments about such a broad range of potential national security threats should reveal a good deal about the scope and magnitude of gender gaps.

The responses of opinion leaders, summarized in table 5.12, provide some evidence of a gender gap in 1992. Women were somewhat more inclined toward a more serious assessment of most of the thirteen threats. In several cases—environmental issues, drug trafficking, armed conflict in the Middle East, and unwarranted American meddling abroad—significant gender differences emerged. But a further analysis of the responses reveals that, except in the case of drug trafficking, the gap disappeared when ideology was introduced into the analysis.

Owing to different response options in the 1996 survey, it is not possible to directly compare responses with those that emerged from the study four years earlier. However, both men and women ranked nuclear proliferation as the most worrisome threat. Beyond agreement on proliferation, the 1996 survey yielded somewhat stronger evidence of a gender gap, notably on judgments about the threats arising from international terrorism, drug trafficking, environmental problems, immigration, and American interventions abroad. Unlike the case four years earlier, however, almost all of the differences between men and women remained statistically significant even after controlling for ideology; only on the perceived threats arising from the growing gap between rich and poor nations did the introduction of ideology into the analysis erase the differences.

Two broad generalizations emerge from the data in table 5.12. Reading it horizontally, women consistently judged each individual threat to be more serious than did men. But if the table is read vertically, a fairly solid consensus emerges on the hierarchy of perceived national security dangers; the rank-order correlations between those of men and women are very high both in 1992 (.96) and four years later (.91).

In summary, opinion leaders tend to resemble the general public with respect to many aspects of gender differences. On some issues—the Persian Gulf War and trade are good examples—the gaps between men and women are substantial, and they do not vanish when other background attributes such as ideological preferences are introduced into the analysis. On many other issues,

TABLE 5.12.   Assessments of Threats to U.S. National Security in the 1992 and 1996 FPLP Surveys: The Impact of Gender

This question asks you to evaluate the seriousness of the following issues as threats to American national security during the remaining years of this century. Please indicate how serious you regard each possible threat.

	Very serious (%)[a]			
	1992		1996	
	Men	Women	Men	Women
Possession of nuclear weapons by Third World countries	—	—	64	68
Possession of nuclear weapons by Third World countries and terrorists	87	88	—	—
An inability to solve such domestic problems as the decay of cities, homelessness, unemployment, racial conflict, and crime	89	91	45	62[b]
International terrorism	—	—	37	57[b]
Uncontrolled growth of the world's population	66	66	38	43
International drug trafficking	72	78[d]	35	52[b]
The federal budget deficit	84	82	33	40[d]
Expansion of Islamic fundamentalism	—	—	30	34
Environmental problems like air pollution and water contamination	76	82[c]	24	46[b]
The development of China as a world power	—	—	27	28
A growing gap between rich nations and poor nations	58	63	24	32[c]
American interventions in conflicts that are none of our business	31	42[c]	15	29[b]
Large numbers of immigrants and refugees coming to the U.S.	—	—	14	29[b]
The military power of Russia	—	—	5	7[d]
Armed conflicts in the Middle East	57	62[c]	—	—
The greenhouse effect and other changes in the global climate induced by human activity	56	66[c]	—	—
Nuclear weapons in republics that seceded from the former Soviet Union	56	61	—	—
Economic competition from Japan and Europe	46	44	—	—
Mass migrations	33	38	—	—
Economic competition from Japan	—	—	6	13[b]
Economic competition from Europe	—	—	3	8[b]

[a]"Extremely serious" plus "very serious" in 1992
[b]Gender differences significant at the .001 level
[c]Gender differences significant at the .001 level, but not after controlling for ideology
[d]Gender differences significant at the .001 level, but only after controlling for ideology

however, gender-based cleavages pale in size and persistence when compared to those defined by other background attitudes. Although gender does not rival ideology and party as a potent source of foreign policy attitudes, it is also not irrelevant. In the light of subsequent events, the 20 percent gender gap on the threat posed by international terrorism stands out. It may also be most relevant on precisely the issues that are central to post–Cold War foreign policy debates on the scope and nature of American international commitments, including trade and interventions abroad.

Other Background Attributes

Education

One of the best-supported generalizations about foreign policy attitudes is that increasing levels of education are associated with stronger support for internationalism. Foreign policy questions during the first decade of systematic polling were largely directed at attitudes toward various aspects of American involvement in world affairs, such as participation in World War II and active participation in international affairs after that conflict, including but not limited to membership in the United Nations. These early surveys found a consistent pattern wherein the least educated segments of the public were also the least likely to support an active international U.S. role (Bruner 1944; National Opinion Research Center 1947). Although immense international changes have occurred in the almost six decades since those pioneering studies, the link between the level of education and internationalism has persisted (Hero 1959, 1969; Watts and Free 1973; B. Hughes 1978). Education is also strongly correlated to interest in international affairs. Among college graduates, the four news categories of highest interest are international, Washington, community, and local government. In contrast, for those with a high school education or less, the comparable categories are crime, community, health, and sports (Pew 2002c, 30).

Even with the development of a more differentiated concept of internationalism—for example, when a distinction is drawn between militant and cooperative internationalism—the link to education has persisted, although in a somewhat modified form. Higher education is strongly correlated with support for cooperative internationalism, but the association with militant internationalism is somewhat weaker and more tenuous (Wittkopf 1990, 37–39; 1995, 14).

The many surveys on the Persian Gulf War provide an opportunity to examine the impact of education on a recent issue. The Gallup polls undertaken before, during, and after military operations against Iraq indicate that even on an issue with strong military internationalist overtones, the links between education and approval of international undertakings persist, although the relationship is not linear. Before the war, levels of support for military action to drive Iraq out of Kuwait were consistently highest among those with some college experience, followed by college graduates, high school graduates, and those with less than a high school diploma. These differences narrowed during the war and in retrospective assessments of the conflict. A July 1991 Gallup survey found that 78 percent of the general public approved of the U.S. decision to go to war; appraisals from the four education-level groups fell within a very narrow range of approval—75 to 79 percent. The most striking differences in these surveys concerned questions about the possible use of tactical nuclear weapons if it would reduce American casualties (50 percent of high school graduates approved versus 35 percent of college graduates) and a hypothetical law to ban peace demonstrations during a war (51 percent of those without a high school diploma agreed, whereas only 16 percent of college graduates did so).

Findings from the second war against Iraq were largely in line with those in 1991, although overall support declined and the range increased somewhat—65 to 77 percent. College graduates—often the most internationalist education group—and those lacking a high school diploma were least supportive of the war at 65 percent and 67 percent, respectively (Jeffrey Jones 2003a).

Because opinion leaders tend to have very high levels of educational attainment, analyses to unearth links between education and foreign policy attitudes are not very meaningful. In both the 1992 and 1996 FPLP surveys, for example, virtually all respondents had graduated from college, and three-fourths of them had earned at least one graduate degree. Analyses based on a differentiation of graduate degrees—for example, distinguishing between the M.A., M.B.A., Ph.D., J.D., M.D. and other degrees—would probably provide a better understanding of the impact of occupation than of the effects of education on foreign policy attitudes.

Region

Region has traditionally been linked to foreign policy attitudes (Lowell 1923, 292). The conventional wisdom has been that midwesterners have an isolationist foreign policy orientation, southerners share internationalist and martial attitudes, and those living on the East and West Coasts are most receptive to such cooperative forms of internationalism as membership in international organizations. On trade issues, the manufacturing North was regarded as the natural home for protectionist sentiments, whereas the agricultural South, dependent on cotton and other exports, was seen as the champion of free trade. Hard evidence supporting these characterizations is often less than definitive, and in some cases it is subject to alternative interpretations. Although systematic survey evidence from the 1919–21 period is lacking, opposition to the Treaty of Versailles and the League of Nations probably was strongest in the Midwest. But ethnicity may provide a plausible alternative to explanations based on geography. German Americans and Irish Americans, two ethnic groups heavily concentrated in the Midwest, tended to oppose the treaty and the league, the former because it placed responsibility for World War I on Germany, the latter because the league was perceived to be an instrument of British policy that would do little to enhance the cause of Irish independence.

Evidence to substantiate the regional thesis is at best mixed. Support in the Midwest for American membership in the United Nations equaled that in other regions (G. H. Gallup 1972, 451–52), and bipartisan cooperation between two midwesterners, Harry S. Truman of Missouri and Arthur Vandenberg of Michigan, contributed significantly to the major undertakings that formed the pillars of an internationalist post–World War II foreign policy, including the Truman Doctrine, the Marshall Plan, and NATO. The experience of World War II; the emergence of national media, first with radio networks and followed by television networks; and the increasing mobility of Americans, a process that was accelerated by World War II, were among the factors that probably contributed to the erosion of whatever distinct regional orientations toward foreign affairs may have existed. Gabriel Almond's analysis of surveys during the early years of systematic polling led him to conclude, "Regional differences in foreign policy attitudes were quite pronounced in the period before World War II, but the evidence for the period since Pearl

Harbor shows regional differences to be of declining importance." In place of a regional explanation, he suggested an alternative geographical thesis that emphasized rural/urban differences (1950, 131, 133; see also Watts and Free 1973; B. Hughes 1978).

Although regionalism appears to be a declining factor in shaping foreign policy attitudes, some evidence indicates that it has not wholly disappeared. Congressional votes have pitted the manufacturing belt against the Sunbelt on foreign policy issues since the 1960s (Trubowitz 1992), and Wittkopf's secondary analyses of the first four CCFR surveys found some regional differences in orientations toward militant and cooperative internationalism, but these variations appear to be situational rather than consistent. While easterners tended to be somewhat more accommodationist than respondents from other regions in all four surveys, for example, both midwesterners and westerners leaned toward three different foreign policy orientations over the course of the twelve-year period (Wittkopf 1990, 39–41, 49).

The Gallup surveys on the Persian Gulf War also provide some support for the regional thesis, but it is very weak. The prewar surveys typically found that southerners were slightly more supportive of military action to drive Iraq out of Kuwait, whereas easterners were slightly less supportive of the military option. Wartime and postwar surveys revealed a further narrowing of the already small regional differences. A few months after the end of military operations, approval for the U.S. decision to go to war with Iraq ranged from 74 percent in the East to 82 percent in the South (G. Gallup Jr. 1991). Regional differences in support for the war that toppled the Saddam Hussein regime in 2003 were also rather modest, ranging between a high of 77 percent in the West to 66 percent in the East (Jones 2003b).

Race

For obvious reasons, much of the attention on race and political attitudes has focused on a broad range of domestic issues that touch in some way on civil rights and efforts to overcome the long legacy of segregation and second-class citizenship for black Americans. It sometimes was assumed that these issues rather than foreign policy topped the political agenda of black Americans and their leaders. Martin Luther King Jr.'s public criticism of the Johnson administration's Vietnam policy may have been something of a watershed event in this respect. Moreover, several developments since the Vietnam War have increased the probability that black Americans would take an active interest in foreign affairs: the end of conscription, leading to a professional military that is both disproportionately black and one of the most effective institutions for professional advancement of minorities; controversy about American policy in Africa, especially but not limited to South Africa; and increasing activism by black Americans within Congress and congressional lobbying groups on such foreign policy issues as sanctions on South Africa and the treatment of refugees from Haiti.

Much of the evidence indicates that black Americans tend to be more isolationist than the public as a whole, but, as one analyst has pointed out, it is sometimes unclear whether there are equally plausible explanations, including class and education, that may account for differences in foreign policy attitudes (Hero 1959; Watts and Free 1973; B. Hughes 1978; Wittkopf 1990, 41, 44; Wittkopf 1995, 14). However, responses to the Persian Gulf surveys appear to indicate that race may well be emerging as one of the more powerful sources of foreign policy cleavages. The evidence summarized in table 5.13 reveals that although the gaps between whites and nonwhite minorities—for example, Asian Americans or Latinos—are consistent but of moderate magnitude, those between white and black Americans can only be described as enormous. The racial chasm was only partially bridged by the onset of the war. Although the United States achieved its goal of forcing Iraq out of Kuwait and did so with minimal casualties, postwar appraisals of the American undertaking yielded striking cleavages that tended to coincide with race. Whereas more than four-fifths of whites approved in retrospect of the decision to initiate the war against Iraq, the comparable figure among black Americans was 37 percent. Race has also been a source of divisions on at least four other recent foreign policy issues: South Africa, Haiti, Somalia, and Bosnia. Compared to whites, black Americans were more supportive of U.S. intervention in the first three cases, whereas the opposite pattern emerged with respect to the civil war in Bosnia.[22]

A survey of more than two thousand Americans during the week following the March 2003 U.S. invasion of Iraq revealed that the differences between various demographic groups remained largely unchanged from the findings summarized earlier. The September 11 terrorist attacks had narrowed most demographic differences because of widespread approval of the intervention in Afghanistan to oust the Taliban regime and to track down al Qaeda leaders. But despite the George W. Bush administration's repeated efforts to link Iraq to al Qaeda, strong overall approval

TABLE 5.13.   Attitudes on Selected Issues Relating to the Persian Gulf Conflict, before, during, and after the War: The Impact of Race

Date	Question	All	White	Nonwhite	Black
Prewar surveys					
Jan. 13, 1991	Do you think the United States made a mistake in sending troops to Saudi Arabia, or not? [% yes]	29	25	34	62
Jan. 13, 1991	Which of the following comes closest to your opinion? Favor: Withdraw; sanctions; war. [% initiate a war]	50	54	42	25
Wartime surveys					
Jan. 20, 1991	Do you approve or disapprove of the U.S. decision to go to war in order to drive the Iraqis out of Kuwait? [% approve]	80	83	81	59
Jan. 26, 1991	Do you favor or oppose using tactical nuclear weapons against Iraq if it might save the lives of U.S. troops? [% favor]	45	45	45	45
Jan. 26, 1991	Would you favor or oppose a law to ban peace demonstrations while U.S. troops are fighting overseas? [% favor]	31	31	27	41
Feb. 17, 1991	Do you favor or oppose the U.S. use of tactical nuclear weapons in the Persian Gulf War? [% favor]	28	29	31	26
Postwar surveys					
July 14, 1991	All in all, was the current situation in the Mideast involving Iraq and Kuwait worth going to war over, or not? [% yes]	66	71	40	37
July 21, 1991	Looking back, do you approve or disapprove of the U.S. decision last January to go to war with Iraq in order to drive the Iraqis out of Kuwait? [% approve]	78	82	46	37

Source: Gallup Organization surveys. The typical survey was spread out over a 3–4-day period. The first column reports the final date of the survey.

(72 percent) for the campaign to oust Saddam Hussein's regime did not extend equally to all groups. Partisan and ideological gaps were very large, whereas those based on gender and region were considerably narrower: Republicans, conservatives, men, and, less strikingly, westerners emerged as the strongest supporters of the military campaign. Responses based on age failed to yield a consistent pattern (table 5.14).

By far the most striking demographic gap on the war in Iraq was the racial one. It may be too early to make any definitive assessment about the persistence or strength of a racial gap on foreign affairs, but the hypothesis that race-based divisions on the use of force abroad are an important feature of the contemporary political landscape receives powerful support from the data in table 5.14. The Bush administration included two highly visible and articulate African American foreign policy officials in Secretary of State Colin Powell and National Security Adviser Condoleezza Rice. Although the latter was a more avid supporter of

TABLE 5.14.   Support for the U.S. War with Iraq: The Impact of Party, Ideology, Gender, Region, Age, and Race

	% Favor	% Oppose
Overall	72	25
Republicans	93	5
Democrats	53	44
Independents	66	31
Conservatives	84	13
Moderates	70	27
Liberals	44	54
Men	78	20
Women	66	32
West	77	21
Midwest	73	24
South	71	26
East	66	32
30–49 years old	75	23
65 years and older	73	25
50–64 years old	69	27
18–29 years old	66	32
White	78	20
Black	29	68
Other race	63	34

Source: Gallup Organization poll conducted March 22–25, 2003 (Jeffrey Jones 2003b).

the war throughout the debates during the months leading up to the invasion of Iraq, both ultimately made the case for the U.S. attack in settings as diverse as the United Nations Security Council and the Sunday talk shows. Despite Powell's and Rice's efforts, a great majority of black Americans conspicuously dissented from the majority that supported the war. In early 2002, after Iraq was identified as part of the "axis of evil" and when top officials in the Bush administration were making almost daily comments about their commitment to ousting Saddam Hussein from power, 76 percent of white respondents favored military action against Iraq, but only 57 percent of nonwhites supported such an operation. When the wording of the question mentioned the possibility of thousands of casualties in a war, the racial gap widened still further, to 61 to 38 percent. The onset of the war did nothing to bridge the chasm between the two groups. Whereas 78 percent of white respondents in a Gallup survey undertaken during the first week of the war supported it, only 29 percent of blacks did so. Thus, the sharp racial divide over the 1991 war to expel the Iraqi invaders from Kuwait, revealed earlier in table 5.13, widened dramatically twelve years later. Indeed, the 49 percent difference may be one of the largest demographic gaps in any major survey on foreign policy issues (Jeffrey Jones 2003b).

A thoughtful analysis of public opinion in five previous U.S. interventions suggests that there may be a common denominator linking the gender and racial gaps on the uses of force abroad: alienation arising from structural features of American society may complement other more specific properties of these two groups (Nincic and Nincic 2002). Whether or not their explanation is valid for a broader range of foreign policy issues, the evidence seems to suggest that race is indeed emerging as an important source of divisions within the American public.

Conclusion

This exploration of the sources of foreign policy opinions began with Destler, Gelb, and Lake's lament of almost two decades ago about the increasingly partisan and ideological character of debates about international issues. The evidence presented here largely sustains their diagnosis, whether the focus is on the general public or opinion leaders. Among both groups, the closely linked attributes of ideology and party identification consistently have been the most powerful correlates of attitudes on a wide range of foreign policy issues, up to and including the 2003 war against Iraq (Jeffrey Jones 2003a). That generalization has withstood repeated multivariate analyses that included other background attributes. Notwithstanding that overall theme, some beliefs transcend party and ideology, and these are far from trivial aspects of international relations—for example, the end of the Cold War and the multipolar nature of the international system that has subsequently emerged. Such events as the demolition of the Berlin Wall and disintegration of the Soviet Union presumably were of such an unambiguous nature and compelling importance that their impact on beliefs transcends partisanship and ideology. Although efforts to claim partisan or ideological advantage from the successful denouement of the Cold War were never in short supply—many a forest has been felled just to print polemics affirming or denying that the Reagan military buildup contributed to the end of the Cold War—the fact of Soviet collapse has not been controversial. Surveys of opinion leaders also have revealed that cleavages on international trade and Middle East issues revolving around Israel and its security divide leaders and the public in other ways. But these are exceptions to the general rule of powerful partisan and ideological cleavages.

In contrast, although the other background factors discussed earlier—gender, generation, region, education, and race—are not irrelevant for explaining foreign policy views, they appear to do so less consistently, and when they do, they only rarely bridge the dominant partisan and ideological cleavages. In the case of race, the most compelling evidence has emerged from attitudes toward the use of force abroad; it remains to be seen whether similar racial gaps characterize public opinion on a wider range of issues. The gender gap is also illustrative. Men and women often differ on specific U.S. security commitments, trade, and the environment, but it is much harder to find comparable evidence of consistent differences on basic orientations toward international affairs, assessments of threats, images of adversaries, the use of force, and foreign aid. More generally, liberal Democrats, whether men or women, usually have similar foreign policy beliefs, which in turn differ sharply from those of conservative Republicans of either sex.

One should nevertheless be cautious about assuming that attributes that contribute only modestly to understanding foreign policy opinions will be equally irrelevant for all issues. Consider the generational hypothesis, wherein it is suggested that because major differences in worldviews are linked to age, the replacement of one cohort with another will account for major changes in attitudes. The evidence has rarely confirmed that this is an especially rewarding way of analyzing U.S. foreign policy attitudes. But other important issues may in fact divide the public, opinion leaders, or both along generational lines. For example, Mayer (1992) has demonstrated that generational replacement had little impact on foreign policy attitudes but constituted a major source of change on some social and cultural issues.

If, as seems likely, the post–Cold War foreign policy agenda will be characterized by a widening array of crucial issues and a continued blurring of the lines between the domestic and international arenas, we might also expect some shifting linkages between foreign policy beliefs and sociodemographic variables. Trade issues may be used to illustrate this hypothesis. Evidence through the mid-1990s indicated that substantial differences existed between the general public and leaders, with the latter far more supportive of efforts to liberalize trade (see table 4.2). The gap no doubt reflected at least in part different personal vulnerabilities to dislocations arising from reduction or removal of trade barriers; blue-collar workers in the textile, shoe, steel, and automobile industries, for example, have been more likely to lose jobs to foreign competition than have bankers, insurance executives, highly educated workers in advanced technology firms, and employees in the "knowledge industries." However, there are also some indications that technological and other changes also may be rendering those in the latter occupational groups increasingly vulnerable; a front-page headline in the *New York Times* proclaimed, "Skilled Workers Watch Their Jobs Migrate Overseas. A Blow to Middle Class: College Educated Foreigners Are Doing High Technology Tasks for Far Less Pay" (August 28, 1995, A:1). Should such trends persist for any significant period beyond the recession that began in 2001, we might well expect that the coalitions supporting and opposing trade liberalization will also change.

In short, although a good deal of stability has existed in the background correlates of foreign policy beliefs during the period since the end of the Vietnam War, including the growth and persistence of partisan and ideological cleavages that have survived the dramatic international changes since the late 1980s, those patterns could change in response to future developments, some of which can only dimly be perceived today.

Finally, what are the linkages between leaders and the general public, particularly with regard to the impact of partisanship and ideology on foreign policy beliefs? This discussion assumes that the relationship between decision makers, opinion leaders, and the general public is better characterized as complex and inter-active rather than simple and unidirectional (as depicted by ei-ther a bottom-up or a top-down model). The latter model has dominated analyses of public opinion and the media at least since Walter Lippmann's early writings, cited in chapter 1, challenged ordinary citizens' ability and willingness to meet the require-ments of classical democratic theory. The central premises of the top-down model are that the general public takes its cues from elites and that the media take theirs from the government. A number of recent studies have raised some serious questions about the adequacy of this model. For example, based on his analysis of the Persian Gulf War, John R. Zaller concluded that "many exaggerated reports of its demise to the contrary, the democratic interplay between leaders and followers was alive and well in the Gulf Crisis" (1994, 271–72). Similarly, a careful analysis of leaders, the media, and public opinion on the 1989 Tiananmen Square massacre and the coup attempt against Mikhail Gorbachev two years later also revealed that the public is capable of taking autonomous positions on foreign policy is-sues that do not merely reflect the views of leaders or the media (Isaacs 1994, 1998).

For purposes of illustrating at least one way of linking leaders and the general public, the hypothesis to be explored here is that

> significant divisions on major issues of national security are usually rooted in ideological differences arising from com-peting views about the proper U.S. role in the world, the major source of threats to national security, and the most ef-fective means and strategies for coping with them; the divi-sions are only secondarily partisan in origin, depending, first, on whether leaders believe that framing the issues in partisan terms will enable them to achieve their goals and, second, on public opinion, actual and anticipated, on these issues.

Leaders may have better informed and more sophisticated worldviews, but these leaders cannot neglect the views of the gen-eral public. Zaller's concept of "anticipated future opinions" (1994, 251)—leaders take policy positions based on their anticipation of future public opinions—serves as a useful way to link leaders and the general public (see also Stimson, MacKuen, and Erikson 1994, 1995). Three examples, sketched in broad strokes rather than fine-grained detail, will illustrate but not adequately test this hypothesis.

During the decade leading up to Pearl Harbor, sharp differences existed about whether and how the United States should deal with the growing military power and increasingly transparent ambitions of expansionist dictatorships in Europe and Asia. To oversimplify, some (including President Roosevelt) feared that aggressive German and Japanese ambitions represented long-term threats to U.S. security and the survival of democracy; it was thus vital for the United States to support the people who were resisting these dictatorships. Critics of this position countered that an active internationalist foreign policy is incompatible with democracy at home. War itself, not the European or Asian balance of power, most directly threatened America's interests and democratic institutions; thus, every effort should be made to avoid once again being drawn into distant conflicts that posed no clear and present danger to the preservation of the republic or its key institutions. (For an excellent and more detailed analysis of public opinion during this period, see Hinckley 1992.)

But these competing worldviews were very imperfectly correlated with party identification, either among leaders or the general public. For example, at the time of his 1937 speech advocating an international "quarantine" of the expansionist powers, President Roosevelt's Democratic Party held overwhelming majorities of 75 to 17 (with 4 "others") in the Senate and 333 to 89 (with 13 "others") in the House. Three years later, when Roosevelt consummated the "destroyer deal" that transferred fifty aged warships to Great Britain by doing an end run around Congress, the Democrats still outnumbered Republicans by three to one in the Senate and by ninety-three seats in the House. Despite these handsome majorities, because foreign policy beliefs in Congress cut across rather than along party lines, Roosevelt repeatedly found himself stymied by various forms of "neutrality legislation" in his efforts to assist the beleaguered allies, even after the collapse of France in the face of the May 1940 German blitzkrieg. Among the president's efforts to build an effective foreign policy coalition across party lines was the replacement in 1940 of his isolationist secretaries of war and the navy with two distinguished Republicans, Henry Stimson and Frank Knox.

The absence of strictly partisan divisions on foreign policy issues was also reflected in the character of several major foreign policy interest groups—the isolationist America First and its internationalist counterparts, the Nonpartisan Committee for Peace through Revision of the Neutrality Laws and the Committee to Defend America by Aiding the Allies, which was led by a newspaper editor with impeccable Republican credentials, William Allen White. Although Roosevelt was never reticent about attacking the GOP when doing so served his political purposes, it would have been self-defeating to frame the key foreign policy issues in partisan terms. Finally, Roosevelt's manifest skill in using the new medium of radio notwithstanding, his efforts to mold public opinion on foreign policy were calculatedly cautious. He interpreted reactions to his "quarantine" speech as unfavorable on balance and, anticipating that the public would be even more critical of concrete steps to help Britain and France, he emphasized repeatedly that he had no intention of permitting the United States to be drawn into war. Thus, despite Roosevelt's personal popularity and public relations skills, his efforts to influence the public on international affairs had a relatively modest impact. As I noted in chapter 1, almost to the eve of Pearl Harbor, strong majorities among the general public favored a wide array of legislative and constitutional efforts to prevent the country from again being pulled into any war for purposes other than defense of the home territory.

The early Cold War period also revealed ideological differences that were less than perfectly correlated with party. Divisions within the GOP pitted such staunch critics of a broadly internationalist foreign policy as Senator Robert Taft and former President Herbert Hoover against the Vandenberg-Dewey-Eisenhower-Dulles faction within the party. Democrats were similarly divided between those supporting Harry Truman, J. William Fulbright, Dean Acheson, and other internationalists and such critics of the U.S. foreign defense policies as Henry Wallace, who bolted the Democrats in 1948 to run for president on the Progressive Party ticket.

The important point, however, is that the internationalists were generally dominant within the leadership of both parties; for example, between 1948 and 1960, presidential candidates of both major parties shared a broad internationalist ideology on foreign affairs. Although sharp partisan differences often existed about which party was best suited to implement that worldview, the principle of active American engagement in world affairs was rarely the basis of partisan debates. That fact no doubt contributed to the absence of striking partisan differences among the general public, at least on many of the important foreign policy issues of the period (see table 5.1). Moreover, many of the major foreign policy interest groups, including the Foreign Policy Association, the United Nations Association, and the Council on Foreign Relations, were largely bipartisan in membership and generally offered support for the internationalist foreign policies of the Truman and Eisenhower administrations. There were, of course, also some critics of internationalism, including the Congress of Industrial Organizations prior to its merger with the American Federation of Labor in 1955, but some of the more vocal critics—for example, the John Birch Society or supporters of Senator Joseph McCarthy—were not primarily partisan in character. Their shotgun charges of treason were aimed at targets in both political parties, and they appealed mostly to those who were prepared to believe in a global communist conspiracy that counted former five-star generals of the army Dwight Eisenhower and George Marshall among its cat's paws.

The late Cold War period, encompassing the two decades prior to demolition of the Berlin Wall, featured sharp divisions within the major political parties. The 1972 Democratic Party presidential nomination of George McGovern represented a repudiation by many Democrats of the Truman-Kennedy-Johnson internationalist policies that, McGovern argued, had ineluctably led to the disaster in Vietnam; it was, therefore, time to "Come home, America." For McGovern's supporters, the most important lesson of Vietnam was that the United States should avoid military engagement in the Third World. Even Fulbright, a stalwart architect and supporter of post–World War II foreign policies, called for rejection of an internationalism that, in his view, had failed to distinguish adequately between vital and peripheral interests.

The Vietnam War and the Nixon-Kissinger policies of trying to contain the USSR by offering carrots (arms control agreements, crisis control measures, expanded trade and credits) as well as sticks (containment and deterrence) also divided Republicans. The Goldwater-Reagan wing of the party narrowly failed to capture the GOP presidential nomination in 1976 but did so four years later. Charging that the détente and arms control policies of his predecessors in the White House, including Republicans Richard Nixon and Gerald Ford, had severely crippled the United

States, if not endangered its survival, Reaganites were no less reluctant than the McGovernites to challenge some foundations of post–World War II foreign and defense policies, albeit from a distinctly different perspective. For them, the lessons of Vietnam included the imperatives of a major military buildup, removal of undue restrictions on the uses of military force, and the desirability of challenging the USSR on the peripheries of its empire (the "Reagan Doctrine").

Thus, whereas the core leadership of the Democratic and Republican Parties during the two decades prior to Vietnam shared some basic axioms about the appropriate U.S. role in world affairs, critics of those premises came to dominate the two major parties in the post-Vietnam years. As a consequence, the partisan cleavages came to be more closely aligned with ideological ones. The Democratic Party tended to be the most congenial home for accommodationists, whereas hard-liners were usually found in the Republican Party. Some prominent hard-line Democrats, including Paul Nitze, Eugene Rostow, and Jeane Kirkpatrick, accepted high positions in the Reagan administration. The convergence of ideological and partisan cleavages was also reflected in some of the major foreign policy interest groups of the period, including the hawkish Committee on the Present Danger, more than three dozen of whose members served in key foreign and defense policy positions in the Reagan administration, and more dovish groups such as the Arms Control Association.

In line, then, with the hypothesis on the ideological origins of foreign policy differences presented previously, partisan cleavages should have widened under these circumstances because as each of the two major parties was becoming more ideologically homogeneous, differences between them were becoming more pronounced. As indicated in tables 5.4 and 5.6, that has been true of opinion leaders. Other evidence also reveals that this has also been true among the general public; for example, the data in table 5.2 reveal sharp partisan cleavages on many foreign policy issues. Finally, this hypothesis appears to offer at least a tentative and partial explanation for the tendency of ideology to dominate party identification among both the opinion leaders (see table 5.8) and the general public (Wittkopf 1990, 1995).

In summary, these brief and sketchy interpretations suggest that major international developments, especially those that revolve around questions of war and peace, often give rise to divergent policy prescriptions rooted in different worldviews. Whether they also divide the country along partisan lines depends on complex interactions between leaders and the public. Despite the dominance of FDR's own party, for example, ideological divisions among leaders and the lack of public support for even modest forms of engagement in emerging conflicts in Europe and Asia required Roosevelt to work toward a bipartisan leadership coalition and to avoid framing foreign policy issues in partisan terms. During the Truman and Eisenhower years, the dominance of an internationalist ideology within both political parties as well as a public that was prepared to accept major international undertakings muted sharp partisan clashes on the fundamental nature of American foreign and defense policies. In contrast, controversies over the Vietnam War gave rise to two internally consistent but mutually exclusive interpretations for why the United States became involved in that conflict, why the United States lost, and what lessons should be learned from the defeat. According to one view, an undiscriminating internationalism drew the United States into an unwinnable conflict that never engaged important national interest. According to the other, the United States appropriately viewed the defense of South Vietnam as a vital interest, the war effort fulfilled a solemn treaty obligation, and the United States could have been victorious but for the media, protests at home, and unwise restrictions on military force imposed by political leaders. These Vietnam postmortems, which also yielded divergent lessons about the future conduct of American foreign and defense policies, tended to fall largely along partisan lines (Holsti and Rosenau 1984). Although that conflict ended three decades ago, the continued convergence of partisan and ideological cleavages appears to be one of its more enduring residues.

This discussion has illustrated only one of the ways that analyses of public opinion can attempt to link leaders and the general public. Moreover, even if the foregoing hypothesis seems plausible, the sketchy and anecdotal evidence is not an adequate substitute for the kind of systematic testing that has not been possible here. Nor does it take into account the possible impact of the September 11, 2001, terrorist attacks. Although barely two years have passed since those tragic events, chapter 6 undertakes an early effort to deal with that question.

CHAPTER 6

A Return to Isolationism and Unilateralism?
Pre– and Post–September 11

In 1995, four years after the disintegration of the Soviet Union, Arthur Schlesinger Jr., a historian, former presidential adviser, and once a vocal critic of American intervention in the Vietnam War, wrote that the age of American internationalism was coming to an end. Looking back on the commitment to collective security during the Cold War, he described the hope that "Americans had made the great turning and would forever after accept collective responsibilities" as "an illusion."

> It is now surely clear that the upsurge in American internationalism during the Cold War was a reaction to what was seen as the direct and urgent Soviet threat to the security of the United States. It is to Joseph Stalin that Americans owe the 40-year suppression of the isolationist impulse. The collapse of the Soviet threat faces us today with the prospect that haunted Roosevelt half a century ago—the return to the womb in American foreign policy.... The isolationist impulse has risen from the grave, and it has taken the new form of unilateralism. (1995, 5)

Schlesinger's essay went on to describe declining support for internationalism across the entire spectrum of American society, from the "housewife in Xenia, Ohio," to members of the Council on Foreign Relations and to many officials in Washington. But Schlesinger was writing at about the midpoint between demolition of the quintessential symbol of the Cold War, the Berlin Wall, and the 2001 terrorist attacks on the United States, as well as eight years prior to the second war against Iraq. Have the September 11 attacks and the regime change in Iraq "changed everything," as some commentators have asserted, or will these events prove to be less than defining moments for the new millennium? The realist critique of democracies and especially of public opinion is that because memories of even dramatic events are short-lived, parochial domestic and personal concerns will ultimately drive international ones to the back burner. If, in fact, the dozen years following the end of the Cold War were marked by a reversion to isolationism and unilateralism, as Schlesinger claimed, then, barring a repetition of terrorist attacks on the homeland, the events of September 11 may well represent a temporary change in a long-term trend away from internationalism and multilateralism. The alternative thesis is that public support for broad and active international engagement, often with the cooperation of allies and through various international institutions, persisted through the years following the disintegration of the Soviet Union. In that case, multilateral impulses are likely to persist into the foreseeable future. For that reason, it is useful to undertake separate analyses of the pre– and post–September 11 periods.

As we are now several years into a new millennium and memories of the Cold War are becoming fainter, are we indeed witnessing a fundamental redefinition of the U.S. role in the world along the lines described in Schlesinger's obituary for "a magnificent dream" (A. Schlesinger 1995, 8)? For more than a half century following Pearl Harbor, many American leaders believed that vital national interests required the United States to play an active leadership role in world affairs; disagreements among elites tended to focus not on the desirability of assuming the burdens—and enjoying the benefits—of international leadership but rather on the goals, strategies, and tactics that should be employed in implementing that role. For example, even the sharp differences between incumbent Jimmy Carter and challenger Ronald Reagan that surfaced during the 1980 presidential campaign were not about whether the United States should take an active position in world affairs but instead concerned the goals, values, and strategies that should inform and guide the country in its international undertakings. Reagan emphasized the need to restore a military posture that he charged had been dangerously compromised by the misguided pursuit of détente and arms control by the Nixon, Ford, and Carter administrations as well as the need to confront more forcefully an evil and expansionist Soviet empire. In contrast, Carter was no more inclined than Reagan to reduce America's internationalist stance, but the incumbent president sought to use that leadership position in the service of rather different goals and values. Carter's definition of a foreign policy in which the American people can take pride included emphasizing arms control rather than arms racing and promoting human rights. Thus, if Schlesinger's diagnosis of post–Cold War American foreign policy correctly unearthed a surge toward isolationism and unilateralism, it would be a watershed in thinking about foreign affairs comparable to that triggered by the attack on Pearl Harbor, which, in the words of Senator Arthur Vandenberg, "ended isolationism for any realist" (1952, 1).

How compelling is the thesis that we are undergoing such a fundamental change in beliefs about the country's appropriate role in the world? What evidence suggests that Schlesinger may in fact have discerned an important transformation in American thinking about foreign affairs? Several points come to mind. First, as Schlesinger and so many others have noted so often that it has almost become a cliché, the United States lost the guiding beacon of the Cold War—opposition to the expansion of Soviet influence was so widely regarded as a vital national interest that it provided a default position for American policymakers that usually prevailed in the absence of a powerful case to the contrary. Not only are the links between core American interests and the outcomes of post–Cold War conflicts such as those in Haiti, Somalia, Bosnia, Rwanda, and Kosovo harder to establish, but it may not be easy even to agree on the indicators of success or failure of military intervention in such conflicts.

Some post–Cold War elections might offer additional grounds for supporting Schlesinger's analysis. The 1994 midterm elections provided the Republicans with majorities in both the Senate and House for the first time in forty-two years. The Republican Contract with America included several provisions with isolationist and unilateralist overtones. Moreover, the presidential candidacies of Patrick Buchanan and H. Ross Perot, while ultimately failing to gain either the Republican nomination or the White House, represented nontrivial alternative conceptions of the general U.S. role in international affairs as well as of preferences on such specific issues as trade and protectionism, alliance commitments, immigration policy, peacekeeping missions, and the like. Despite the results of the 1992 and 1996 elections, these candidacies did not represent the final acts of semi-isolationist and unilateralist challenge within either major political party. Ralph Nader's 2000 independent presidential campaign, like those of Buchanan and Perot, was grounded in a critique of globalization and especially in the consequences of trade liberalization. And, as will be noted later in this chapter, George W. Bush's successful 2000 presidential campaign staked out a foreign policy position with more than a few unilateralist overtones.

Although generational theses have rarely provided wholly persuasive explanations of continuity and change in foreign policy, the 1990s in fact witnessed a major change at the leadership level that might plausibly be linked to ways of thinking about international affairs. The defeats of George H. W. Bush and Bob Dole in the 1992 and 1996 elections represented the last hurrah of a generation that came to adulthood during World War II, a conflict in which both Bush and Dole served with valor. Indeed, until Bill Clinton's inauguration, all post–World War presidents save Ronald Reagan had combat experience. In contrast, many leaders in Washington, including former President Clinton, President George W. Bush, Vice President Richard Cheney, and former Senate Minority Leader Trent Lott, share an important common experience—extraordinary efforts to avoid military service in Vietnam. Although several leading senators in both parties served in that conflict, unless John Kerry or Wesley Clark wins the 2004 Democratic nomination, John McCain and Al Gore, both unsuccessful presidential candidates in 2000, may turn out to have been the last serious contenders for the White House who saw active duty in Vietnam.

But the case for a fundamental post–Cold War change in American orientations toward world affairs is not entirely compelling because there are also some reasons to suspect that continuity has not fully given way to change during recent years. As figure 3.1 reveals, surveys of the general public reveal that a substantial majority of Americans continue to support an "active role in world affairs," a point acknowledged by Schlesinger but dismissed as little more than lip service to "euphonious generalities in support of internationalism" because of declining public enthusiasm for some more specific international goals (A. Schlesinger 1995, 7). Nor have opinion leaders, the most internationalist stratum of American society for many decades, shown much inclination to abandon their views in this respect. Eight Chicago Council on Foreign Relations (CCFR) and six Foreign Policy Leadership Project (FPLP) surveys of American opinion leaders, spanning the Cold War and post–Cold War eras (1974–2002), do not offer much evidence that leaders' internationalist impulses collapsed in tandem with the ebbing Soviet threat.

More detailed studies, drawing on evidence from the late 1980s and 1990s, have generally found that even the startling events marking the end of the Cold War, culminating in disintegration of the USSR, did not give rise to equally dramatic changes in public opinion. Appraisals of quite specific aspects of foreign affairs—for example, the perceived level of threat from the Soviet Union—may have changed to reflect international realities, but the basic structures of attitudes toward foreign affairs proved quite resistant to change (Murray 1996). If the spectacular developments of 1989–91 did not yield substantial changes in foreign policy orientations, are there compelling reasons to believe that such changes subsequently have occurred? For example, several acute observers of the American political arena noted in the early 1980s that the formulation of American foreign policy had become increasingly marked by strident partisan and ideological bickering (Destler, Gelb, and Lake 1984). There is little evidence that the end of the Cold War or events of the post–Cold War period—including the military campaign to remove the Saddam Hussein regime in Iraq—have softened, much less bridged, these partisan and ideological cleavages (see tables 5.2–5.7). More specifically, it is not wholly clear that recent years have witnessed the emergence of a bipartisan post–Cold War consensus favoring either isolationism or unilateralism.

Finally, is it possible that the attacks of September 11, 2001, have created a new internationalist foreign policy consensus in which international terrorists and terrorist organizations will play the same role that the Axis powers did during World War II and the Soviet Union did during the Cold War? Has the enormity of the attacks convinced a vast majority of American policymakers, opinion leaders, and the general public that the path to success against terrorism must entail consultation, collaboration, and cooperation with other countries on a scale not seen since the height of the Cold War, when the United States played a key role in formation of the United Nations and the North Atlantic Treaty Organization (NATO), the Marshall Plan for economic reconstruction of Europe, and resistance to aggression in Korea? Alternatively, have these attacks persuaded significant segments of the public that an America with fewer international entanglements will also be a less inviting target for violently disaffected terrorist groups—what one analyst has called "blowback" (Johnson 2000)? The recency of the attacks suggests considerable caution in projections about their long-run consequences, but at least some preliminary observations are possible.

There are two key terms in Schlesinger's lament about U.S. foreign policy. *Isolationism* refers to policies that seek to limit or reduce the country's international engagements to the extent that it is possible to do so. Admonitions by George Washington and Thomas Jefferson to shun permanent entangling alliances were efforts to protect the weak, young nation from dangerous embroilments in Europe's frequent wars. *Unilateralism,* which may or may not be a part of an isolationist stance, attempts to engage the world with as few constraints as possible from norms, treaties, agreements, international organizations, and other countries. Its proponents point to the ability to pursue self-defined national interests, undiluted by the need to compromise, and the preservation of the country's sovereign prerogatives as its primary virtues. Flexibility and the ability to act with speed are touted as additional benefits of unilateralism.

A preference for unilateralism may be part of an effort to reduce engagement abroad, as it was during the 1920s and 1930s, when the United States failed to ratify the Treaty of Versailles, torpedoed the London International Economic Conference of 1933, and adopted various types of "neutrality legislation" to prevent the country from being drawn into conflicts abroad in ways that it allegedly had been in 1917. But unilateralism may also characterize the policies of a nation that is highly engaged with the world across virtually all issue areas—that is, one that has clearly rejected the isolationist path. In this case, unilateralism takes the form of a country using its power to impose its rules of engagement whenever there is a possibility that treaties, agreements, norms, or international organizations might require consultation, cooperation, or compromise with others; might impinge on a broad definition of sovereignty; or might in other ways limit the country's freedom of action. American exceptionalism lies at the heart of many briefs on behalf of the unilateral path to coping with global issues. According to its advocates, multilateralism and its attending constraints may be necessary for the weak, who can pursue their vital interests only in conjunction with allies and for whom treaties, agreements, and international organizations provide a rational way to impose some limits on the powerful. But there is no reason for the powerful—and certainly not for a superpower—to accept that logic because, like F. Scott Fitzgerald's description of the rich, they are different. Indeed, the overarching goal, as one analyst points out, is to "invoke America's global mission to limit the prerogatives of other nations but not the United States" (Judis 2003, 22).

Post–Cold War America is not lacking in articulate voices for greatly reduced engagement abroad and their primary arguments are not unlike those of their ideological brethren in earlier eras. A central theme is that the welfare of the United States and its democratic institutions are at an unreasonable—perhaps even fatal—risk as a result of excessive entanglements with the rest of the world, whether because the country will be swamped by floods of immigrants seeking better economic opportunities or because American meddling in conflicts that have only a marginal relationship to vital national interests breeds resentment and invites attacks (Buchanan 2002; Schwarz and Layne 2002). Neoisolationists have cited the events of September 11 as dramatic proof that such fears are well founded. These arguments notwithstanding, the proponents of isolationism are still on the margins rather than at the core of contemporary political debates within either of the two major political parties. For this reason, the remainder of this discussion will focus on the issue of unilateralism, with only secondary attention to isolationism.

This chapter addresses these issues in three stages. The first section examines the policy proclivities of the George W. Bush administration, both before and after the 2001 terrorist attacks. That survey must necessarily summarize major trends rather than undertake detailed descriptions of all aspects of foreign and defense policy. The next section analyzes the views of opinion leaders. There is ample evidence that, compared to the general public, leaders have typically been more inclined to support internationalist and multilateralist policies across a fairly wide range of issues. Any recent change in this respect would therefore provide especially telling support for the Schlesinger thesis. Surveys conducted by the CCFR and the FPLP provide the bulk of the evidence about opinion leaders. The third section assesses the views of the general public as revealed in surveys conducted by Gallup, the CCFR, the Pew Research Center for the People and the Press, the Program on International Policy Attitudes (PIPA) at the University of Maryland, and others.

Bush Administration Foreign and Defense Policies

The George W. Bush administration came to office following the closest and most controversial presidential election since 1876. During the electoral campaign, members of the Bush team asserted that they would present a dramatically different orientation toward world affairs than that of the outgoing Clinton administration. The Bush administration's goals, strategies, and tactics would be characterized by a "hardheaded realism" that placed core national interests ahead of such vague and elusive goals as "nation building," "peacekeeping," and what one critic described derisively as "international social work" worthy of Mother Teresa but not of the world's only superpower (Mandelbaum 1996). In one of the televised presidential debates, candidate Bush expressed the need for the United States to be humble rather than arrogant in exercising its global leadership, but it was also clear that U.S. interests would be self-defined rather than compromised or diluted by any perceived need to accommodate allies, international agreements, or international institutions, much less anything as vague as "world opinion." For example, shortly before the election, Condoleezza Rice, a key member of the Bush foreign policy team who would subsequently be named National Security Adviser, asserted that U.S. peacekeeping troops in parts of the former Yugoslavia would be withdrawn should Bush be elected. Such rhetoric is of course not always a reliable guide to the policies of a new administration, a point amply demonstrated by candidate Bill Clinton's attacks on the policies of incumbent President George H. W. Bush in 1992; after denouncing Bush's actions with respect to refugees from Haiti, the civil war in Bosnia, and most-favored-nation trade status for China, Clinton subsequently adopted policies that varied only slightly from those of his predecessor.

Thus, two questions remain. Was the pattern described by former Secretary of State Warren Christopher as the "anti-predecessor syndrome" (2002, 4) repeated in the transition between Clinton and his successor? How did the events of September 11 affect the foreign and defense policy orientations of the present administration?

President Bush and his advisers did not invariably follow the path favored by the most vocal isolationists and unilateralists, including former Senate Foreign Relations Committee Chair Jesse Helms; journalist–presidential candidate Patrick Buchanan; syndicated columnists Charles Krauthammer, George Will, and William Safire; many libertarians; and others who argued that the end of the Cold War at last freed the United States from having to waste its resources supporting ungrateful allies, the United Nations, NATO, and other such Cold War relics. Most notably, the new administration accepted some key aspects of globalization that had been championed by the previous Bush and Clinton administrations, including trade liberalization and permanent normal trade status for China. Bush's administration also rejected the xenophobic anti-immigrant policies favored by many Republicans, including Buchanan and former California Governor Pete Wilson.

These points aside, the Bush administration also undertook some major steps that put it at odds with most of America's closest allies. Among the most visible actions was a firm commitment to deploying a national missile defense system even in advance of tests that would demonstrate its technical feasibility. To critics who argued that the missile defense system would require withdrawal from one of the foundations of the Cold War arms control regime, the Antiballistic Missile Treaty, Secretary of Defense Donald Rumsfeld and others argued that international conditions had changed fundamentally since the agreement was signed in 1972, that the other party to it had ceased to exist with the disintegration of the USSR, and, most importantly, that the administration would not permit any treaty to stand in the way of a program that would, in the Bush advisers' view, materially enhance the country's security.

Of the other major unilateralist steps, withdrawal from the Kyoto Protocol on global warming drew strong criticism from America's allies, most of whom were among the 178 countries that had reached agreement on the issue in July 2001. Because the United States is the major source of such suspected causes of global warming as carbon dioxide emissions, the American withdrawal represented a significant setback on efforts to deal with the issue. In reply, administration critics of the Kyoto Protocol raised questions about whether there really is a global warming problem, whether human-created emissions are among its major sources, and whether it is just to impose less demanding requirements on such developing countries as India and China. Most importantly, Bush made clear his unwillingness to accept an agreement that might impose any costs on the U.S. economy. Although the Kyoto Protocol would have faced a steep uphill battle in the Senate, the administration also reneged on its campaign promise to work toward a modified agreement that might accommodate major U.S. reservations. To underscore its position, the administration did not take part in negotiations in Marrakech, Morocco, in 2001 to revive the accord by finding common ground (Joyner 2003). A report from the Environmental Protection Agency that had been reviewed by other agencies concluded that human-created emissions were major sources of global warming. Submitted to the

United Nations in June 2002, the report outlined the ways in which the United States would be changed, mostly for the worse, as a result of such emissions. Nevertheless, the administration reiterated its opposition to the Kyoto Protocol and asserted that it would be better to adapt to the negative consequences of global warming than to take actions to prevent or mitigate it. When asked about the global warming study produced by his administration, the president scornfully replied, "I have read the report put out by the bureaucracy" (Seeyle 2002, A19). With the 2002 Canadian ratification of the Kyoto Protocol, it was only one nation shy of becoming law in more than one hundred countries. The heart of the agreement, an emissions trading system closely resembling the original U.S. proposal, is set to begin on a full scale in 2005 (Pohl 2003).

In May 2002 the administration announced that it was withdrawing all support for the International Criminal Court (ICC), which since July of that year has had jurisdiction over charges of genocide, crimes against humanity, and war crimes. The Clinton administration had signed the ICC Treaty during the president's final month in office, although officials were aware that the treaty had little chance of obtaining Senate approval. The United States would refuse to provide any information that might be used to bring a case against any individuals even though the 1969 Vienna Convention on the Law of Treaties requires states not to take steps to undermine treaties that they sign. The ICC has strong support from most U.S. allies, especially Canada, which played a leading role in the court's creation. Bush administration opponents assert that the ICC would hamper the war on terrorism because it might be used to undertake politically motivated prosecutions of American officials and military personnel. According to Secretary of Defense Rumsfeld, "By putting U.S. men and women in uniform at risk of politicized prosecutions," the ICC "could well create a powerful disincentive for U.S. military engagement in the world" (Lewis 2002, A9). The U.S. position is thus that it has the right to try others' military personnel without ceding that right to any international body.[1] To derail the ICC, the Bush administration threatened to veto continuation of United Nations operations in Bosnia in July 2002 and left open the possibility that it would veto all United Nations peacekeeping operations. A last-minute compromise effectively provided American peacekeeping personnel a one-year exemption from prosecution by the ICC. The Security Council renewed the exemption for another year by a 12-0 vote—France, Germany, and Syria abstained—on July 12. Furthermore, the administration, with strong congressional support, notified all signatories to the treaty except for NATO members, Israel, and a very few others that they would lose all military assistance unless they signed bilateral agreements exempting all American personnel from the jurisdiction of the new court. Legislation signed in 2002 prohibits American cooperation with the ICC and authorizes the president to use any necessary means to free covered persons held by or on behalf of the court (Joyner 2003). The United States has taken this position in spite of the fact that the ICC's jurisdiction is severely circumscribed: it may act only in cases of suspected genocide or crimes against humanity and even then only if the accused's government fails to bring the person to trial within its legal system. According to military analyst Andrew Bacevich (2002), a retired U.S. Army colonel with experience in peacekeeping operations, the effort to drive a single stake simultaneously through the heart of the ICC and peacekeeping operations was motivated largely by a desire to placate the "nationalist right," whose members have consistently and vocally expressed their opposition to any use of the military for purposes other than war fighting and for whom any treaty that binds the United States is anathema.

The Bush administration has also opposed international efforts to cope with other issues that cross national frontiers. "Offshore" banking has become a major industry for several ministates, including the Cayman Islands. These countries permit nonresidents to open unregistered accounts that offer confidentiality and lie outside the purview of tax and other officials. Shortly after the Bush administration came to office in 2001, Secretary of the Treasury Paul O'Neill testified before the Senate that the United States would oppose any international efforts to monitor these banking activities, although there were strong reasons to suspect that many of the accounts served as tax-avoidance havens and vehicles for money laundering by drug dealers and other illicit activities. The stated reason was that by easing tax collection from those with such accounts, monitoring was a form of tax increase. The Cayman Islands alone boasted more than a million offshore accounts and businesses, fewer than 1 percent of which were disclosed and legal, resulting in estimated U.S. losses of seventy billion dollars per year in taxes (Johnston 2001, A1). It was later revealed that the Houston-based energy firm Enron had some nine hundred accounts in the Caymans. Although the United States belatedly took steps to stop banking activities by suspected terrorist organizations, including "charities" that may be covers for terrorist fund-raising, there has been no serious U.S. attempt to revive international efforts toward comprehensive regulation of offshore banking (Thachuk 2002).

Another example illustrates the administration's propensity for putting the parochial interests of favored domestic interest groups ahead of international cooperation. The Small-Arms Control Pact is intended to slow the flow of small arms and assault weapons, mostly to Third World nations, where such weapons are responsible for about a half million deaths annually, more than 70 percent of them women and children. The agreement would not infringe on Americans' right to acquire and bear arms, but strident opposition from Attorney General John Ashcroft and the National Rifle Association, whose leaders have been quite vocal in reminding the president that their members put him into the White House in the tightly contested 2000 election, guaranteed that the United States would oppose the measure. In his address to the plenary session of the Small-Arms conference, Undersecretary of State John R. Bolton not only criticized the draft program of action but also asserted, "Neither will we, at this time, commit to beginning negotiations and reach agreement on any legally binding instrument" (2001, 3). The United States, the only member of the General Assembly to oppose the United Nations Agreement to Curb the International Flow of Illicit Small Arms, is the leading exporter of such weapons, with sales of about $1.2 billion in 1998. U.S. opposition also provides a convenient cover for international sales by Russian and Chinese arms producers.

Additional examples of the Bush administration's determination not be bound by multilateral agreements, especially those that might be opposed by significant domestic constituents, include the following (Joyner 2003):

> Elimination of the minuscule funding (thirty-four million dollars) for the United Nations Population Fund, much to the delight of U.S. antiabortion groups, although independent investigations have demonstrated the falsity of the claim that such funds are used for abortions in China.
> Opposition to the Convention on Rights of the Child, an agreement to which, among United Nations members, only the United States and Somalia are not parties.

Opposition to the Comprehensive Nuclear Test Ban Treaty.

Refusal to become party to the Land Mines Convention.

Refusal to strengthen the 1972 Biological and Toxic Weapons Convention, to which the United States is already a party.

Finally, the president's September 2002 approval of the National Security Strategy doctrine is the most important example of American exceptionalism. Existing rights to preemptive self-defense require that the threat must be imminent, immediate, or overwhelming. Instead, the National Security Strategy permits the administration to undertake a preventive war if it believes that at some future time another government might strike the United States. The administration presumably would be loathe to extend a similar right to other states—for example, India or Pakistan—even if they could also claim, with some justification, that they face a potential threat (Byers 2003). Indeed, India and Pakistan have inflicted far more casualties upon each other than the United States suffered on September 11.

The 2001 terrorist attacks energized the Bush administration to form an international coalition to destroy Osama bin Laden's al Qaeda organization, which was responsible for the attacks on New York and Washington, and to uproot the Taliban regime in Afghanistan that provided a haven for al Qaeda. Many NATO allies provided vital help ranging from special forces personnel deployed in combat and peacekeeping missions in Afghanistan to intelligence about al Qaeda, an organization whose trained members are believed to reside in scores of nations. Indeed, for the first time in its history, NATO invoked Article V—the provision that an attack on one is an attack on all. In addition, a number of countries near or adjoining Afghanistan—Pakistan, Russia, several other republics of the former Soviet Union, and China—offered valuable assistance, including intelligence, bases and staging areas for U.S. and other military personnel, and overflight rights. In short, the logic of events and geographic realities left the Bush administration little choice but to eschew unilateralism in favor of a multilateral approach. Indeed, the president made it clear that others had an obligation to assist in the war against terrorists. In this sense, he was correct when he denied at a news conference that his was a unilateralist administration: "I asked them for help, didn't I?"

But if multilateralism means more than demanding help from

allies—as the president stated repeatedly, "You are either with us or with the terrorists"—then the tenor of the administration's approach to foreign affairs is less clear. If multilateralism also implies a habit of taking seriously the vital interests of allies and of being prepared to offer quid pro quos in appropriate circumstances, then it is not clear that the terrorist attacks led the president and his key advisers to experience an epiphany similar to that Senator Arthur Vandenberg experienced when he learned of the attack on Pearl Harbor six decades earlier. Although an administration cannot be held accountable for the rhetoric of its most ardent cheerleaders in the media and elsewhere, the follow-up to the events of September 11 has confirmed for them not only that the United States is the world's only superpower but also that it best serves its own interests by severing any constraints that might be imposed by acting in cooperation with less red-blooded allies. Two months prior to the terrorist attacks, in one of his more restrained essays on that theme, syndicated columnist Charles Krauthammer, a staunch proponent of a unilateral approach to foreign affairs since the end of the Cold War, wrote,

> After eight years during which foreign policy success was largely measured by the number of treaties the president could sign and the number of summits he could attend, we now have an administration willing to assert American freedom of action and the primacy of American national interests. Rather than contain American power within a vast web of constraining international agreements, the new unilateralism seeks to strengthen American power and unashamedly deploy it on behalf of self-defined global ends. Ends such as a defense against ballistic missiles. . . . And the most flamboyant demonstration of the new unilateralism was Bush's out-of-hand rejection of the Kyoto Protocol on global warming, a refreshing assertion of unwillingness to be a party to farce, no matter how multilateral. . . .
>
> An unprecedented dominant United States, however, is in the unique position of being able to fashion its own foreign policy. After a decade of Prometheus playing pygmy, the first task of the new administration is precisely to reassert American freedom of action. . . .
>
> The new unilateralism recognizes the uniqueness of the unipolar world we now inhabit and thus marks the real

beginning of American post–Cold War foreign policy. (2001, A29)

The terrorist attacks and the debates about how best to deal with the Saddam Hussein regime only increased the vehemence of his insistence that the United States pursue its interests on a "go it alone" basis, untrammeled by the interests or preferences of others. Similar assessments and prescriptions have emerged consistently from others who count themselves among the administration's strongest supporters, including William Safire, George Will, the editorial pages of the *Wall Street Journal, Weekly Standard,* and Fox News.

In its pronouncements and actions, the Bush administration — particularly Secretary of State Colin Powell—has often been somewhat more measured in its language, but little evidence indicates that Washington has accorded much weight to allies' views. Simply parading foreign leaders to the White House or to the president's ranch in Texas is not a compelling indicator of multilateralist impulses. As a former European specialist on the National Security Council, Ivo Daalder, put it, "The notion that you can just act in the way you did 25 years ago—which is that we'll assert our leadership and expect others to follow—just doesn't play anymore. [Multilateralism] has nothing to do with whether you're willing to talk to people. It's whether you are willing to take their views into account" (Brunt 2001, A10). The events of September 11 are not likely to alter that reality permanently, nor have they apparently had an impact on many aspects of U.S. foreign policy. For example, there are no indications of any second thoughts about the issues previously described briefly: national missile defense, environmental issues, the ICC, or small-arms trafficking. Even the evidence that al Qaeda owes some of its success to its ability to move its assets around in various shadowy banking institutions has not given rise to new American interest in comprehensive international efforts to pierce the veil of secrecy offered by offshore banks.

The second Bush administration has also been quite insensitive to the domestic political needs of allied leaders, most of whom are accountable to parliaments and electorates. Rhetoric from the president and his economic advisers has consistently supported steps toward liberalizing world trade, but post–September 11 actions have often followed a rather different path. In response to demands from the domestic steel industry, in 2002 the administration imposed harsh tariffs ranging from 8 to 30 percent on imported steel. The tariff increases were subsequently rescinded on a few steel products, but not enough to mitigate their negative impact on some of America's closest allies not only during the Cold War but also in the current campaign against terrorists, including members of the European Union, Japan, Brazil, South Korea, and Russia. In March 2003, the World Trade Organization ruled that the steel tariffs were illegal, but the United States asserted that it would appeal the decision (Becker 2003). When faced with European Union and Japanese threats to retaliate against U.S. goods from such key electoral states as Florida and Michigan, the Bush administration lifted the steel tariffs on December 3, 2003.

Twenty-seven percent duties on softwood lumber imports were targeted at Canada, costing some twenty thousand workers in British Columbia their jobs. In percentage terms, this is equivalent to the loss of two hundred thousand U.S. jobs. On May 27, 2003, a World Trade Organization panel sided with Canada on the issue, but that isn't likely to be the end of it. Similarly, the huge subsidies in the 2002 U.S. farm bill—another instance in which President Bush's free-market rhetoric as well as pledges made at the international economic conference in Doha, Qatar in 2001, gave way to partisan electoral calculations—will almost surely ruin many Canadian farmers. According to a Canadian foreign policy analyst, the grassroots view north of the U.S. border is that whatever the rhetoric coming out of the Oval Office, its occupant "doesn't hesitate to knife 'allies and best friends' in the back if it placates the American right wing," a view echoed by a member of the Canadian Parliament who stated, "The Americans have forgotten who their friends are" (private communication, May 2002; Simon 2002, A14).

Although Pervez Musharraf's government in Pakistan has taken considerable domestic risks in assisting U.S. efforts to combat the Taliban and al Qaeda, the United States has made no moves to lift American duties on Pakistani textile exports. Powerful domestic political concerns led to each of these actions; for example, the steel industry in Ohio, Pennsylvania, and West Virginia—three key electoral swing states—will reap handsome rewards from the stiff tariffs on steel imports, while many other industries, such as automobile manufacturers, and all U.S. consumers will bear the costs. These are certainly not the first or last times that trade policy has been driven by perceived domestic political concerns, but even the Clinton administration, often accused of being excessively driven by electoral considerations, refused to meet the steel industry's demands.

U.S. pressures in 2003 on Turkey, a loyal NATO ally in conflicts spanning a half century since the Korean War, to permit stationing a large military force that would attack Iraq from the north provides a final case of insensitivity to the political interests of other countries. Sizable Kurdish populations live in both southern Turkey and northern Iraq, and for many years the Turkish government endured a bloody civil war with its Kurdish minority. Moreover, Kurds in northern Iraq made it clear that they would oppose with force any Turkish military involvement in the campaign to topple Saddam Hussein. Despite U.S. use of carrots (a huge aid and loan package) and sticks (threats to withdraw support for such major Turkish goals as entry into the European Union), Turkey's democratically elected parliament narrowly rejected the U.S. demands. Washington made it clear that Ankara would pay a price for this decision even though it was quite predictable that the northern invasion would have little impact on the outcome of the war because Iraq's third-rate military forces would be quickly routed by the invasion from Kuwait. In effect, the United States was demanding that the Ankara government commit an act of political self-immolation because its refusal to cave in to American demands faithfully reflected the Turkish public's overwhelming opposition (83 percent) to allowing the United States and its allies to use bases in Turkey for military action against Iraq (Pew 2002d, 3). Turkey's decision may well have spared the country from a renewal of its civil war, and its unwillingness to become a participant in the war also contributed to the relative postwar stability in Kurdish areas of Iraq that compared favorably to the chaos in Baghdad and other parts of Iraq.

In summary, the evidence suggests that Schlesinger's fears of an American reversion to unilateralism were not wholly off the mark. Although he was writing in the mid-1990s, when neither the accession of George W. Bush to the presidency in 2001 nor the terrorist attack nine months later could have been foreseen, subsequent events have provided at least some support for his lament. It remains to be seen whether the views of American opinion leaders and the general public have been a driving force behind or at least a willing supporter of the new unilateralism.

American Opinion Leaders

As discussed in chapter 4, opinion leaders have been more internationalist than the general public, with respect both to general foreign policy orientation and to more specific undertakings. Furthermore, several students of public opinion have emphasized the important differences between unilateral and multilateral approaches to world affairs. Consequently, these analysts have criticized some analytic schemes on the grounds that they have been insufficiently sensitive to the distinction between those who would seek to gain international goals through multilateral efforts in conjunction with allies and through international institutions, on the one hand, and, on the other, those who prefer that the United States pursue its interests unilaterally, unfettered by the need to consult, coordinate policies, and compromise with other countries.

To gain some insight about the extent to which the end of the Cold War has given rise to unilateral preferences among opinion leaders, this section initially examines some data from the 1996 FPLP survey. The analysis then turns to results from the 2002 CCFR poll with a view to assessing the impact of the terrorist attacks of the previous year.

Ten questions in the 1996 FPLP survey were used to construct a unilateral/multilateral scale. Listed in table 6.1, these items address several aspects of this dimension. Two general questions focus on the most appropriate U.S. foreign policy orientation and the best ways to deter aggression. Other questions address several "hot button" issues at the core of debates among proponents and opponents of multilateralism, including the role of the United Nations, the appropriate circumstances for American participation in peacekeeping missions abroad, under whose command U.S. troops in such undertakings should be permitted to serve, and the wisdom of ceding some aspects of sovereignty to strengthen the United Nations and other international organizations. The ten items form a reliable scale with an alpha coefficient of .81, well in excess of the conventional standard of .70.

Two of the questions elicited very limited support for a multilateral approach to world affairs. A mere one opinion leader in five judged that strengthening the United Nations and international organizations provided a "very effective" approach to peace, and only about one-third of the respondents agreed that the United States and other countries should "cede some of their sovereignty to strengthen the power of the United Nations."

In contrast to these very skeptical views of international organizations, the remaining eight questions brought forth responses that ranged from moderate to exceptionally strong support for a multilateral approach to contemporary world affairs. The general proposition that "countries will have to act together to deter and resist aggression" gained the approval of 90 percent of the opinion leaders. Contrary to the opinions of those who regard NATO as a Cold War relic that has outlived its original purpose of deterring the USSR in Europe, the alliance continued to maintain strong support: an overwhelming 85 percent of those surveyed agreed that the United States should contribute troops to NATO peacekeeping missions. Despite the critical assessments of international organizations, an overwhelming majority of opinion leaders also

TABLE 6.1. Unilateralism/Multilateralism Scale: 1996 FPLP Survey of American Opinion Leaders

	Reported Response	All Respondents (%) ($N = 2{,}141$)
U.S. armed forces should be used in response to requests from the United Nations for peacekeeping forces	Agree	75
U.S. armed forces should be used in response to requests from NATO for peacekeeping forces	Agree	85
Strengthening the United Nations and other international organizations [as an approach to peace]	Very effective	20
If interests compel the U.S. to intervene militarily, it should be undertaken as part of a multilateral operation	Agree	80
Unilaterally reducing the U.S. share of contributions to the UN budget	Agree	39
Increasingly countries will have to act together to deter and resist aggression	Agree	90
What we need is a new foreign policy that puts America first, second, and third as well	Agree	30
The time is ripe for the U.S. and other countries to cede some of their sovereignty to strengthen the power of the UN and other international organizations	Agree	34
The U.S. [should] accept a commander appointed by the United Nations when U.S. troops take part	Should accept	54
The U.S. [should] accept a commander appointed by NATO when U.S. troops take part	Should accept	68

Correlations: Range = .10 to .62, mean = .30; Alpha = .81.

agreed that the United States should contribute peacekeeping forces in response to United Nations requests. In light of the hammering that the United Nations occasionally took from the Clinton administration and more frequently has received from the Republican leadership, as well as the myth that the UN secretary-general ordered U.S. troops into a firefight that killed eighteen Americans in Somalia, it may seem somewhat surprising that a majority of the respondents (54 percent) expressed a willingness to have American military personnel serve under a UN-appointed commander in peacekeeping undertakings.

As a partial test of its utility, the unilateral/multilateral scale can be combined with the scales on the two types of internationalism—militant and cooperative—originally developed by Eugene R. Wittkopf (1990). Doing so creates a classification scheme of eight types: that is, each of the four MI/CI groups (*hard-liners, isolationists, accommodationists,* and *internationalists*) would be further divided into unilateralist and multilateralist subgroups. Unless it can be shown, however, that this further subdivision enhances our insight into thinking about international affairs, the value of doing so is rather limited. Evidence from the 1996 FPLP survey in fact supports the value of a distinction between preferences for unilateralism or multilateralism. This point may be illustrated by a cluster of items, presented in table 4.6, asking respondents to appraise the effectiveness of various approaches to world peace. As table 6.2 indicates, the further division of the four MI/CI does reveal consistently significant differences. For example, within the internationalist group (those who support both militant and cooperative internationalism), the multilateralists were consistently more inclined than the unilateralists to rate as "very effective" approaches that require acting in conjunction with other countries—arms control, trade, international organizations, international communication, collective security, narrowing the rich nation–poor nation gap, and so forth—while expressing less support for such unilateral measures as military superiority. Similar patterns of differences can be discerned between the unilateralist and multilateralist variants within the hard-liners, isolationists, and accommodationists.

Finally, responses to the ten-item scale may be used to describe the distribution of opinion leaders on the multilateral/unilateral scale as well as to assess how preferences for each of these approaches are linked to other political beliefs and to partisan and ideological self-descriptions. The scale was divided into four equal

TABLE 6.2. Approaches to Peace Assessed by Opinion Leaders in 1996: Groups Defined by Foreign Policy Orientations

How effective do you consider each of the following as an approach to world peace?

	Isolationists		Hard-Liners		Accommodationists		Internationalists	
% "Very effective"	Uni.	Multi.	Uni.	Multi.	Uni.	Multi.	Uni.	Multi.
Military superiority of the United States	57	44	81	72	61	32	77	61
Collective security through alliances	22	30	28	41	36	39	45	51
Trade, technical cooperation, and economic interdependence	36	32	19	28	39	50	36	48
Arms control	9	14	5	7	24	31	22	30
Narrowing the gap between rich and poor nations	6	15	4	5	21	39	10	23
Strengthening the United Nations and other international organizations	0	9	0	7	6	32	3	26
Political efforts to achieve a balance of power within regions and between great powers	7	10	8	12	19	21	15	23
Better communications and understanding among peoples	25	33	22	22	49	54	46	57

Note: Differences among groups significant at the .001 level for all items.

Key: Uni. = Unilateralists, Multi. = Multilateralists

intervals, one endpoint of which was defined as multilateralist responses to each of the ten items and the other defined as unilateralist responses to all of them. As table 6.3 reveals, the 2,141 opinion leaders who took part in the survey were predominantly on the multilateral side of the scale. More specifically, they were distributed among the four categories as follows: 31.7 percent strong multilateralists, 41.3 percent moderate multilateralists, 21.4 percent moderate unilateralists, and 5.7 percent strong unilateralists.

Further analysis also reveals strong links between preferences for multilateral or unilateral approaches to foreign affairs and other political beliefs. The figures in table 6.2 suggested that the multilateral/unilateral scale can usefully be combined with the MI/CI scheme to provide eight distinct ways of thinking about foreign affairs, but there are also clear links between them. For example, unilateralists are also predominantly hard-liners and isolationists, whereas multilateralists are more likely to be either internationalists or accommodationists. Multivariate analyses reveal, however, that the unilateral/multilateral and MI/CI scales are sufficiently different that both make an independent contribution to responses, not only to the questions summarized in table 6.2 but also to a much broader range of other foreign and defense policy issues.

Similarly strong links exist between the multilateral/unilateral scale and a domestic issues classification scheme described in chapter 4. As one moves from the most multilateral to the most unilateral categories, the number of conservatives rises and the number of liberals falls. The smaller libertarian and populist groups are more evenly divided in their placement on the multilateral/unilateral scale. In light of these strong relationships, it does not come as a surprise that strong relationships also exist between multilateral or unilateral policy preferences and party identification and self-placement on a standard ideology scale. Unilateralists are predominantly Republicans and conservatives, Democrats and liberals tend to support multilateralism, and independents constitute about one-fifth to one-quarter of the opinion leaders in each category. But these four categories do not include equal numbers of opinion leaders. Thus, while the 121 strong unilateralists are overwhelmingly Republican (72 percent), they are outnumbered by the members of the GOP who constitute 36 percent of the moderate multilateralists.

These data address Schlesinger's fears, published in 1995, that powerful demands from opinion leaders are pushing the country

TABLE 6.3. Unilateralists and Multilateralists: Relationship to Other Beliefs, Party, and Ideology in the 1996 FPLP Survey of American Opinion Leaders

	Foreign Policy Beliefs	%	Domestic issues	%	Party	%	Ideology	%
Strong multilateralists (N = 679)	Hard-liners	—a	Conservatives	9	Republican	12	Very conservative	1
	Isolationists	3	Libertarians	6	Democrat	64	Somewhat conservative	10
	Internationalists	21	Populists	8	Independent	21	Moderate	26
	Accommodationists	76	Liberals	76	Other	3	Somewhat liberal	43
							Very liberal	19
	phi = .61		phi = .56		phi = .46		phi = .61	
Moderate multilateralists (N = 884)	Hard-liners	8	Conservatives	32	Republican	36	Very conservative	6
	Isolationists	10	Libertarians	13	Democrat	36	Somewhat conservative	32
	Internationalists	34	Populists	15	Independent	23	Moderate	33
	Accommodationists	48	Liberals	40	Other	4	Somewhat liberal	23
							Very liberal	5
Moderate unilateralists (N = 457)	Hard-liners	30	Conservatives	64	Republican	62	Very conservative	19
	Isolationists	19	Libertarians	9	Democrat	17	Somewhat conservative	47
	Internationalists	35	Populists	11	Independent	19	Moderate	25
	Accommodationists	16	Liberals	16	Other	3	Somewhat liberal	8
							Very liberal	*
Strong unilateralists (N = 121)	Hard-liners	63	Conservatives	89	Republican	72	Very conservative	47
	Isolationists	21	Libertarians	6	Democrat	1	Somewhat conservative	40
	Internationalists	11	Populists	3	Independent	26	Moderate	10
	Accommodationists	5	Liberals	2	Other	2	Somewhat liberal	3
							Very liberal	0
	phi = .61		phi = .56		phi = .46		phi = .61	

Note: Owing to rounding error, column totals may not equal 100%.

aFewer than 0.5%

TABLE 6.4. Unilateralism and Multilateralism: CCFR Survey of American Opinion Leaders, 2002 (in percentages)

With respect to its commitment to NATO, the U.S. should		1998	1994	1990
Increase it	8	7	6	3
Keep as it is now	69	64	57	35
Decrease but remain in NATO	20	25	34	57
Withdraw from NATO	3	3	3	4

In responding to international crises, do you think the U.S. should or should not take action alone if it does not have the support of its allies?		1998
Should act alone	40	44
Should not act alone	53	48
Not sure/decline	7	8

When the U.S. is asked to be part of a UN international peacekeeping force in a troubled part of the world, do you think we should

Take part	79
Leave this job to other countries	12
Depends on circumstances [VOL]	8
Not sure/decline	1

There has been some discussion about whether the U.S. should use its troops to invade Iraq and overthrow the regime of Saddam Hussein. Which of the following positions is closest to yours?

The U.S. should not invade Iraq	26
The U.S. should invade Iraq only with UN approval and the support of its allies	49
The U.S. should invade Iraq even if we have to go it alone	22
Not sure/decline	3

Do you favor or oppose the U.S. paying its UN dues in full?

Favor	87
Oppose	11
Not sure/decline	2

Do you think the U.S. should or should not participate in the following treaties and agreements:

Kyoto agreement to reduce global warming	
Should participate	63
Should not participate	35
Not sure/decline	2
The treaty that bans all use of land mines	
Should participate	74
Should not particpate	24
Not sure/decline	2

TABLE 6.4.—*Continued*

The treaty that would prohibit nuclear weapon test explosions worldwide	
Should participate	82
Should not participate	17
Not sure/decline	1
The agreement to establish an International Criminal Court that would try individuals for war crimes, genocide, or crimes against humanity if their own country won't try them	
Should participate	65
Should not participate	33
Not sure/decline	2

Note: The figures for 1990, 1994, and 1998 are also drawn from CCFR surveys.

toward reducing its role in world affairs and pursuing its international interests unencumbered by allies and international institutions, but the data do so only through 1996. Thus they cannot address questions about the impact of the September 11 terrorist attacks five years later.

Table 6.4 summarizes responses in the 2002 CCFR survey of opinion leaders to questions that touch on unilateralism and multilateralism. The item about NATO indicates growing rather than eroding support for that alliance. In 1990, as the Cold War was winding down and the Soviet Union was experiencing the convulsions that would lead to its disintegration a year later, more than 60 percent of respondents to the CCFR survey favored reducing the U.S. commitment to NATO or withdrawing altogether. In contrast, twelve years later, more than three-fourths of the opinion leaders expressed support for maintaining or increasing the U.S. commitment to the alliance.

Preferences for acting in conjunction with allies rather than for going it alone also emerged from a general question on coping with crises and on a specific item on the use of American troops to overthrow the Saddam Hussein regime in Iraq. With respect to the latter undertaking, only 22 percent favored the "go it alone" option. However, had that question been posed eight months later, during the run-up to the attack on Iraq, the results would probably have revealed some shift of sentiment toward the option of taking action alone or with only the support of Great Britain.

The other items in table 6.4 provide little support for the thesis that multilateralist sentiments have been ebbing since the end of the Cold War. Support for the United Nations, whether by participation in peacekeeping operations or by paying dues in full, was at an impressive level. It is again likely that a similar survey during the days prior to the invasion of Iraq would have revealed a somewhat less sanguine view of the United Nations after Washington, unable to gain much Security Council support for demands to disarm Iraq by force and to force the ouster of Saddam Hussein, withdrew its resolution on the issue.

Finally, the 2002 CCFR survey asked opinion leaders about the desirability of participating in treaties and agreements pertaining to global warming, land mines, nuclear weapons testing, and the ICC. In each case, the treaties gained approval from substantial majorities, although about one-third of the opinion leaders opposed the Kyoto Protocol on global warming and the ICC—both the targets of strident Bush administration attacks—whereas opposition to the other two treaties fell below 25 percent.

The General Public

Have members of the general public, whose internationalist proclivities typically trail those of the opinion leaders, regarded the end of the Cold War and the outbreak of brutal local and regional conflicts, often triggered by "failed states," as sufficient reason to pull back from what Schlesinger described as the "magnificent dream" (A. Schlesinger 1995, 8) of collective security? How, if at all, have the events of September 11 affected public attitudes toward international engagement?

Figure 3.1 showed that contrary to the conventional description of public opinion as "volatile," the American people have shown a quite stable preference for an "active role" in world affairs despite the fact that the six decades in question constitute a period of unprecedented international turbulence. At the same time, compared to leaders, the public has also shown considerable disquiet about several aspects of internationalism. Specifically, trade liberalization and globalization, both of which have typically garnered strong support among leaders, have engendered less enthusiasm among the public, and the same pattern of differences can be seen in most surveys about foreign aid, with leaders expressing stronger approval for both economic and military assistance programs (table 4.3). Similarly, the public has generally had a more selective view of when and in defense of whom U.S. troops should be deployed abroad (table 4.4).

Nevertheless, there is also a good deal of evidence that those who portray the post–Cold War mood of the American people as isolationist and unilateralist are in fact "misreading the public" (Kull and Destler 1999). Data from several surveys, including Pew, Gallup, CCFR, and PIPA, yield a much more subtle and variegated picture of public opinion, even before the dramatic events of September 11. Several important generalizations emerge from these data.

Most Americans are uneasy with such international roles as the "world's police force" that imply that because of its predominant military and economic resources, the United States has the means to impose its solutions on most international problems. Such observers as Charles Krauthammer, William Safire, and George Will offer the unilateralist/triumphalist argument that because of the U.S. power position, which outranks all others as far back as the Roman empire at the height of its power, only a lack of wisdom and courage prevents the United States from pursuing its interests irrespective of the views of allies or adversaries. Aside from the fact that the thesis is historically dubious—U.S. economic and military predominance during 1945–49, when the United States produced almost half of the world's goods and services and enjoyed a monopoly on nuclear power, in fact exceeded that of the contemporary era—it has not found an especially receptive public reaction. Most Americans prefer that the country work actively with others, most notably with allies, to cope with the plethora of security, humanitarian, and other issues that have surfaced in recent decades. *Burden sharing* is probably the best term to describe predominant public preferences on a wide range of international undertakings, whereas going it alone, the essence of unilateralism, is the much less popular path. The 2002 CCFR survey offered respondents several opportunities to express their views on the proper U.S. role in the post-9/11 world. When asked about "the more important lesson of September 11," 61 percent stated that it was the U.S. "need to work more closely with other countries," whereas only 34 percent stated that it was the U.S. "need to act on its own more." Further probes reinforced these results. In connection with the U.S. status as the sole remaining superpower, 71 percent of respondents asserted that "the United States should do its share to solve international problems together with other countries," whereas only one respondent in six preferred for the United States to "be the preeminent leader in solving international problems." Finally, two-thirds of the respondents agreed that the United States "is playing the role of world policeman more than it should be," whereas about one-third disagreed.

Additional evidence on this score emerged from six Pew surveys conducted between 1993 and 2001. Two of the studies took place just days before and about five weeks after September 11 (August 25–September 5 and October 15–21). The results confirm that an overwhelming majority of Americans prefer a "shared leadership role" to that of the "single world leader," both before and after the terrorist attacks (table 6.5). The Gallup Organization posed a similar question about preferred international roles each year starting in 2001. Although wording of the questions and response options differed somewhat from those in the Pew surveys, the results were quite similar over the three-year period. Few respondents in either survey expressed much interest in retrenchment to a minor role or in withdrawing altogether from any leadership role in world affairs. Rather, majorities wanted the United States to have a "shared leadership role" (Pew) or "a major role but not the leadership role" (Gallup). Both studies spanned the 9/11 assaults on Washington and New York, but in neither case did these attacks appear to have had much impact on responses. The data in table 6.5, in short, provide further evidence that public attitudes are better characterized as stable rather than volatile. Another question in the Pew surveys asked, "How should the United States determine its policy with regard to the war on terrorism?" Prior to September 11, a plurality of 48 percent of respondents preferred that the United States "strongly take into account the interests of its allies," whereas 38 percent stated that the policy should be based "mostly on the national interests of the United States." When the same question was posed after the terrorist attacks, the margin in favor of strongly considering the interests of allies increased to almost two to one (59 to 30 percent) (Pew, 2001a, 1).

These findings are quite robust. A PIPA survey revealed a majority of 73 to 24 percent in favor of a multilateral approach to the war on terrorists, even though the question specifically mentioned the primary objection of the unilateralists: "it would be better not to get these countries involved, because if we did, the operation would get bogged down by having to make decisions together with these countries" (PIPA 2001b, 2). An earlier *Los Angeles Times* poll, undertaken just days after the attacks, found that six in ten respondents agreed that U.S. action "should only be undertaken as part of a cooperative effort" (Richardson 2001,

6). Support for the multilateral approach is probably sustained in part by the belief—espoused by 75 percent of respondents to a Pew poll—that the United States is "getting the support that we need from our traditional allies" (Pew, 2001a).

Although the United Nations has rarely been able to achieve the lofty goals of its founders—the few exceptions are in such specialized areas as some programs of the World Health Organization—public support for that organization remains high. Indeed, the CCFR surveys indicate that the general public accords a higher degree of support than elites do for "strengthening the United Nations" as an important foreign policy goal. A majority of the general public believes that the United States should pay its United Nations dues, including the large overdue payments.

TABLE 6.5. America's Role in the World, 1993–2003 (in percentages)

A. "What kind of leadership role should the United States play in the world?"

	Sept. 1993	Oct. 1993	June 1995	Sept. 1997	Early Sept. 2001	Oct. 2001
Be the single world leader	10	9	13	12	13	12
A shared leadership role:	81	78	74	73	75	79
Most active leading nation		27	23	25	22	25	33
About as active as other leading nations		52	53	47	50	49	45
Don't know/refused		2	2	2	1	1	1
Shouldn't play any leadership role	7	9	9	11	8	3
Don't know/refused	2	4	4	4	4	6

Source: Pew Research Center for the People and the Press, *America's New International Point of View,* December 2001.

B. "We would like you to think about the role the United States should play in trying to solve international problems. Do you think the U.S. should":

	Feb. 3–6, 2001	Feb. 4–6, 2002	Feb. 1–4, 2003
Take the leading role in world affairs	16	26	26
Take a major role but not the leading role	57	52	53
Take a minor role	21	16	16
Take no role in world affairs	4	4	3

Source: Gallup Poll Social Series: World Affairs, 2003, 7.

And when interventions abroad are under consideration, most Americans prefer acting under auspices of and in cooperation with the United Nations or NATO rather than acting alone. This is another manifestation of the strong preference for sharing the burdens of important international undertakings. Public preferences for multilateral action may also be rooted in a feeling that military action in conjunction with NATO or the United Nations endows a greater legitimacy on the use of force, but the survey data are inadequate on this point.

The previously cited Pew surveys conducted in early September and mid-October 2001 also revealed that goal priorities for American foreign policy remained remarkably stable during the period encompassing the terrorist attacks. Not surprisingly, nearly all (93 percent) post-9/11 respondents rated "taking measures to protect the United States from terrorist attacks" as a top policy priority, but even in the pre-9/11 survey that goal had earned the highest number (80 percent) of "top priority" ratings. Of the fourteen goals in the Pew survey, responses to only half changed by as much as 6 percent. The rank order of the top eight goals—antiterrorism, antiproliferation of weapons of mass destruction, job protection, energy security, reducing the spread of AIDS and other infectious diseases, anti–drug trafficking, getting other countries to pay more of the costs of maintaining world order, and protecting groups and nations against genocide—were identical in the two surveys; the pre- and post-9/11 rank-order correlation for the fourteen items was an exceptionally high .97. The trend toward declining interest in altruistic international goals persisted in these two surveys, with reduced importance attributed to improving the standard of living in less developed countries, reducing hunger, and reducing the spread of AIDS and other infectious diseases. Skepticism about promoting American values and institutions was also evident as fewer than 30 percent of the respondents assigned a "top priority" to promoting either democracy or human rights abroad (Pew, 2001a, 14).

The 2002 CCFR survey provides the most recent and complete evidence on foreign policy goals. Because seventeen of the items also appeared in the comparable survey four years earlier, they provide at least some basis for assessing the impact of the September 11 attacks. Moreover, the identical items were included in a smaller survey of leaders. The results are summarized in table 6.6. It is hardly surprising that combating terrorism and preventing nuclear proliferation ranked as the top goals for both leaders

TABLE 6.6. The Importance of American Foreign Policy Goals: Assessments by the General Public and Leaders in the 1998 and 2002 CCFR Surveys (percentage of "very important" ratings)

For each [foreign policy goal], please say whether you think that it should be a very important foreign policy goal of the United States, a somewhat important foreign policy goal, or not an important goal at all.

	1998		2002	
	General Public	Leaders	General Public	Leaders
World-order security issues				
Preventing the spread of nuclear weapons	82	85	90	89
Combating international terrorism	79	74	91	87
Strengthening the United Nations	45	32	57	28
Protecting weaker nations against aggression	32	29	41	27
Strengthening international law and institutions	—	49	43	49
World-order economic and environmental issues				
Combating world hunger	62	56	61	59
Improving the global environment	53	46	66	43
Helping to improve the standard of living in less developed countries	29	36	30	42
Safeguarding against global financial instability	—	49	54	49
U.S. economic interest issues				
Stopping the flow of illegal drugs into the U.S.	81	57	81	45
Protecting the jobs of American workers	80	45	85	35
Securing adequate supplies of energy	64	55	75	51
Controlling and reducing illegal immigration	55	21	70	22
Reducing the U.S. trade deficit with foreign countries	50	34	51	21
Protecting the interests of American business abroad	—	—	49	23
U.S. values and institutional issues				
Promoting and defending human rights in other countries	39	41	47	46
Promoting market economics abroad	34	36	36	27
Helping to bring a democratic form of government to other nations	29	27	34	33
Cold War/security issues				
Maintaining superior military power worldwide	59	58	68	52
Defending our allies' security	44	58	57	55

Source: Rielly 1999; Bouton and Page 2002.

and the general public, but this did not represent a significant post-9/11 change, as these had been among the most important foreign policy goals four years earlier.

As had been the case in previous CCFR surveys, including the one conducted in 1998, issues revolving around U.S. economic interests continued to receive a very high number of "very important" assessments from the general public. Drug trafficking, job protection, energy security, immigration control, and the trade deficit received the top rating from a majority of the respondents, and protecting the interests of U.S. businesses abroad barely failed to do so. The gaps between leaders and the general public on these goals were enormous, ranging from 24 percent to 50 percent or more on the related issues of job protection and immigration control. In every case, the general public–leader gap increased materially during the four-year interval between the two surveys. The focus on U.S. economic interests might be cited by proponents of the Schlesinger thesis as evidence that the public is indeed turning inward, but responses to many of the other questions would appear to contradict that conclusion. For example, in comparison to 1998, assessments of many other goals also recorded significant increases of 8 percent or more: protecting weaker nations against aggression, strengthening the United Nations, improving the global environment, defending allies, maintaining U.S. military superiority, and promoting human rights abroad. The picture that emerges from table 6.6 is of a U.S. public that not merely is focused on self-regarding interests but also seems prepared to support a rather wide range of international undertakings. In every case save two, goal ratings increased between 1998 and 2002, and the two exceptions—on drug trafficking and world hunger—recorded changes of 1 percent or less.[2] In the post-9/11 survey, the leaders' attributions of importance outstripped those of the general public on only two of the foreign policy goals: strengthening international law and institutions and helping to improve the standard of living in less developed countries.

Most public opinion surveys rank foreign aid at or near the top of programs whose budgets should be reduced rather than increased, and the proposition that "taking care of problems at home is more important than giving aid to foreign countries" elicited agreement from 84 percent of respondents to a 2001 PIPA poll. The gap between leaders and the general public with respect to support for foreign aid has been consistently high, but there is also quite persuasive evidence that the preferences of the latter group are based on substantial misinformation about the actual size of U.S. foreign aid budgets. Many people erroneously believe that such expenditures constitute one of the largest items in the federal budget—the median estimate was 20 percent—although the correct amount is less than 1 percent. When asked what would be a "fair share" for foreign aid, the median figure is approximately ten times greater than the current allocations. When respondents are informed of the actual level of economic and technical assistance, support for foreign aid rises sharply (Kull and Destler 1999; PIPA 2001a). Humanitarian impulses are an important consideration in preferences about foreign aid. More than three-fourths of the public agreed that too much aid is allocated to undemocratic governments with poor records on human rights. When asked whether aid should be sent only to areas where the United States has security interests or should be allocated to parts of the world where the United States has no security interests but hunger is a problem, the latter option was preferred by a margin of 63 to 34 percent (PIPA 2001a).

The most recent CCFR survey reinforced these findings of a gap between perceptions and reality on foreign aid. When asked about the percentage of the federal budget that goes to foreign aid, the median and mean responses were about 20 percent. When respondents were asked about the appropriate level of foreign assistance, the comparable figures were 10 percent and 17 percent. These results again confirm the fact that sentiments for reducing foreign aid—one of the constants of virtually all surveys that deal with the issue—are based on vastly exaggerated conceptions about actual American outlays for such programs.

Public approval for deployment of U.S. forces abroad has generally lagged behind that of leaders (table 4.4). There is stronger support for sending troops to protect the victims of aggression—for example, in response to Iraq's 1990 invasion of Kuwait—than for interventions to cope with internal conflicts, such as the civil wars arising from the disintegration of the former Yugoslavia (Jentleson 1992; Eichenberg 2002). Moreover, the public expresses greater approval for troop deployments in such areas of traditional American interests as Europe than, for example, in Africa. To date, U.S. military personnel have not been deployed in peacekeeping operations in the conflict between Israel and its neighbors. Nothing in the long and troubled history of the conflict suggests that any peacekeeping mission is likely to yield quick or easy success. Nevertheless, should there be a peace agreement between

Israel and the Palestinian Authority, more than three-fourths of the American public would support U.S. participation to enforce such an agreement if it were undertaken with other countries under United Nations sponsorship (PIPA, 2002a, 5).

The 2002 CCFR survey asked both the general public and leaders about the circumstances under which they would be willing to deploy U.S. troops abroad. The questions at the top of table 6.7 have a very distinct post-9/11 tenor, probing for attitudes on sending military forces to the Philippines, Afghanistan, Iraq, Pakistan, and Saudi Arabia. When we compare these results with those of earlier surveys that focused on the use of troops to protect allied countries against attack from their neighbors, the impact of the terrorist attacks seems quite clear. Whereas the public has consistently exhibited much less enthusiasm than leaders have for such actions on behalf of most allies, the gap between the two groups has narrowed significantly in situations that might seem to be linked to a war against terrorists. There was a strong consensus in support of using U.S. troops to prevent genocide, for peacekeeping in Afghanistan, for fighting terrorism in the Philippines, to overthrow the Saddam Hussein government in Iraq, and, to a somewhat lesser degree, to protect the regime in Pakistan. In two instances, there was a striking divergence of views between the public and leaders, and interestingly, in both cases a majority of public approved the use of U.S. troops, whereas leaders did not. Two-thirds of the public supported military action against drug lords in Colombia, whereas fewer than one-third of the leaders did so. The two groups were also on opposite sides on the question of preventing the overthrow of the government in Saudi Arabia. The revelation that fifteen of the nineteen September 11 hijackers were Saudi subjects and the Riyadh government's rather lukewarm assistance to the United States has opened up a debate in Washington about the future of U.S.-Saudi relations that would have been unthinkable only a few years ago. Indeed, after the war against Iraq, all U.S. military personnel, save for a small token force, were withdrawn from Saudi Arabia. A survey taken just prior to that decision found strong public support (67 percent) for such a withdrawal (PIPA 2003).

The middle part of table 6.7 provides further evidence that the post-9/11 era has been marked by an erosion of public opposition to the use of U.S. troops abroad. (The question was not included in the survey of leaders, but there is no reason to believe that their responses would have deviated dramatically from those of

the general public.) Earlier surveys revealed public support for
coming to the aid of specific allies who might be subject to attack
by Cold War adversaries. The results in table 6.7 indicate strong
support for the use of armed forces in more general undertakings, including coping with famine, liberating hostages, and up-
holding international law. As revealed in many other surveys,

TABLE 6.7.   The Uses of U.S. Troops Abroad: 2002 CCFR Survey

Would you favor or oppose the use of U.S. troops	Percent who favor	
	General Public	Leaders
To stop a government from committing genocide and killing large numbers of its own people	77	85
To assist the Philippine government to fight terrorism	78	70
To be part of an international peacekeeping force in Afghanistan	76	88
To overthrow Saddam Hussein's government in Iraq	75	—
To fight drug lords in Colombia	66	31
To be part of an international peacekeeping force to enforce a peace agreement between Israel and the Palestinians	65	79
If the government of Pakistan requested our help against a radical Islamic revolution	61	61
If the government of Saudi Arabia requested our help against an attempt to overthrow it	54	41

Would you approve or disapprove of the use of U.S. military troops:	Percent who approve	
	General Public	Leaders
To destroy a terrorist camp	92	—
To assist a population struck by famine	81	—
To liberate hostages	77	—
To uphold international law	76	—
To ensure the supply of oil	65	—
To help bring peace to a region where there is a civil war	48	—

There has been some discussion about whether the U.S. should use its troops to invade
Iraq and overthrow the government of Saddam Hussein. Which of the following positions is closest to yours?

	General Public	Leaders
The U.S. should not invade Iraq	13	26
The U.S. should only invade Iraq with UN approval and the support of its allies	65	49
The U.S. should invade Iraq even if we have to go it alone	20	22
Not sure/decline	2	3

Source: CCFR Survey, June 2002; Bouton and Page 2002

there was considerably less enthusiasm for intervention in civil wars.

The conventional wisdom that the public will reject armed interventions abroad if they involve casualties received very little support when the question was posed in connection with the post–September 11 deployment of ground troops in Afghanistan. Hypothetical questions about acceptable losses must be viewed with more than the usual level of caution, especially if the somewhat ambiguous term *casualties* rather than *deaths* or *killed* is used. Virtually every poll posed a question about the use of ground troops in the war against terrorists, and support for this option ranged upward of 60 percent. Even when follow-up questions raised the prospect of heavy casualties, support remained quite high. For example, a Pew survey shortly after the terrorist attacks revealed that 82 percent of respondents favored the use of ground troops, while only 8 percent opposed that option. When a revised version of the question added the phrase, "even if we might suffer thousands of casualties," supporters of military action still outnumbered opponents by 77 to 9 percent (Pew 2001b, 3). Polls taken after the introduction of ground troops into Afghanistan, including questions that specifically mentioned battle deaths, found only a moderate decline in support for the ground war. Although evidence of public sensitivity to casualties abounds, responses to the events of September 11 indicate a public willingness to bear the costs if the goals are seen as desirable and feasible, as they clearly were in the case of the intervention in Afghanistan.

These results suggest persisting public support for an active international role but with a decided preference for multilateralism rather than going it alone. What could account for the disjunction between the administration's policies and public preferences on these issues? One explanation—that the president and his advisers lack sufficient polling data—can be ruled out. Despite vowing to govern "based on principle and not polls and focus groups," the Bush administration spent about one million dollars on surveys during 2001. The results of the polls are used less to align decisions with public sentiments and more to develop effective rhetorical strategies to sell preferred policies. Because pollsters do not rank high on the list of most admired professions, the Bush administration has this in common with those of Franklin Roosevelt, John Kennedy, and Richard Nixon—the existence of polling operations and the resulting data are kept very close to the vest (Green 2002).

Although the evidence about long-run impact of the September 11 terrorist attacks on public attitudes is far from conclusive at this point, that which is available would certainly not appear to sustain the charge of a reversion to traditional American isolationism or unilateralism. The war to root out the Taliban regime in Afghanistan and to destroy the al Qaeda network has continued to enjoy widespread support despite the ability of many al Qaeda leaders to evade capture. Although analogies between the Pearl Harbor and World Trade Center/Pentagon attacks are sometime overdrawn, most Americans have reacted to the two events in the same way—with a determination to punish the perpetrators. Nor has the hypothesis that the public will not support any undertaking that involves body bags gained greater credence; however, the level of U.S. casualties in Afghanistan remained quite low to this point and thus the conventional wisdom has not been put to a very rigorous test. Unlike in the war in Iraq, to be discussed later in this chapter, the United States has been fortunate in the strong support it has garnered from most of its allies and from strategically located countries in the war against the Taliban and al Qaeda; thus, questions of unilateralism and multilateralism did not surface as a major issue until debates about invading Iraq. Should the war on terrorists ultimately involve deployment of U.S. troops in a large number of foreign countries, result in eroding support from allies, and give rise to mounting casualties—that is, if the effort takes on some of the characteristics of the Vietnam quagmire three decades ago—then public support might well decline. That erosion of support appears to be taking place with respect to the Iraq undertaking. Continuing turmoil and violence in the areas surrounding Baghdad have inflicted steady casualties on U.S. military personnel and public support, as measured by Gallup polls, fell rather steadily during the summer and fall of 2003 (Gallup 2003, 1–3). By November, although a small majority of 54 percent stated that it had been worth going to war against Iraq, 61 percent felt that things there were going badly. According to Gallup, 48 percent wished to begin withdrawing some or all U.S. troops (Moore 2003, 1–5), and almost 40 percent of PIPA respondents favored reduction of American forces from Iraq (PIPA 2003e).

Finally, strong support for the war on terrorists has not been accompanied by much enthusiasm for suppressing domestic debate about the conflict. Few people have been inclined to agree with administration officials who considered any questions about the conduct of the war a breach of bipartisanship or, worse, support for terrorists. According to a survey conducted shortly after the terrorist attacks, overwhelming majorities of the public (75 percent) believed that critics should be allowed to express their views, even if doing so took the form of antiwar protests (71 percent) (Pew 2001b). Similar sentiments surfaced during the weeks prior to the invasion of Iraq, when, in response to the question, "How much have you heard from war opponents?" 42 percent replied "too little" and only 24 percent selected "too much." Even those supporting the use of force against Iraq preferred the "too little" option by a margin of 35 to 30 percent (Pew 2003a, 24).

The final stage of this analysis examines how, if at all, the Iraq issue that culminated in the invasion of that country in March 2003 may have affected public preferences for pursuing foreign policy goals in conjunction with allies or doing so alone. The Bush administration repeatedly stated that removal of the Saddam Hussein regime in Iraq was a top priority because it possessed threatening weapons of mass destruction and, in a campaign timed for the traditional Labor Day beginning of the 2002 election season, gained strong support for military action from both the House and Senate. During the months between the September 11 terrorist attacks and the invasion of Iraq, almost all polling organizations regularly asked the public about whether the United States should use force to effect a regime change in Iraq. When the question of removing Saddam Hussein from power was posed as a "support-oppose" choice, the results were exceptionally consistent; every survey yielded a majority that would support using force to oust Saddam's government. As usual, variations in the precise wording of the questions have affected the results, but only enough to change the size of the majority that favors toppling Saddam Hussein, not the majority itself. The controversies surrounding the issue, then, have centered not on the desirability of removing the Iraqi dictator from power but rather on whether doing so should be contingent on support from the U.N. Security Council, major U.S. allies in NATO, or both.

Table 6.8 presents some evidence from Gallup and Pew surveys undertaken during the two years prior to March 2003: the 1992 Gallup results indicate that the preference for regime change in Baghdad dates back to the aftermath of the first Gulf War. The later surveys found majorities ranging between 52 percent (seven months prior to September 11 attacks) and 68 percent in favor of military action versus Iraq. Six of the Pew polls also asked advocates of military action whether their support was

TABLE 6.8. Support for Invasion of Iraq with or without Support of Allies, 2001–2003 (in percentages)

Would you favor or oppose taking military action in Iraq to end Saddam Hussein's rule? If favor, should we attack Iraq only if our major allies agree to join us, or attack Iraq even if allies do not want to join us?

	Mar. 13–16, 2003	Feb. 2003	Jan. 2003	Dec. 2002	Nov. 2002	Late Oct. 2002	Early Oct. 2002	Sept. 2002	Aug. 2002	June 2002	Nov. 2001	Feb. 2001	Mar. 1992
Favor	59	66	68	65	62	55	62	64	64	59	74	52	55
Even if allies won't join	38	38	26			27		33	30				
Only if allies agree	16	22	37			23		25	30				
Don't know/refused	5	6	5			5		6	4				
Oppose	30	26	25	25	26	34	28	23	21	34	20	42	40
Don't know/refused	11	8	7	10	12	11	10	13	15	7	6	6	5

Source: March 1992–June 2002: Gallup; August 2002–March 2003: Pew Research Center for the People and the Press.

Gallup wording: "Would you favor or oppose sending American troops back to the Persian Gulf in order to remove Saddam Hussein from power in Iraq?"

When it comes to Iraq, do you think the United States should do what it thinks is right no matter what its allies think, or should the U.S. take into account the view of allies before taking action?

	Mar. 7–9, 2003	Mar. 4–5, 2003	Feb. 24–25, 2003
Do what it thinks is right	36	38	27
Take allies into account	60	56	70
Don't know/no answer	4	6	3

Source: CBS/*New York Times* surveys.

conditional on the support of major allies or whether they favored acting "even if allies won't join"; in none of these surveys did the "go it alone" option gain a majority. In the mid-March 2003 Pew (Pew 2003b, 6) survey, completed just days prior to the U.S.-British invasion of Iraq, more than a quarter of the 59 percent who supported military action conditioned approval on the agreement of major allies to join the war effort. None of these or other surveys appear to have asked whether consistent support from Tony Blair's Labour government in London was sufficient to qualify as assistance from "major allies."

The second part of table 6.8 reports responses to a question, posed by the *New York Times*/CBS poll during the month prior to the invasion of Iraq, about whether the United States should or should not "take into account the views of allies before taking action" against Iraq. In each instance, solid majorities favored that option rather than "doing what [the United States] thinks is right no matter what its allies think."

By the autumn of 2003, the Anglo-American military campaign had removed Saddam Hussein and his Baath Party from power in Iraq. While military success may give rise to some reconsideration of the relative merits of "going it alone" versus burden sharing with allies, the evidence available to date suggests that neither the September 11 terrorist attacks nor the debates about how to cope with the Saddam Hussein regime in Iraq have given rise to strong unilateralist sentiments among the general public. To the contrary, the evidence consistently portrays a public that accepts an active global role for the United States (figure 3.1) while strongly preferring to share the burdens of that role with allies and major international organizations. Even in the absence of direct poll evidence on the question, it seems reasonable to assume that support for the postwar occupation of Iraq would have witnessed less erosion if the costs in lives and resources were shared among a much broader coalition of allies.

Even postwar surveys, which might have been expected to validate unilateralist policies in light of the predictable ease with which U.S. and U.K. forces initially crushed those of Iraq, found continued support for multilateralism in general and, more specifically, for the United Nations. To be sure, two-thirds of the respondents felt that if the United States were to become a more dominant force in the world as a result of the war, that would be "something positive." Yet a strikingly large majority (76 percent) also agreed that "the United States should do its share in efforts to solve international problems together with other countries," whereas only 12 percent asserted that "the United States should continue to be the preeminent world leader in solving international problems." Contrary to the claims of Krauthammer and many other conservative pundits that the United Nations has rendered itself wholly irrelevant because the Security Council failed to support the U.S. position on Iraq, only a third of those taking part in the PIPA survey agreed that, in the future, the United States "should feel more free to use force without United Nations authorization," and 88 percent of respondents felt that trying to get United Nations authorization to take military action against Iraq "was the right thing to do" (PIPA 2003a).

Several postwar surveys of Americans have yielded a mixed scorecard for the United Nations. An August 2003 Gallup poll found that 60 percent rated the job that organization is doing as "poor," whereas only 37 percent assessed it as "good." This is the lowest rating received by the United Nations since Gallup began asking the question in 1953 (Jeffrey Jones 2003c). At about the same time, however, a Pew survey revealed that 70 percent of Americans—including 68 percent of Republicans and 71 percent of Democrats—wanted the United Nations to "play a significant role in rebuilding Iraq." Forty-four percent preferred that the United Nations "have the most say" in that process, twice the number who wanted the United States to have the dominant voice on the issue (Pew 2003c, 1–2).

Conclusion

Recent U.S. foreign and defense policies reflect a greater degree of unilateralism than at any time since Pearl Harbor. In this sense, Schlesinger's diagnosis and forecast of the mid-1990s has turned out to be rather prescient. But to the extent that his analysis located the roots of isolationism and unilateralism in irresistible pressures from the general public ("the housewife in Xenia, Ohio") or opinion leaders ("members of the Council on Foreign Relations"), the evidence is much less kind to his thesis. Both pre- and post-9/11 surveys indicate greater persistence than change in public attitudes toward foreign affairs since the end of the Cold War: opinion leaders continue to be more internationalist than the general public on most issues; the general public has shown little indication of a mindless retreat toward isolationism and even less support for unilateralism in preference to action in cooperation with NATO or the United Nations. Although consultation and cooperation with others may sometimes seem less efficient than acting alone, as vocal unilateralists in the media and elsewhere constantly remind us, most Americans seem to prefer that path. The public has shown little support for crusades to make the world over in the American image (tables 3.3a, 3.3b, and 6.6) but also has not jumped on the bandwagon of those who would bypass or withdraw from NATO, the United Nations, and most other international organizations; reduce or eliminate foreign aid; withdraw most American forces stationed abroad; and otherwise seek to cut the ties that have enmeshed the United States in the global system.

Thus, although the data reveal declining support for some international endeavors and ripples of disquiet about the effects of economic globalization—a concern that predates the end of the Cold War—evidence of continuity in public opinion dominates signs of sharp change. Even with respect to the most controversial post–Cold War undertakings—military interventions abroad that may pose the risk of casualties—the public is selectively supportive rather than reflexively opposed. Support is most likely for interventions in such areas of traditional concern as Europe, when the purpose is to prevent or punish aggression, and when there is a reasonable prospect of success. Less approval may be forthcoming when the goal is to promote American values and institutions or to effect a change in leadership abroad. The clear links between Afghanistan and the al Qaeda terrorists underlay support for military intervention in that country following the 9/11 attacks. Conditional support for toppling Saddam Hussein is an exception to general skepticism about interventions for purposes of regime change; Iraq's previous invasions of Iran and Kuwait no doubt contributed to support for removal of the Baath Party regime. Public concern about and willingness to deal forcefully with terrorist threats is not merely a post-9/11 phenomenon. Compared to opinion leaders, a higher proportion of the general public rated terrorist attacks as a significant threat (table 4.2). Moreover, whereas in 1998 the public was generally unenthusiastic about using U.S. troops abroad in a number of hypothetical scenarios, the same CCFR survey revealed that 57 percent favored "attacks by U.S. ground troops against terrorist training camps and other facilities," and by 2002 that figure had increased to 91 percent. Whether or not one agrees with these preferences, they bear considerably greater resemblance to traditional realism than to isolationism. Indeed, they are less stringent than the Weinberger Doctrine, a set of six preconditions—including the support of Congress and the public—for military interventions abroad proposed by the secretary of defense in 1984 and opposed by his cabinet colleague, George Shultz (Weinberger 1984; Shultz 1993).

Domestic politics certainly have complicated and sometimes damaged Washington's ability to conduct foreign affairs and to demonstrate essential leadership in attempting to cope with the post–Cold War international arena. This is not an unfamiliar pattern. Periods of crisis and conflict, when there is an accretion of power by the executive branch, are often followed by congressional efforts to restore legislative prerogatives and, more generally, by the intrusion of domestic political concerns into the conduct of foreign affairs. The years following the Revolutionary War, Civil War, World War I, and the Vietnam War illustrate this pattern, and the post–Cold War era appears to be no exception.

But where is the primary focus of the problem? Is it in a public that, at least until the 2001 terrorist attacks, focused more attention on domestic issues than on international ones? Or in intensified partisanship in Congress? Or in the willingness of some congressional leaders to engage in such damaging frivolities as withholding payments of legitimate dues to the United Nations or holding up ambassadorial and other appointments for reasons that are unrelated to the qualifications of the nominees? Or in the print and electronic media that have drastically reduced coverage of foreign affairs in recent years (Emery 1989; Norris 1995; Robinson and Livingston 2003)? Or in parochial single-issue interest groups that found it easier to thrive in the absence of an overriding international threat after the disintegration of the USSR and whose post–September 11 activities often have been directed at persuading public officials that pet projects, no matter how far removed from foreign policy or homeland security, are in fact an integral part of the "war on terrorism"? Many of these actors state that they accurately reflect public preferences. Media leaders assert that in focusing on domestic issues and entertainment, they are merely giving the public what it wants. Many senators and representatives argue that their opposition to peacekeeping operations, foreign aid, or the United Nations and other international institutions reflects the views of an increasingly isolationist public that has lost patience with recalcitrant allies, inefficient international organizations, and Third World kleptocracies that look to America to bail them out of problems of their own making.

Compelling evidence demonstrates that foreign and defense policy issues have lost a good deal of their salience for the general public except in time of crisis or war. At least until the terrorist attacks in 2001, domestic issues seemed to impinge more directly than foreign ones on most citizens' daily lives, and the print and electronic media's declining coverage of international affairs reinforces and exacerbates the public tendency to focus on problems at home in the absence of wars, crises, and other dramatic events abroad. In virtually every post–Gulf War and pre–September 11 survey asking, "What are the major problems facing the country today?" the list of answers was dominated by such issues as health care, corporate malfeasance, unemployment, drugs, crime, education, poverty, immorality, the economy, Social Security, and similar concerns. Even during the months leading up to the 2003 invasion of Iraq, most polls revealed that the weak state of the U.S. economy ranked at the top of public concerns, and postwar surveys have shown an even higher priority accorded to economic issues (Pew 2003d, T-8). The paucity of international issues near the top of public concerns is not, however, necessarily an unambiguous or even especially valid indicator of isolationism. Indeed, public inattention to international problems during the closing years of the twentieth century derived at least in part from a general sense of satisfaction with the conduct of foreign affairs. Not only did former President Clinton's overall approval ratings remain at a remarkably high level, but respondents to the 1998 CCFR survey, conducted during House impeachment proceedings against Clinton, gave him the highest percentage of "very successful" ratings for his foreign policies of any post–World War II president. When "somewhat successful" responses are included, Clinton ranked second only to his immediate predecessor, George H. W. Bush (Rielly 1999, 36–37; Lipset and Bowman 2000; Walt 2000).

George W. Bush's exceptionally high approval ratings are a direct consequence of his leadership in the war on terrorists and the war against Iraq rather than a groundswell of support for his domestic agenda. These responses seem to point to a public that is rather poorly informed about the world (as usual), inattentive most of the time, generally satisfied with the conduct of foreign affairs—but not necessarily leading a charge "back to the womb." Not surprisingly, the events of September 11 and their aftermath dominated public attention to the news. According to the Pew News Interest Index, eight of the ten stories to which Americans paid the most attention in 2001 involved those events and subsequent U.S. actions against terrorism (Kohut 2002, 15; Pew 2001e, 1). Except in the immediate aftermath of crises, the public mood is perhaps most accurately described as "apathetic internationalism" (Lindsay 2000, 4).

The absence of sustained public attention to international issues is not without important policy consequences, for it eases the task of policymakers who employ emotional appeals to drum up public support for favored undertakings. The public relations campaign during the run up to the invasion of Iraq is a case in point. The core of the administration's indictment was that the Baghdad regime possessed weapons of mass destruction that posed an imminent national security danger to the United States and further that Iraq's ties to the al Qaeda terrorist group gave rise to the threat that these weapons could well fall into the hands of those who planned future terrorist attacks on the United States. Although persuasive evidence was not forthcoming on either of these points prior to the March 2003 invasion, repeated assertions by the president and his top advisers, reinforced by Saddam Hussein's well-deserved reputation for unusual brutality, resulted in a public that was prepared to believe both charges. Postwar investigations may yet uncover evidence that the administration's case was valid, but to date (February 2004) they have not done so.

Nevertheless, although the war received massive media coverage, 41 percent of respondents surveyed immediately after the war believed that WMDs had in fact been found and 22 percent stated that Iraq had used such weapons against the United States during the conflict (PIPA 2003b). Even about four months after the end of hostilities almost one half of Americans believed that evidence had been discovered to show that Saddam Hussein was working closely with al Qaeda terrorists, almost one quarter believed that the United States had uncovered weapons of mass destruction in Iraq, and a quarter believed that world public opinion favored the United States going to war against Iraq. An analysis of news sources upon which respondents relied revealed some striking differences. Those relying primarily on Fox News had significantly more misperceptions, those who depended on National Public Radio/Public Broadcasting System had significantly fewer misperceptions, and those whose primary news sources were other networks fell in between. Respondents who relied on the print media were less likely than average to misperceive the three facts about the Iraq situation (PIPA 2003c).

Where does that leave any administration that seeks to have the United States play an effective leadership role in world affairs? Although one should exercise great caution in attempting to draw historical parallels, it may be instructive to recall the half decade immediately following the end of World War II. Some pioneering opinion analysts of that period feared that a fickle and poorly informed public, weary of the sacrifices imposed by four years of war, would resist any efforts to continue shouldering the burdens of world leadership. In a memo to President Roosevelt, just prior to his departure for the Yalta Conference in 1945, his personal pollster Hadley Cantril warned that "it is unrealistic to assume that Americans are international-minded. . . .The present internationalism rests on rather unstable foundations: it is recent, it is not rooted in broad or long range conceptions of self-interest, it has little intellectual basis" (1967, 76). Gabriel Almond (1960) examined responses to questions about the "most important problems facing the country." Noting that wartime concerns with international issues had been replaced by domestic concerns, he concluded that a volatile and inattentive public provided a shaky foundation on which to sustain global leadership. Yet, during 1945–50, the public came to support a number of unprecedented undertakings that have been described by William G. Carleton (1963) as the "revolution in American foreign policy," suggesting that there is a significant difference between an inattentive and an isolationist public. Effective presidential leadership, often bridging partisan lines, generated public support for innovative undertakings, some of which ran counter to such deeply embedded axioms as George Washington's admonition in his "Farewell Address" "to steer clear of permanent alliances with any portion of the foreign world."

We should be wary of pushing too far the parallels between 1945–50 and the present. The most striking difference is that Stalin's Soviet Union posed a threat to vital interests far greater than any that exists today, even when the activities of terrorist organizations or the "axis of evil" are taken into account. Nevertheless, the example suggests that because even a poorly informed and inattentive public is not necessarily isolationist or unilateralist, it can be persuaded to support an American leadership role in a broad range of international undertakings if it can be shown that such a role is both desirable and feasible. A critical element is a presidential leadership that is capable of making an effective case for its foreign policy agenda; of avoiding the mendacity that all too often has marred efforts to use the "bully pulpit" to gain public support, with the consequence that public trust in government has declined precipitously during the past several decades; and of reading the public accurately rather than misreading it.

History suggests that active cooperation with other countries may be the most effective and rewarding form of world leadership. In the years after World War II, many American leaders of both political parties rejected the "Fortress America" concept of national security in favor of multilateralism. The United Nations, the World Bank, the International Monetary Fund, the Truman Doctrine, the Marshall Plan, NATO, and resistance to aggression in Korea were among the more important milestones along the multilateral path to a more stable international order. Much to the surprise of many experts of that era, the American public was persuaded, largely through the concerted efforts of effective leaders in both parties, to abandon its traditional preference for limited peacetime international obligations and to embrace an unprecedented set of multilateral commitments. The multilateral path also made the vast preponderance of power enjoyed by the United States in the aftermath of World War II more palatable and less threatening to allies, thereby contributing in no small way to acceptance abroad of America's international leadership role (Ikenberry 2001).

There would appear to be food for thought in the words of an author who is not widely known for an excessive deference to liberal perspectives and prescriptions on foreign affairs or to the merits or multilateralism as an approach for all seasons and all reasons:

> If the United States could move past the anxiety engendered by this inaccurate sense of constraint [from European allies], it could begin to show more understanding for the sensibilities of others, a little generosity of spirit. It could pay its respects to multilateralism and the rule of law and try to build some international political capital for those moments when multilateralism is impossible and unilateral action unavoidable. It could, in short, take more care to show what the founders called "a decent respect for the opinions of mankind." (Kagan 2002, 28)

The evidence reviewed here reveals that even a "decent respect for the opinions" of a much smaller group, the American public, might give policymakers reason to pause as they weigh the longer-term costs and benefits of unilateralism.

But is multilateralism, with its sensitivity to the vital interests of countries whose citizens do not vote in the United States, a realistic path toward electoral success at home? All first-term presidents since Rutherford B. Hayes, save those who died in office (James A. Garfield, Warren G. Harding, and John F. Kennedy), have sought election to a second term. The most improbable success in this respect was the startling victory by Harry S. Truman in 1948. According to a recent study, his foreign policy actions during the year prior to the election, including the Marshall Plan and the Berlin airlift to bring food and fuel to the beleaguered citizens of that city, probably brought him enough votes to win the election (Zaller 2004). Perhaps the American public, for all its apathy and other well-documented weaknesses, appreciates a generosity of spirit and can be persuaded to reward it on election day.

CHAPTER 7

Public Opinion and Foreign Policy: Where Do We Go from Here?

A few days before President Bill Clinton ordered American troops to invade Haiti in September 1994, Jeff MacNelly of the *Chicago Tribune* published an editorial cartoon depicting a loaded military landing craft approaching the coast of Haiti. Among those on board was Clinton, who was depicted as saying, "Shouldn't the pollsters go in first?" To be sure, in the case of Haiti, President Clinton took action in the face of substantial evidence of public and congressional opposition to any military intervention there. But the cartoon reflects the widely held belief that the Clinton administration's frequent threats of strong action, followed by retreats over Somalia and most-favored-nation trade status for China were significantly influenced by public opinion and especially by widespread disquiet about any deployment of American troops abroad. Indeed, at about the same time, another cartoonist, Garry Trudeau, creator of the *Doonesbury* comic strip, began depicting President Clinton as a waffle.

It is not altogether clear that these cartoons accurately depicted the Clinton administration's decision making on foreign affairs—Clinton ultimately sent armed forces into Haiti, Bosnia, and Kosovo in efforts to cope with egregious human rights violations despite the absence of powerful public sentiments that he do so—but there is a good deal of evidence that, for better or worse, public opinion had a substantial impact on the foreign policies of recent administrations. Some of this evidence was reviewed in chapter 3. This chapter will focus on two related points. First, I will develop the thesis that the terrorist attacks of September 11, 2001, notwithstanding, whatever may have been true in earlier periods, public opinion during the post—Cold War era is likely to become a more rather than less potent force in shaping American foreign relations. If the reverse were true, then there would be scant reason for students of international relations and foreign policy to direct additional attention to public opinion.

Policymakers' growing use of polling data testifies to the perceived importance of public opinion. We cannot, however, rule out the possibility that attention to the public can be motivated not only by a desire to bring policy into concordance with public sentiments but also by manipulative goals. An excellent recent study by Lawrence Jacobs and Robert Shapiro (2000), drawing on both archival evidence and interviews, provides a sobering reminder on this score. Focused on the health care policy of the Clinton administration and the Newt Gingrich–led "Republican revolution" of the mid-1990s, Jacobs and Shapiro's study found ample evidence that polling data were used primarily as the means for crafting messages to manipulate the public.[1] Furthermore, foreign affairs, especially in time of war or crisis, provide even greater opportunities in this respect, especially if officials succumb to the temptation to depict any questions about or challenges to administration policy as tantamount to giving aid and comfort to the enemy. President George W. Bush, Vice President Richard Cheney, and Attorney General John Ashcroft did so with respect to the war on terrorists, but in this they are only the latest in an unfortunately long list of American leaders, dating back to the late eighteenth century, who have attempted to demonize those with even modestly dissenting views about foreign affairs.

If the hypothesis about an increasing role for public opinion is valid, it leads to the second point to be considered in this chapter: what might be done to understand better the relationship between public opinion and foreign policy? The second section of the chapter will consider several approaches that might contribute to that goal, including case studies to assess causal relationships, cross-national comparative analyses, and standardized questions.

Public Opinion in the Post–Cold War Era

The realist thesis, some features of which were described in chapter 1, holds that public opinion can contribute very little to the effective conduct of foreign affairs. In some versions of the realist position, public opinion is depicted as an ill-informed, volatile, and mood-driven force that, if heeded, would often deflect leaders from the steady pursuit of the long-range interests and goals that constitute the essence of the country's national interests. In other contexts, the realist position views public opinion as pushing the government into ill-considered undertakings that have little, if any, relationship to those national interests. One variant of this thesis points to the so-called CNN effect, wherein the media, especially television, play a critical role in arousing the public, which in turn pressures policymakers to act (Kennan 1993). However, a careful study of post–Cold War cases largely discounts this explanation for U.S. interventions. According to Warren Strobel,

> Clinton's dispatch of troops to Bosnia, like his deployment of forces to Haiti the year before, is continuing testimony to the power of the chief executive to lead, at least in the short run, in ways that are not automatically in line with prevailing sentiment. The push in this case came not from the television-driven public opinion that so worries George Kennan and others, but from government leaders who chose to exercise that leadership at the expense of short-term popularity or political capital. (1997, 215)

Government officials may at times also exercise leadership as a way of enhancing popularity or political capital. This may be perceived as an attractive strategy if the adversary is an especially nasty and widely hated tyrant—for example, Manuel Noriega or Saddam Hussein—whose military forces seem incapable of putting up serious and protracted resistance. Other critiques agree that the public is poorly informed about international affairs but also focus on the alleged rigidity rather than volatility of public opinion. The public is described as so firmly set in its ways of thinking that serious attention to public preferences would make it impossible for policymakers to act with sufficient flexibility and dexterity to cope effectively with international opportunities and challenges (see, for example, Dallek 1983). In his classic *Study of War* (1942), first published when the Axis powers had reached the outer limits of their conquests in Europe and Asia, Quincy Wright wrote that democracies were hampered in their attempts to cope with the imperatives of an anarchical international environment:

> Executive freedom of action has been hampered by an active and independent public opinion, by indirect checks on the control of appropriations, by certain direct checks, such as legislative participation in treaty-making and general

responsibility of the executive to parliament and the electorate. These limitations have seriously affected the capacity of the more democratic nations to conduct foreign policy efficiently when that policy must be conducted in a balance of power system. (1965, 265)

More specifically, the essence of the case against public opinion is that effective diplomacy requires three important features, none of which is enhanced by more active public participation: *secrecy, speed,* and *flexibility*. Moreover, policymakers must often rely on confidential information that cannot be shared with the public. Critics—not all of whom are realists—deem all of these requirements as essential to bargaining and negotiating effectively with other countries, meeting external challenges and taking advantage of opportunities as they arise, maneuvering adroitly in a rapidly changing global system, and, most importantly, avoiding war. Senator J. William Fulbright expressed some of these reservations: "Statesmen and scholars have long since discovered that the kind of thinking which makes for the successful conduct of foreign-policy is all too often diametrically opposed to prevailing public attitudes." He went on to assert that the public prefers "a hero to a horsetrader and, knowing this, the diplomat is under the strongest pressure to strike postures rather than bargains" (Battle 1995).

The case for the importance of these features in the conduct of foreign affairs is most plausible in times of war, crisis, and confrontation. Without in any way suggesting that traditional security concerns have vanished with the end of the Cold War and the disintegration of the Soviet Union, it seems increasingly likely that the top echelons of the U.S. foreign policy agenda during the post–Cold War era will also encompass some issues on which it is difficult to make a compelling case for excluding the public and its representatives from involvement in the policy process. This agenda will probably include but not be limited to a number of issues on which the public is likely to have strong views and on which the thesis that the "president knows best" may appear less compelling than, for example, during World War II or the Cold War (Yankelovich 1978; Clough 1994). The long-term impact of the terrorist attacks on New York and Washington is not yet wholly clear. The war on terrorists could create an extended crisis atmosphere reminiscent of the coldest days of the Cold War, with enhanced power for the executive branch and a concomitant constriction of the role of the public and those representing it. Alternatively, although the war on terrorists is unlikely to result in a clearly defined victory in the near future, if ever, efforts to subordinate permanently all other issues to that undertaking may fail. Among the issues on which the case for executive dominance over other domestic political actors is not likely to be wholly compelling are trade, immigration, the environment, and intrastate conflicts abroad that may touch on the interests of various groups of hyphenated Americans.

Trade.   As I noted in chapter 4, the general public has diverged sharply from the views of elites on questions of trade liberalization versus protectionism as well as on such specific trade agreements as the North American Free Trade Agreement (NAFTA) and the General Agreement on Tariffs and Trade/World Trade Organization (GATT/WTO) pact. Moreover, because such a varied array of opponents of trade liberalization, from H. Ross Perot, Patrick Buchanan, and Ralph Nader to Senators Ernest Hollings and Jesse Helms and Representative Dick Gephardt, have consistently argued that there is a direct negative relationship between trade liberalization and the number of good jobs in the United States, the issue is likely to continue to engage the interest of the public, especially when major trade agreements or other trade-related issues are being negotiated or are before Congress for ratification. Buchanan's vehement attacks on free trade and his promise to cancel the NAFTA agreement if elected president contributed to his successes in the early 1996 Republican presidential primary elections. His dismal showing and the spoiler role played by Ralph Nader in the 2000 election probably ended their political careers, but the public protests against globalization at major trade meetings in Seattle, Washington; Davos, Switzerland; and elsewhere suggest that trade issues will not disappear. The Republican Congress denied President Clinton "fast track authority" to negotiate trade agreements that can be approved or rejected but not amended. Congress restored that power, renamed "trade promotion authority," to President Bush in 2002 but did so only after adding some protectionist amendments to meet the demands of legislators from textile-producing states. The recession that began in March 2001 provided additional ammunition for those who assert that trade liberalization merely accelerates the loss of American jobs to low-wage areas. Measures to protect the steel, lumber, textile, and farm industries, described in the previous chapter, indicate that free trade principles and rhetoric will continue to give way to interest-group pressures, at least on a se-lective basis. Moreover, trade is not an issue on which public apa-thy can be assumed. "Protecting the jobs of American workers" has consistently ranked among the public's top foreign policy goals (tables 3.3 and 6.6).

Refugees and immigration.   Right-wing parties in Europe scored some stunning electoral victories in 2001 and 2002 by focusing on opposition to immigrants and by demanding tighter restrictions on those allowed to enter the country. Virtually all Americans are immigrants or descendants of immigrants, but sentiments against specific groups have periodically been aroused in the United States. Examples include the Alien and Sedition Acts of 1798; the 1850s Know-Nothing movement, which targeted Catholics; vari-ous types of legislation in California and other states against Asians; and quota systems in the 1907, 1924, and 1952 immigra-tion acts that were highly biased against Eastern Europeans and Asians. Although some of the most discriminatory acts have been mitigated, strong public sentiments on questions of refugees and immigration have not altogether disappeared, especially in states and regions that have been the more popular destinations of those entering the United States — the Southeast for those arriv-ing from Haiti and Cuba and the Southwest for those arriving from Mexico and Central America.[2] Several states have sued the federal government to recover the alleged costs of providing services to illegal immigrants, and immigration was probably the most potent issue in the 1994 California gubernatorial election. Even if the measure is ultimately declared unconstitutional, the overwhelming public support for California's Proposition 187, which would deny educational, medical, and social services to all persons who have entered the United States illegally, is not likely to be the last such effort to deal with the issue. The response to Proposition 187 encouraged California Governor Pete Wilson to make immigration control the centerpiece of his 1996 presiden-tial campaign; Patrick Buchanan proposed even more restrictive measures — including erection of a high wall along the Mexican border — to stem the flow of immigrants into the United States. Although Wilson's presidential bid was aborted soon after its in-ception, the issue will almost surely survive for the foreseeable future. During the early months of 2001 it appeared that the United States would ease restrictions on immigration from Mex-ico as part of a Bush administration effort to increase the GOP's appeal to Hispanic voters, but the terrorist attacks and subsequent revelations of laxity and incompetence in the Immigration and Naturalization Service are almost sure to strengthen the hands of those who favor more rather than less restrictive immigration policies, and the administration has placed on the back burner any efforts to negotiate a settlement with Mexico on the issue. Furthermore, the country's refusal to back the Iraq war reduces the likelihood that Mexican concerns regarding immigration will receive a high priority in Washington in the near future.

Environmental issues. Environment-related issues, especially those that may involve further regulation of major industries or trigger NIMBY (not in my back yard) responses, are likely to remain controversial. Environmental and trade issues also have been linked, especially by opponents of the NAFTA in 1993 and the GATT/WTO agreement a year later. Many environmental groups and activists charged that these agreements would prevent the United States from enforcing environmental standards that are more stringent than those of its trade partners. The war on terrorists has heightened the intensity of debates about how best to reduce American dependence on oil from such major foreign suppliers as Saudi Arabia, home of fifteen of the nineteen 9/11 airline hijackers. Proponents of both conservation and expanded oil drilling in Alaska pointed to the events of September 11, 2001, as proving the superiority of their preferred policies. By mid-2003 it appeared that neither side could claim victory. Congress rejected efforts, led by Senator John McCain, to raise automobile fuel standards over the coming decade but also refused to authorize oil drilling in the Alaskan National Wildlife Reserve, one of the centerpieces of the Bush administration's energy policy. California mandated that auto manufacturers must meet certain modest fleet fuel-efficiency standards by producing electric cars, but the success of these efforts is far from assured, as the Bush administration has joined the auto industry in opposing them.

Ethnic, racial, religious, and nationalist conflicts and civil wars. It is also clear, however, that post–Cold War foreign policy leaders will not have the luxury of focusing all of their energies on international economic, social, and environmental issues, if only because of the persistence of ethnic, racial, religious, nationalist, and tribal civil wars in many regions. The disintegration of the Soviet Union and its withdrawal from its Eastern European empire have also opened up opportunities for sometimes ancient rivalries and hatreds to resurface as civil wars. Some, such as the conflicts in the Russian province of Chechnya or in the Uighur areas of western China, are unlikely to engage American interests, especially as they have been framed by Presidents Vladimir Putin and Jiang Zemin as part of the larger global war against terrorists, an assessment with which Washington has concurred. But at least some of these intrastate conflicts are also likely to stimulate political activity by ethnic and other interest groups in the United States, thereby magnifying the impact of at least parts of the public. Efforts of the American-Israeli Political Action Committee on behalf of Israel, of Greek-Americans following the Turkish invasion of Cyprus, of TransAfrica in connection with conflicts within South Africa and Haiti, of Irish-Americans with respect to Northern Ireland, and Polish-Americans in support of NATO expansion to include Poland illustrate forms of political activity that are likely to become more rather than less frequent. According to such realists as Kennan (1993), internal conflicts abroad are often precisely the types of issues on which the public, aroused by television images of unspeakable suffering at the hands of local tyrants or competing warlords, may push the United States and international organizations into well-intentioned but hopeless and probably dangerous undertakings—for example, nation building in Somalia or restoring democracy in Haiti.

Of course, the terrorist attacks also have affected the post–Cold War foreign policy agenda. During the 2000 presidential campaign, George W. Bush and members of his foreign policy team made it clear that nation building was a Clintonian snare and delusion that his administration would avoid. President Bush's 2002 State of the Union address focused attention on a group of highly authoritarian states—Iran, Iraq, and North Korea—that he dubbed the "axis of evil" because of their efforts to acquire weapons of mass destruction and because they had given aid and comfort to international terrorist groups. But the events of September 11 also highlight a competing or supplementary hypothesis: "failed states"—those that suffer not from excessively centralized political power but in fact lack any semblance of a legitimate and effective governing authority—may be especially attractive havens for international terrorist groups. Examples of such failed states include but are not limited to Afghanistan, Somalia, and Sudan. The war against the Osama bin Laden's network and the

Taliban in Afghanistan has inevitably raised the question of what role the United States should play in that country during the post-Taliban era. Will the United States once again abandon Afghanistan, as it did under the elder President Bush's administration after the Soviet invaders had been driven out, leaving a power vacuum and civil war that led the Taliban to gain power in Kabul? Alternatively, will the United States make a long-term commitment of the financial and other resources—including peacekeeping forces—to give the post-Taliban government a decent chance of creating a viable state? That is, will the United States engage in nation building? In early 2002, two-thirds of the public favored keeping military forces in Afghanistan "to maintain civil order there," whereas only one-quarter opposed doing so (Pew 2002a, 20). There are nevertheless signs that the administration is not prepared to expend the personnel or material resources necessary to create a stable and secure Afghanistan, much less to establish a democratic country with a viable economy. Through the early summer of 2003 most Americans favored keeping U.S. forces in Iraq until a stable post–Saddam Hussein regime can be established in Baghdad (PIPA 2003c, 6; *Washington Post*-ABC News 2003, 5), but continued violence targeted at U.S. military personnel began to erode that support—even before the November 2 downing of a Chinook helicopter with the loss of sixteen lives (Gallup 2003, 1–3).

If we are indeed entering a period of fewer crises and confrontations among the major powers with greater attention paid to post–Cold War issues such as those listed here—and ample survey data demonstrate that much of the American public believed this was true even before the end of the Cold War (*Americans Talk Security* 1987–90)—it is also likely to be an era in which public opinion plays a more autonomous role. Even those who do not fully subscribe to the thesis that the public is merely the hapless object of elite manipulations would acknowledge that crises and confrontation abroad provide a setting in which opportunities and temptations for elite manipulation of the public are far greater than on nonsecurity issues. Such issues are typically resolved over a longer time period, thus providing greater opportunities for the public, interest groups, the media, Congress, and other domestic actors to play a significant role. Nonsecurity issues also tend to be more resistant to claims that the needs for secrecy, flexibility, and speed of action, as well as the president's constitutional role as commander-in-chief of the armed forces, make it both necessary and legitimate for the executive to have a relatively free hand and to withhold vital information from Congress and the public. In short, despite the prospect of a protracted and possibly inconclusive war on terrorists and temptations to define all other issues, including those discussed earlier, as merely facets of that war, we may be moving into a period in which the relationship between public opinion and foreign policy takes on added rather than diminished significance.

Public Opinion in the Foreign Policy Process

The argument that public opinion is likely to play a more potent role in the future than in the past, however plausible, is a hypothesis to be tested rather than a firmly established fact. This raises some questions about research strategies. Important elements of any effective strategy will include continuing performance of the tasks that have dominated public opinion research since the mid-1930s, including gathering and summarizing data about public attitudes, correlating them with important international events and foreign policy decisions, depicting major trends, describing the concepts around which attitudes are structured, identifying the demographic and other correlates of attitudes, and the like. No doubt there is room for important substantive and technical developments that will enable us to have more confidence in the validity and reliability of the resulting data—for example, devising survey methods that will provide a better sense of what the public is thinking (Fishkin 1991, 1992, 1994; Yankelovich 1991; Kay 1992a, b; Yankelovich and Destler 1994); dealing with the problem of nonresponses to surveys (Brehm 1993); improving the quality of longitudinal analyses (D. Taylor 1980; Stimson 1991); combining survey research with experimental designs (Sniderman 1993); identifying the sources of response variability (Alvarez and Brehm 2002); bringing new theoretical perspectives and concepts to the study of public opinion (Gaubatz 1995); and devising multipronged research designs to explore the relationship between public opinion and elite perceptions or misperceptions of public preferences (Kull and Destler 1999). As befits a vibrant field of inquiry, the past two decades have witnessed quite substantial progress in these respects.

However, as I noted in chapter 3, by far the least well developed of the areas of public opinion research has been the opinion-policy link. This is also arguably the most important aspect of the topic. Some impressive correlational studies exist; in several cases, they span decades rather than just a few years and reveal that when public policies change, the shifts occur predominantly in the direction favored by the public. But these findings do not exhaust the relevant questions, which include but are not limited to the following:

Did policymakers rule out certain courses of action because of a belief that lack of public support would reduce or eliminate the prospects of success?

Did policymakers decide on certain foreign policy undertakings, even when the chances of success were deemed very slight, because of a belief that the public demanded some form of action? Because of a belief that they would benefit politically from a public tendency to "rally round the flag"? Because doing so was perceived as an effective strategy for deflecting public attention from such domestic problems as a flagging economy?

How, if at all, did expectations of future public reactions affect decision makers' appraisal of policy options?

How, if at all, did calculations about the electoral consequences of certain decisions restrain or motivate policymakers?

On what indicators, if any, of public sentiments did leaders rely?

Were the timing of foreign policy decisions and the choice of means to carry out an undertaking influenced by beliefs about what the public would or would not accept, would or would not demand?

What strategies and tactics did leaders use to persuade the public to support their favored policies? What role did polling data play in such efforts?

Answers to these and related questions require more substantial evidence of a causal nature. Case studies employing archival research, interviews with policymakers, or both, are virtually indispensable for assessing the impact of public opinion. But as noted earlier, those employing interviews and archives must also be sensitive to possible validity problems.

Moreover, the brief review of some case studies in chapter 3 revealed quite mixed results; in some instances, the evidence indicated that public opinion had a negligible impact, whereas other studies showed the public's effects to be highly significant. These varied findings, while scarcely surprising, suggest the need for research strategies and designs that can capture adequately the variations that may be found across cases and that can help to explain the sources of those differences. The case studies also need to be designed in ways that will enhance cross-case comparisons by employing, for example, the method of "structured, focused comparison" (George 1979) or other research designs employing qualitative data (King, Keohane, and Verba 1994).

Case studies designed to assess the impact of public opinion on foreign policy are likely to be enhanced by sensitivity to certain distinctions in research designs, including not only the type of issue, as noted earlier, but also the stage of the policy process, the decision context, and policymakers' beliefs about and sensitivity to public opinion. Although all post–World War II presidential administrations have had access to immense amounts of survey data about public attitudes, increasingly generated by and paid for by the administration, it should not be assumed that this information is taken uniformly into account in policy deliberations. Just as policymakers may vary substantially in their sensitivity to public opinion, they also may have quite different conceptions of the most relevant and useful indicators of public attitudes. Moreover, decision makers at varying levels of the government hierarchy may be sensitive to public opinion to different degrees. Political appointees are more likely than civil servants to pay attention to public sentiments, and elected officials are likely to be even more sensitive.

Stage in the policy process.   Thomas Graham (1989, 1994) analyzed the impact of public opinion on four arms control issues spanning seven American administrations from Presidents Truman through Carter. The four cases—international control of atomic energy, the Limited Test Ban Treaty, the SALT I/ABM treaties, and SALT II—varied in outcomes, ranging from unsuccessful negotiations with the USSR to negotiated treaties that received approval from the U.S. Senate and went into effect. Graham distinguished between four stages in the policy process: getting the issue on the agenda, negotiating the issue, ratifying the treaty, and implementing the treaty. Although the evidence revealed that public opinion had an important impact in all of the cases, this impact varied according to the stage in the policy process. Public opinion had a direct impact on getting the issues on the agenda and on ratification of agreements but only an indirect effect on negotiations and implementation.

Graham's study focused on strategic nuclear arms control, but Douglas Foyle's (1999) intensive analysis of four cases spanning a broader range of foreign and defense policy episodes during the Eisenhower administration provided further support for the proposition that a distinction between stages is important for understanding the ways in which public opinion may affect the policy process. In the four Eisenhower cases, public opinion had limited impact on problem representation but became a focus of policymakers' concern during consideration of policy options.

Decision context.   The cases in the Foyle study included four decision contexts: *crisis* (the 1954 Formosa Straits confrontation with China), *reflexive* (the 1954 Dien Bien Phu case in which Eisenhower decided against military intervention to assist France in the climactic battle of the war in French Indochina), *innovative* (the 1957–58 response to the successful Soviet launching of the *Sputnik* space satellite), and *deliberative* (the 1954 "New Look" defense policy by which the United States proposed emphasizing nuclear weapons and deemphasizing conventional military forces to contain the USSR and its allies).[3] The impact of public opinion varied across the four cases. In the Formosa Straits crisis, for example, decision makers focused on fears about how the public eventually would react to developments in the episode rather than on specific indicators of current public views. During the deliberative case, in contrast, Eisenhower administration officials anticipated the need to confront the issue and, having a long time to cope with it, were more comfortable with attempting to generate public support for their preferred policy options.

Beliefs about public opinion.   Even a cursory reading of memoirs, biographies, and accounts of many important decisions reveals that top-ranking American leaders have shown wide variations in their assessments of, sensitivity to, and strategies for dealing with public opinion. Moreover, although elected officials never can be utterly indifferent to public opinion, they may have quite different assessments of what constitute the most valid and politically significant indicators of those attitudes.

The latter point has become more relevant during recent years because the number of potential sources of information about the public has increased sharply. The menu of choices available in earlier eras may have included little more than legislative sentiments, newspapers, conversations with influential citizens, mail, and some limited contacts with the general public. Policymakers have often regarded newspapers as the best indicator of public opinion. A former newspaper editor, Warren G. Harding, relied heavily on the press as a gauge of public sentiments, as did his key advisers. Secretary of State Charles Evans Hughes asserted, "The sentiment of our people is expressed by our press, which gives the point of view of our composite population, the fidelity of the general picture making up for inaccuracies in the detail of the drawing" (E. Williams 1996). During the Washington Conference of 1921–22, the Harding administration established the Subcommittee on Public Opinion, which used newspaper editorials and letters from the public as sources of information. Some policymakers may still regard newspapers as important indicators of public sentiments, but the range of potential sources of public opinion data has expanded dramatically during the past seven decades. The most important innovation during that period clearly has been the advent of systematic polling, but the electronic age also has opened up new possibilities that have yet to be fully developed.

These innovations have, of course, also opened up vast new opportunities for official efforts to influence the public. Theodore Roosevelt's description of the White House as a "bully pulpit" (which could apply equally well to 10 Downing Street and many other official executive residences), does not fully capture the range of tools available to top leaders today. Roosevelt's distant cousin, Franklin, revealed an uncanny ability to deal with the public. FDR mastered the new technology of the day—the radio—but the means at his disposal were quite limited compared to those available to his successors. Ronald Reagan asserted that the most important lesson he learned as governor of California was the value of "making an end run around the legislature by going directly to the people" (1990, 234). According to two observers, the "Reagan entourage possessed an unprecedented sophistication in the technology of discerning what the public wanted and then giving it to them" (Weiler and Pearce 1992, 39). Assisted by pollster Richard Wirthlin, the Reagan presidency revealed that "influencing public opinion by broadly based appeals and image building has become not only a way of campaigning but a way of governing" (Weiler and Pearce 1992, 94). This assessment was validated by two White House insiders who wrote that "opinion polls are at the core of presidential decision making" (Beal and Hinckley 1984, 74; for a contrasting view, see Fischer 1997).

Even the nature of polling has changed significantly since the pioneering surveys conducted by George Gallup, Archibald Crossley, and Elmo Roper in the mid-1930s. These developments include a vast increase in the number of polls and countries where they can be conducted, the ability to get almost instantaneous public reactions to developing situations, and, perhaps most important, the widespread publicity accorded poll results. As noted earlier, major newspapers and television networks are today among the major producers of information about public opinion (see Mann and Orren 1992, especially Ladd and Benson 1992). Consequently, news reports not only describe major events but also can insert data on public opinion directly into even the most rapidly breaking crises. CNN routinely asks its audiences to express their views on controversial current issues as they are being covered in telecasts; however, although the number of responses may be quite large, the results hardly represent a valid sample of the American public. Moreover, the extensive use of polls to assess presidential performance and popularity—rather than surveys that focus on specific issues—may add to the influence of public opinion. Even presidents who may be reluctant to place much weight on how the public feels about foreign policy issues are not likely to be indifferent to surveys that assess presidential performance. Thus, "impression management" is likely to remain an important aspect of day-to-day White House activities. Yet it would be a mistake to assume that technical improvements in polling have uniformly increased survey data's impact on policymakers. An anecdotal examination of some evidence about the uses of information about public opinion by a few American presidents suggests the need for skepticism on that score.

Most accounts of Franklin Roosevelt's administration depict the president as intensely interested in public opinion. He relied on multiple sources of information, including analyses of mail to the White House (Sussmann 1963), press opinion, and conversations with visitors. Roosevelt's long tenure coincided with the advent of scientific polling, however, and he was the first president to make extensive use of the resulting information. Indeed, few of his successors appear to have matched FDR's intense interest in public opinion surveys, although, as noted in chapter 1, he was quite skeptical about the impartiality of poll data provided by George Gallup (Casey 2001). This interest was especially manifest in the areas of foreign and defense policy, including such issues as aid to Britain during the period between the outbreak of World War II and the attack on Pearl Harbor that brought the United States into the conflict. Roosevelt took a special interest in charts that plotted trends in public opinion.

FDR was not merely a consumer of data produced by Gallup and other surveys, however. To satisfy his desire for frequent information about public attitudes, he commissioned polling pioneer Hadley Cantril to conduct nationwide surveys. With all expenses covered by financial support from Gerald Lambert, a drug company heir, Cantril established a secret organization, Research Council Incorporated, to conduct surveys for the president. Cantril (1948) summarized some of the trend analyses available to the president based on data from multiple survey organizations. Both admirers and critics agree that FDR's actions were strongly influenced by public opinion. A passionate critic, Representative Claire Boothe, contemptuously compared FDR to Churchill, asserting that whereas the latter's symbol was two upheld fingers in the form of a V, Roosevelt's was a wet finger held to the wind. But even a sympathetic biographer concluded that "Roosevelt would lead—but not by more than a step. He seemed beguiled by public opinion, by its strange combination of fickleness and rigidity, ignorance and comprehension, by rapidly shifting optimism and pessimism" (Burns 1970, 66; see also Casey 2001).

Roosevelt's successor, Harry S. Truman, provides an interesting contrast to FDR. Both presidents were confronted with a predominantly Republican press that was less than supportive, especially on domestic issues, and thus the two men shared a somewhat skeptical view about newspapers as indicators of public attitudes. Truman also paid close attention to mail and telegrams after his speeches, but in contrast to FDR, Truman's enthusiasm for polls was very limited. In one of his more colorful observations, he asserted,

> Some people think that public relations should be based on polls. That is nonsense. I wonder how far Moses would have gone if he had taken a poll in Egypt? What would Jesus Christ have preached if he had taken a poll in the land of Israel? Where would the reformation have gone if Martin Luther had taken a poll? It isn't polls or public opinion of the moment that counts. It is right and wrong, and leader-

ship—men with fortitude, honesty and a belief in the right that makes epochs in the history of the world. (Hechler 1982, 219–20)

In an assessment of the ten presidents between Roosevelt and George H. W. Bush, Graham gave Roosevelt an "extensive" rating on two criteria: levels of presidential understanding of public opinion and successful presidential use of public opinion. In contrast, Graham gave Truman a "poor" score on both counts (1994, 198). These ratings seem valid, but they may also underscore the limits of focusing on a single dimension of leadership. Truman's modest public relations abilities notwithstanding, his administration achieved what has sometimes been called a revolution in American foreign policy, including such innovative undertakings as membership in the United Nations, the Marshall Plan, and the formation of NATO. Perhaps a president more cowed by the fear that the public would not tolerate broad international commitments—as predicted in Cantril's 1945 report to Roosevelt—or by the 1946 congressional elections, which gave the Republicans control of both the House and Senate, might not have attempted such pathbreaking undertakings.

Although the differences between Roosevelt and Truman reflected their different leadership styles, their attitudes toward public opinion polls may also have been reinforced by their different experiences with election surveys. Gallup had established his reputation as a pollster by forecasting that Roosevelt would win his 1936 reelection bid with a landslide victory over Republican nominee Alf Landon. Gallup's prediction was especially noteworthy because it flew in the face of a contrary forecast by the established and respected *Literary Digest* that Landon would be swept into the presidency by a large margin. In contrast to Roosevelt's experience in 1936, Truman had seen Gallup and the other polls confidently confirm the widespread expectation that Thomas Dewey would ride a Republican tidal wave into the White House in the 1948 presidential election. Although Gallup's forecast missed the size of the Democratic vote by a greater margin in 1936 (6.8 percent) than in 1948 (5.4 percent), is it any wonder that Truman never came to share his predecessor's fascination with public opinion surveys?

Members of a single presidential administration may harbor quite different views about representations of public opinion. President Eisenhower relied on multiple indicators, including informal dinner meetings with leaders from government, business, publishing, the professions, agriculture, the arts, labor, and education, "as a means of gaining information and intelligent opinion" (Eisenhower 1965, 265). He also relied on polls conducted by the U.S. Information Agency. In contrast, his Secretary of State, John Foster Dulles, felt that although "we can't get too far ahead of public opinion and we must do everything we can to bring it along with us," polls were of limited value. The State Department under Dulles discontinued the use of survey questions on foreign affairs; evidence about public opinion was derived from articles and editorials in one hundred daily newspapers, columnists, radio and television commentators, letters to the editor, materials from nongovernmental organizations, and speeches in Congress (Berding 1965, 140).[4] Our understanding of the various ways in which public opinion is measured and used by top officials has also been enhanced by archival research on the administrations of Presidents Herbert Hoover (Eisinger 2000), Richard Nixon (Katz 1997), and Jimmy Carter (Katz 2000).

Leaders also may have quite varied reasons for being interested in evidence about public opinion, not the least of which may be to develop more effective strategies for manipulating domestic audiences on behalf of preferred policies and strategies (Jacobs and Shapiro 1995–96, 2000). In other cases, public opinion may be used as a lever for dealing with governments abroad. Midway through the crisis precipitated by Egyptian nationalization of the Suez Canal in 1956, President Eisenhower attempted to head off the use of force by the British. In a letter to Prime Minister Anthony Eden, Eisenhower wrote,

> I regard it as indispensable that if we are to proceed to the solution of this problem, public opinion in our several countries must be overwhelmingly in its support. I must tell you frankly that American public opinion flatly rejects the thought of using force. . . . I must say frankly that there is as yet no public opinion in this country which is prepared to support such a move, and the most significant public opinion that there is seems to think that the United Nations was formed to prevent this very thing. (Eisenhower 1965, 667–70)

Similarly, Paul Warnke reported that he used survey data as a bargaining instrument in arms control negotiations with his counterpart from the Soviet Union: Soviet Deputy Foreign Minister Vladimir S. Semenov

> would always take the position that we were asking too much in the way of verification, and I would continually point out that as indicated by the polls and not necessarily reflecting my own feeling, there still was a wide distrust within the American public; therefore, verification and their acceptance of our verification position was a *sine qua non* to getting a SALT Treaty approved. (quoted in A. Cantril 1980, 143)

In other cases, public opinion may tip the balance in favor of one policy option or rule out another that seems destined to arouse strong public disapproval. Despite John Kennedy's doubts about the realism of U.S. policy toward China, according to Dean Rusk, "fearing the issue might divide Congress and the American people, [Kennedy] decided that potential benefits of a more realistic China policy didn't warrant risking a severe political confrontation" (1990, 283). The anticipation of public responses also appears to have played a role in President George H. W. Bush's decision to use military force to drive Iraq out of Kuwait because he feared that the public would be unwilling to accept the deployment of American forces in Saudi Arabia for a sufficient time to ensure the success of economic sanctions, and American military strategy in the Kosovo war in 1999 and during the anti-terrorist campaign in Afghanistan appears to have been driven at least in part by the anticipation that casualties would severely erode public support.

In still other cases, policymakers may undertake visible efforts to seek guidance from the public on decisions that, in fact, were already made for reasons that had little if anything to do with public preferences. According to one of his biographers, a "favorite technique" of Richard Nixon's was "pretending to canvass public opinion on a decision on which he had already made up his mind" (Ambrose 1989, 258). A variant of that technique is to use public opinion data for guidance on the best ways to depict the rationale for decisions that have been arrived at for reasons that do not necessarily reflect public sentiments. The surveys conducted during the period immediately following Iraq's invasion of Kuwait helped the administration to identify the public's strongest concern about Iraq—its nuclear weapons program—but appear to have had limited impact on the decision to launch a war against the Baghdad regime when it failed to comply with an ultimatum to withdraw its forces from Kuwait.

This brief survey is by no means a comprehensive analysis of the role that public opinion may play in the foreign policy process. This section may, however, illustrate the important general point that the public opinion–policy relationship is usually complex, variable, and interactive rather than simple, constant, and unidirectional. Research designs that fail to take into account the possible impacts of issue, decision context, stage of the policy process, and policymakers' beliefs about public opinion and the uses to which it may be put are thus likely to overlook important aspects of the relationship.

Cross-National Research

Because of the focus of this book, the theories and findings discussed here are almost wholly confined to the United States. But many of the questions addressed here are obviously of much broader concern. Debates between supporters and critics of the Tocqueville thesis that democracies are at an inherent disadvantage in the conduct of foreign policy often revolve around competing conceptions of the contribution of public opinion to the quality of foreign policy; these debates clearly have implications for countries other than the United States, especially in an era of expanding democracy.

Another issue also points to the need for public opinion research in which evidence about the United States is placed in a broader comparative context. The role of public opinion in foreign policy is often a central aspect of the contemporary debates about the "democratic peace"—the finding that liberal democracies rarely if ever go to war against each other (Doyle 1986). The vast literature on that important question is too extensive to review here. Suffice it to say that a vigorous debate revolves around two questions. First, does the democratic peace actually exist, or are the studies purporting to have uncovered it definitionally or methodologically unsound? Second, what institutions, processes, or norms may have rendered democracies unlikely to go to war with each other?

A related question centers not on the propensity of democracies to avoid war but on their high success rate once they initiate a conflict. According to a recent study that draws heavily on the

American experience, "For better or worse, democratic foreign policy is driven by public desires rather than by fundamental pacifism" (Reiter and Stam 2002, 145). Public opinion, or what the authors call the "contemporary consent model," is at the heart of the analysis. Democratic leaders, fearful of the domestic consequences of losing a conflict, initiate only winnable wars, and, aware that public support is likely to erode over time, they seek quick victories. Further, because covert actions by democracies are undertaken outside the "bright light of public scrutiny," thus resembling wars initiated by nondemocracies, such actions are less likely to be successful. The analysis is strengthened by demonstrating empirically the flaws in alternative explanations for victory—for example, that democracies have larger economies or that they are able to mobilize larger percentages of their populations into their armed forces. Whether these hypotheses will be sustained by analysis of a wider range of cases, including non-American ones, remains to be demonstrated; for purposes of the present discussion, they present an interesting alternative to many realist theories, including those reviewed in chapters 1 and 2, that emphasize the negative consequences of engaging the public in foreign affairs.

It is at least a plausible working hypothesis that the nature of public opinion, the channels through which it enters the policy process, and its impact may vary across countries and political systems. A good many other issues that have been discussed in the preceding chapters, including questions about how foreign policy attitudes are structured, would benefit from comparative research designed to identify common elements and differences.

Examples of innovative comparative research on public opinion include studies by Martin Abravanel and Barry Hughes (1973); Richard C. Eichenberg (1989, 2000); Don Munton (1989, 1991, 1992); Robert Mandel (1991); Thomas Risse-Kappen (1991); Lawrence R. Jacobs (1992); Jon Hurwitz, Mark Peffley, and Mitchell Seligson (1993); Hans Rattinger and Don Munton (1991); Lisa Catherine Olga Brandes (1994); Ronald D. Asmus (1995); Philip Everts (2000); Natalie La Balme (2000); Richard Sobel (2000); and Pierangelo Isernia, Zoltan Juhasz, and Hans Rattinger (2002); and Sobel and Eric Shiraev (2003). Risse-Kappen found that although public opinion was important in each of the four countries he studied—France, Japan, West Germany, and the United States—its impact was significantly affected by domestic institutions and coalition-building processes among elites.

Contrasting findings emerged from Richard C. Eichenberg and Richard Stoll's (2003) five-nation study of post–Cold War defense budgets. The study tested James A. Stimson's (1999) hypothesis that because public opinion is free of institutions, results from one country should transfer across national boundaries. Eichenberg and Stoll also drew on Christopher Wlezien's (1995, 1996) metaphor that public reactions to spending resemble a thermostat. Although the United States, Great Britain, France, Germany, and Sweden have quite different institutional structures, Eichenberg and Stoll found that in four of the five countries (Sweden was the exception), "public support at some prior moment is the most consistent predictor of change in defense spending across countries" (2003, 415). A single study of five countries on one issue cannot foreclose the possibility that institutional structures elsewhere, on other issues, may influence whether and how public opinion influences policy outcomes, but studies of this kind clearly take us a substantial distance toward a fuller and finer-grained understanding of opinion-policy linkages. Dramatic political changes, notably in Eastern Europe and the former Soviet Union, open up possibilities for a range of comparative analyses that would have been quite unthinkable as recently as the late 1980s (A. Miller, Reisinger, and Hesli 1993; Gibson 1994; A. Miller, Hesli, and Reisinger 1995). Studies by William Zimmerman (2002) and his colleagues in Russia, in some cases posing questions identical to those used in American studies, exemplify some of the interesting possibilities.

Jacobs and Shapiro (1994b) have provided a useful framework for comparative research, both across countries and across issues or administrations within a single country, based on the divergent ways in which opinion and leadership responsiveness can be combined. *Responsive leadership* is characterized by strong impact of opinions on leaders and of leaders on opinion. *Bureaucratic rule* takes place when opinion provides low direction and there is a low leadership response. When leaders defer to strong, sustained public preferences, the result is *democratic responsiveness*. The fourth combination, when leaders pursue their own convictions and the role of the public is restricted, is described as *charismatic direction*.

Standard Questions

Ample evidence shows that the wording of questions and the context in which they are posed can significantly affect responses.[5] An example of the importance of wording emerges from two questions that were frequently asked during the 1990–91 crisis arising from Iraq's invasion of Kuwait. One question, "All in all, is the current situation in the Mideast worth going to war over, or not?" yielded an almost even division between positive and negative answers in each of nine Gallup surveys during the five months preceding the start of Operation Desert Storm. Another survey organization posed a slightly different question: "Do you agree or disagree that the United States should take all action necessary, including the use of military force, to make sure that Iraq withdraws its forces from Kuwait?" Responses to the latter question in sixteen ABC/*Washington Post* surveys resulted in majorities ranging between two to one and more than three to one in favor of the use of force (Mueller 1994, 208, 217).

Even the order in which questions are posed may affect the results. Consider a simple example of two hypothetical questions: "How great is the threat posed by Saddam Hussein's efforts to acquire weapons of mass destruction?" and "Should the United States take military action to remove Saddam Hussein from power in Iraq?" If posed in that order, the first question may prime the respondent to think of the second question from a particular perspective. In this hypothetical case, it seems that this sequence is likely to produce higher support for military action against Iraq than the if the questions are asked in the reverse order (see also Bartels 2002; Moore 2002).

Moreover, the suspicion that pollsters can craft questions to elicit whatever results their clients prefer is not wholly unfounded (Moore 1992). Indeed, rare is the voter who has not at some time received a "questionnaire" or telephone call at dinner time asking such challenging questions as "Do you believe that the administration should squander your hard-earned tax dollars for wasteful programs that have never worked?" or "Do you believe that the government should restrict the right of law-abiding citizens to protect themselves so that only the criminals will be able to get guns?"—along with a request for a contribution to pay for "tabulating the results." More seriously, one might question the disinterestedness of Louis Harris, a prominent pollster who has been closely associated with Democratic candidates and who is reported to have boasted, "I elected one President, one prime minister, about 28 governors and maybe close to 60 U.S. Senators" (Moore 1992, 78).[6] These are, of course, extreme examples, but they underscore the point that surveys may be used to generate data in support of virtually any predetermined position. The issue of bias in constructing survey instruments may not be limited to commercial firms. The questions raised by Philip Tetlock (1994b) in a broader context—"political psychology or politicized psychology?"—are not irrelevant to survey research (see also the further discussion in Kroeger and Sapiro 1994; Sears 1994; Sniderman 1994; Tetlock 1994a). Aside from the issue of bias, a skeptical position on survey data validity has been summarized by John Mueller's observation that "the poll interview is a rather primitive stimulus-response social situation in which poorly–thought out responses are casually fitted to questions that are overly ingenuous" (1973, 265; see also Zaller 1992, 76–96; Mueller 1994, 1–11).

Even if this warning may be somewhat overstated with respect to the best surveys, it appropriately reminds us to be cautious about drawing conclusions from any single datum on public opinion. It is permissible to be more venturesome in making inferences about trends on specific issues, but doing so assumes that the questions from which the trends are adduced have remained constant, providing control over at least one potential threat to valid results. Gallup and other major polling organizations have asked certain standard political questions at quite regular intervals—for example, items asking respondents to assess presidential performance. However, as noted in chapter 3, even slight variations in the wording of this question brought forth consistently different results in Gallup and Harris surveys about President Reagan's performance in dealing with the Soviet Union.

Questions focusing on foreign or defense policy issues have not been posed with comparable regularity. During and immediately after World War II, the public was regularly asked about the desirability of an active U.S. role in the world, but interest in that issue appears to have waned by the mid-1950s, perhaps because by then the United States seemed to be firmly committed to a broadly internationalist foreign policy; the question was asked only once during the 1960s (see fig. 3.1). The question was revived in the wake of the war in Vietnam, when U.S. global activism once again became controversial; since 1973, it has been posed quite regularly except for a four-year gap between 1978 and 1982.

Many other important foreign and defense policy issues that might well have been the subject of surveys at regular intervals were in fact ignored for long periods. For example, the Gallup poll asked the public to assess the appropriate level of defense spending in 1950 and 1953. During the next sixteen years, the question was asked only once, in 1960, when presidential candidate John F. Kennedy criticized the Eisenhower administration for allegedly having neglected defense needs and for being dangerously complacent about the development of a "missile gap" that supposedly favored the Soviet Union. Since 1969 the question has been asked quite regularly, with a frequency largely determined by the extent to which the defense budget has been controversial. For example, Gallup asked questions about the Pentagon budget five times in 1982–83, when public support for the massive Reagan administration defense buildup was waning. In still other cases, promising time series data have been rendered suspect by wording changes. In 1956, the Gallup survey made a "minor" alteration to its standard item asking about support for U.S. foreign aid programs by adding the phrase "to prevent [the recipients of aid] from going communistic" at the end of the question, giving it a quite different tenor than it previously had.

Among the many useful features of the eight quadrennial Chicago Council on Foreign Relations (CCFR) studies (Rielly 1975–99; Bouton and Page 2002) has been a carryover of certain questions from survey to survey. The cluster of items asking respondents to rate the importance of a series of possible U.S. foreign policy goals has been especially useful for analysts with an interest in tracing trends in public opinion (tables 3.3a, 3.3b, and 6.6). Responses to these questions have played a central role in several secondary analyses of the CCFR data (for example, Wittkopf 1990). Many of the goals items have also been picked up by several other surveys, including those of the Foreign Policy Leadership Project, the Pew Research Center for the People and the Press, and the Gallup Organization, thereby greatly enhancing the questions' value.

With a few exceptions, however, the independent surveys that have been undertaken recently appear to have taken relatively little note of questions in other studies that might provide the basis for comparative analyses. In one sense this is understandable: an important rationale for independent surveys is to undertake probes that have been overlooked by others. But it is also regrettable that there appears to have been rather limited communication at the planning stage among people designing surveys. The development of even a handful of standard foreign and defense policy questions that would be included in all such surveys would be highly desirable.

Richard Sobel (1996) has made a useful contribution toward this end with a proposed list of thirty standard questions for polling on foreign policy crises. The questions are clustered into nine groups that deal with respondents' opinions on the importance of the issue, attention to the issue, U.S. interests at stake, presidential approval on dealing with the issue, responsibility for coping with the crisis, policy options, likely outcomes, the impact of costs and casualties, and retrospective appraisals. The focus on crises makes these questions more appropriate for commercial or news organizations that are capable of conducting surveys with little advance notice. Surveys that are undertaken at regular and more distant intervals—for example, the American National Election Study, the General Social Survey, or the CCFR studies—are less suited to dealing with crises. It would be useful for them to use a somewhat different set of standard questions that might, for example, focus on

foreign policy goals (the CCFR cluster of goal items, mentioned several times previously, is a good starting point);

U.S. interests in various areas and countries;

threats to vital interests and security (the questions should include a broader list than traditional military threats by including terrorism, trade, immigration, the environment, drug trafficking, epidemics such as AIDS, SARS, and so on);

assessment of institutions such as the United Nations, the World Health Organization, the WTO, NATO, the World Bank, and others;

proper allocation of resources for recurring lines in the budget, including the Defense Department, foreign aid, intelligence gathering, international peacekeeping, and the like;

questions that pose trade-offs (for example, reducing the budget deficit versus the budget allocations for a broad range of foreign, defense, and domestic programs versus tax cuts).

Widespread use of such questions, using standard wording, would go a long way toward improving a less than outstanding record of cumulative findings.

In summary, although recent decades have witnessed a remarkable and productive renaissance of interest in public opinion, a number of steps could further enhance our understanding of the topic, especially on the most important and least well developed areas of systematic knowledge. As noted several times, many of these questions center on the impact of public opinion on foreign policy.

Public Opinion and Foreign Policy after the Cold War

Not only has most of the evidence cited here come from the United States, but a substantial part of it also emerged from a period dominated first by World War II and soon thereafter by the Cold War. One can plausibly argue that this period is sufficiently atypical to raise questions about at least some generalizations relating to public opinion. Ronald Hinckley has argued persuasively that some discussions about the post-Vietnam breakdown of a foreign policy consensus are misdirected if they assume that broad disagreement about international affairs is an abnormal state of affairs in American politics. As he put it, "What has appeared since Vietnam is not dissensus but the reemergence of the basic and fundamentally different attitudinal beliefs that Americans have held and debated for some time" (1992, 10; see also Schneider 1992).

More generally, we need to address questions about whether and how the end of the Cold War may have affected or even rendered obsolete much of what we have learned about public opinion and foreign policy. At the most obvious level, there has been a sea change in public attitudes toward many of the issues and some of the key actors that dominated the Cold War era. Indeed, in many respects, changing public attitudes may have preceded rather than followed those at the pinnacles of government on such issues as the appropriate level of defense spending, the primary threats to American national security, assessments of Mikhail Gorbachev's goals, and the motivations underlying Soviet foreign policy (*Americans Talk Security* 1987–90; Holsti 1991). Well before the demolition of the Berlin Wall or the disintegration of the Soviet Union, the public ranked the danger to American national security from the USSR in seventh place, tied with the greenhouse effect (*Americans Talk Security* 1988, 51–54).

The end of the Cold War also raises some questions about the structuring of foreign policy attitudes. Substantial evidence indicates that assessments of the Soviet Union have played a key role in foreign policy belief structures: for example, they are a central element in the hierarchical model developed by Hurwitz and Peffley (1990) as well as in Eugene R. Wittkopf's (1986, 1990) militant internationalism dimension. Some interesting questions arise from the collapse of the Soviet Union and the dramatic change in relations between Washington and Moscow. Will these events result for many in a loss of structure and a consequent disorientation about foreign affairs? Are the structures of foreign policy beliefs likely to differ among the many democracies that joined forces to contain the USSR? Will there be a search for a replacement of the Soviets by another adversary such as China or the "axis of evil" countries—Iran, Iraq, and North Korea—featured in President George W. Bush's 2002 State of the Union address? Are there segments of the public or leadership groups who, if deprived of one enemy, will seek to find another? Alternatively, are the key concepts that structured beliefs about foreign affairs during the Cold War era sufficiently generic and robust that they will survive the dramatic international changes of the past decade? Will they be adequate for an expanded agenda of post–Cold War issues? For conflict with adversaries, notably terrorist organizations, that are strikingly different from traditional territorial nation-states?

Some evidence indicates that such dimensions as militant internationalism, cooperative internationalism, and unilateralism/ multilateralism may continue to structure foreign policy attitudes, but the changes we have witnessed since the late 1980s are of such unprecedented magnitude that this must be treated as a hypothesis that requires systematic testing. In short, we may be entering into a period in which the relationship between public opinion and foreign policy takes on added significance, but we should also be wary of assumptions that the theories, evidence, and linkages that emerged from research during the World War II and Cold War eras are sufficiently robust to be transported intact into a period of strikingly different circumstances. Some years will need to pass before it will be possible to undertake archival research on the impact of public opinion during the post–Cold War era, but judicious use of open sources, memoirs, and interviews should make it possible at least to explore the hypothesis that public sentiments are playing a greater or at least different role than they did during the half century between Pearl Harbor and the disintegration of the Soviet Union. President Bush's November 2001 executive order to overturn legislation requiring most presidential papers to be opened after twelve years will obviously complicate such research, as will his administration's expansive definition of what information may be withheld on the grounds of protecting the confidentiality of advice to the president.

Some Concluding Thoughts

Chapters 1 and 2 summarized very briefly the competing positions in the venerable and persisting differences between realists and liberals on the proper role of public opinion in international affairs. It was noted that critical events, including two world wars and the long, controversial conflict in Vietnam, have often played an important role in igniting debates and framing the terms of the discourse between these schools of thought. The end of the Cold War has been no less significant in stimulating interest in and arousing controversies about the topic. The debate about the "democratic peace" is but one such example. These are not merely continuations of prior disputes in the memoirs of retired Cold War policymakers—for example, between George Shultz (1993) and Caspar Weinberger (1990)—or esoteric debates carried on between the covers of obscure academic journals. The democratic peace issue has found its way into the press ("Democracies and War" 1995) as well as into official foreign policy blueprints (U.S. President 1994). Such post–Cold War events as conflicts in Bosnia, Somalia, Haiti, Kosovo, Afghanistan, and Iraq have also brought forth a flurry of op-ed articles and rejoinders in mass circulation newspapers, lamenting or defending the public's role in shaping foreign policy (see, for example, Kennan 1993; Koppel 1994; Wines 1994; and the rejoinders to them in "letters to the editor" sections).

This conclusion is not intended to bring definitive evidence to bear on these issues, nor would it be possible to do so within the confines of a few pages, but a few general observations are appropriate. First, debates about the proper role of public opinion on foreign policy ought not be framed in terms that posit, on the one hand, a bottom-up, direct democracy model in which public officials are merely the agents for carrying out whatever public preferences emerge from the latest Gallup poll and, on the other hand, a vision of skilled and knowledgeable elites, shielded from the television-aroused passions of an ill-informed public, carefully deliberating the great international issues of the day. Unfortunately, even such thoughtful observers of international affairs as George Kennan (1993) sometimes slip into this style of discourse.

Framing the alternatives in such a dichotomous fashion trivializes an important issue in democratic theory, precluding the considered discussion that the topic deserves.

Second, the cursory—and admittedly selective—sample of foreign and defense policy episodes that follows suggests that the realist thesis against public participation in international affairs may be somewhat less persuasive than some of its staunchest advocates would have us believe—or at least it is not so compelling that the case should be considered closed. A list of the more successful American international undertakings since World War II might arguably include the Marshall Plan (1947), the formation of NATO (1949), and the Limited Test Ban Treaty (1963). In each instance, the administration made a forceful case for the policies in question but did so without resorting to gross distortions or suppression of vital information, tactics that are unfortunately not unknown in such cases. Before approving these undertakings, Congress engaged in extensive debates, and substantial majorities of the public ultimately were persuaded that the policies were in the national interest. Whether public opinion played a significant role in these undertakings is certainly open to discussion, but the outcomes hardly square with Walter Lippmann's charges, leveled soon after the Marshall Plan and NATO debates and a few years before the test ban treaty, that the proper balance between the executive and the legislature in Washington had been destroyed and that the public "has shown itself to be a dangerous master of decision when the issues are life and death" (1955, 20).

Conversely, a list of the foreign policy disasters of the Cold War period would almost surely include the Vietnam War and the Iran-contra episode. In the former case, evidence that the Johnson and Nixon administrations were less than forthright with the public—or even with the Congress—is not hard to find. Nor did prescient warnings about public opinion have an impact. Clark Clifford recounts one such episode during the summer of 1965, as the Johnson administration was moving toward fateful decisions regarding Vietnam.

> When I entered, George Ball was speaking. "We can't win," he said, his deep voice dominating the Cabinet Room. "The war will be long and protracted, with heavy casualties. The most we can hope for is a messy conclusion. We must measure the long-term price against the short-term loss that will result from withdrawal." Producing a chart that correlated

public opinion with American casualties in Korea, Ball predicted that the American public would not support a long and inconclusive war. (1991, 412)

Ball's warnings were dismissed, perhaps because they were viewed as the predictable gloomy diagnoses of the house devil's advocate.

The central figures in the Iran-contra affair, notably Lieutenant Colonel Oliver North, repeatedly engaged in secret and patently illegal maneuverings, often with shady intermediaries and arms brokers who enriched themselves without advancing any U.S. interests in the area. Not only did North and his collaborators fail to achieve any of their stated goals with respect to establishing links with "moderates" in Iran or in freeing the American hostages who were believed to be held by groups under control of the Tehran government, but when the facts of the arms deliveries to Iran became known, they resulted in a powerful public backlash against the Reagan administration, reflected most dramatically in a record decline in the president's performance ratings. As Reagan had pledged during his campaign for the presidency in 1980 that he would never negotiate with terrorists, the revelations were especially damaging to his reputation. Even a heavy-handed public relations campaign by the president to gain support for assistance to the contras in Nicaragua—at one point the rebel group was described as the "moral equal of the [U.S.] Founding Fathers"(Sobel 1993, 35)—failed to arouse substantial public enthusiasm (Sobel 2001). Would a more realistic appreciation of the public's disapproval of shipping arms to Iran or negotiating with terrorists have averted a policy disaster? It is, of course, impossible to answer this question definitively or, more broadly, to establish beyond reasonable doubt a causal link between inattention to or contempt for public opinion and policy decisions and outcomes.

Such a highly selective group of cases, focusing on a small sample of successes and failures, does not constitute an adequate discussion of the public's role in foreign policy. Nor does it address at least one other aspect of the relationship between public opinion and foreign policy that merits some discussion. Deliberate efforts by public officials to manipulate the public have been mentioned earlier. One variant of that strategy warrants attention because many public officials, even those who have generally leveled with the public, have succumbed at one time or another to a temptation to engage in "oversell" with a view to gaining public support, be it for an election or a specific policy objective.

Leaders who ascribe the most importance to public opinion and are most sensitive to public preferences may also be the most likely to engage in oversell. The temptation may appear all the more attractive if the costs of hyperbolic or misleading rhetoric are not adequately appreciated at the time or if it is believed that these costs will not have to be paid until much later—perhaps even by another administration. Examples from several episodes involving relations with the Soviet Union can be used to illustrate a problem, although it is not confined to the three administrations in question.

Throughout much of World War II, Franklin Roosevelt was often less than frank with the American public in describing the nature of the Soviet regime or in acknowledging divergent American and Soviet interests on such issues as the postwar status of Poland. For example, after the Nazi invasion of its erstwhile Soviet ally in 1941 but before the Japanese attack on Pearl Harbor had brought the United States into World War II, Roosevelt depicted the Stalin regime's policy toward religion in glowing but quite inaccurate terms as a means of defusing arguments used by opponents of American aid to Moscow. At a press conference on September 30, 1941, the president asserted that the USSR's constitution guaranteed freedom of conscience: "Freedom equally to use propaganda against religion, which is essentially what is the rule in this country, only we don't put it quite the same way" (Dallek 1979, 297). Roosevelt's optimistic public expressions with respect to the Soviet Union no doubt contributed to maintenance of the Allied coalition against Hitler—they may even have been necessary to prevent the coalition from fracturing before the defeat of the Third Reich—but they also may have poorly prepared the public to face realistically the policy differences between Washington and Moscow that would almost inevitably emerge when the guns had stopped firing.

Two years after the defeat of Germany, the Truman administration faced an urgent request to provide assistance to beleaguered Greek and Turkish governments in the wake of a British decision to reduce its traditional commitments in that area. When Senator Arthur Vandenberg told Truman that it would be necessary to "scare the hell" out of Congress to assure appropriation of the funds for Greece and Turkey, the president did so in his March 12, 1947 "Truman Doctrine" address to that body. Congress quickly approved the four hundred million dollar aid package, and Gallup polls revealed that a majority of both Republicans and Democrats supported the program. Nevertheless, the open-ended commitments implied by Truman's rhetoric may have served longer-term national interests less well.

Finally, as part of a broad effort to restructure American foreign policy, the Nixon administration pursued a policy of détente with the Soviet Union under which carrots would supplement sticks as strategies aimed at stabilizing relations between the superpowers and creating incentives for the Soviet Union to contain itself. President Nixon and national security adviser Henry Kissinger succumbed to the temptation to oversell détente during the 1972 presidential campaign with such declarations as "The Cold War is over." While this may have proved an effective short-run strategy for Nixon's successful reelection campaign, it also set the stage for a public backlash against détente when subsequent events, including the 1973 Yom Kippur War, revealed that Washington and Moscow held quite different conceptions of the meaning of *détente*, especially in connection with rivalries in the Third World. According to the author of the most comprehensive study of American-Soviet relations during the period in question,

> One reason for the disintegration of consensus in favor of détente in the United States was the failure of leadership to explain its limitations as well as its promises to the public. . . . When the expectations of the public, aroused by the hyperbole about the benefits of peace and détente, were not met, disillusion set in — and so did the natural temptation to blame the other side. (Garthoff 1985, 1088; see also Homet 1990)

A few anecdotes do not constitute definitive analyses or give rise to timeless prescriptions about such complex and enduring issues as the proper role of public opinion in the formulation and implementation of American foreign policy. Nevertheless, if we are indeed entering into a period in which the public will be increasingly vocal in expressing its policy preferences, especially on a growing agenda of issues that fall at the intersection of domestic and foreign affairs, perhaps it is worth contemplating whether there is less to be gained by tactics for bypassing, manipulating, or misleading the public to ease the short-term tasks of policymakers than by frank efforts to engage the public in constructive debates about the proper American role in the world, definitions of the national interest, and the appropriate strategies (if not necessarily

the tactics) for pursuing them. Is such a suggestion evidence of ter-
minal woolly headed idealism or of a realistic appraisal of the necessary conditions for the effective pursuit of long-range interests?
Opponents and skeptics will no doubt play their strongest card
against such proposals by pointing to the indisputable fact that the
American public is poorly informed on even some of the most
basic facts about the world and international affairs. In fairness,
however, it should be pointed out that some of these critics also
take a very broad view of what information it is permissible to
withhold from the public because of "national security concerns."

Can efforts to provide the public with better international education improve what Daniel Yankelovich (1991) calls "public
judgment"? If international education consists primarily of providing more factual information of the kind that might improve
students' performances on a television game show, then one might
well share Alan F. Kay's pessimistic conclusion that "efforts to
remedy this situation by educational programs of any kind clearly
seem headed for failure" (1992b, 14). It is not clear that knowing
the name of the foreign minister of Israel, the countries added to
NATO since the end of the Cold War, or the nations that have
held democratic elections in Africa since 2000 will add substantially to the public's ability to render more informed judgments on
major international issues.

The general public today is less frequently described in the
frightening terms that dominated thinking during the 1950s. One
of the classic studies of recent years is entitled "The Rational Public," and another has coined the phrase *low information rationality* to describe the manner in which the public deals with a complex world (Page and Shapiro 1992; Popkin 1991). Moreover,
opportunities for gaining information about the world have never
been greater. Cheap international travel, dramatically rising graduation rates from secondary schools and universities, and new information technologies that even dedicated science fiction fans of
the 1950s could hardly have imagined have contributed to these
opportunities. Indeed, James N. Rosenau (1990), a distinguished
political scientist, a former president of the International Studies
Association, and onetime skeptic about the role that the public
could play in foreign affairs, has written that the electronic-infor-
mation revolution has provided general publics with the information and analytical skills necessary to become vital players in
global affairs.

Nevertheless, there are also reasons for disquiet. The possibility that increasing survey data will merely be used by leaders to manipulate the public has already been mentioned. A closely related concern is the persistent poverty of international knowledge. Many studies reveal that levels of information about foreign affairs among publics in the industrial world remain abysmally low, most notably in the United States (Dimock and Popkin 1996). One disturbing example illustrates the point. Gallup surveys commissioned by the National Geographic Society in 1948 and 1988 revealed that basic geographic knowledge—for example, identification of the largest country in the world or location of Great Britain on a map—declined during the forty-year interval between surveys (National Geographic Society 1988). Yet this was a period of dramatic increases in the level of educational attainment, whether measured by the percentage of high school diplomas, college graduates, or graduate and professional degrees earned by Americans. Considering that geography has virtually dropped out of school curricula and that many universities no longer house geography departments, perhaps those troubling results are not especially surprising. Only 10 percent of Americans could identify any of the nations involved in the first round of post–Cold War expansion of NATO (Pew 1997, 98), and no doubt even some of those would have been unable to locate Hungary, Poland, and the Czech Republic on a map. In those circumstances, could a principled debate have occurred in the United States on adding new members to NATO? There are many reasons to applaud the more benign and realistic view of the general public that has emerged from several decades of research, but it is hardly a time for complacency. At what point does low information rationality become no information irrationality?

But even if we acknowledge that the public is not well informed, is it fruitless to engage the public with a view to a better understanding of at least some aspects of foreign policy? Foreign aid, an issue discussed at some length in earlier chapters, may provide a case in point. Two facts—foreign aid accounts for less than 1 percent of the federal budget (it is not the largest item in the budget, as many people in several recent polls believed), and most of the foreign assistance funds are spent in the United States—may be relevant. But these facts alone may not be sufficient to engage the public on the issue or to raise the discussion above the "foreign aid is money down the rathole" thesis propounded by former Senate Foreign Relations Committee Chair Jesse Helms. When respondents receive additional information about foreign aid outlays, attitudes toward assistance programs become substantially more favorable (Kull 1995a; Kull and Destler 1999; PIPA 2001a). Moreover, when discussions of foreign aid are linked to other vital concerns of the American public—for example, immigration, jobs supported by foreign purchases in the United States, stability in the Middle East, dismantling of nuclear weapons in parts of the former Soviet Union, and efforts to combat international terrorism—the discourse may take a different tone. Intense skepticism about some forms of foreign assistance no doubt would still exist, especially with regard to regimes that exhibit a callous disregard for the most basic human rights, but such distinctions do not seem beyond the capabilities of the public.

Perhaps it is appropriate to give the final word on this point not to ivory tower idealists but to Elihu Root, a hardheaded conservative whose career was spent in the rough-and-tumble arenas of a Wall Street law firm, the War Department, the State Department, and the U.S. Senate.

That way [to prevent a people from having an erroneous opinion] is to furnish the whole people, as a part of their ordinary education, with correct information about their relations to other peoples, about the limitations upon their own rights, about their duties to respect the rights of others, about what has happened and is happening in international affairs, and about the effects upon national life of the things that are done or refused as between nations; so that the people themselves will have the means to test misinformation and appeals to prejudice and passion based upon error. (1922, 5)

Notes

Chapter 1

1. CBS conducts surveys with the *New York Times*, ABC with the *Washington Post*, and NBC with the *Wall Street Journal*. In addition, CNN regularly commissions the Gallup Organization to conduct surveys.

2. The description that follows emphasizes differences between these two schools of thought and devotes less attention to the views of those who have taken intermediate positions or attempted to bridge the differences.

3. Bevin, speech to the House of Commons, November 1945, quoted in Bartlett 1955, 926. The liberal position on questions of international relations is effectively summarized and analyzed in Doyle 1986; 1997.

4. Locke argued that issues of security and foreign affairs properly are a function of the executive. Foreign policy requires a consistency that derives only from the vision of one person rather than from the diverse interests of the public (Locke 1988, 365–66).

5. These efforts stimulated the creation of a new field of inquiry—propaganda analysis—that subsequently engaged the interest of such leading social scientists as Harold Lasswell and Alexander L. George.

6. Woodrow Wilson, quoted in Carr 1941, 44. (Carr cites the R. S. Baker edition of Wilson's papers, Baker, 1:259, as the source for this quotation, but I could not find it there.)

7. The role of liberals, Protestants, Irish-Americans, and public culture in the League of Nations debate has been examined in Helbich 1967–68; Lancaster 1967–68; Maxwell 1967–68; Levering 1991; and Tony Smith 2000.

8. Root was not unmindful of the realist thesis that the mass public's passions and prejudices can complicate international negotiations and contribute to conflict. For example, he wrote in 1907 (nine years after the Spanish-American War), that "it sometimes happens that governments are driven into war against their will by the pressure of strong popular feeling . . . because a large part of the people in both countries maintain an uncompromising and belligerent attitude, insisting upon the supreme and utmost views of their own right in a way which, if it were to control national actions, would render peaceable settlement impossible" (Root 1907, 1). See also Root 1917.

9. An indication of Lippmann's continuing influence is the fact that *Public Opinion* has remained in print. It was republished in a paperback edition

in 1965 and by 2002 was available in editions from three publishers. Evidence of his influence as a columnist emerged during the tensest days of the Cuban missile crisis. His *Washington Post* column on October 25, 1962, the fourth day of the public phase of the crisis, proposed a trade of U.S. missiles in Turkey for the Soviet missiles in Cuba. Although many in President Kennedy's ExComm opposed the trade, that proposal became a crucial part of the deliberations in the final stages of the crisis.

10. Although it is widely recognized that an unrepresentative sample led the *Literary Digest* astray in 1936, scholars and pollsters still debate the specific details of the debacle. See, for example, Squire 1988.

11. For an excellent history and analysis of survey research in the United States, see Jean Converse 1987.

12. From the transcript of Roosevelt's recording of the meeting. I am grateful to Steve Casey of the London School of Economics for providing this information in a private communication, March 21, 2002. Roosevelt's views on Gallup and, more generally, on the impact of public opinion on his wartime policies are carefully analyzed in Casey 2001.

13. Even before the U.S. entry into World War II, a majority of the public supported the Soviet Union rather than Germany. In 1938, the margin was 83 to 17 percent, and after the Nazi attack on its erstwhile ally the margin was 72 to 4 percent. In July 1941, Gallup asked whether respondents favored a peace in which Germany would keep "only territory won from Russia" and give up its other conquests; only 34 percent of respondents accepted that proposition (Gallup 1972, 128–29, 288, 296).

14. All of the following survey results are drawn from Gallup 1972, vol. 1.

Chapter 2

1. Had American officials responsible for conduct of the war in Vietnam paid serious attention to the Strategic Bombing Survey, they might have been less sanguine about the prospect of bombing North Vietnam into submission. According to one historian, the U.S. and British bombing campaigns against Germany were driven in part by "the public's affection for air power, the term usually given to strategic bombardment, and its fear of heavy casualties. The polls made this clear, survey after survey showing that the bomber was America's favorite weapon" (O'Neill 1993, 304).

2. This report is undated, but internal evidence indicates that the survey was conducted in September 1947.

3. Almond's use of the term *mood* differs from that of Frank Klingberg. Almond refers to short-term shifts of attention and preferences, whereas Klingberg has used the term to explain American foreign policy in terms of generation-long societal swings between introversion and extroversion. For the latter usage of the term, see Klingberg 1952, 1979, 1983; Holmes 1985.

4. In less than five years, Almond was backing away from his most pessimistic diagnoses; see Almond 1960.

5. Kennan's critical assessment of U.S. policy-making was also an important theme in the fourteen lectures that he delivered at the National War College between September 16, 1946, and December 18, 1947. The texts of these lectures may be found in Harlow and Maerz 1991.

6. Some of the more notable examples include Joseph Jones 1955 on the Truman Doctrine and Marshall Plan; Wohlstetter 1962 on Pearl Harbor; George 1955 and Paige 1968 on the decision to resist aggression in Korea; Neustadt 1970 on the Suez crisis and cancellation of the Skybolt missile program; Allison 1971 on the Cuban missile crisis; and George and Smoke 1974 on challenges to U.S. deterrence policy.

7. The exceptions include Cohen 1957; Bauer, Pool, and Dexter 1963; and Cottam 1977.

Chapter 3

1. In addition to a large number of individual studies of the general public, a number of long-term projects on public opinion and foreign policy were initiated during this period. The Chicago Council on Foreign Relations undertook its first survey in 1974 and has conducted similar studies every four years through 2002. These findings have been summarized in Rielly 1975, 1979, 1983, 1987, 1991, 1995, 1999; Bouton and Page 2002. Some of the data are also available at www.ccfr.org. Steven Kull and his colleagues at the University of Maryland's Program on International Policy Attitudes (PIPA) have been conducting surveys since 1993; the fullest summary of their findings appears in Kull and Destler 1999. PIPA also provides reports (available at www.pipa.org) on specific topics that include not only PIPA's data but also those from other surveys. Under the leadership of Andrew Kohut, the Pew Research Center for the People and the Press (formerly the Times Mirror Center for the People and the Press) has since 1993 conducted periodic surveys that have been published under such titles as "America's Place in the World" (see www.people-press.org).

The foreign policy views of opinion leaders have received greater attention since the 1970s. The Chicago Council surveys described earlier include a smaller sample of leaders in various institutions. Some of the PIPA and Pew studies also include leaders. The Foreign Policy Leadership Project, directed by Ole Holsti and James Rosenau, conducted six large-sample surveys of opinion leaders at four-year intervals beginning in 1976. For descriptions of the samples in these and other studies of leaders, see table 4.1.

2. Valuable book-length, post-Vietnam works that explore the nature, sources, trends, and other important aspects of public opinion include Levering 1978; Foster 1983; Deibel 1987; Wittkopf 1990; Mayer 1992; Page and Shapiro 1992; Price 1992; Zaller 1992; Murray 1996; Foyle 1999; Jacobs and Shapiro 2000. See also three excellent unpublished dissertations: Graham 1989; Brandes 1994; Isaacs 1994.

3. For additional evidence from this research program, see Page and Shapiro 1983, 1984, 1992; Page, Shapiro, and Dempsey 1987; Shapiro and Page 1988, 1994. A somewhat different assessment of stability and change in American public opinion appears in Mayer 1992.

4. For additional evidence about the rational public, the stability of policy preferences, and issue voting, see S. Bennett 1972; Free and Watts 1980; Graham 1988, 1989, 1994; Krosnick 1988a, 1988b, 1990, 1991; Russett 1990, 1993; Popkin 1991; Peffley and Hurwitz 1992; Marcus and Hanson 1993.

5. Other studies confirm the limited knowledge of public affairs despite

rising levels of education. In some cases, they even indicate that factual knowledge has declined during recent years. See Graham 1988; S. Bennett 1989; Delli Carpini and Keeter 1996; Jennings 1996.

6. For a somewhat similar effort to categorize the American public in the post–Cold War era, see Kohut and Toth 1994. Using questions on the approval or disapproval of using force abroad for oil security and humanitarian assistance, they classified respondents as *interventionists* (approve the use of force for both purposes), *noninterventionists* (disapprove force for both), *oneworlders* (approve for humanitarian, disapprove for oil), and *U.S.- centrics* (approve for oil, disapprove for humanitarian).

7. Good starting points are Bauer, Pool, and Dexter 1963; Rosenau 1963, 1974; B. Hughes 1978; Zaller 1992; Powlick and Katz 1998.

8. Not surprisingly, many of the existing studies have been conducted by historians. In addition to those cited in the following pages, see May 1959, 1964; Benson 1967–68; Small 1970; Levering 1978, 1989; E. Williams 1996.

9. The public differences between Defense Secretary Weinberger and Secretary of State Shultz, described in the opening pages of chapter 1, were also evident in private policy discussions.

10. Public opinion analysts have long focused on American attitudes toward the Soviet Union and Russia. See, for example, Walsh 1944; Levering 1976; Tom Smith 1983; Holsti 1991; Richman 1991.

11. A study by Russian, Chinese, and American scholars based on archival materials from Moscow confirms the hypothesis that Stalin knew of and in 1950 approved Kim Il Sung's plan to invade South Korea, although Stalin had earlier refused to give Kim the go-ahead for an invasion (Goncharov, Lewis, and Xue Litai 1993).

12. The thesis that Ronald Reagan won the 1980 election despite rather than because of his foreign policy positions is developed in Schneider 1983.

13. The *Los Angeles Times, Washington Post,* and Harris Organization also asked for appraisals of China in four surveys between 1983 and 2001, but because the response options differed from those offered by Gallup, these surveys are excluded from figure 3.3.

Chapter 4

1. For example, Barton 1974–75, 1980; Sussman 1976; Koopman, Snyder, and Jervis 1989, 1990; Chittick, Billingsley, and Travis 1990; Times Mirror Center 1993; Pew 1997. Despite the military's importance in foreign and defense policy, it is not included in the samples of some leadership surveys. Studies that focus on military leaders include Kinnard 1975; Russett and Hanson 1975; Holsti 1998, 2001; Davis 2001.

2. The occupations listed in table 4.1 are those specifically targeted by the sampling design. This list does not include other occupations or groups that may also be represented in the samples. For example, in the course of sampling among various occupational groups, the Times Mirror sample included substantial numbers of women. Thus, it should not be assumed that the Times Mirror data preclude analyses directed at possible gender-based differences. Similarly, the FPLP surveys include lawyers who may have been included as part of random samples of leaders drawn from general directo-

ries (*Who's Who in America*) or because they qualified for inclusion by other criteria, such as foreign policy experts who have published in major foreign affairs journals.

3. For a scathing critique of what the 1994 CCFR survey reveals about the American public, see A. Schlesinger 1995, 7: "The latest public opinion survey by the Chicago Council on Foreign Relations and the Gallup Organizations shows that, while Americans are still ready to endorse euphonious generalities in support of internationalism, there is a marked drop-off when it comes to committing not just words but money and lives." Schlesinger is among several articulate liberals who criticized expansive definitions of American national interests two decades ago but are now strong proponents of a more active U.S. leadership role in such areas as Bosnia. *New York Times* columnist Anthony Lewis shared these views.

4. I am indebted to Ronald Hinckley for the 1812 example.

5. The question about using U.S. troops was also included in the 1974 CCFR survey, but the wording seems sufficiently different to raise questions about comparability with the four subsequent surveys. Hence, table 4.4 begins with data from the 1978 CCFR survey.

6. Steven Kull, private communication, October 2000.

7. Unfortunately, the "cooperation" question was dropped from the CCFR surveys of the public after 1974. In that survey, the gap in "very important" ratings between leaders and the public was 19 percent (86 percent to 67 percent).

A comparison of responses to the CCFR and FPLP surveys reveals that consistently higher proportions of leaders in the CCFR studies accorded arms control a "very important" rating. That gap may result largely from one significant difference in the CCFR and FPLP samples. The latter included military officers, an occupational group that has generally expressed somewhat less enthusiasm for arms control than most others, whereas descriptions of the CCFR samples indicate that they did not include military officers.

8. More extended discussion of public and leadership views on human rights and democracy promotion abroad as foreign policy goals may be found in Holsti 2000a, b.

9. The centrality of attitudes toward the Soviet Union in structuring foreign policy beliefs emerges from many studies, including those cited in chapter 3.

10. To take the intensity of attitudes into account, each response was transformed into a scale of 1.00 to −1.00: "agree strongly" (1.00) to "disagree strongly" (−1.00), or "very important" (1.00) to "not at all important" (−1.00). Scores were then summed to place each leader on the two scales.

11. A more extensive analysis that assesses the relationship of the MI/CI scheme to a broader set of issues appears in Holsti and Rosenau 1993.

12. For a critique of international relations theorists and their failure to predict the end of the Cold War, see Gaddis 1992–93. However, Gaddis could perhaps equally well have aimed his critique at students of comparative politics.

13. In the 1999 TISS survey, the item on the Equal Rights Amendment was replaced by one about encouraging mothers to stay at home rather than to work outside the home. As a result, agreement with six items was scored

as a "liberal" answer and agreement with the other six was scored as a "conservative" one.

14. As with the MI and CI scales, each response received a score between 1.00 and −1.00, depending on the intensity of the attitude: "agree strongly" (1.00) to "disagree strongly" (−1.00). Responses to the twelve items were then summed to place each leader on the social and economic issues scales.

15. Ronald Hinckley has taken this classification scheme and expanded it into a two-by-two-by-two scheme by categorizing respondents according to their answers to three questions—whether the government should be more or less involved in economic, social, and value engineering. The resulting eight groups range from *libertarians* (who believe that the government is doing too many things in all three areas) to *statists* (who believe that the government should do more in all of them). The other six groups are: *conservatives, egalitarians, materialists, populists, moralists,* and *liberals.*

A very similar classification scheme using two dimensions to describe *liberals, conservatives, populists,* and *libertarians* appears in Janda, Berry, and Goldman 1994, 26. These authors plan to replace the term *populist* with *communitarian.*

Still another effort to classify respondents on domestic politics is described in *U.S. News and World Report* 1995. The seven groups are described as *populist traditionalists, stewards, liberal activists, dowagers, conservative activists, ethnic conservatives,* and *agnostics.*

For one of the earliest efforts of this kind, see Lowell 1923, 271–89, on "classification of dispositions."

Chapter 5

1. See chapter 3, including table 3.1 and figure 3.2, for evidence of changing public attitudes toward the Soviet Union.

2. Responses to almost three hundred questions on the Persian Gulf War, many of which were asked several times, are reported and analyzed in Mueller 1994. Almost half of that book consists of tables reporting aggregate responses to these questions. However, neither the tables nor the text examines the demographic correlates of opinions on the war. Other studies that deal with public opinion during the Persian Gulf War include Idelson 1991; Kagay 1992; Renshon 1993; W. Bennett and Paletz 1994; Nacos 1994.

3. For effective summaries of the circumstances under which the "rally round the flag" phenomenon is likely to occur, see Brody and Shapiro 1989; Lian and Oneal 1993.

4. These measures received strong support in Congress. In each case, votes in support exceeded 70 percent, and in the cases of the Marshall Plan and NATO, the favorable votes ranged from 80 to 86 percent.

5. Foster 1983, 112. For evidence of partisan differences on foreign policy during the period immediately following Truman's dismissal of MacArthur, see Belknap and Campbell 1951–52.

6. For the most detailed assessment of public support for the wars in Korea and Vietnam, see Mueller 1973. Verba et al. 1967 report that even after the Vietnam War became controversial, party identification was not an important determinant of attitudes on the war.

7. Gaubatz 1995 also found important intransitivities in public preferences regarding the various U.S. policy options for responding to the Iraqi invasion of Kuwait: withdrawal, multilateral economic sanctions, unilateral military intervention, and multilateral military intervention.

8. Gallup special survey of leaders listed in *Who's Who in America,* May 22, 1955 (Gallup 1972, 1152).

9. The following paragraphs discuss only some highlights of similarities and differences between Democrats and Republicans who participated in the 1992 leadership survey. For tables that provide more detailed data, see Holsti and Rosenau 1994.

10. Drew 1978, 116–17. Many others regarded the views of the "Vietnam generation" as the best hope for this nation's future. "What the country may have learned is that it should listen to its young. They never saw the cables. They read the handwriting on the wall. The Vietnam generation was 'the best and the brightest,' the term David Halberstam applies to the glittering Kennedyites who got us into the war in the first place" (McGrory 1975, 31).

11. An article on the African policy staff of the State Department described its leading members as follows: "The four are in the same age group—39–46—and they share a common experience of disillusionment with and then opposition to the Vietnam War. All remain highly skeptical about United States military involvement, direct and indirect, in areas where they feel the national interest is not obviously at stake" (Hovey 1978, A3; see also Roberts 1982).

12. See, for example, comments by Samuel P. Huntington (Hoffmann 1981, 3–27) and Representative Thomas Downey's assertion that the "children of Vietnam are the adults of El Salvador" (Roberts 1983, D26).

13. The percentages in the text are recalculated from the data in Mandelbaum and Schneider 1979, table 1.

14. The data in this paragraph are drawn from Gallup surveys, January 24–26, February 12–14, and February 26–28, 1993 (G. Gallup Jr. 1993, 41, 43).

15. Sigmund Neumann has defined a political generation as all those who underwent essentially similar historical experiences during the crucial formative years between ages seventeen and twenty-five (1942, 235–36). The importance of this period in the life cycle is emphasized by many others; see, for example, Barber 1972.

16. In the six FPLP surveys, the correlations (phi) between generation and foreign policy orientation were consistently weak: .19, .09, .12, .08, .10, and .10.

17. In two-way analyses of variance, occupational differences were significant at the .001 level for all four of these questions. None of the differences across generations reached that level, although those for the United Nations question approached it.

18. For further evidence on this point, see Holsti and Rosenau 1984, 153–63.

19. Other relevant studies on gender include Tom Smith 1984; Zur and Morrison 1989; Rapaport, Stone, and Abramowitz 1990; E. Cook and Wilcox 1991; Bardes 1992; Gallagher 1992.

20. The data in this paragraph are drawn from Americans Talk Security

surveys 2, 3, and 6 (1988) and from Gallup polls in February, May, June, and July 1992 (G. Gallup Jr. 1993, 43, 116, 117, 127).

21. The correlations between gender and foreign policy orientations (phi) for the six surveys are .11, .06, .03, .08, .06, and .06.

22. Data on racial differences with respect to these issues were drawn from the following sources: South Africa (G. Gallup Jr. 1991, 133–34); Haiti (G. Gallup Jr. 1992, 32–33); Somalia (G. Gallup Jr. 1993, 175); and Bosnia (G. Gallup Jr. 1993, 41–42).

Chapter 6

1. The United States has taken the position that the captured members of the Taliban and al Qaeda who have been incarcerated at the Guantanamo Naval Base in Cuba are trained terrorists and thus are not entitled to protections accorded to prisoners of war under the Geneva Convention.

2. These increases, however, may have been the result of a switch from all in-person interviews in 1998 to some telephone interviews in 2002. Respondents in the two modes ranked the goals almost identically, but those in the telephone interviews were quicker to rate all goals as "very important." I am indebted to Benjamin Page, Co-Director of the 2002 CCFR survey, for this information in a personal communication, September 2003.

Chapter 7

1. For other coauthored case studies that touch on manipulation of public opinion, see Jacobs and Shapiro 1994a, b, 1995, 1995–96, 1999, 2000.

2. For a study that links attitudes toward immigration to broader aspects of U.S. identity and nationalism, see Citrin et al. 1994.

3. This distinction between decision contexts is drawn from Hermann 1969.

4. If the executive views congressional moods as expressions of public opinion, it opens up another very large body of evidence on intervening variables between public opinion and foreign policy. For recent studies that explore these linkages on the Strategic Defense Initiative, weapons procurement, and sanctions on South Africa, see Lindsay 1990, 1991; Hill 1993. Other issues are considered in Ripley and Lindsay 1993.

5. The literature on these topics is enormous; see, for example, Bishop, Tuchfarber, and Oldendick 1978; Bishop, Oldendick, and Tuchfarber 1984; Kagay and Elder 1992. Graham 1989 presents a somewhat different view on the importance of identically worded questions.

6. The Nixon administration considered Gallup a friendly pollster and Harris an adversarial one. In an effort to gain some control over data released by these organizations, the White House took various measures, including awarding a contract to Harris (Jacobs and Shapiro 1995–96).

References

Abramson, Paul, John H. Aldrich, and John Rohde. 1990. *Change and Continuity in the 1988 Election.* Washington, DC: Congressional Quarterly Press.

Abravanel, Martin, and Barry Hughes. 1973. "The Relationship between Public Opinion and Governmental Foreign Policy: A Cross-National Study." In *Sage International Yearbook of Foreign Policy Studies,* edited by Charles W. Kegley Jr. and Patrick J. McGowan, 4:107–33. Beverly Hills, CA: Sage.

Achen, Christopher H. 1975. "Mass Political Attitudes and the Survey Response." *American Political Science Review* 69:1218–31.

Aldrich, John H., John L. Sullivan, and Eugene Borgida. 1989. "Foreign Affairs and Issue Voting: Do Presidential Candidates 'Waltz before a Blind Audience?'" *American Political Science Review* 83:123–41.

Allison, Graham T. 1970–71. "Cool It: The Foreign Policy of Young America." *Foreign Policy* 1:144–60.

Allison, Graham T. 1971. *The Essence of Decision: Explaining the Cuban Missile Crisis.* Boston: Little, Brown.

Allport, Floyd H. 1937. "Toward a Science of Public Opinion." *Public Opinion Quarterly* 1:7–23.

Almond, Gabriel. 1956. "Public Opinion and National Security." *Public Opinion Quarterly* 20:371–78.

Almond, Gabriel. 1960 [1950]. *The American People and Foreign Policy.* New York: Praeger.

Altschuler, Bruce E. 1986. "Lyndon Johnson and the Public Polls." *Public Opinion Quarterly* 50:285–99.

Alvarez, R. Michael, and John Brehm. 2002. *Hard Choice, Easy Answers: Values, Information, and American Public Opinion.* Princeton: Princeton University Press.

Ambrose, Stephen. 1989. *Nixon: The Triumph of a Politician.* New York: Simon and Schuster.

Americans Talk Issues: Serial National Surveys of Americans on Public Policy Issues. 1991–95. Washington, DC: Americans Talk Issues Foundation.

Americans Talk Security: Fourteen National Surveys on National Security Issues. 1987–90. Winchester, MA: Americans Talk Security.

Angle, Paul M., ed. 1991. *Created Equal? The Complete Lincoln-Douglas Debates of 1858.* Chicago: University of Chicago Press.

Asmus, Ronald D. 1995. *Germany's Geopolitical Maturation: Public Opinion and Security Policy in 1994.* Santa Monica, CA: RAND.

Bacevich, Andrew. 2002. Discussion about peacekeeping on *The Connection.* National Public Radio, July 5.

Bailey, Thomas A. 1948. *The Man in the Street: The Impact of American Public Opinion on Foreign Policy.* New York: Macmillan.

Bailey, Thomas A. 1950. *A Diplomatic History of the American People.* 4th ed. New York: Appleton-Century-Crofts.

Baker, Roy Stannard. 1925. *The Public Papers of Woodrow Wilson,* Vol. I. New York: Harper.

Barber, James David. 1972. *The Presidential Character: Predicting Performance in the White House.* Englewood Cliffs, NJ: Prentice-Hall.

Bardes, Barbara A. 1992. "Women and the Persian Gulf War: Patriotism and Emotion." Paper presented at the Brookings Institution Conference on Public Opinion and the Persian Gulf Crisis, Washington, DC, February 28.

Bardes, Barbara A., and Robert W. Oldendick. 1978. "Beyond Internationalism: A Case for Multiple Dimensions in the Structure of Foreign Policy Attitudes." *Social Science Quarterly* 59:496–508.

Bardes, Barbara A., and Robert W. Oldendick. 1990. "Public Opinion and Foreign Policy: A Field in Search of a Theory." *Research in Micropolitics* 3:227–47.

Bartels, Larry M. 1991. "Consistency Opinion and Congressional Policy Making: The Reagan Defense Buildup." *American Political Science Review* 85:457–74.

Bartels, Larry M. 2002. "Question Order and Declining Faith in Elections." *Public Opinion Quarterly* 66:67–79.

Bartlett, John. 1955. *Familiar Quotations.* 13th ed. Boston: Little, Brown.

Barton, Allen H. 1974–75. "Conflict and Consensus among American Leaders." *Public Opinion Quarterly* 38:507–30.

Barton, Allen H. 1980. "Fault Lines in American Elite Consensus." *Daedalus* 109:1–24.

Battle, Joseph. 1995. Communication with author, July 7.

Bauer, Raymond A., Ithiel de Sola Pool, and Lewis A. Dexter. 1963. *American Business and Public Policy: The Politics of Foreign Trade.* New York: Atherton.

Baum, Matthew A. 2002. "Sex, Lies, and War: How Soft News Brings Foreign Policy to the Inattentive Public." *American Political Science Review* 96: 91–109.

Baum, Matthew A., and Samuel Kernell. 2001. "Economic Class and Popular Support for Franklin Roosevelt in War and Peace." *Public Opinion Quarterly* 65:198–229.

Baxter, Sandra, and Marjorie Lansing. 1980. *Women and Politics: The Invisible Majority.* Ann Arbor: University of Michigan Press.

BBC News Online. 2001. "U.S. Blocks Small Arms Control." July 10.

Beal, Richard S., and Ronald H. Hinckley: 1984. "Presidential Decision Making and Opinion Polls." *Annals* 472:1272–84.

Becker, Elizabeth. 2003. "W.T.O. Rules against U.S. on Steel Tariff." *New York Times,* March 27.

Beckman, Peter R., and Francine D'Amico, eds. 1994. *Women, Gender, and World Politics: Perspectives, Policies, and Prospects.* Westport, CT: Bergin and Garvey.

Belknap, George, and Angus Campbell. 1951–52. "Political Party Identification and Attitudes toward Foreign Policy." *Public Opinion Quarterly* 15: 601–23.

Bennett, Stephen Earl. 1972. "Attitudes Structure and Foreign Policy Opinions." *Social Science Quarterly* 55:732–42.

Bennett, Stephen Earl. 1989. "Trends in Americans' Political Information, 1967–1987." *American Politics Quarterly* 17:422–435.

Bennett, Stephen Earl. 1992. "The Persian Gulf War's Impact on Americans' Political Information." Paper presented at the National Election Studies Conference on the Political Consequences of the War, Washington, DC, February 28.

Bennett, W. Lance, and David L. Paletz, eds. 1994. *Taken by Storm: The Media, Public Opinion, and U.S. Foreign Policy in the Gulf War.* Chicago: University of Chicago Press.

Benson, Lee. 1967–68. "An Approach to the Scientific Study of Past Public Opinion." *Public Opinion Quarterly* 31:522–67.

Bentham, Jeremy. 1962. *Works of Jeremy Bentham.* 11 vols. New York: Russell and Russell.

Berding, Andrew H. 1965. *Dulles on Diplomacy.* Princeton, NJ: Van Nostrand.

Berelson, Bernard R., Paul F. Lazarsfeld, and William N. McPhee. 1954. *Voting: A Study of Opinion Formation in a Presidential Campaign.* Chicago: University of Chicago Press.

Bernays, Edward L. 1945. "Attitude Polls—Servants or Masters?" *Public Opinion Quarterly* 3:264–68.

Billington, James H. 1987. "Realism and Vision in American Foreign Policy." *Foreign Affairs* 65:630–52.

Bishop, George F., Robert W. Oldendick, and Alfred J. Tuchfarber. 1984. "Interest in Political Campaigns: The Influence of Question Order and Electoral Context." *Political Behavior* 6:159–69.

Bishop, George F., Alfred J. Tuchfarber, and Robert W. Oldendick. 1978. "Change in the Structure of American Political Attitudes: The Nagging Question of Question Wording." *American Journal of Political Science* 22:250–69.

Blechman, Barry M., and Tamara Cofman Wittes. 1999. "Defining Moments: The Threat and Use of Force in American Foreign Policy." *Political Science Quarterly* 114:1–30.

Bobrow, Davis, and Neal E. Cutler. 1967. "Time-Oriented Explanations of National Security Beliefs: Cohort, Life-Stage, and Situation." *Peace Research Society (International) Papers* 8:31–57.

Bolton, John R. 2001. "Statement to the UN Conference on the Illicit Trade in Small Arms and Light Weapons in All Its Aspects." July 9. U.S. Department of State. Available at www.state.gov/t/us/rm/janjuly /4038.htm.

Bouton, Marshall, and Benjamin Page. 2002. *Worldviews 2002: American*

Public Opinion and Foreign Policy. Chicago: Chicago Council on Foreign Relations.

Boyce, Louis. 1985. "The Role of Gender in Recent Presidential Elections: Reagan and the Reverse Gender Gap." *Presidential Studies Quarterly* 15: 372–85.

Brace, Paul, and Barbara Hinckley. 1992. *Follow the Leader: Opinion Polls and Modern Presidents.* New York: Basic Books.

Brandes, Lisa Catherine Olga. 1994. "Public Opinion, International Security Policy, and Gender." Ph.D. diss., Yale University.

Brehm, John. 1993. *The Phantom Respondents: Opinion Surveys and Political Representation.* Ann Arbor: University of Michigan Press.

Brody, Richard A., and Catherine R. Shapiro. 1989. "A Reconsideration of the Rally Phenomenon in Public Opinion." In *Political Behavior Annual,* edited by Samuel Long, 2:77–102. Boulder, CO: Westview.

Bruner, Jerome S. 1944. *Mandate from the People.* New York: Duell, Sloan, and Pearce.

Brunt, Frank. 2001. "Easygoing Words and a Hard Line: Bush Speaks of Consultation but Budges Little on Issues." *New York Times,* June 18. A10.

Buchanan, Patrick J. 1990. "America First—and Second, and Third." *National Interest* 19:77–92.

Buchanan, Patrick J. 1998. *The Great Betrayal: How American Sovereignty and Social Justice Are Being Sacrificed to the Gods of the Global Economy.* Boston: Little, Brown.

Buchanan, Patrick J. 2002. *The Death of the West: How Dying Populations and Immigrant Invasions Imperil Our Country and Civilization.* New York: Thomas Dunne.

Bundy, McGeorge, transcriber, and James G. Blight, ed. 1987–88. "October 27, 1962: Transcripts of the Meetings of the ExComm." *International Security* 12 (winter): 30–92.

Burns, James M. 1970. *Roosevelt: The Soldier of Freedom.* New York: Harcourt, Brace, Jovanovich.

Burstein, Paul. 1998. "Bringing the Public Back In: Should Sociologists Consider the Impact of Public Opinion on Public Policy?" *Social Forces* 77: 27–62.

Bush, George, and Brent Scowcroft. 1998. *A World Transformed.* New York: Knopf.

Byers, Michael. 2003. "Preemptive Self-Defense: Hegemony, Equality, and Strategies of Legal Change." *Journal of Political Philosophy* 11:171–90.

Campbell, Angus, Philip E. Converse, Warren E. Miller, and Donald E. Stokes. 1964. *The American Voter.* New York: Wiley.

Cantril, Albert H. 1980. *Polling on the Issues: A Report from the Kettering Foundation.* Cabin John, MD: Seven Locks.

Cantril, Hadley. 1948. "Trends of Opinion during World War II: Some Guides to Interpretation." *Public Opinion Quarterly* 12:30–44.

Cantril, Hadley. 1967. *The Human Dimension: Experiences in Policy Research.* New Brunswick, NJ: Rutgers University Press.

Carleton, William G. 1963. *The Revolution in American Foreign Policy.* New York: Random House.

Carr, Edward Hallett. 1940. *The Twenty Years' Crisis, 1919–1939: An Introduction to the Study of International Relations.* London: Macmillan.

Casey, Steven. 2001. *Cautious Crusade: Franklin D. Roosevelt, American Public Opinion, and the War against Nazi Germany.* New York: Oxford University Press.

Caspary, William R. 1970. "The 'Mood Theory': A Study of Public Opinion and Foreign Policy." *American Political Science Review* 64:536–47.

Chanley, Virginia A. 1999. "U.S. Public Views of International Involvement from 1964 to 1993." *Journal of Conflict Resolution* 43:23–44.

Cherington, Paul T. 1949. "Opinion Polls as the Voice of Democracy." *Public Opinion Quarterly* 4:236–38.

Chittick, William O. 1970. *State Department, Press, and Pressure Groups: A Role Analysis.* New York: Wiley.

Chittick, William O., and Keith R. Billingsley. 1989. "The Structure of Elite Foreign Policy Beliefs." *Western Political Quarterly* 42:201–24.

Chittick, William O., Keith R. Billingsley, and Rick Travis. 1990. "Persistence and Change in Elite and Mass Attitudes toward U.S. Foreign Policy." *Political Psychology* 11:385–402.

Chittick, William O., Keith R. Billingsley, and Rick Travis. 1995. "A Three-Dimensional Model of American Foreign Policy Beliefs." *International Studies Quarterly* 39:313–31.

Christopher, Warren. 2002. *Foreign Policy of the Bush Administration: A One-Year Assessment.* Working Paper 28. Los Angeles: Burkle Center for International Relations.

Churchill, Winston S. 1951. *The Grand Alliance.* Boston: Houghton Mifflin.

Citrin, Jack, Ernst B. Haas, Christopher Muste, and Beth Reingold. 1994. "Is American Nationalism Changing? Implications for Foreign Policy." *International Studies Quarterly* 38:1–32.

Clifford, Clark, with Richard Holbrooke. 1991. *Counsel to the President: A Memoir.* New York: Random House.

Clough, Michael. 1994. "Grass-Roots Policymaking." *Foreign Affairs* 73:191–96.

Cohen, Bernard C. 1957. *The Political Process and Foreign Policy: The Making of the Japanese Peace Settlement.* Princeton: Princeton University Press.

Cohen, Bernard C. 1973. *The Public's Impact on Foreign Policy.* Boston: Little, Brown.

Conover, Pamela Johnston. 1988. "Feminists and the Gender Gap." *Journal of Politics* 50:985–1010.

Conover, Pamela Johnston, and Stanley Feldman. 1984. "How People Organize the Political World: A Schematic Model." *American Journal of Political Science* 28:95–126.

Converse, Jean. 1987. *Survey Research in the United States: Roots and Emergence, 1890–1960.* Berkeley: University of California Press.

Converse, Philip E. 1964. "The Nature of Belief Systems in Mass Publics." In *Ideology and Discontent,* edited by David E. Apter, 206–61. New York: Free Press.

Converse, Philip E. 1970. "Attitudes and Non-Attitudes: Continuation of a Dialogue." In *The Quantitative Analysis of Social Problems,* edited by Edward R. Tufte, 168–89. Reading, MA: Addison-Wesley.

Converse, Philip E. 1975. "Public Opinion and Voting Behavior." In *Handbook of Political Science,* edited by Fred Greenstein and Nelson Polsby, 4:75–169. Reading, MA: Addison-Wesley.

Converse, Philip E. 1987a. "Changing Conceptions of Public Opinion in the Policy Process." *Public Opinion Quarterly* 51:S12–24.

Converse, Philip E. 1987b. "The Enduring Impact of the Vietnam War on American Public Opinion." In *After the Storm: American Society a Decade after the Vietnam War,* 53–75. Taipei: Academic Sinica.

Converse, Philip E., and Howard Schuman. 1970. "Silent Majorities and the Vietnam War." *Scientific American* 222:17–25.

Cook, Elizabeth Adell, and Clyde Wilcox. 1991. "Feminism and the Gender Gap—A Second Look." *Journal of Politics* 53:1111–22.

Cook, Fay Lomax, Jason Barabas, and Benjamin I. Page. 2002. "Invoking Public Opinion: Policy Elites and Social Security." *Public Opinion Quarterly* 66:235–64.

Cornwell, Elmer E. 1959. "Wilson, Creel, and the Presidency." *Public Opinion Quarterly* 23:189–202.

Cottam, Richard. 1977. *Foreign Policy Motivation: A General Theory and a Case Study.* Pittsburgh: University of Pittsburgh Press.

Cottrell, Leonard S., Jr., and Sylvia Eberhart. 1948. *American Opinion on World Affairs in the Atomic Age.* Princeton: Princeton University Press.

Crabb, Cecil. 1976. *Policy-Makers and Critics: Conflicting Theories of American Foreign Policy.* New York: Praeger.

Cutler, Neal E. 1970. "Generational Succession as a Source of Foreign Policy Attitudes: A Cohort Analysis of American Opinion, 1946–1966." *Journal of Peace Research* 7:33–47.

Dallek, Robert. 1979. *Franklin D. Roosevelt and American Foreign Policy, 1932–1945.* New York: Oxford University Press.

Dallek, Robert. 1983. *The American Style of Foreign Policy: Cultural Politics and Foreign Affairs.* New York: Knopf.

D'Amico, Francine, and Peter R. Beckman, eds. 1995. *Women in World Politics: An Introduction.* Westport, CT: Bergin and Garvey.

Danielian, Lucig H., and Benjamin I. Page. 1994. "The Heavenly Chorus: Interest Group Voices on TV News." *American Journal of Political Science* 38:1056–78.

Davies, Joseph E. 1941. *Mission to Moscow.* New York: Simon and Schuster.

Davis, James A. 1987. "The Future Study of Public Opinion: A Symposium." *Public Opinion Quarterly* 51:S178–79.

Davis, James A. 2001. "Attitudes and Opinions among Senior Military Officers and a U.S. Cross-Section, 1998–99." In *Soldiers and Civilians,* edited by Peter D. Feaver and Richard H. Kohn. Cambridge: MIT Press.

DeConde, Alexander. 1992. *Ethnicity, Race, and American Foreign Policy: A History.* Boston: Northeastern University Press.

Deese, David. 1994. *The New Politics of American Foreign Policy.* New York: St. Martin's.

Deibel, Terry L. 1987. *Presidents, Public Opinion, and Power: The Nixon, Carter, and Reagan Years.* New York: Foreign Policy Association.

Delli Carpini, Michael, and Scott Keeter. 1996. *What Americans Know about Politics and Why It Matters.* New Haven: Yale University Press.

"Democracies and War: The Politics of Peace." 1995. *Economist,* April 1, 17–18.

De Stefano, Linda. 1990. "Looking ahead to the Year 2000." Princeton, NJ. Gallup Organization.

Destler, I. M., Leslie H. Gelb, and Anthony Lake. 1984. *Our Own Worst Enemy: The Unmaking of American Foreign Policy.* New York: Simon and Schuster.

Devine, Donald J. 1970. *The Attentive Public: Polyarchical Democracy.* Chicago: Rand McNally.

DiMaggio, Paul, John Evans, and Bethany Bryson. 1996. "Have American's Social Attitudes Become More Polarized?" *American Journal of Sociology* 102:690–755.

Dimock, Michael A., and Samuel L. Popkin. 1996. "Political Knowledge in a Comparative Perspective." In *Do the Media Govern?* Edited by Shanto Iyengar and Richard Reeves, 217–24. Thousand Oaks, CA: Sage.

Doyle, Michael W. 1986. "Liberalism and World Politics." *American Political Science Review* 80:1151–70.

Doyle, Michael W. 1997. *Ways of War and Peace.* New York: Norton.

Drew, Elizabeth. 1978. "A Reporter at Large (Zbigniew Brzezinski)." *New Yorker,* May 1, 90–130.

Ehrenreich, Barbara. 1984. "The Real and Ever-Widening Gender Gap." *Esquire,* June, 213–17.

Eichenberg, Richard C. 1989. *Public Opinion and National Security in Western Europe.* Ithaca: Cornell University Press.

Eichenberg, Richard C. 2000. "NATO and European Security after the Cold War: Will European Citizens Support a Common Security Policy?" In *Decisionmaking in a Glass House,* edited by Brigitte Nacos, Robert Y. Shapiro, and Pierangelo Isernia, 155–75. Lanham, MD: Rowman and Littlefield.

Eichenberg, Richard C. 2003. "Gender Differences in Public Attitudes toward the Use of Force by the United States, 1990–2003." *International Security* 28:110–41.

Eichenberg, Richard C., and Russell J. Dalton. 1993. "Europeans and the European Community: The Dynamics of Public Support for European Integration." *International Organization* 47:507–34.

Eichenberg, Richard C., and Richard Stoll. 2003. "Representing Defense: Democratic Control of the Defense Budget in the United States and Western Europe." *Journal of Conflict Resolution* 47:399–422.

Eisenhower, Dwight D. 1965. *Waging Peace, 1956–1961: The White House Years.* Garden City, NY: Doubleday.

Eisinger, Robert M. 2000. "Gauging Public Opinion in the Hoover White House: Understanding the Roots of Presidential Polling." *Presidential Studies Quarterly* 30:643–61.

Elder, Robert E. 1957. "The Public Studies Division of the Department of State: Public Opinion Analysts in the Formulation and Conduct of American Foreign Policy." *Western Political Quarterly* 10:783–92.

Emery, Michael. 1989. "An Endangered Species: The International News Hole." *Gannett Center Journal* 3:151–64.

Entman, Robert M., and Susan Herbst. 2000. "Reframing Public Opinion as We Have Known It." In *Mediated Politics: Communication in the Future of Democracy,* edited by W. Lance Bennett and Robert M. Entman, 203–25. New York: Oxford University Press.

Erikson, Robert S. 1978. "Constituency Opinion and Congressional Behavior:

A Reexamination of the Miller-Stokes Data." *American Journal of Political Science* 22:511–35.

Erskine, Hazel. 1970. "The Polls: Is War a Mistake?" *Public Opinion Quarterly* 34:134–50.

Erskine, Hazel. 1972. "The Polls: Pacifism and the Generation Gap." *Public Opinion Quarterly* 36:617–27.

Everts, Philip. 2000. "Public Opinion after the Cold War: A Paradigm Shift." In *Decisionmaking in a Glass House,* edited by Brigitte Nacos, Robert Y. Shapiro, and Pierangelo Isernia, 177–94. Lanham, MD: Rowman and Littlefield.

Fagen, Richard R. 1960. "Some Assessments and Uses of Public Opinion in Diplomacy." *Public Opinion Quarterly* 24:448–57.

Feaver, Peter D., and Christopher Gelpi. 1999. "How Many Deaths Are Acceptable? A Surprising Answer." *Washington Post,* November 7, B3.

Ferguson, Thomas. 1986. "The Right Consensus." *International Studies Quarterly* 30:411–23.

Fiorina, Morris P. 1981. *Retrospective Voting in American National Elections.* New Haven: Yale University Press.

Fischer, Beth A. 1997. *The Reagan Reversal: Foreign Policy and the End of the Cold War.* Columbia: University of Missouri Press.

Fishkin, James S. 1991. *Democracy and Deliberation: New Directions for Democratic Reform.* New Haven: Yale University Press.

Fishkin, James S. 1992. "The Idea of a Deliberative Opinion Poll." *Public Perspective* 3:26–34.

Fishkin, James S. 1994. "Britain Experiments with the Deliberative Poll." *Public Perspective* 5:27–29.

Fite, David, Marc Genest, and Clyde Wilcox. 1990. "Gender Differences in Foreign Policy Attitudes: A Longitudinal Analysis." *American Politics Quarterly* 18:492–513.

Foster, H. Schuyler. 1983. *Activism Replaces Isolationism: U.S. Public Attitudes, 1940–1975.* Washington, DC: Foxhall Press.

Foyle, Douglas C. 1999. *Counting the Public In: Presidents, Public Opinion, and Foreign Policy.* New York: Columbia University Press.

Free, Lloyd, and William Watts. 1980. "Internationalism Comes of Age . . . Again." *Public Opinion* 3:46–50.

Friedman, Thomas L. 1995. "The No-Dead War." *New York Times,* August 23.

Gabel, Matthew J. 1998. *Interests and Integration: Market Liberalization, Public Opinion, and European Union.* Ann Arbor: University of Michigan Press.

Gaddis, John Lewis. 1992–93. "International Relations Theory and the End of the Cold War." *International Security* 17 (winter): 5–58.

Gallagher, Nancy W. 1993. "The Gender Gap in Popular Attitudes toward the Use of Force." In *Women and the Use of Military Force,* edited by Ruth Howes and Michael Stevenson, 23–37. Boulder, CO: Lynn Reiner.

Gallup, George, Jr. 1985–2001. *The Gallup Poll.* Wilmington, DE: Scholarly Resources.

Gallup, George H. 1972. *The Gallup Poll: Public Opinion, 1935–1971.* 3 vols. New York: Random House.

Gallup, George H. 1978. *The Gallup Poll: Public Opinion, 1972–1977.* 2 vols. Wilmington, DE: Scholarly Resources.

Gallup, George H. 1979–84. *The Gallup Poll.* Wilmington, DE: Scholarly Resources.

Gallup, George H., and Saul Rae. 1940. *The Pulse of Democracy: The Public-Opinion Poll and How It Works.* New York: Simon and Schuster.

Gallup Organization. 2001a. "Attack on America: Key Trends and Indicators." December 18. Available at www.gallup.com/poll/release/pr010926c.asp? Version=p.

Gallup Organization. 2001b. "Most Americans Satisfied with the U.S. Position in the World." March 8. Available at www.gallup.com/subscription /?m=f&c_id=9842.

Gallup Organization. 2003. "Americans Grow More Doubtful About Iraq War." September 23. Available at www.gallup.com/poll/release/pr030923 .asp?Version=p.

Gamson, William A., and Andre Modigliani. 1966. "Knowledge and Foreign Policy Opinions: Some Models for Consideration." *Public Opinion Quarterly* 30:187–99.

Garthoff, Raymond L. 1985. *Détente and Confrontation: American-Soviet Relations from Nixon to Reagan.* Washington, DC: Brookings Institution.

Gaubatz, Kurt Taylor. 1995. "Intervention and Intransitivity: Public Opinion, Social Choice, and the Use of Military Force Abroad." *World Politics* 47: 534–54.

Gaubatz, Kurt Taylor. 1999. *Elections and War: The Electoral Incentive in the Democratic Politics of War and Peace.* Stanford, CA: Stanford University Press.

Genco, Stephen J. 1984. "The Attentive Public and American Foreign Policy." Ph.D. diss., Stanford University.

George, Alexander L. 1955. "American Policy-Making and the North Korean Aggression." *World Politics* 2:209–32.

George, Alexander L. 1979. "Case Studies and Theory Development: The Method of Structured, Focused Comparison." In *Diplomacy: New Approaches in History, Theory, and Policy,* edited by Paul Gordon Lauren, 43–68. New York: Free Press.

George, Alexander L., and Richard Smoke. 1974. *Deterrence in American Foreign Policy: Theory and Practice.* New York: Columbia University Press.

Gergen, Kenneth J., and Kurt W. Back. 1965. "Aging, Time Perspective, and Preferred Solutions to International Conflicts." *Journal of Conflict Resolution* 9:177–86.

Gibson, James L. 1994. "Survey Research in the Past and Future USSR: Reflections on the Methodology of Mass Opinion Surveys." *Research in Micropolitics* 4:87–114.

Ginsberg, Benjamin. 1986. *The Captive Public: How Mass Opinion Promotes State Power.* New York: Basic Books.

Goldstein, Joshua. 2001. *War and Gender.* Cambridge: Cambridge University Press.

Goncharov, Sergei, John W. Lewis, and Xue Litai. 1993. *Uncertain Partners: Stalin, Mao, and the Korean War.* Stanford, CA: Stanford University Press.

Graber, Doris A. 1968. *Public Opinion, the President, and Foreign Policy: Four Case Studies from the Formative Years.* New York: Holt, Rinehart, and Winston.

Graebner, Norman A. 1983. "Public Opinion and Foreign Policy: A Pragmatic View." In *Interaction: Foreign Policy and Public Policy,* edited by E. D. Piper and R. J. Tercheck, 11–34. Washington, DC: American Enterprise Institute.

Graham, Thomas W. 1988. "The Pattern and Importance of Public Knowledge in the Nuclear Age." *Journal of Conflict Resolution* 32:319–34.

Graham, Thomas W. 1989. "The Politics of Failure: Strategic Nuclear Arms Control, Public Opinion, and Domestic Politics in the United States, 1945–1980." Ph.D. diss., Massachusetts Institute of Technology.

Graham, Thomas W. 1994. "Public Opinion and U.S. Foreign Policy Decision Making." In *The New Politics of American Foreign Policy,* edited by David A. Deese, 190–215. New York: St. Martin's.

Green, Joshua. 2002. "The Other War Room." *Washington Monthly,* April, 11–16.

Gunn, J. A. W. 1995. "Public Opinion in Modern Political Science." In *Political Science in History: Research Programs and Political Traditions,* edited by James Farr, John S. Dryzek, and Stephen T. Leonard, 99–122. New York: Cambridge University Press.

Hamill, Ruth, Milton Lodge, and Frederick Blake. 1985. "The Breadth, Depth, and Utility of Class, Partisan, and Ideological Schemata." *American Journal of Political Science* 29:850–70.

Hamilton, Alexander, John Jay, and James Madison. 1937 [1788–88]. *The Federalist.* New York: Modern Library.

Handberg, Roger B., Jr. 1972–73. "The 'Vietnam Analogy': Student Attitudes on War." *Public Opinion Quarterly* 36:612–15.

Harlow, Giles D., and George C. Maerz, eds. 1991. *Measures Short of War: The George F. Kennan Lectures at the National War College, 1946–47.* Washington, DC: National Defense University Press.

Hartley, Thomas, and Bruce Russett. 1992. "Public Opinion and the Common Defense: Who Governs Military Spending in the United States?" *American Political Science Review* 86:905–15.

Hechler, Ken. 1982. *Working with Truman: A Personal Memoir of the White House Years.* New York: Putnam.

Heith, Diane J. 1998. "Staffing the White House Public Opinion Apparatus, 1969–1988." *Public Opinion Quarterly* 62:165–89.

Helbich, Wolfgang J. 1967–68. "American Liberals in the League of Nations Controversy." *Public Opinion Quarterly* 31:568–96.

Herman, Edward S., and Noam Chomsky. 1988. *Manufacturing Consent: The Political Economy of the Mass Media.* New York: Pantheon.

Hermann, Charles F. 1969. "International Crisis as a Situational Variable." In *International Politics and Foreign Policy,* edited by James N. Rosenau, 409–21. New York: Free Press.

Hero, Alfred O., Jr. 1959. *Americans in World Affairs.* Boston: World Peace Foundation.

Hero, Alfred O., Jr. 1969. "Liberalism-Conservatism Revisited: Foreign vs. Domestic Federal Policies, 1937–1967." *Public Opinion Quarterly* 33:399–408.

Herrmann, Richard K. 1986. "The Power of Perceptions in Foreign Policy Decision Making." *American Journal of Political Science* 30:841–75.

Herrmann, Richard K., and Jonathan W. Keller. 2004. "Beliefs, Values and Strategic Choice: U.S. Decisions to Engage, Contain and Use Force in an Era of Globalization." *Journal of Politics* 66:557–80.

Herrmann, Richard K., Philip E. Tetlock, and Matt N. Diascro. 2001. "How Americans Think about Trade." *International Studies Quarterly* 45:191–218.

Higgs, Robert, and Anthony Kilduff. 1992. "Public Opinion: A Powerful Predictor of U.S. Defense Spending." *Defense Economics* 4:227–38.

Hilderbrand, Robert C. 1981. *Power and the People: Executive Management of Public Opinion in Foreign Affairs, 1897–1921.* Chapel Hill: University of North Carolina Press.

Hill, Kevin A. 1993. "The Domestic Sources of Foreign Policymaking: Congressional Voting and American Mass Attitudes toward South Africa." *International Studies Quarterly* 37:195–214.

Hinckley, Ronald H. 1988. "Public Attitudes toward Key Foreign Policy Events." *Journal of Conflict Resolution* 32:295–318.

Hinckley, Ronald H. 1992. *People, Polls, and Policy-Makers: American Public Opinion and National Security.* New York: Lexington.

Hinckley, Ronald H. 1993. "Public Opinion and Foreign Policy in Comparative Perspective." Paper presented at the annual meeting of the International Studies Association, Acapulco, Mexico, March 24–28.

Hinckley, Ronald H. 1995. Private communication with author, July 26.

Hoffmann, Stanley, Samuel P. Huntington, Ernest R. May, Richard N. Neustadt, and Thomas C. Schelling. 1981. "Vietnam Reappraised." *International Security* 6 (summer): 3–26.

Holmes, Jack E. 1985. *The Mood/Interest Theory of American Foreign Policy.* Lexington: University Press of Kentucky.

Holsti, Ole R. 1979. "The Three-Headed Eagle: The United States and System Change." *International Studies Quarterly* 23:339–59.

Holsti, Ole R. 1988. "What Are the Russians Up to Now: The Beliefs of American Leaders about the Soviet Union and Soviet-American Relations, 1974–1984." In *East-West Conflict: Elite Perceptions and Political Options,* edited by Michael D. Intriligator and Hans-Adolf Jacobsen, 45–105. Boulder, CO: Westview.

Holsti, Ole R. 1991. "American Reactions to the USSR: Public Opinion." In *Soviet-American Relations after the Cold War,* edited by Robert Jervis and Seweryn Bialer, 23–47. Durham, NC: Duke University Press.

Holsti, Ole R. 1998. "A Widening Gap between the U.S. Military and Civilian Society? Some Evidence, 1976–96." *International Security* 23:5–42.

Holsti, Ole R. 2000a. "Democracy Promotion as Popular Demand?" In *American Democracy Promotion: Impulses, Strategies, and Impacts,* edited by Michael Cox, G. John Ikenberry, and Takashi Inogushi, 151–80. New York: Oxford University Press.

Holsti, Ole R. 2000b. "Public Opinion and Human Rights in American Foreign Policy." In *The United States and Human Rights: Looking Inward and Outward,* edited by David P. Forsythe, 127–47. Lincoln: University of Nebraska Press.

Holsti, Ole R. 2001. "Of Chasms and Convergences: Attitudes and Beliefs of

Civilians and Military Elites at the Start of a New Millennium." In *Soldiers and Civilians,* edited by Peter D. Feaver and Richard H. Kohn, 15–99. Cambridge: MIT Press.

Holsti, Ole R., and James N. Rosenau. 1979. "Vietnam, Consensus, and the Belief Systems of American Leaders." *World Politics* 32:1–56.

Holsti, Ole R., and James N. Rosenau. 1981. "The Foreign Policy Beliefs of Women in Leadership Positions." *Journal of Politics* 43:326–47.

Holsti, Ole R., and James N. Rosenau. 1984. *American Leadership in World Affairs: Vietnam and the Breakdown of Consensus.* Boston: Allen and Unwin.

Holsti, Ole R., and James N. Rosenau. 1986. "The Foreign Policy Beliefs of American Leaders: Some Further Thoughts on Theory and Method." *International Studies Quarterly* 30:473–84.

Holsti, Ole R., and James N. Rosenau. 1988. "The Domestic and Foreign Policy Beliefs of American Leaders." *Journal of Conflict Resolution* 32:248–94.

Holsti, Ole R., and James N. Rosenau. 1990. "The Structure of Foreign Policy Attitudes among American Leaders." *Journal of Politics* 52:94–125.

Holsti, Ole R., and James N. Rosenau. 1993. "The Structure of Foreign Policy Beliefs among American Opinion Leaders—After the Cold War." *Millennium* 22:235–78.

Holsti, Ole R., and James N. Rosenau. 1994. "The Post–Cold War Foreign Policy Beliefs of American Leaders: Persistence or Abatement of Partisan Cleavages?" In *The Future of American Foreign Policy,* edited by Eugene R. Wittkopf, 127–47. New York: St. Martin's.

Holsti, Ole R., and James N. Rosenau. 1995. "Gender and the Political Beliefs of American Opinion Leaders." In *Women and World Politics,* edited by Francine D'Amico and Peter Beckman, 113–42. Amherst, MA: Bergin and Garvey.

Holsti, Ole R., and James N. Rosenau. 1996. "Liberals, Populists, Libertarians and Conservatives: The Link between Domestic and International Affairs." *International Political Science Review* 17:29–55.

Holsti, Ole R., and James N. Rosenau. 1998. "The Political Foundations of Elites' Domestic and Foreign Policy Beliefs." In *The Domestic Sources of American Foreign Policy,* edited by Eugene R. Wittkopf and James M. McCormick, 33–50. Lanham, MD: Rowman and Littlefield.

Homet, Roland S., Jr. 1990. *The New Realism: A Fresh Beginning in U.S.-Soviet Relations.* New York: HarperCollins.

House, Karen Elliott. 1980. "Reagan's World: Republican's Policies Stress Arms Buildup, a Firm Line to Soviet." *Wall Street Journal,* June 3.

Hovey, Graham. 1978. "Architects of U.S. African Policy Privately Worried by Carter's Attacks on Moscow." *New York Times,* June 4.

Howe, Neil, and William Strauss. 1992. "The New Generation Gap." *Atlantic,* December, 67–89.

Hughes, Barry B. 1978. *The Domestic Context of American Foreign Policy.* San Francisco: Freeman.

Hughes, Thomas L. 1980. "The Crack-Up: The Price of Collective Irresponsibility." *Foreign Policy* 40:33–60.

Hugick, Larry, and Alec H. Gallup. 1991. "Rally Events and Presidential Approval." *Gallup Poll Monthly,* June, 15–31.

Hull, Cordell. 1936. Speech at the Pan American Conference, Buenos Aires, December 5, 1936. Reprinted in the *New York Times*, December 6.

Huntington, Samuel P. 1974. "Paradigms of American Politics: Beyond the One, the Two, and the Many." *Political Science Quarterly* 89:1–26.

Hurwitz, Jon, and Mark Peffley. 1987. "How Are Foreign Policy Attitudes Structured? A Hierarchical Model." *American Political Science Review* 81:1099–120.

Hurwitz, Jon, and Mark Peffley. 1990. "Public Images of the Soviet Union and Its Leaders: The Impact on Foreign Policy Attitudes." *Journal of Politics* 52:3–28.

Hurwitz, Jon, Mark Peffley, and Mitchell A. Seligson. 1993. "Foreign Policy Belief Systems in Comparative Perspective: The United States and Costa Rica." *International Studies Quarterly* 37:245–70.

Idelson, Holly. 1991. "National Opinion Ambivalent as Winds of War Stir Gulf." *Congressional Quarterly Weekly*, January 5, 14–17.

Ikenberry, G. John. 2001. *After Victory: Institutions, Strategic Restraint, and the Rebuilding of Order after Major Wars.* Princeton: Princeton University Press.

Inglehart, Ronald, J.-R. Rabier, and K. E. Reif. 1987. "The Evolution of Public Attitudes toward European Integration, 1970–86." *Journal of European Integration* 10:135–55.

Inter-Parliamentary Union. 2003. "Women in National Parliaments." Available at www.ipu.org/wmn-e/classif.htm.

Isaacs, Maxine. 1994. "The Independent American Public: The Relationship between Elite and Mass Opinions on American Foreign Policy in the Mass Communication Age." Ph.D. diss., University of Maryland.

Isaacs, Maxine. 1998. "Two Different Worlds: The Relationship between Elite and Mass Opinion on American Foreign Policy." *Political Communication* 15:323–45.

Isernia, Pierangelo, Zoltan Juhasz, and Hans Rattinger. 2002. "Foreign Policy and the Rational Public in Comparative Perspective." *Journal of Conflict Resolution* 46:210–24.

Jacobs, Lawrence R. 1992. "The Recoil Effect: Public Opinion and Policy Making in the U.S. and Britain." *Comparative Politics* 24:199–217.

Jacobs, Lawrence R., and Robert Y. Shapiro. 1994a. "Issues, Candidate Image, and Priming: The Use of Private Polls in Kennedy's 1960 Presidential Campaign." *American Political Science Review* 88:527–40.

Jacobs, Lawrence R., and Robert Y. Shapiro. 1994b. "Studying Substantive Democracy." *PS: Political Science and Politics* 27:9–17.

Jacobs, Lawrence R., and Robert Y. Shapiro. 1995. "The Rise of Presidential Polling: The Nixon White House in Historical Perspective." *Public Opinion Quarterly* 59:163–95.

Jacobs, Lawrence R., and Robert Y. Shapiro. 1995–96. "Presidential Manipulation of Polls and Public Opinion: The Nixon Administration and Pollsters." *Political Science Quarterly* 110:519–38.

Jacobs, Lawrence R., and Robert Y. Shapiro. 1999. "Lyndon Johnson, Vietnam, and Public Opinion: Rethinking Realist Theory of Leadership." *Presidential Studies Quarterly* 29:592–616.

Jacobs, Lawrence R., and Robert Y. Shapiro. 2000. *Politicians Don't Pander:*

Political Manipulation and the Loss of Democratic Responsiveness. Chicago: University of Chicago Press.

Janda, Kenneth, Jeffrey M. Berry, and Jerry Goldman. 1994. *The Challenge of Democracy: Government in America.* 4th ed. Boston: Houghton Mifflin.

Jennings, M. Kent. 1987. "Residues of a Movement: The Aging of the American Protest Generation." *American Political Science Review* 81:367–82.

Jennings, M. Kent. 1992. "Ideological Thinking among Mass Publics and Political Elites." *Public Opinion Quarterly* 56:419–41.

Jennings, M. Kent. 1996. "Political Knowledge over Time." *Public Opinion Quarterly* 60:228–52.

Jentleson, Bruce W. 1992. "The Pretty Prudent Public: Post-Vietnam American Opinion on the Use of Military Force." *International Studies Quarterly* 36:49–73.

Jentleson, Bruce W. 1996. "Who, Why, What, and How: Debates over Post–Cold War Military Intervention." In *Eagle Adrift: American: American Foreign Policy at the End of the Century,* edited by Robert J. Lieber, 266–81. New York: HarperCollins.

Jentleson, Bruce W., and Rebecca L. Britton. 1998. "Still Pretty Prudent: Post–Cold War American Public Opinion and the Use of Military Force." *Journal of Conflict Resolution* 42:395–417.

Johnson, Chalmers A. 2000. *Blowback: The Costs and Consequences of American Empire.* New York: Metropolitan.

Johnston, David Cay. 2001. "Tax Enforcer Says Cheating Is on the Rise." *New York Times,* July 19.

Jones, Jeffrey M. 2003a. *Blacks Show Biggest Decline in Support for War Compared with 1991: Other Traditional Democratic Groups Also Much Less Supportive of Current Iraq War.* Princeton, NJ: Gallup Organization.

Jones, Jeffrey M. 2003b. *Blacks Showing Decided Opposition to War.* Princeton, NJ: Gallup Organization.

Jones, Jeffrey M. 2003c. "Six in Ten Americans Say United Nations Doing a Poor Job." Princeton, NJ: Gallup Organization.

Jones, Joseph M. 1955. *Fifteen Weeks.* New York: Viking.

Joyner, Christopher C. 2003. "United States' Unilateralism: Implications for Contemporary International Law." Paper presented at the International Studies Association convention, Portland, OR, February 26–March 1.

Judis, John B. 2003. "History Lesson." *New Republic* June 9:19–23.

Kagan, Robert. 2002. "Power and Weakness." *Policy Review* 113:3–28.

Kagay, Michael R. 1992. "Variability without Fault: Why Even Well-Designed Polls Can Disagree." In *Media Polls in American Politics,* edited by Thomas E. Mann and Gary R. Orren, 95–124. Washington, DC: Brookings Institution.

Kagay, Michael R., and Janet Elder. 1992. "Numbers Are No Problem for Pollsters. Words Are." *New York Times,* August 9.

Kant, Immanuel. 1983 [1796]. *Perpetual Peace and Other Essays on Politics, History, and Morals.* Translated with an introduction by Ted Humphrey. Indianapolis: Hackett.

Katz, Andrew Z. 1997. "Public Opinion and Foreign Policy: The Nixon Administration and the Pursuit of Peace with Honor in Vietnam." *Presidential Studies Quarterly* 27:496–513.

Katz, Andrew Z. 2000. "Public Opinion and the Contradictions of Jimmy Carter's Foreign Policy." *Presidential Studies Quarterly* 30:662–87.

Katz, Elihu. 1957. "The Two-Step Flow of Communication: An Up-to-Date Report on an Hypothesis." *Public Opinion Quarterly* 21:61–78.

Katz, Elihu, and Paul F. Lazarsfeld. 1955. *Personal Influence: The Part Played by People in the Flow of Mass Communications.* Glencoe, IL: Free Press.

Kaufmann, Karen M., and John R. Petrocik. 1999. "The Changing Politics of American Men: Understanding the Sources of the Gender Gap." *American Journal of Political Science* 43:864–87.

Kay, Alan F. 1992a. "Discovering the Wisdom of the People." *World Business Academy Perspectives* 6:19–28.

Kay, Alan F. 1992b. *Uncovering the Public View on Policy Issues: Evidence that Survey Research Can Address Intractable Problems in Governance.* Washington, DC: Americans Talk Issues Foundation.

Kegley, Charles W., Jr. 1986. "Assumptions and Dilemmas in the Study of Americans' Foreign Policy Beliefs: A Caveat." *International Studies Quarterly* 30:447–71.

Kegley, Charles W., Jr. 1993. "The Neoidealist Moment in International Studies? Realist Myths and the New International Realities." *International Studies Quarterly* 37:131–46.

Kelman, Herbert C. 1965. "Social-Psychological Approaches to the Study of International Relations: The Question of Relevance." In *International Behavior: A Social-Psychological Analysis,* edited by Herbert C. Kelman, 565–607. New York: Holt, Rinehart, and Winston.

Kelman, Steven J. 1970. "Youth and Foreign Policy." *Foreign Affairs* 48:414–26.

Kennan, George F. ["X"]. 1947. "Sources of Soviet Conduct." *Foreign Affairs* 25:566–82.

Kennan, George F. 1951. *American Diplomacy, 1900–1950.* Chicago: University of Chicago Press.

Kennan, George F. 1993. "Somalia, through a Glass Darkly." *New York Times,* September 30.

Kennedy, David M. 1999. *Freedom from Fear: The American People in Depression and War, 1929–1945.* New York: Oxford University Press.

Key, V. O., Jr. 1961. *Public Opinion and American Democracy.* New York: Knopf.

Kinder, Donald R. 1983. "Diversity and Complexity in American Public Opinion." In *Political Science: The State of the Discipline,* edited by Ada W. Finifter, 389–425. Washington, DC: American Political Science Association.

Kinder, Donald R., and David O. Sears. 1985. "Public Opinion and Political Action." In *Handbook of Social Psychology,* 3d ed., edited by Elliot Aronson and Gardner Lindzey, 659–741. New York: Random House.

King, Gary, Robert O. Keohane, and Sidney Verba. 1994. *Designing Social Inquiry: Scientific Inference in Qualitative Research.* Princeton: Princeton University Press.

Kinnard, Douglas. 1975. "Vietnam Reconsidered: An Attitudinal Survey of U.S. Army General Officers." *Public Opinion Quarterly* 39:445–56.

Kissinger, Henry. 1994. *Diplomacy.* New York: Simon and Schuster.

Klein, Ethel. 1984. *Gender Politics: From Consciousness to Mass Politics.* Cambridge: Harvard University Press.

Klingberg, Frank L. 1952. "The Historical Alternation of Moods in American Foreign Policy." *World Politics* 4:239–73.

Klingberg, Frank L. 1979. "Cyclical Trends in American Foreign Policy Moods and Their Policy Implications." In *Challenges to America: United States Foreign Policy in the 1980s*, edited by Charles W. Kegley Jr. and Patrick J. McGowan, 37–56. Beverly Hills, CA: Sage.

Klingberg, Frank L. 1983. *Cyclical Trends in American Foreign Policy Moods: The Unfolding of America's World Role*. Lanham, MD: University Press of America.

Knight, Thomas J. 1977. "The Passing of the Cold War Generation." *Intellect* 105:236–41.

Kohut, Andrew. 1999. *Retropolitics: The Political Typology*. Washington, DC: Pew Research Center for the People and the Press.

Kohut, Andrew. 2001. *2000*. Washington, DC: Pew Research Center for the People and the Press.

Kohut, Andrew. 2002. *Public Opinion in a Year for the Books*. Washington, DC: Pew Research Center for the People and the Press.

Kohut, Andrew, and Robert C. Toth. 1994. "Arms and the People." *Foreign Affairs* 73:47–61.

Kolko, Gabriel, and Joyce Kolko. 1972. *The Limits of Power: The World and United States Foreign Policy, 1945–1954*. New York: Harper and Row.

Koopman, Cheryl, Jack Snyder, and Robert Jervis. 1989. "American Elite Views of Relations with the Soviet Union." *Journal of Social Issues* 45:119–38.

Koopman, Cheryl, Jack Snyder, and Robert Jervis. 1990. "Theory-Driven versus Data-Driven Assessment in a Crisis." *Journal of Conflict Resolution* 34:694–722.

Koppel, Ted. 1994. "The Perils of Info-Democracy." *New York Times*, July 1.

Krauthammer, Charles. 1990–91. "The Unipolar Moment." *Foreign Affairs* 70:23–33.

Krauthammer, Charles. 2001. "The New Unilateralism." *Washington Post*, June 8.

Krauthammer, Charles. 2002. "OK—We've Made Our Point." *Raleigh News and Observer*, February 21.

Kriesberg, Martin. 1949. "Public Opinion: Dark Areas of Ignorance." In *Public Opinion and Foreign Policy*, edited by Lester Markel, 49–64. New York: Harper.

Kroeger, Brian, and Virginia Sapiro. 1994. "Oh, Ye of Little Faith: Philip Tetlock's Road to Hell." *Political Psychology* 15:557–66.

Krosnick, Jon A. 1988a. "Attitude Importance and Attitude Change." *Journal of Experimental Social Psychology* 24:240–55.

Krosnick, Jon A. 1988b. "The Role of Attitude Importance in Social Evaluation: A Study of Policy Preferences, Presidential Candidate Evaluations, and Voting Behavior." *Journal of Personality and Social Psychology* 55:196–210.

Krosnick, Jon A. 1990. "Americans' Perceptions of Presidential Candidates: A Test of the Projection Hypothesis." *Journal of Social Issues* 46:159–82.

Krosnick, Jon A. 1991. "The Stability of Political Preferences: Comparisons of Symbolic and Nonsymbolic Attitudes." *American Journal of Political Science* 35:547–76.

Krosnick, Jon, and Catherine Carnot. 1988. *Identifying the Foreign Affairs Attentive Public in the U.S.: A Comparison of Competing Theories.* Columbus: Ohio State University.

Kuklinski, James H., Paul J. Quirk, David W. Schwieder, and Robert F. Rich. 1998. "Just the Facts, Ma'am: Political Facts and Public Opinion." *Annals of the American Academy of Political and Social Science* 560:143–54.

Kull, Steven. 1995a. *America and Foreign Aid: A Study of American Public Attitudes.* College Park, MD: Center for International and Security Studies.

Kull, Steven. 1995b. *American Public Attitudes on Sending U.S. Troops to Bosnia.* College Park, MD: Center for International and Security Studies.

Kull, Steven. 1995c. *Americans on Bosnia: A Study of U.S. Public Attitudes.* College Park, MD: Center for International and Security Studies.

Kull, Steven. 1995–96. "What the Public Knows That Washington Doesn't." *Foreign Policy* 101:102–15.

Kull, Steven, and I. M. Destler. 1999. *Misreading the Public: The Myth of a New Isolationism.* Washington, DC: Brookings Institution Press.

Kull, Steven, and Clark Ramsay. 1993. *U.S. Public Attitudes on Involvement in Somalia.* College Park, MD: Center for International and Security Studies.

Kull, Steven, and Clark Ramsay. 1994a. *U.S. Public Attitudes on Involvement in Bosnia.* College Park, MD: Center for International Security Studies.

Kull, Steven, and Clark Ramsay. 1994b. *U.S. Public Attitudes on Involvement in Haiti.* College Park, MD: Center for International and Security Studies.

Kull, Steven, and Clark Ramsay. 1994c. *U.S. Public Attitudes on UN Peacekeeping.* Part 1, *Funding.* College Park, MD: Center for International and Security Studies.

Kusnitz, Leonard A. 1984. *Public Opinion and Foreign Policy: America's China Policy, 1949–1979.* Westport, CT: Greenwood.

Kuzma, Lynn M. 2000. "The Polls: Terrorism in the United States." *Public Opinion Quarterly* 64:90–105.

La Balme, Natalie. 2000. "Constraint, Catalyst, or Political Tool? The French Public and Foreign Policy." In *Decisionmaking in a Glass House,* edited by Brigitte Nacos, Robert Y. Shapiro, and Pierangelo Isernia, 265–78. Lanham, MD: Rowman and Littlefield.

Ladd, Everett Carll, and John Benson. 1992. "The Growth of News Polls in American Politics." In *Media Polls in American Politics,* edited by Thomas E. Mann and Gary R. Orren, 19–31. Washington, DC: Brookings Institution.

LaFeber, Walter. 1977. "American Policy-Makers, Public Opinion, and the Outbreak of the Cold War, 1945–1950." In *The Origins of the Cold War in Asia,* edited by Yonosuke Nagia and Akira Iriye, 43–65. New York: Columbia University Press.

Lancaster, James L. 1967–68. "The Protestant Churches and the Fight for Ratification of the Versailles Treaty." *Public Opinion Quarterly* 31:597–619.

Larson, Eric V. 1996. *Casualties and Consensus.* Santa Monica, CA: RAND.

Larson, James F. 1984. *Television's Window on the World: International Affairs Coverage on the U.S. Networks.* Norwood, NJ: Ablex.

Layne, Christopher. 1997. "From Preponderance to Offshore Balancing: America's Future Grand Strategy." *International Security* 22 (summer): 86–124.

Lazarsfeld, Paul F., Bernard R. Berelson, and Hazel Gaudet. 1944. *The People's Choice.* New York: Duell, Sloan, and Pearce.

Leigh, Michael. 1976. *Mobilizing Consent: Public Opinion and American Foreign Policy, 1937–1947.* Westport, CT: Greenwood.

Levering, Ralph B. 1976. *American Opinion and the Russian Alliance, 1939–1945.* Chapel Hill: University of North Carolina Press.

Levering, Ralph B. 1978. *The Public and American Foreign Policy, 1918–1978.* New York: Morrow.

Levering, Ralph B. 1989. "Public Opinion, Foreign Policy, and American Politics since the 1960s." *Diplomatic History* 13:383–93.

Levering, Ralph B. 1991. "Public Culture and Public Opinion: The League of Nations Controversy in New Jersey and North Carolina." In *The Wilson Era: Essays in Honor of Arthur S. Link,* edited by John Milton Cooper and Charles E. Neu, 159–97. Arlington Heights, IL: Harlan Davidson.

Lewis, Neil A. 2002. "U. S. Rejects All Support for New Court on Atrocities." *New York Times,* May 7.

Lian, Bradley, and John R. Oneal. 1993. "Presidents, the Use of Military Force, and Public Opinion." *Journal of Conflict Resolution* 37:277–300.

Lindsay, James M. 1990. "Parochialism, Policy, and Constituency Constraints: Congressional Voting on Strategic Weapons Systems." *American Journal of Political Science* 34:936–60.

Lindsay, James M. 1991. "Testing the Parochial Hypothesis: Congress and the Strategic Defense Initiative." *Journal of Politics* 53:860–76.

Lindsay, James M. 2000. "The New Apathy: How an Uninterested Public Is Reshaping Foreign Policy." *Foreign Affairs* 79:2–8.

Lippmann, Walter. 1920. *Liberty and the News.* New York: Harcourt, Brace, and Howe.

Lippmann, Walter. 1922. *Public Opinion.* New York: Macmillan.

Lippmann, Walter. 1925. *The Phantom Public.* New York: Harcourt Brace.

Lippmann, Walter. 1955. *Essays in the Public Philosophy.* Boston: Little, Brown.

Lippmann, Walter, and Charles Merz. 1920. "A Test of the News." *New Republic,* special supplement, 23:1–42.

Lipset, Seymour Martin. 1966. "The President, the Polls, and Vietnam." *Trans-Action,* September–October, 19–24.

Lipset, Seymour Martin, and Karlyn H. Bowman. 2000. "Clinton: Assessing the 42nd President." *Public Perspective* 11:5–13.

Lipset, Seymour Martin, and Everett Carll Ladd Jr. 1971. "College Generations from the 1930s to the 1960s." *Public Interest* 25:99–113.

Literary Digest. 1936. October 31, 5–6.

Locke, John. 1988 [1690]. *Two Treatises of Government.* Edited by Peter Laslett. New York: Cambridge University Press.

Logan, Carolyn J. 1996. "U.S. Public Opinion and the Intervention in Somalia." *Fletcher Forum of World Affairs* 20:155–80.

Lowell, A. Lawrence. 1923. *Public Opinion in War and Peace.* Cambridge: Harvard University Press.

Lowi, Theodore J. 1967. "Making Democracy Safe for the World: National

Politics and Foreign Policy." In *Domestic Sources of Foreign Policy*, edited by James N. Rosenau, 295–331. New York: Free Press.

Lowi, Theodore J. 1985. *The Personal President: Power Invested, Promise Unfulfilled*. Ithaca: Cornell University Press.

Lunch, William, and Peter W. Sperlich. 1979. "American Public Opinion and the War in Vietnam." *Western Political Quarterly* 32:21–44.

Luttbeg, Norman R. 1968. "The Structure of Beliefs among Leaders and the Public." *Public Opinion Quarterly* 32:398–409.

Luttbeg, Norman R., and Michael M. Gant. 1985. "The Failure of Liberal/Conservative Ideology as a Cognitive Structure." *Public Opinion Quarterly* 49:80–93.

Luttwak, Edward N. 1994. "Where Are the Great Powers?" *Foreign Affairs* 73:23–29.

Mandel, Robert. 1991. "Public Opinion and Superpower Strategic Arms." *Armed Forces and Society* 17:409–27.

Mandelbaum, Michael. 1996. "Foreign Policy as Social Work." *Foreign Affairs* 75:16–32.

Mandelbaum, Michael, and William Schneider. 1979. "The New Internationalism." In *Eagle Entangled: U.S. Foreign Policy in a Complex World*, edited by Kenneth A. Oye, Robert J. Lieber, and Donald Rothchild, 40–63. New York: Longman.

Mann, Thomas E., and Gary R. Orren, eds. 1992. *Media Polls in American Politics*. Washington, DC: Brookings Institution.

Mannheim, Karl. 1952. *Essays in the Sociology of Knowledge*. Edited by Paul Kecskemeti. London: Routledge and Kegan Paul.

Manza, Jeff, and Fay Lomax Cook. 2002. "A Democratic Polity? Three Views of Policy Responsiveness to Public Opinion in the United States." *American Politics Research* 30:630–67.

Marcus, George E., and Russell L. Hanson, eds. 1993. *Reconsidering the Democratic Public*. University Park: Pennsylvania State University Press.

Margolis, Michael, and Gary A. Mauser, eds. 1989. *Manipulating Public Opinion: Essays on Public Opinion as a Dependent Variable*. Pacific Grove, CA: Brooks/Cole.

Markel, Lester. 1949. "Opinion — A Neglected Instrument." In *Public Opinion and Foreign Policy*, 3–46. New York: Harper.

Marra, R. F., C. W. Ostrom, and D. M. Simon. 1990. "Foreign Policy and Presidential Popularity." *Journal of Conflict Resolution* 34:558–623.

Maxwell, Kenneth R. 1967–68. "Irish-Americans and the Fight for Treaty Ratification." *Public Opinion Quarterly* 31:620–41.

May, Ernest R. 1959. *The World War and American Isolation, 1914–1917*. Cambridge: Harvard University Press.

May, Ernest R. 1964. "An American Tradition in Foreign Policy: The Role of Public Opinion." In *Theory and Practice in American Politics*, edited by William H. Nelson, 101–22. Chicago: University of Chicago Press.

Mayer, William G. 1992. *The Changing American Mind: How and Why American Public Opinion Changed between 1960 and 1988*. Ann Arbor: University of Michigan Press.

McCloskey, Herbert, Paul J. Hoffmann, and Rosemary O'Hara. 1960. "Issue Conflict and Consensus among Party Leaders and Followers." *American Political Science Review* 54:406–27.

McGrory, Mary. 1975. "The Young People Had It Right." *Boston Globe,* May 1.

Mead, Walter R. 2001. *Special Providence: American Foreign Policy and How It Changed the World.* New York: Knopf.

Meernik, James, and Peter Waterman. 1996. "The Myth of the Diversionary Use of Force by American Presidents." *Political Research Quarterly* 49: 573–90.

Mill, James. 1913 [1821]. *On Liberty of the Press for Advocating Resistance to Government: Being Part of an Essay Written for the Encyclopedia Britannica.* 6th ed. New York: Free Speech League.

Miller, Arthur H., Vicki L. Hesli, and William M. Reisinger. 1995. "Mass and Elite Belief Systems in Russia/Ukraine." *Public Opinion Quarterly* 59: 1–40.

Miller, Arthur H., William M. Reisinger, and Vicki L. Hesli, eds. 1993. *Public Opinion and Regime Change: The New Politics of Post-Soviet Societies.* Boulder, CO: Westview.

Miller, Steven E. 2002. "The End of Unilateralism or Unilateralism Redux?" *Washington Quarterly* 25:15–29.

Miller, Warren E. 1967. "Voting and Foreign Policy." In *Domestic Sources of Foreign Policy,* edited by James N. Rosenau, 213–30. New York: Free Press.

Miller, Warren E., and Donald E. Stokes. 1963. "Constituency Influence in Congress." *American Political Science Review* 57:45–56.

Molyneux, Guy. 1994. "NAFTA Revisited: Unified 'Opinion Leaders' Best a Reluctant Public." *Public Perspective* 5:28–30.

Monroe, Alan D. 1979. "Consistency between Public Preferences and National Policy Decisions." *American Politics Quarterly* 7:3–19.

Monroe, Alan D. 1998. "Public Opinion and Public Policy, 1980–1993." *Public Opinion Quarterly* 62:6–28.

Moore, David W. 1992. *The Superpollsters: How They Measure and Manipulate Public Opinion in America.* New York: Four Walls and Eight Windows.

Moore, David W. 2002. "Measuring New Types of Question-Order Effects." *Public Opinion Quarterly* 66:80–91.

Moore, David W. 2003. "Public Steady on Iraq: Evenly Divided on Whether to Withdraw or Keep Troops in Iraq." Washington, DC: Gallup Organization. November 7.

Morgenthau, Hans J. 1978. *Politics among Nations.* 5th ed. New York: Knopf.

Mueller, John E. 1973. *War, Presidents, and Public Opinion.* New York: Wiley.

Mueller, John E. 1993. "American Public Opinion and the Gulf War: Some Polling Issues." *Public Opinion Quarterly* 57:80–91.

Mueller, John E. 1994. *Policy and Opinion in the Gulf War.* Chicago: University of Chicago Press.

Mueller, John E. 2000. "Public Opinion as a Constraint on U.S. Foreign Policy: Assessing the Perceived Value of American and Foreign Lives." Paper presented at the annual convention of the International Studies Association, Los Angeles, March.

Munton, Don. 1989. "Threat Perceptions and Shifts of Public Attitudes,

1960s–1980s." In *Western Perceptions of Soviet Goals: Is Trust Possible?* edited by Klaus Gottstein, 97–134. Frankfurt am Main: Campus; Boulder, CO: Westview.

Munton, Don. 1991. "NATO Up against the Wall: Changing Security Attitudes in Germany, Britain, and Canada, 1960s to the 1980s." In *Debating National Security: The Public Dimension,* edited by Hans Rattinger and Don Munton, 343–77. Frankfurt am Main: Peter Lang.

Munton, Don. 1992. "Up (or Down) in Arms: American and Canadian Public Attitudes in the Mid-1980s." In *East-West Arms Control: Challenges for the Western Alliance,* edited by David Dewitt and Hans Rattinger, 212–44. London: Routledge.

Murray, Shoon Kathleen. 1996. *Anchors against Change: American Opinion Leaders' Beliefs after the Cold War.* Ann Arbor: University of Michigan Press.

Murray, Shoon Kathleen, and Peter Howard. 2002. "Variation in White House Polling Operations: Carter to Clinton." *Public Opinion Quarterly* 66:527–57.

Nacos, Brigitte Lebens. 1994. "Presidential Leadership during the Persian Gulf War." *Presidential Studies Quarterly* 24:543–61.

National Geographic Society. 1988. *Geography: An International Gallup Survey.* Princeton, NJ: Gallup Organization.

National Opinion Research Center. 1947. *Cincinnati Looks at the United Nations.* Report 37. Chicago: National Opinion Research Center.

Neuman, W. Russell. 1986. *The Paradox of Mass Politics: Knowledge and Opinion in the American Electorate.* Cambridge: Harvard University Press.

Neumann, Sigmund. 1942. *Permanent Revolution: The Total State in a World at War.* New York: Harper.

Neustadt, Richard. 1970. *Alliance Politics.* New York: Columbia University Press.

Nevitte, Neil, and Roger Gibbins. 1987. "The Ideology of Gender." Paper presented at the tenth annual meeting of the International Society of Political Psychology, San Francisco, July 4–7.

"The New Americans: A New *U.S. News* Poll Shatters Old Assumptions about American Politics." 1995. *U.S. News and World Report,* July 10, pp. 18–23.

Newport, Frank. 1995. *Presidential Address on Bosnia Changed Few Minds.* Princeton, NJ: Gallup Organization.

Nie, Norman H., and Kristi Anderson. 1974. "Mass Belief Systems Revisited: Political Change and Attitude Structure." *Journal of Politics* 36:540–91.

Nie, Norman H., Sidney Verba, and John R. Petrocik. 1976. *The Changing American Voter.* Cambridge: Harvard University Press.

Niemi, Richard G. 1986. "The Dynamics of Public Opinion." In *Political Science: The Science of Politics,* edited by Herbert Weisberg, 225–40. New York: Agathon.

Nincic, Miroslav. 1988. "The United States, the Soviet Union, and the Politics of Opposites." *World Politics* 40:452–75.

Nincic, Miroslav. 1992. *Democracy and Foreign Policy: The Fallacy of Political Realism.* New York: Columbia University Press.

Nincic, Miroslav. 1997. "Loss Aversion and the Domestic Context of Military Intervention." *Political Research Quarterly* 50:97–120.

Nincic, Miroslav, and Donna J. Nincic. 2002. "Race, Gender, and War." *Journal of Peace Research* 39:547–68.

Norris, Pippa. 1995. "The Restless Searchlight: Network News Framing of the Post–Cold War Period." *Political Communication* 12:357–70.

Nye, Joseph S., Jr. 2002. *The Paradox of American Power.* New York: Oxford University Press.

Oldendick, Robert W., and Barbara Ann Bardes. 1982. "Mass and Elite Foreign Policy Opinions." *Public Opinion Quarterly* 46:368–82.

O'Neill, William L. 1993. *A Democracy at War: America's Fight at Home and Abroad in World War II.* New York: Free Press.

Page, Benjamin I. 1994. "Democratic Responsiveness? Untangling the Links between Public Opinion and Policy." *PS: Political Science and Politics* 27: 25–29.

Page, Benjamin I. 2002. "The Semi-Sovereign Public." In *Navigating Public Opinion: Polls, Policy, and the Future of American Democracy,* edited by Jeff Manza, Fay Lomax Cook, and Benjamin I. Page, 325–44. New York: Oxford University Press.

Page, Benjamin I., and Robert Y. Shapiro. 1982. "Changes in Americans' Policy Preferences, 1935–1979." *Public Opinion Quarterly* 46:24–42.

Page, Benjamin I., and Robert Y. Shapiro. 1983. "Effects of Public Opinion on Policy." *American Political Science Review* 77:175–90.

Page, Benjamin I., and Robert Y. Shapiro. 1984. "Presidents as Opinion Leaders: Some New Evidence." *Policy Studies Journal* 12:649–61.

Page, Benjamin I., and Robert Y. Shapiro. 1992. *The Rational Public: Fifty Years of Trends in Americans' Policy Preferences.* Chicago: University of Chicago Press.

Page, Benjamin I., Robert Y. Shapiro, and G. R. Dempsey. 1987. "What Moves Public Opinion." *American Political Science Review* 81:23–43.

Paige, Glenn D. 1968. *The Korean Decision: June 24–30, 1950.* New York: Free Press.

Parker, Suzanne. 1995. "Toward Understanding the 'Rally' Effects: Public Opinion in the Persian Gulf War." *Public Opinion Quarterly* 59:526–46.

Parry, R., and P. Kornbluh. 1988. "Iran-Contra's Untold Story." *Foreign Policy* 72:3–30.

Paterson, Thomas G. 1979. "Presidential Foreign Policy, Public Opinion, and Congress: The Truman Years." *Diplomatic History* 3:1–18.

Peffley, Mark A., and Jon Hurwitz. 1992. "International Events and Foreign Policy Beliefs: Public Responses to Changing Soviet-U.S. Relations." *American Journal of Political Science* 36:431–61.

Percy, Charles. 1981–82. "The Partisan Gap." *Foreign Policy* 45:3–15.

Pew Research Center for the People and the Press. 1997. *America's Place in the World II.* Washington, DC: Pew Research Center.

Pew Research Center for the People and the Press. 2001a. *America's New Internationalist Point of View.* Washington, DC: Pew Research Center.

Pew Research Center for the People and the Press. 2001b. "American Psyche Reeling from Terror Attacks." September 19. Available at www.people -press.org/reports/display.php3?ReportID=3.

Pew Research Center for the People and the Press. 2001c. *Public Opinion in a Year for the Books*. Washington, DC: Pew Research Center.

Pew Research Center for the People and the Press. 2001d. "Terror Coverage Boosts News Media's Image: But Military Censorship Backed." November 28. Available at www.people-press.org/reports/display.php3?ReportID =143.

Pew Research Center for the People and the Press. 2001e. "Terrorism Transforms News Interest." December 18. Available at www.people-press.org /reports/print.php3?ReportID=146.

Pew Research Center for the People and the Press. 2002a. "Americans Favor Force in Iraq, Somalia, Sudan, and ... Washington, DC." January 22. Available at www.people-press.org/reports/display.php3?ReportID=148.

Pew Research Center for the People and the Press. 2002b. "Unusually High Interest in Bush's State of the Union: Public Priorities Shifted by Recession and War." January 17. Available at www.people-press.org/reports /display.php3?ReportID=147.

Pew Research Center for the People and the Press. 2002c. "Public's News Habits Little Changed by Sept. 11." Washington, DC. June 9.

Pew Research Center for the People and the Press. 2002d. "What the World Thinks in 2002." Washington, DC. December 4.

Pew Research Center for the People and the Press. 2003a. "U.S. Needs International Backing." Washington, DC. February 20.

Pew Research Center for the People and the Press. 2003b. "America's Image Further Erodes, Europeans Want Weaker Ties." Washington, DC. March 18.

Pew Research Center for the People and the Press. 2003c. "Give U.N. Control, in Order to Get More Foreign Troops." Washington, DC. September 23.

Pew Research Center for the People and the Press. 2003d. "Evenly Divided and Increasingly Polarized: 2004 Political Landscape." Washington, DC. November 5.

PIPA (Program on International Policy Attitudes). 2001a. "Americans on Foreign Aid and World Hunger: A Study of U.S. Public Attitudes." February 2. Available at www.pipa.org/OnlineReports/BFW/toc.html.

PIPA (Program on International Policy Attitudes). 2001b. "Americans on the War on Terrorism: A Study of U.S. Public Attitudes." November 13. Available at www.pipa.org/OnlineReports/Terrorism/WarOnTerr .html.

PIPA (Program on International Policy Attitudes). 2002a. "Americans on the Israel/Palestine Conflict." May 8.

PIPA (Program on International Policy Attitudes). 2002b. "Americans on Defense Spending and the War on Terrorism." August 2.

PIPA (Program on International Policy Attitudes). 2003a. "Americans on America's Role in the World after the Iraq War." April 29.

PIPA (Program on International Policy Attitudes). 2003b. "Strong Majority Continues to Approve of War with Iraq." May 14–18.

PIPA (Program on International Policy Attitudes). 2003c. "Americans on Iraq." July 23.

PIPA (Program on International Policy Attitudes). 2003d. "Misperceptions, the Media and the Iraq War." October 2.

PIPA (Program on International Policy Attitudes). 2003e. "Americans Reevaluate Going to War with Iraq." November 13.

Pohl, Otto. 2003. "U.S. Left Out of Emissions Trading." *New York Times,* April 10.

Popkin, Samuel L.1991. *The Reasoning Voter: Communication and Persuasion in Presidential Campaigns.* Chicago: University of Chicago Press.

Powlick, Philip J. 1991. "The Attitudinal Bases for Responsiveness to Public Opinion among American Foreign Policy Officials." *Journal of Conflict Resolution* 35:611–41.

Powlick, Philip J. 1995. "The Sources of Public Opinion for American Foreign Policy Officials." *International Studies Quarterly* 39:427–52.

Powlick, Philip J., and Andrew Z. Katz. 1998. "Defining the American Public Opinion/Foreign Policy Nexus." *Mershon International Studies Review* 42, supplement 1:29–61.

Price, Vincent. 1992. *Public Opinion.* Newbury Park, CA: Sage.

Prothro, James, and Charles Grigg. 1960. "Fundamental Principles of Democracy: Bases of Agreement and Disagreement." *Journal of Politics* 22:276–94.

Quirk, Paul J., and Joseph Hinchliffe. 1998. "The Rising Hegemony of Mass Opinion." *Journal of Policy History* 10:19–50.

Randall, Vicky. 1982. *Women and Politics: An International Perspective.* New York: St. Martin's.

Rapaport, Ronald B., Walter J. Stone, and Alan I. Abramowitz. 1990. "Sex and the Caucus Participant: The Gender Gap and Presidential Nominations." *American Journal of Political Science* 34:725–40.

Rattinger, Hans, and Don Munton. 1991. *Debating National Security: The Public Dimension.* New York: P. Lang.

Reagan, Ronald W. 1990. *An American Life.* New York: Simon and Schuster.

Reiter, Dan, and Allan C. Stam. 2002. *Democracies at War.* Princeton: Princeton University Press.

Renshon, Stanley A., ed. 1993. *The Political Psychology of the Gulf War: Leaders, Publics, and the Process of Conflict.* Pittsburgh: University of Pittsburgh Press.

Richardson, Jill Darling. 2001. "Poll Analysis: Americans Support Military Action, Think Attack Plans Should Have Been Exposed." *Los Angeles Times,* September 16.

Richman, Alvin. 1991. "The Polls: Poll Trends: Changing American Attitudes toward the Soviet Union." *Public Opinion Quarterly* 55:135–48.

Richman, Alvin. 1995. "When Should We Be Prepared to Fight?" *Public Perspective* 6:44–47.

Rielly, John E., ed. 1975. *American Public Opinion and U.S. Foreign Policy, 1975.* Chicago: Chicago Council on Foreign Relations.

Rielly, John E., ed. 1979. *American Public Opinion and U.S. Foreign Policy, 1979.* Chicago: Chicago Council on Foreign Relations.

Rielly, John E., ed. 1983. *American Public Opinion and U.S. Foreign Policy, 1983.* Chicago: Chicago Council on Foreign Relations.

Rielly, John E., ed. 1987. *American Public Opinion and U.S. Foreign Policy, 1987.* Chicago: Chicago Council on Foreign Relations.

Rielly, John E., ed. 1991. *American Public Opinion and U.S. Foreign Policy, 1991.* Chicago: Chicago Council on Foreign Relations.

Rielly, John E., ed. 1995. *American Public Opinion and U.S. Foreign Policy, 1995.* Chicago: Chicago Council on Foreign Relations.

Rielly, John E., ed. 1999. *American Public Opinion and U.S. Foreign Policy, 1999.* Chicago: Chicago Council on Foreign Relations.

Rintala, Marvin. 1962. *Three Generations: The Extreme Right Wing in Finnish Politics.* Bloomington: Indiana University Press.

Ripley, Randall B., and James M. Lindsay, eds. 1993. *Congress Resurgent: Foreign and Defense Policy on Capitol Hill.* Ann Arbor: University of Michigan Press.

Risse-Kappen, Thomas. 1991. "Public Opinion, Domestic Structure, and Foreign Policy in Liberal Democracies." *World Politics* 43:479–512.

Roberts, Steven V. 1982. "A Critical Coterie on Foreign Policy." *New York Times,* April 5.

Roberts, Steven V. 1983. "The Focus Turns to Foreign Policy." *New York Times,* May 3.

Robinson, Lucas, and Steven Livingston. 2003. "No News and Foreign News: U.S. Media Coverage of the World." Paper presented at the International Studies Association convention, Portland, OR, February 26–March 1.

Rogers, William C., Barbara Stuhler, and Donald Koenig. 1967. "A Comparison of Informed and General Public Opinion on U.S. Foreign Policy." *Public Opinion Quarterly* 31:242–52.

Root, Elihu. 1907. "The Need of Popular Understanding of International Law." *American Journal of International Law* 1:1–3.

Root, Elihu. 1917. "The Effects of Democracy on International Law." *Proceedings of the American Society of International Law* 1917:2–11.

Root, Elihu. 1922. "A Requisite for the Success of Popular Diplomacy." *Foreign Affairs* 1:1–10.

Rosenau, James N. 1961. *Public Opinion and Foreign Policy: An Operational Formulation.* New York: Random House.

Rosenau, James N. 1963. *National Leadership and Foreign Policy: A Case Study in the Mobilization of Public Support.* Princeton: Princeton University Press.

Rosenau, James N., ed. 1967. *Domestic Sources of Foreign Policy.* New York: Free Press.

Rosenau, James N. 1974. *Citizenship between Elections: An Inquiry into the Mobilizable American.* New York: Free Press.

Rosenau, James N. 1990. *Turbulence in World Politics: A Theory of Change and Continuity.* Princeton: Princeton University Press.

Rosenberg, Milton J. 1967. "Attitude Change and Foreign Policy in the Cold War Era." In *Domestic Sources of Foreign Policy,* edited by James N. Rosenau, 111–60. New York: Free Press.

Roskin, Michael. 1974. "From Pearl Harbor to Vietnam: Shifting Generational Paradigms and Foreign Policy." *Political Science Quarterly* 89: 563–88.

Rosner, Jeremy D. 1995–96. "The Know-Nothings Know Something." *Foreign Policy* 101:116–29.

Rusk, Dean. 1990. *As I Saw It.* As told to Richard Rusk. Edited by Daniel S. Papp. New York: Norton.

Russett, Bruce M. 1975. "The Americans' Retreat from World Power." *Political Science Quarterly* 90:1–21.

Russett, Bruce M. 1990. *Controlling the Sword: The Democratic Governance of National Security.* Cambridge: Harvard University Press.

Russett, Bruce M. 1993. *Grasping the Democratic Peace.* Princeton: Princeton University Press.

Russett, Bruce M., and Elizabeth C. Hanson. 1975. *Interest and Ideology: The Foreign Policy Beliefs of American Businessmen.* San Francisco: Freeman.

Russett, Bruce, Thomas Hartley, and Shoon Kathleen Murray. 1994. "The End of the Cold War, Attitude Change, and the Politics of Defense Spending." *PS: Political Science and Politics* 27:17–21.

Russett, Bruce, and Samuel Shye. 1993. "Aggressiveness, Involvement, and Commitment in Foreign Policy Attitudes." In *Diplomacy, Force, and Leadership: Essays in Honor of Alexander L. George,* edited by Dan Caldwell and Timothy J. McKeown, 41–60. Boulder, CO: Westview.

Saad, Lydia. 1995. *Americans Back Clinton's Plan to Keep the Peace in Bosnia.* Princeton, NJ: Gallup Organization.

Saad, Lydia, and Frank Newport. 1995. "Americans Want To Keep at Arms Length from Bosnian Conflict." *Gallup Monthly,* July, 16–18.

Sanders, Lynn M. 1999. "Democratic Politics and Survey Research." *Philosophy of the Social Sciences* 29:248–80.

Schlesinger, Arthur, Jr. 1995. "Back to the Womb?" *Foreign Affairs* 74:2–8.

Schlesinger, James R. 1975. "Now—A Tougher U.S." *U.S. News and World Report,* May 26, p. 25.

Schneider, William. 1983. "Conservatism, Not Interventionism: Trends in Foreign Policy Opinion, 1974–1982." In *Eagle Defiant: United States Foreign Policy in the 1980s,* edited by Kenneth Oye, Robert J. Lieber, and Donald Rothchild, 33–64. Boston: Little, Brown.

Schneider, William. 1992. "The Old Politics and the New World Order." In *Eagle in a New World,* edited by Kenneth A. Oye, Robert J. Lieber, and Donald Rothchild, 35–68. New York: HarperCollins.

Schuman, Howard, and Cheryl Rieger. 1992. "Historical Analogies, Generational Effects, and Attitudes toward War." *American Sociological Review* 57:315–26.

Schwarz, Benjamin, and Christopher Layne. 2002. "A New Grand Strategy." *Atlantic Monthly,* January, 36–42.

Schwarzkopf, H. Norman, with Peter Petre. 1992. *It Doesn't Take a Hero: General H. Norman Schwarzkopf, the Autobiography.* New York: Bantam.

Sears, David. 1994. "Ideological Bias in Political Psychology: The View from Scientific Hell." *Political Psychology* 15:547–56.

Seeyle, Katherine Q. 2002. "President Distances Himself from Global Warming Report." *New York Times,* June 5.

Sestanovich, Stephen. 2001. "The Challenges of Alliance with Russia." *New York Times,* October 5.

Shapiro, Robert Y. 1998. "Public Opinion, Elites, and Democracy." *Critical Review* 14:501–28.

Shapiro, Robert Y., and Lawrence R. Jacobs. 1989. "The Relationship between Public Opinion and Public Policy: A Review." In *Political Behavior Annual,* edited by Samuel Long, 2:149–79. Boulder, CO: Westview.

Shapiro, Robert Y., and Lawrence R. Jacobs. 2000. "Who Leads and Who Follows? U.S. Presidents, Public Opinion, and Foreign Policy." In *Decision-*

making in a Glass House, edited by Brigitte Nacos, Robert Y. Shapiro, and Pierangelo Isernia, 223–45. Lanham, MD: Rowman and Littlefield.

Shapiro, Robert Y., and Harpreet Mahajan. 1986. "Gender Differences in Policy Preferences: A Summary of Trends from the 1960s to the 1980s." *Public Opinion Quarterly* 50:42–61.

Shapiro, Robert Y., and Benjamin I. Page. 1988. "Foreign Policy and the Rational Public." *Journal of Conflict Resolution* 32:211–47.

Shapiro, Robert Y., and Benjamin I. Page. 1994. "Foreign Policy and Public Opinion." In *The New Politics of American Foreign Policy,* edited by David A. Deese, 216–35. New York: St. Martin's.

Shogan, Robert. 1995. *Hard Bargain: How FDR Twisted Churchill's Arm, Evaded the Law, and Changed the Role of the American Presidency.* New York: Scribner.

Shultz, George P. 1993. *Turmoil and Triumph: My Years as Secretary of State.* New York: Scribner's.

Sigelman, Lee, and Pamela Johnston Conover. 1981. "Knowledge and Opinions about the Iran Crisis: A Reconsideration of Three Models." *Public Opinion Quarterly* 45:477–91.

Simon, Bernard. 2002. "Washington's Farm Bill Adds to a Rising Canadian Anger over Trade." *New York Times,* May 23.

Small, Melvin, ed. 1970. *Public Opinion and Historians: Interdisciplinary Perspectives.* Detroit: Wayne State University Press.

Smith, Tom W. 1983. "The Polls: American Attitudes toward the Soviet Union and Communism." *Public Opinion Quarterly* 47:277–92.

Smith, Tom W. 1984. "The Polls: Gender and Attitudes toward Violence." *Public Opinion Quarterly* 48:384–96.

Smith, Tom W. 1985. "The Polls: America's Most Important Problems: National and International." *Public Opinion Quarterly* 49:264–74.

Smith, Tony. 2000. *Foreign Attachments: The Power of Ethnic Groups in the Making of American Foreign Policy.* Cambridge: Harvard University Press.

Sniderman, Paul M. 1993. "The New Look in Public Opinion Research." In *Political Science: The State of the Discipline II,* edited by Ada W. Finifter, 219–45. Washington, DC: American Political Science Association.

Sniderman, Paul M. 1994. "Burden of Proof." *Political Psychology* 15:541–46.

Sniderman, Paul M., and Philip E. Tetlock. 1986. "Interrelationship of Political Ideology and Public Opinion." In *Political Psychology,* edited by Margaret G. Hermann, 62–96. San Francisco: Jossey-Bass.

Sobel, Richard. 1989. "Public Opinion about United States Intervention in El Salvador and Nicaragua." *Public Opinion Quarterly* 53:114–28.

Sobel, Richard, ed. 1993. *Public Opinion in U.S. Foreign Policy: The Controversy over Contra Aid.* Lanham, MD: Rowman and Littlefield.

Sobel, Richard. 1995. "What People Really Say about Bosnia." *New York Times,* November 22.

Sobel, Richard. 1996. "Polling on Foreign Policy Crises: Creating a Standard Set of Questions." *Public Perspective* 7:13–15.

Sobel, Richard. 2000. "To Intervene or Not Intervene in Bosnia: That Was the Question for the United States and Europe." *In Decisionmaking in a Glass House,* edited by Brigitte Nacos, Robert Y. Shapiro, and Pierangelo Isernia, 111–31. Lanham, MD: Rowman and Littlefield.

360   *References*

Sobel, Richard. 2001. *The Impact of Public Opinion on U.S. Foreign Policy since Vietnam: Constraining the Colossus.* New York: Oxford University Press.

Sobel, Richard, and Eric Shiraev, eds. 2003. *International Public Opinion and the Bosnia Crisis.* Lanham, MD: Lexington.

Spiro, Peter J. 2000. "The New Sovereigntists." *Foreign Affairs* 79:9–15.

Spitzer, Alan B. 1973. "The Historical Problem of Generations." *American Historical Review* 78:1353–85.

Spivak, Jonathan. 1981a. "Changes in Poland's Communist Party Show Switch to a Younger Generation." *Wall Street Journal,* September 3.

Spivak, Jonathan. 1981b. "Generation Gap: Polish Crisis Is a Clash of Old and Entrenched with Impatient Youth." *Wall Street Journal,* February 11.

Squire, Peverill. 1988. "Why the 1936 *Literary Digest* Poll Failed." *Public Opinion Quarterly* 52:125–33.

Steel, Ronald. 1980. *Walter Lippmann and the American Century.* Boston: Little, Brown.

Steele, Richard W. 1974. "The Pulse of the People: Franklin D. Roosevelt and the Gauging of American Public Opinion." *Journal of Contemporary History* 9:195–216.

Steele, Richard W. 1985. *Propaganda in an Open Society: The Roosevelt Administration and the Media, 1933–1941.* Westport, CT: Greenwood.

Stimson, James A. 1999. *Public Opinion in America: Moods, Cycles, and Swings.* 2d ed. Boulder, CO: Westview.

Stimson, James A., Michael B. MacKuen, and Robert S. Erikson. 1994. "Opinion and Policy: A Global View." *PS: Political Science and Politics* 27:29–35.

Stimson, James A., Michael B. MacKuen, and Robert S. Erikson. 1995. "Dynamic Representation." *American Political Science Review* 89:543–65.

Stouffer, Samuel A., et al. 1949. *The American Soldier.* 2 Vols. Princeton: Princeton University Press.

Strauss, William, and Neil Howe. 1991. *Generations: The History of America's Future, 1584 to 2069.* New York: Morrow.

Strobel, Warren P. 1997. *Late-Breaking Foreign Policy: The News Media's Influence on Peace Operations.* Washington, DC: United States Institute of Peace Press.

Sullivan, John L., James E. Pierson, and George E. Marcus. 1978. "Ideological Constraint in the Mass Public: A Methodological Critique and Some New Findings." *American Journal of Political Science* 22:233–49.

Sussman, Barry. 1976. "Elites in America." *Washington Post,* September 26–30.

Sussmann, Leila A. 1956. "FDR and the White House Mail." *Public Opinion Quarterly* 20:5–15.

Sussmann, Leila A. 1963. *Dear FDR: A Study of Political Letter Writing.* Totowa, NJ: Bedminister.

Taylor, D. Garth. 1980. "Procedure for Evaluating Trends in Public Opinion." *Public Opinion Quarterly* 44:86–100.

Taylor, Stan A., and Robert S. Wood. 1966. "Image and Generation: A Social-Psychological Analysis of the Sino-Soviet Dispute." *Brigham Young University Studies* 7:143–57.

Tetlock, Philip. 1994a. "How Politicized Is Political Psychology and Is There Anything We Should Do about It?" *Political Psychology* 15:567–77.

Tetlock, Philip. 1994b. "Political Psychology or Politicized Psychology: Is the Road to Scientific Hell Paved with Good Moral Intentions?" *Political Psychology* 15:509–30.

Thachuk, Kimberly L. 2002. "Terrorism's Financial Lifeline: Can It Be Severed?" *Strategic Forum,* May.

Thucydides. 1876. *History of the Peloponnesian War.* London: Longman's, Green.

Tien, Charles, and James A. Nathan. 2001. "American Ambivalence toward China." *Public Opinion Quarterly* 65:124–38.

Times Mirror Center for the People and the Press. 1993. *America's Place in the World: An Investigation of the Attitudes of American Opinion Leaders and the American Public about International Affairs.* Washington, DC: Times Mirror Center.

Tocqueville, Alexis de. 1958. *Democracy in America.* Vol. 1. New York: Vintage.

Trubowitz, Peter. 1992. "Sectionalism and American Foreign Policy: The Political Geography of Consensus and Conflict." *International Studies Quarterly* 36:173–90.

Turner, Henry A. 1957. "Woodrow Wilson and Public Opinion." *Public Opinion Quarterly* 21:505–20.

U.S. Department of Commerce. 1994. *Statistical Abstract of the United States.* Washington, DC: U.S. Government Printing Office.

U.S. News and World Report. 1995. "Seven Tribes." 119:24–32.

U.S. President. 1994. *A National Security Strategy of Engagement and Enlargement.* Washington, DC: U.S. Government Printing Office.

U.S. Strategic Bombing Survey. 1947. *The Effects of Strategic Bombing on German Morale.* Vol. 1. Washington, DC: U.S. Strategic Bombing Survey.

Vandenberg, Arthur H., Jr., ed. 1952. *The Private Papers of Senator Vandenberg.* Boston: Houghton Mifflin.

Verba, Sidney. 1996. "The Citizen as Respondent: Sample Surveys and American Democracy." *American Political Science Review* 90:1–7.

Verba, Sidney, and Richard A. Brody. 1970. "Participation, Policy Preferences, and the War in Vietnam." *Public Opinion Quarterly* 34:325–32.

Verba, Sidney, Richard A. Brody, Edwin B. Parker, Norman H. Nie, Nelson W. Polsby, Paul Ekman, and Gordon S. Black. 1967. "Public Opinion and the War in Vietnam." *American Political Science Review* 61:317–33.

Walsh, Warren B. 1944. "What the American People Think of Russia." *Public Opinion Quarterly* 8:513–22.

Walt, Stephen. 2000. "Two Cheers for Clinton's Legacy." *Foreign Affairs* 79: 63–79.

Waltz, Kenneth N. 1967. "Electoral Punishment and Foreign Policy Crises." In *Domestic Sources of Foreign Policy,* edited by James N. Rosenau, 263–94. New York: Free Press.

Washington Post-ABC News. 2003. "War in Iraq." July 11. Available at www .washingtonpost.com/wp-srv/politics/polls/vault/stories/data071103.htm.

Watts, William, and Lloyd A. Free. 1973. *State of the Nation.* New York: Universe.

Weiler, Michael, and W. Barnett Pearce, eds. 1992. *Reagan and Public Discourse in America.* Tuscaloosa: University of Alabama Press.

Weinberger, Caspar. 1984. "Excerpts from Address of Weinberger." *New York Times,* November 29, A5.

Weinberger, Caspar. 1990. *Fighting for Peace: Seven Critical Years in the Pentagon.* New York: Warner.

White, Lincoln. 1959. "The News Division of the Department of State." *Department of State Bulletin* 40 (June 22): 921–25.

Wildavsky, Aaron. 1966. "The Two Presidencies." *Trans-Action,* December, 7–14.

Will, George F. 1989. "Europe's Second Reformation." *Newsweek,* November 20, p. 90.

Williams, Erin M. 1996. "Sources of New Era Foreign Policy: Public Opinion, Congress, and the Harding Administration, 1921–1923." Ph.D. diss., Emory University.

Williams, Frederick W. 1945. "Regional Attitudes on International Cooperation." *Public Opinion Quarterly* 9:38–50.

Willkie, Wendell L. 1943. *One World.* New York: Simon and Schuster.

Wilson, Woodrow. 1917. "Text of the President's Address." *New York Times,* April 3.

Wines, Michael. 1994. "Washington Is Really in Touch: We're the Problem." *New York Times,* October 16.

Wirls, Daniel. 1986. "Reinterpreting the Gender Gap." *Public Opinion Quarterly* 50:316–30.

Wittkopf, Eugene R. 1986. "On the Foreign Policy Beliefs of the American People: A Critique and Some Evidence." *International Studies Quarterly* 30:425–45.

Wittkopf, Eugene R. 1990. *Faces of Internationalism: Public Opinion and American Foreign Policy.* Durham, NC: Duke University Press.

Wittkopf, Eugene R. 1995. "The Faces of Internationalism Revisited." Paper presented at the annual meeting of the American Political Science Association, Chicago, August 31–September 3.

Wlezien, Christopher. 1995. "The Public as Thermostat: Dynamics of Preferences for Spending." *American Journal of Political Science* 39:981–1000.

Wlezien, Christopher. 1996. "Dynamics of Representation: The Case of U.S. Spending on Defence." *British Journal of Political Science* 26:81–103.

Wohlstetter, Roberta. 1962. *Pearl Harbor: Warning and Decision.* Stanford, CA: Stanford University Press.

Wood, Floris W., ed. 1990. *An American Profile: Opinions and Behavior, 1972–1989.* Detroit: Gale Research.

Woodward, Julian L. 1945. "Public Opinion Polls as an Aid to Democracy." *Political Science Quarterly* 61:238–46.

Wright, Quincy. 1965. *A Study of War.* 2d ed. Chicago: University of Chicago Press.

Yankelovich, Daniel. 1978. "Farewell to 'the President Knows Best.'" *Foreign Affairs* 57:670–93.

Yankelovich, Daniel. 1991. *Coming to Public Judgment: Making Democracy Work in a Complex World.* Syracuse, NY: Syracuse University Press.

Yankelovich, Daniel, and I. M. Destler, eds. 1994. *Beyond the Beltway: Engaging the Public in U.S. Foreign Policy.* New York: Norton.

Zaller, John R. 1992. *The Nature and Origins of Mass Opinion*. New York: Cambridge University Press.

Zaller, John R. 1994. "Strategic Politicians, Public Opinion, and the Gulf Crisis." In *Taken by Storm: The Media, Public Opinion, and U.S. Foreign Policy in the Gulf War*, edited by W. Lance Bennett and David L. Paletz, 250–76. Chicago: University of Chicago Press.

Zaller, John R. 2004. "Floating Voters in U.S. Presidential Elections, 1948–2000." In *The Issue of Belief: Essays in the Intersection of Non-Attitudes and Attitude Change*, edited by Paul Sniderman and Willem Saris. Princeton: Princeton University Press.

Zimmerman, William. 2002. *The Russian People and Foreign Policy: Russian Elite and Mass Perspectives, 1993–2000*. Princeton: Princeton University Press.

Zur, Ofer, and Andrea Morrison. 1989. "Gender and War: Reexamining Attitudes." *American Journal of Orthopsychiatry* 59:528–33.

Index

ABC/*Washington Post* polls, 79, 85,
    311, 325n. 1
ABM Treaty. *See* Antiballistic Missile (ABM) Treaty
Abortion, 152
Abramowitz, Alan, 331n. 19
Abramson, Paul, 60
Abravanel, Martin, 309
Accommodationists, 52, 54, 130,
    260–65
Achen, Christopher H., 47, 49
Acheson, Dean, 236
Adams, John, 65
Afghanistan, 2, 9, 63, 70, 77–78,
    82–83, 97, 124, 229, 274, 276,
    282, 297, 307
Age, as source of foreign policy
    attitudes. *See* Generation
Agenda for future research,
    289–324
Aideed, Mohamed Farah, 122
AIDS, 107
Aldrich, John H., 60–61
Alien and Sedition Acts, 294
Allison, Graham T., 197, 204, 327n. 6
Almond, Gabriel, 22, 26, 28–31, 34,
    37, 42, 47, 95, 99, 148–49, 208,
    226, 286, 326nn. 3–4
Almond-Lippmann consensus,
    25–40, 48, 71–72, 101–2
challenges to, 41–97
Al Qaeda, 2, 9, 80, 229, 253, 277,
    282, 285, 332n. 1
Altschuler, Bruce, 58
Alvarez, R. Michael, 298
Ambrose, Stephen, 307

America First, 236
American Federation of Labor
    (AFL), 237
American Institute of Public Opinion. *See* Gallup poll
American-Israeli Political Action
    Committee (AIPAC), 296
Americans Talk Issues, 192, 212
Americans Talk Security, 77, 83–84,
    192, 210, 213–14, 297, 315,
    331–32n. 20
Anderson, Kristi, 50
Andropov, Yuri, 70
Angle, Paul M., 37
Angola, 169
Antiballistic Missile (ABM) Treaty,
    66, 249, 300
Arab-Israeli conflict, 107
Arms control, 81–82, 329n. 7
Arms Control Association, 238
Ashcroft, John, 252, 290
Asmus, Ronald D., 309
Augustine (saint), 5
"Axis of evil," 57, 286, 296, 316

Back, Kurt W., 197
Bacevich, Andrew, 251
Bailey, Thomas A., 22, 26–28, 31, 37
Baker, Roy Stannard, 325n. 6
Ball, George, 122, 318–19
Barber, James David, 331n. 15
Bardes, Barbara Ann, 51, 331n. 19
Bartels, Larry M., 61, 311
Barton, Allen H., 149, 328n. 1
Battle, Joseph, 292
Bauer, Raymond A., 327n. 7, 328n. 7